ASPECTS OF COMPOSITION

Aspects of
Composition

Billie Andrew Inman
Ruth Gardner
UNIVERSITY OF ARIZONA

Harcourt, Brace & World, Inc.
NEW YORK · CHICAGO · SAN FRANCISCO · ATLANTA

ISBN: 0-15-503840-0

Library of Congress Catalog Card Number: 79-111321

Printed in the United States of America

Picture Credits

Inc. Reprinted from the November 1956 issue of *Harper's Magazine* by permission of the author.

271: Bernie Boston, © 1967 *Washington Star*. Reprinted by permission.

392: George Tames, *The New York Times.*

COLOR SECTION

Infrared Thermogram. Courtesy of Barnes Engineering Company.

Distant Thunder, Andrew Wyeth. Courtesy of Mrs. Norman B. Woolworth.

The Poet Reclining, Marc Chagall. The Tate Gallery, London. Permission ADAGP by French Reproduction Rights, 1969.

Big Julie (1945), Fernand Léger. Collection, The Museum of Modern Art, New York. Acquired through the Lillie P. Bliss Bequest.

Preface

The chief aim of ASPECTS OF COMPOSITION is to teach students to write the most common type of essay published today—an essay in which the author describes and interprets a situation of particular concern to him and to his audience.

The book and Instructor's Manual grew out of a three-year experimental program in freshman composition at the University of Arizona, in which 136 instructors and 5,200 students in 176 classes participated. Four times during the experiment, instructors and students made detailed evaluations of the program, and instructors also made many suggestions during informal discussions. In this manner, through trial, evaluation, and modification, a course evolved that was varied in content and method, reflecting the preferences of both teachers and students. ASPECTS OF COMPOSITION incorporates the types of semantical, grammatical, visual, and literary material that proved most interesting and effective in this experimental course.

The book is organized according to four types of development: *factual detail, exemplification, comparison,* and *explanation.* These four types of development are not discrete, but cumulative: that is, factual detail may be used in exemplification; exemplification, perhaps including factual detail, may be used in comparison, and comparison in explanation. And of course factual detail, exemplification, and comparison may be used separately in explanation, the most complex of the four types. Part I is concerned with descriptive reports based on observation and reports that combine descriptions, statistics, and quotations. Part II is concerned with the development of classifications, definitions, and generalizations by examples. In Part III, development by comparison is applied to comparisons in kind and in degree, and to analogies. In Part IV, development by explanation is applied to interpretations of situations in life and art.

To us, development consists of logic, arrangement, sentence construction, and diction. In this book, therefore, these four elements are taught as aspects of each type of development rather than as separate topics in independent chapters. For example, one kind of inductive logic, reasoning from specifics to a generalization, is taught in Part II, Exemplification, because it is integral to the conception of examples. Similarly, the construction of cumulative sentences is taught in Part I, Factual Detail, because cumulative sentences are especially good vehicles for reporting descriptive details.

In this book, grammar is not presented for its own sake, simply because there is not time in most college schedules to teach both grammar and composition in one course. Since the main concern in this book is composition, only grammatical facts that support instruction in the rhetoric of the sentence are included. The emphasis in grammar is upon large-constituent modifiers, especially upon how these modifiers function to produce particular effects.

Finally, while the written and visual materials included here are meant to be thought-provoking, it is the writer's own observations and experiences outside the classroom and the ideas he forms from them that are the most important sources for his compositions. Our intention is to help him develop skills to express *his* ideas effectively.

For their willingness to try new approaches and for their cooperation in meeting common objectives, we are grateful to all the instructors who participated in the experiment that made this book possible, and especially to Susan Rosowski, Robert Terry, and Johnnie Raye Harper. We are grateful to students who have permitted us to reprint their compositions. We appreciate the support given the experimental program by the Department of English of the University of Arizona, under the chairmanship of A. Laurence Muir, and the time allowed by the University for the preparation of the manuscript.

For encouragement and much practical help in preparing the manuscript, we say a special thanks to our husbands, George D. Inman and Leon Gardner.

BILLIE ANDREW INMAN
RUTH GARDNER

Contents

Contents:
EXERCISES and SELECTIONS

PART II   *Exemplification*   159

Classification   161

Definition   186

PART III   *Comparison*   219

Application   365

ASPECTS OF COMPOSITION

Introduction

One of the chief occupations of literate men and women is interpreting and judging situations in which they find themselves and more remote situations that influence them. A father may want to know why his fifth-grade son's mark in social studies dropped from an A to a C during the past nine weeks. A teen-ager may want to know why several women in the community have recently organized a citizen's censorship committee to examine books in the high-school library. A college student may want to know why the enrollment in some of the under-graduate courses in his program runs as high as two hundred. A group of drivers may want to know why there are more traffic accidents at Sixth and Bradford than at any other intersection in town. Many citizens of the United States want to know why so many whites are moving into the suburbs of cities and so many blacks are moving into the hearts of cities; why tranquilizers and pep pills are in such vogue; why so many college students are protesting administrative poli-cies; and why millions of people in this affluent society are hungry. The usual reason for wanting to know why a situation exists is to take some sort of action to remedy it or to show appreciation of it: for example, vote in an appropriate way, sign a petition, write a letter to an editor or a legislator, make a persuasive speech before the City Council, the school board, or some other group, or write a persuasive article for publication.

Businessmen, lawyers, physicians, nurses, teachers, ministers, legislators, wel-fare workers, psychologists, administrators, coaches, researchers, journalists—indeed all persons who are called upon in their vocations to make decisions—are continually engaged in interpretation of data and observations, and often they are expected to explain their conclusions and recommendations in writing. Any college student who is becoming a participating citizen and who wishes to be effective in a vocation can expect to be frequently explaining his interpretations and evaluating interpretations made by other people.

1

The overriding purpose of this book is to teach ways of evaluating and writing interpretations of aspects of life. This purpose cannot be satisfied in one easy lesson, because people do not learn to evaluate and to write such interpretations by reading general advice on the subject or by following six or seven general rules. They can learn, however, by practicing types of development that constitute parts of effective explanation and by performing the various processes that pertain to each of these.

The first step toward interpreting a situation is perceiving it clearly; the first step toward writing an interpretation of a situation is writing a report on the situation, using factual detail—descriptions, statistics, and quotations—as appropriate to the situation. Accordingly, Part I of this book teaches means of developing reports, emphasizing description because it is the most difficult of these means to master. A precise report on a situation gives the reader the background needed to understand the main ideas in the interpretation of it. Whether the interpretation is convincing or not depends primarily upon the support given its main ideas. It is easy to tell people to develop their ideas through factual detail, exemplification, and comparison; but just telling them does little good. Each of these types of development requires a different rationale and a different arrangement of parts; therefore, each is the subject of detailed and extensive instruction in this book.

When you reach Part IV, you will be ready to develop your ideas through the use of factual detail, exemplification, and comparison. In Part IV, you will add another type of development, enumeration of reasons, to these three types. You will also study an inductive process of reasoning that allows you to form interpretive conclusions; and through a comprehensive type of development called explanation, you will learn to combine factual detail, exemplification, comparison, and enumeration of reasons, as needed, to support your conclusions. In short, you will write interpretations developed by explanation.

Thus far we have been discussing development in writing as if it consisted of only two processes, thinking and arranging types of support. Two other processes that are integral to development are the construction of sentences within the given plan of arrangement and the choice of words within the structures of the sentences. Sentence structure and diction (choice of words) are often treated in composition books in chapters separate from those treating thinking and arrangement. In this book, however, sentences and diction are taken up when they can be most readily applied. In other words, this book coordinates instruction in thinking, arrangement, sentence structure, and diction.

In every course, there are certain special abilities that are so fundamental they must be assured before the instruction proper can begin. In this course, the ability to distinguish statements of fact from inferences and value judgments, the ability to distinguish concrete words from nonconcrete words and specific words from general words, and the ability to discern basic grammatical patterns in sentences are special and fundamental. The instruction in Preliminary Distinctions aims at developing these abilities. You will probably already have mastered some of the processes to be treated there, but since it cannot be assumed that all of the students who will use this book have mastered all of the processes, all must be taught. As you proceed from one to another you may not see any relationship among them; but you will see later that they all apply to the writing you will be asked to do in Part I and in succeeding parts of the book.

Two modes of instruction, discussion and dialog, are used repeatedly in this book. In the discussions the main ideas are stated first and supported with factual details, examples, comparisons, and reasons—the kinds of support that you will be using in your own compositions. Each dialog is a series of questions and answers moving from the specifics of a subject to general conclusions; in other words, its procedure is inductive. This type of dialog is like an instructional program, except that the answers are not always as obvious as in a program. There is nothing to keep you from simply reading the dialogs, but you will learn more from them if you participate as the answerer and use the printed answers to check yourself. The exercises in the book are intended to reinforce the instruction; and the readings, though you may enjoy them for their content, have been selected primarily to illustrate forms of development, types of thinking, organization, sentence structure, or diction within a form. The photographs are used primarily to stimulate thought. The suggested writing assignments are objectives toward which all of the other material is aimed.

Preliminary Distinctions

Distinguishing Types
of Statements Semantically

DIALOG 1

Three Types of Statements

Refer to the sets below as you answer the questions that follow.

Set 1
A. These eight spearheads were found buried among the bones of this skeleton—a mammoth's.
B. The mammoth whose skeleton we see here was killed by prehistoric Indians.
C. The Indians had a right to kill the mammoth for food.

Set 2
D. An instructor says, "Sam answered twenty questions out of twenty-five incorrectly; the questions were drawn from one chapter in the textbook."
E. The same instructor, who never sees Sam outside of class, remarks, "Sam did not read the chapter that I assigned for outside reading."
F. The instructor, with statement D in mind, says, "Sam is the most uncooperative student in this class."

Set 3
G. The lungfish has internal nostrils connecting with the mouth.
H. A creature like the lungfish is the ancestor of all land animals.
I. Whoever believes that men are descended from lungfish is going to Hell.

Set 4
J. ". . . *to do* for to cheat has been traced to 1789, *to frisk* for to search to 1781, *to grease* for to bribe to 1557, and *to blow* for to boast to *c.* 1400.

Among nouns, *gas* for empty talk has been traced to 1847, *jug* for prison to 1834, *lip* for insolence to 1821 . . . *grub* for food to 1659, *rot-gut* to 1597 and *bones* for dice to *c.* 1386."[1]

K. Slang words may remain in the language for centuries.
L. My lousy English teacher lied to me when she said that slang words drop out of use after a few years.

Try to answer each question below before looking at its answer. Read the first set before reading the first question.

1. What do statements A, B, and C (in Set 1) have in common?	They concern a mammoth.
2. Who might have made the first statement?	The archeologist who discovered the skeleton.
3. If you asked him how he knew the spearheads were found among the bones, what would he reply?	I saw them.
4. Suppose that the same archeologist made statement B. If you asked him how he knew the mammoth was killed by prehistoric Indians, could he say that he had seen the mammoth killed?	No.
5. What would he say?	I assume from the position of the spearheads that the mammoth was killed by spears; I know that only men throw spears and that the only men who lived in this region in prehistoric times are called Indians.
6. Upon what does the archeologist base his answer to the question in number 3 above?	Seeing.
7. Upon what does the archeologist base his answer to the question in number 4 above?	Reasoning from what he has seen and from historical knowledge.
8. I doubt that an archeologist would make statement C, but if he did, upon what would the statement be based?	Acceptance of statement B, that Indians had killed the mammoth with spears, plus his approval of the killing.

[1]H. L. Mencken, "The Nature of Slang," *The American Language* (New York: Knopf, 1937), p. 566.

9. We have been using the term *historical knowledge*. Do you know that President Kennedy was assassinated on November 22, 1963?	Yes.
10. How do you know?	I heard of this event on the day it happened (read about it in newspapers, saw the funeral on television, and so forth).
11. Do you know that President Lincoln was shot on April 14, 1865?	Yes.
12. How do you know?	I have read about the assassination in history books.
13. Were the historians you have read alive when Lincoln died?	Probably not.
14. Where did they get their information?	Ultimately, from records written at the time.
15. And what were these based on?	Seeing, hearing.
16. Is all historical knowledge traced to its source based on perceptions?	Yes.
17. Does knowledge have to be in a history book to be called historical?	No, if it happened in the past, even in the immediate past, and if it is remembered by someone, it is historical knowledge.
18. What do statements D, E, and F have in common?	They concern Sam's performance on an examination.
19. Assuming that the instructor knows the answers to the questions on the examination, upon what is his first statement based?	Upon seeing Sam's answers and performing a calculation.
20. Does the instructor know for sure that Sam did not read the chapter?	No.
21. Upon what is his statement in E based?	Reasoning from a result (Sam's performance), which he has seen, to a probable cause.
22. Upon what is his statement in F based?	Upon seeing and calculating, reasoning, and disapproving.

23. What do statements A, D, G, and J have in common?	They testify to seeing.
24. Let's call statements A, D, G, and J *statements of fact.* A statement of fact is a statement based on perception. Are statements A, D, G, and J necessarily true?	No.
25. What makes a statement of fact true?	Corroboration by testimony of other people.
26. Can we always judge whether a statement of fact is true or false?	No, if a thing happens only once and is seen by only one person, the statement about it cannot be proved true or false.
27. What do statements B, E, H, and K have in common?	They are based on historical knowledge plus reasoning.
28. Let's call statements B, E, H, and K *statements of inference.* Can all statements of inference be proved true or false?	No.
29. Why can statements B and H not be proved true or false?	They refer to a time before written records were kept, that is, before statements of fact could be preserved.
30. Why can statement K not be proved true or false?	It pertains to the future as well as to the present and the recorded past, and there are, of course, no statements of fact about the future.
31. Can the instructor's statement in E be proved true or false?	Probably. Sam can state whether he did or did not read the chapter.
32. Then there may no longer be a reason for the instructor to infer that Sam did not read the chapter?	No. The instructor either accepts Sam's statement or he does not.
33. What can you conclude about the verifiability of inferences?	Some inferences can be investigated and proved true or false.
34. What do statements C, F, I, and L have in common? What can they be called?	They reveal approval or disapproval and can therefore be called value judgments.

35. To sum up the lesson, give definitions of a *statement of fact*, a *statement of inference*, and a *statement of value judgment*.	A statement of fact is a statement reportedly based on perception plus, at times, a mathematical calculation. A statement of inference is a statement based on perception and historical knowledge plus reasoning. A statement of value judgment is a statement that may be based partly on statements of fact and/or partly on inference, but that, in any case, expresses approval or disapproval.

OTHER TYPES OF STATEMENTS

Not all declarative statements can be classified semantically (according to meaning) as statements of fact, inference, or value judgment, or mixtures of these. When a mother says, "Bobby, you are a good boy," she may not actually be stating a value judgment; she may be giving a directive or building in Bobby's mind a desirable image of himself. Leaders of organizations sometimes praise the membership more in hope than in conviction, their apparent value judgments actually being directives to "work as a team," "give generously," "increase the enrollment," and so forth.

Some hypothetical statements—for example, "If I were brighter, I would become an astronaut"—are wishes that cannot be classified as one of our three types of statements. Hypothetical statements that begin "If I were you" are directives. A hypothetical statement may be a statement of fact in disguise, however, as you will see when you read "Color Blind from Birth."

Books of myths are full of statements that appear to be facts ("The heaven of the Greek gods was the summit of an ideal mountain called Olympus") and value judgments ("Jupiter was the supreme ruler of the universe, wisest of the divinities and most glorious"),[2] but the modern reader knows that the meanings of all such statements relate only to the minds that created them, not to the world as he knows it.

---

[2]Charles Mills Gayley, *The Classical Myths in English Literature and Art* (Boston: Ginn & Company, 1939), p. 18 (first quotation) and p. 19 (second quotation).

Types of Statements

A. Decide whether each of the following statements is one of fact, inference, or value judgment.

　　1. Continental's Flight 91 arrived at O'Hare sixteen minutes early this evening.

　　2. That new Corvair is beautiful.

3. Our football team is sure to win the regional championship this year.
4. Eleven percent of the freshmen who took Introductory Composition at this university last fall made A's.
5. Professor Ralls said in his lecture this morning that the scientific method had been a greater blessing to man than any of the world's religions had been.

      6. Students who stage riots on college campuses should be treated like other criminals.

      7. Rioting by students on campuses in the United States will cease soon after the Vietnam War has ended.

      8. Earth originated more than four billion years ago as a ball of gases hurled into space from the sun.

      9. Jules Verne wrote *From the Earth to the Moon and a Trip Around It* one hundred and three years before astronauts from the United States orbited the moon.

    10. The space program is worth the money that it costs the American people, since it is their chief source of national pride.

B.

      1. Please look at the photograph on page 12. What do you infer to be the boy's attitude toward the cat? State your inference, and list the factual details upon which you base it.

      2. Do you think that your inference is perhaps true, probably true, or almost certainly true? Explain.

C. What do you infer to be the situation in the photograph on page 13? Which details support your inference (or cluster of inferences)?

**EXAMINATION OF TYPES OF STATEMENTS
IN A REPORT**

The following article is a report on relations between blacks and whites in the Virgin Islands. After reading the article, you will be asked to examine statements in several of the paragraphs.

Color Blind from Birth

Eleanor Heckert

St. Thomas, V.I.

1 If you had an accident in the Virgin Islands, and were rushed to the hospital for emergency surgery, the chances are four to one that your surgeon would be black, and only one of your three nurses would be white. Should you

COLOR BLIND FROM BIRTH   Reprinted by permission of the author and her agent, James Brown Associates, Inc. Copyright © 1968 by Eleanor Heckert.

wish later to pursue the legal niceties of the accident, you would know that of the 200 policemen who might investigate the case, 196 are black, and that the chances were even that a black judge would hear your case in municipal court. Eighty per cent of newspaper coverage of your adventure would be controlled by blacks.

2 And if you had arrived recently from the States, where "burn, baby, burn" vies with "law and order" and Huey Newton confronts George Wallace across an impasse of hate, you might be afraid. But you would not need to be. In these island outposts of the United States, your white skin would not be held against you. Neither, however, would it gain you an advantage. And of course you would be outnumbered five to one.

3 Integration is an almost ancient fact in these islands, a strange sort of integration wherein the white man has come to seek acceptance from the black. A few more statistics and then a little history: Of the estimated 54,000 residents of the Virgin Islands, 17 per cent are white. In the public schools about 70 per cent of students and 75 per cent of teachers are black. Three out of five principals are white. About 90 per cent of the students at the new College of the Virgin Islands are black, but the faculty is about half white.

4 Of the fifteen Senators in the Virgin Islands legislature, twelve are black. On the other hand, of the sixteen American Governors appointed (by the U.S. President) since the United States bought the islands from Denmark in 1917, only three have been black, and those in fairly recent years. The smart money here says that the first elected governor will be a white man, but not because he is white. He is native.

5 The intended implication is that the largest part of such discrimination as does exist here is of an older sort, not drawn on lines of color but according to whether one was born here or came from somewhere else. And it happens that, while a good many natives are white (mostly of French, Dutch and Danish origin), a large part of the immigrant population (from neighboring British and French islands, where work is scarce and wages are incredibly low) is black.

6 Integration came to these islands (the U.S. Virgins, comprising St. Thomas, St. John and St. Croix) before the Americans took possession fifty one years ago. In 1835, Peter von Scholten, the Danish Governor-General, invited intelligent and well-tutored slaves to his formal dinner parties. Foreseeing the certainty of emancipation, von Scholten was eager to establish social possibilities between responsible Negroes and the whites they would have to deal with, once free. His first attempt failed; the white guests, having heard of his plan, did not show up. But the Danish colonists were essentially a liberal lot, and from the time of the second attempt at an integrated dinner party until the present, Government House has been the scene of mixed gatherings. Von Scholten's mistress, a free colored woman, was his hostess at both political and social functions.

7 Von Scholten is given much of the credit for obtaining King Christian's signature on a bill (in July, 1847) proclaiming all children henceforth born of slaves to be free. The bill stated further, however, that the slaves themselves were to remain in bondage for twelve more years, so that they could be educated for their

freedom. The promise of freedom was not enough for the slaves and they threatened to revolt unless they had freedom now. They got it within the year, and from 1848 the blacks of these three islands have been not only free but possessed of goods and a very real power to control their own destiny.

8 Like the Governor-General, other influential Danes had openly loved, and often married, their Negro women. As a result, the larger part of the islands' real estate was owned by citizens of mixed blood when the Stars and Stripes were hoisted over Fort Christian.

9 For a good many years integration—complete integration as far as one can tell—was quietly and innocently practiced as daily routine. Marriage and social congress between the races were not considered unusual. There were occasional complaints of discrimination when the white U.S. military personnel (for Washington recognized the islands' strategic advantages) were generous with their seed but unwilling to assume the responsibilities of an integrated family life. But for the most part, black and brown and white moved about without giving much thought to color.

10 The integration that was a natural state in this primitive community turned into an economic necessity about twenty years ago with the considerable ingress of white entrepreneurs from the United States and Europe. These businessmen saw a potential that had escaped the imagination of all but a very few natives: tourism. The newcomers were possessed of capital, business ideas, energy and faith in the growth of the islands. As they began to prosper, so did the large majority of heretofore desperately poor natives; the per capita income for the Virgin Islands became (and remains) the highest in the entire Caribbean area. Thus the now powerful black middle class was born.

11 And with the incredibly rapid growth of tourism came an unspoken knowledge that complete racial concord, or at least the appearance of it, was essential to the islands' economic foundation. When there is racial disturbance, the visitor almost never gets a whiff of it. In fact, the proofs of working integration are so dazzling and refreshing to the newcomer that he is easily led to imagine a perfection that does not exist.

12 In the last year there have been several minor racial conflicts and the murder of two whites by blacks. (Most local opinion would say, perhaps defensively, that these were the direct results of agitation from stateside black militants.) The first murder took place immediately following the news that Martin Luther King had been killed. It was very simple: a black man walked into a restaurant in St. Croix and killed (by his own admission) the first white man he saw. The second was the killing of the publisher of a local liberal and controversial magazine by a Negro who had displayed "kill whites" signs on his taxi several months earlier, and who had for that reason been removed from the streets by black policemen. It is generally thought that the man is insane. Everyone concerned about the island's future thinks of these incidents as horrible exceptions to an otherwise nearly satisfactory situation.

13 Rumors have been circulating, some of which seem reliable, that certain Black Power groups will be the first to bring the notion of real racism to the islands—that in fact the basic strategy for infiltration has already been laid.

I discount any strong possibility of success for such movements. I am not, of course, speaking of those groups whose aim in the States is to forward the cause of integration; here they would find the situation far too advanced to be worth their efforts. But anyone or any group devoted to violence as a means of achieving black separation would lack the slogans that would mean anything to anyone. It is a simple fact that equality of opportunity is a way of life here—in education, in housing, in jobs, in social situations. The kind of discrimination that is in fact a problem (i.e., that displayed by "natives" toward "off-islanders," black or white) would only, I think, work against any attempt by outside militant groups to change the present situation.

14 But this in turn suggests one group that might be susceptible to the arguments of militants from the States: the off-island blacks, who have indeed been faced with living conditions comparable (in some ways) to the ghettos in America. About 12,000 bonded aliens work in the U.S. Virgin Islands. Black and white islanders employ aliens almost exclusively as domestics, and aliens swell the rank of businesses that are in need of menial or hard labor. Natives tend to eschew such work, preferring such jobs as driving their own taxis or office work. Here the alien is at a disadvantage and is made to feel it—in the already over-crowded housing and hospital facilities and in the schools.

15 There is a great deal of social interaction between blacks and whites in the upper economic strata. The educated, affluent Negro appears to accept his white counterpart without challenge. If he has hidden misgivings, they most probably stem from a fear of losing his island culture and heritage. Blacks of this class have been forced to develop a razor-sharp sense of tolerance, for they have in most cases been exposed to long periods of white arrogance during stateside education, military service or business dealings.

16 No statistics, alas, are available concerning interracial sexual drives in the islands; and since the subject is bound to lurk in the back of most readers' minds, I offer a personal sampling of opinion. One black woman friend voiced a feeling I have heard expressed commonly: "I could be attracted to white guys here, but I simply won't let myself. I have the distinct impression that a white man wouldn't value me or take me seriously. He doesn't in the States; why should he here?" A white woman's response to the question of her inclination toward black men: "I've been involved that way, but never again. The attraction on their part is spurious. I doubt that a Negro would ever trust my motives, even though *I* know he has good reason to." And from a black man: "I've reached the point where I don't want to go out with white women any more. In the beginning I suppose my desire for them was mostly curiosity. But a lot of these tourist chicks come running down here on a fling and they think a black man's here for them to use. There's a sign on them that says 'look at me, I'm liberal' but when it's all over they shake hands and are as businesslike as a Cuban prostitute. No thanks, not for me." And from a white man: "White women ought to take a lesson from the colored girls I know. White women tend to let you take something for a price—oh, not a monetary price but a psychological one. Colored women have a more giving nature."

17 Today, less than half the real estate (and only a small portion of the

real value) of the islands is owned by blacks. Along the main streets it is easy to see that the white man definitely controls retail business. Of white owners, mainlanders rather than natives are in the majority, but several vast business empires are owned or controlled by white natives. It is said that all but a few Virgin Islanders have been too close to the woods to see the big bills growing on the trees. It is also said that they feel a deep resentment of the whites to whom they have sold the vineyard.

18 And what about the wealthy stateside black businessmen? If our spring is so sweet and pure, why have so few of them come to taste the water? Here I must rely on the voice of one Negro from the States who had been very successful in business on St. Thomas, but eventually sold his interests and returned home. He said he had left the islands so that his children could have the benefits of a more cultural atmosphere. When I asked him if the discrimination he would face back home was worth the exchange, he smiled and asked, "What discrimination? It's 'in' to be black today."

19 Many of the bright younger black natives are leaving the islands for a wider variety of job opportunities and very few mainland blacks are coming to take their places. Some blacks from the States say the local natives resent them (which is true) and make it difficult for them to live and work here. Some say the cost of living is disproportionate to the low salaries, and still others say the islands have nothing to offer the black man except a good climate and a very groovy spot for retirement.

20 White tourists (and why almost all the tourists here *are* white is a matter that has puzzled me for years) often forget to leave their racial hang-ups at home, and this sometimes presents problems for all of us who live here. A black doctor friend tells me of a white woman who was brought to the hospital after an automobile accident. Only emergency surgery could save her life. As she was being wheeled along the corridor she became conscious and cursed my friend and the nurses, telling them all to keep their black hands off her. I asked the doctor if he had not been tempted to do just that, and let her bleed to death. "We have to be tolerant of people like that," he said softly. "Before she left the hospital she even liked us."

21 More recently, after another automobile accident, a teen-age son of white islanders found himself in the emergency room, where the black nurses and doctor treating him began to talk about race relations in the States. As the doctor took a stitch in the patient's eyebrow, he hesitated. Looking into the boy's eyes he grinned broadly and said: "You better believe black is beautiful."

---

1. Reread paragraph 6 and list, in the words of the source, five statements of fact.
2. Reread paragraph 3 and list six statements of statistical fact, not necessarily using the words of the source.
3. Paragraph 1 describes a hypothetical not a factual incident, but it is based on statistical fact. State in a percentage the statistical fact underlying this

hypothetical statement: "If you had an accident in the Virgin Islands, and were rushed to the hospital for emergency surgery, the chances are four to one that your surgeon would be black . . . ."

4. Why do you think Eleanor Heckert opened her report with hypothetical statements instead of statements of statistical fact based on percentages?

5. Quote three inferences from paragraph 2.

6. The first clause of the following sentence from paragraph 4 is a mixture of types: "The smart money here says that the first elected governor will be a white man, but not because he is white." It is a reported fact that certain gamblers predict that the first elected governor will be white. Their prediction is which kind of statement? Which word shows that Mrs. Heckert thinks the prediction is probably right?

7. One of Mrs. Heckert's most important inferences is stated in paragraph 13. Through it she refutes rumors that "certain Black Power groups will be the first to bring the notion of real racism to the islands." What is her inference? What does she do in the remainder of the paragraph, after she has stated the inference?

8. When Mrs. Heckert lacks statistics to elucidate a subject, as in paragraph 16, she uses quotations from individuals interviewed. These quotations combine statements of fact, inference, and value judgment. Illustrate these three types of statement in the second quotation. Mrs. Heckert does not draw conclusions from the quotations. Is she wise not to?

9. Mrs. Heckert seems not to have written the last two paragraphs primarily to give information. What seems to have been her main purpose?

MORE ON VALUE JUDGMENTS

Sometimes a value judgment rests at the center of an idea; the whole statement of that idea can therefore be called a value judgment. All of the value judgments in the four sets of statements at the beginning of Dialog 1 are of this type. For example, in "The Indians had a right to kill the mammoth for food" and "Sam is the most uncooperative student in this class," the value judgments are in the central predications—"had a right to kill" and "is the most uncooperative student."

Such value statements are often strengthened by the inclusion of words that are almost universally recognized as value terms and that therefore tend to stir the reader's emotions or at least to draw the reader into the author's mood. In the following quotation the writer gives little precise information, but because in expressing his distaste for the appearance of American cities he uses value terms that almost everyone reacts to unfavorably—*corrupted, ugliness, conformity, neglect*—he tends to win the reader's assent:

The American landscape has been badly corrupted. European writers no longer even notice the natural wonder of it, they are so put off by the ugliness and conformity of the towns. But worse than the ugliness and conformity is the neglect that baffles pride of place. Our poets try to move themselves by nostalgically repeating the names of towns: "Biloxi and Natchez, Pascagoula and Opelousas" —but beware of paying a visit.[3]

In this quotation the first three sentences are value statements, since the value judgments are the central ideas expressed; and the last clause of the last sentence is an implied judgment.

Not all value judgments are expressed through value statements, however. Statements of fact can be slanted favorably or unfavorably by the addition of value terms. The first passage below is paragraph 7 from "Color Blind from Birth." All of the statements in it are purely factual except the first, in which *credit* carries a favorable judgment:

Von Scholten is given much of the credit for obtaining King Christian's signature on a bill (in July, 1847) proclaiming all children henceforth born of slaves to be free. The bill stated further, however, that the slaves themselves were to remain in bondage for twelve more years, so that they could be educated for their freedom. The promise of freedom was not enough for the slaves and they threatened to revolt unless they had freedom now. They got it within the year, and from 1848 the blacks of these three islands have been not only free but possessed of goods and a very real power to control their own destiny.

Without changing the factual content of this paragraph, one can slant it unfavorably by adding value terms and a connector that is often significant to the context of judgments—*but*:

Von Scholten should be given the full blame for obtaining King Christian's signature on a bill (in July, 1847) proclaiming all children henceforth born of slaves to be free. The bill stated that the slaves themselves were to remain in bondage for twelve more years, so that they could be educated for freedom. But the promise of freedom was not enough for these ungrateful slaves, and they threatened to revolt unless they had freedom now. Unfortunately, they got it within a year, and from 1848 the blacks of these islands have not only been free, but have been the successful wielders of Black Power.

In this passage the value terms behave characteristically; that is, *blame, ungrateful*, and *unfortunately*, which normally express unfavorable judgments, do so here.

Words to which most persons generally react favorably can express unfavorable value judgments, however, when they are put in inappropriate contexts. There are two examples of such reverses in "Color Blind from Birth." Watch what happens in the following sentences to *generous* and *businesslike*:

[3]Paul Goodman, *Growing Up Absurd* (New York: Random House, Vintage Books, 1960), p. 109.

There were occasional complaints of discrimination when the white U.S. military personnel (for Washington recognized the islands' strategic advantages) were generous with their seed but unwilling to assume the responsibilities of an integrated family life (paragraph 9).

There's a sign on them that says 'look at me, I'm liberal' but when it's all over they shake hands and are as businesslike as a Cuban prostitute (paragraph 16).

Since we expect *generous* and *businesslike* to be used in favorable contexts, we say that they are ironic when used in unfavorable contexts. Any "good" value term can be used ironically.

The word that slants a fact need not be one easily recognizable as a value term like *blame, ungrateful, unfortunately, generous,* or *businesslike,* or a vague, emotive term like *Black Power.* A value judgment can be conveyed by one nondescript modifier in a statement in which the central idea is a fact, as the third sentence of the following passage from Stephen Leacock's *Mark Twain* illustrates:

The other occasion is equally historic—memorable in its utter and awful failure. For the time it crushed Mark Twain with a dead weight of despair. The scene was the dinner given on December 17, 1877, by the staff of the *Atlantic* to the aged poet Whittier on his seventieth birthday.[4]

What function does *aged* serve in the third sentence? Since Whittier's age is stated, *aged* is not needed to give information. In the full context it is plain that Leacock wants the reader to think Whittier so senile that he is unable to appreciate Mark Twain. Throughout the paragraph Leacock belittles Whittier and other Eastern writers who misjudge Mark Twain the Westerner. *Aged* fits a pattern of adverse judgment.

Though value judgments are usually expressed by direct statements of judgment, by use of value terms as modifiers, or by contextual transformation of nondescript terms into value terms, special linguistic devices can also convey judgments. As you read the following review of *A Dandy in Aspic,* notice how the reviewer uses an overly precise term, a metaphor, and a cliché to belittle the "idyllic interludes," and colloquial diction, alliteration, pun, and rhyme to belittle the hero.

Like the western, the international spy story usually falls into one of two categories: the Spoof or the Morality Play. *A Dandy in Aspic* offers a little of one and a lot of the other. The anti-hero has his moments of fun during a few idyllic interludes in the percales with some warm-blooded British birds; the rest of the time he is trapped in a plot as inexorable as fate.

Haughty, dandified Eberlin (Laurence Harvey) is outwardly a London snob and secretly a top British agent. He is also a Russian assassin named Krasnevin who

[4]New York: Appleton-Century-Crofts, 1933, p. 95.

for 18 years has been knocking off other British agents as he knocks down a smashing double salary. Homesick, he begs his Red superiors to let him quit. *Nyet:* he must go on. And his job is getting tougher all the time. His British bosses have got wind of Krasnevin's existence—though they don't know what he looks like—and they want him expunged. As just the man for the job, Eberlin winds up with the unenviable assignment of tracking down and killing himself in Berlin, when all he wearily wants to be is the spy who came in from the gold.

Aspic was almost as cursed as Eberlin. Director Anthony Mann died before it was finished and Laurence Harvey took over, maintaining the film's tense, glossy style. But the Mann-Harvey combination could not quite cope with *Aspic's* thin and often incoherent content. No one in the film is properly motivated; nearly everyone is unremittingly evil. For the viewer, as for Eberlin, there is no one to trust.

As the haggard, laggard spy, Harvey is a stereotypical pawn of the politburo; as his most persistent bedmate, Mia Farrow is a soft sprite whose eyes are larger than her role. The stars are outshone by the supporting players, including Tom Courtenay as a psychotic British agent and Per Oscarsson as his junkie Russian counterpart, hopelessly in love with the heroin. Fortunately, they give *Aspic* some flavor as it moves toward a credibly tragic end, when Harvey suspects the game is up and utters the burnt-out lament: "I feel like a whore in a creaking bed."[5]

Some readers may think that the judgments in the central predications here—such as, "the Mann-Harvey combination could not quite cope with *Aspic's* thin and often incoherent plot"—are enough and that the piling on of abuse through linguistic devices is too much, but other readers may enjoy the linguistic antics.

It is as common to encounter slanted statements of inference as slanted statements of fact. Rachel Carson's *Silent Spring* stirred a heated controversy among scientists when it appeared because, although it proposes to be a scientific work, its central idea is a value judgment—that promoters of the use of chemical insecticides on a large scale are responsible for killing many desirable forms of life and for injuring men and their progeny. The following statements from *Silent Spring* blend value judgment with inference:

For the first time in the history of the world, every human being is now subjected to contact with dangerous chemicals from the moment of conception until death.[6]

For mankind as a whole, a possession infinitely more valuable than individual life is our genetic heritage, our link with past and future. Shaped through long eons of evolution, our genes not only make us what we are, but hold in their minute beings the future—be it one of promise or threat. Yet genetic deterioration through man-made agents is the menace of our time, "the last and greatest danger to our civilization."[7]

---

[5] *Time*, Vol. XCI, No. 15 (April 12, 1968), p. E3
[6] Boston: Houghton Mifflin, 1962, p. 15.
[7] *Ibid.*, p. 208.

In the passage below, Sir Winston Churchill assesses the reasons the bombing of England by Germany failed to achieve its objective:

The third ordeal was the indiscriminate night-bombing of our cities in mass attacks. This was overcome and broken by the continued devotion and skill of our fighter pilots, and by the fortitude and endurance of the mass of the people, and notably the Londoners, who, together with the civil organizations which upheld them, bore the brunt. But these noble efforts in the high air and in the flaming streets would have been in vain if British science and British brains had not played the ever-memorable and decisive part which this chapter records.[8]

The reasons Sir Winston gives for the failure of the bombing are substantial inferences, stated in a way entirely complimentary to British fighter pilots, civilians, and scientists.

SUGGESTED WRITING ASSIGNMENT

Rewriting Objectively or with a Different Slant

Read the following essay—John Corry's "God, Country, and Billy Graham"—noting passages that you feel to be objective (that is, passages that consist of statements of fact only) and passages that you think to be slanted favorably or unfavorably by value judgments. Then select a passage (a paragraph or two) of 200 to 300 words to rewrite. If the passage is objective, slant it favorably or unfavorably. If it is slanted, rewrite it objectively or with the opposite slant. Be sure to give an exact reference to the passage. After rewriting, add a paragraph stating your purpose and listing the means you have used to achieve that purpose.

God, Country, and Billy Graham

John Corry

1 Billy Graham is speaking. He jabs with the right hand, while the left disappears into the pocket of his jacket. Then both hands come straight out, hanging there only a moment before they disappear behind his back. They stay

---

[8]Sir Winston Churchill, *The Second World War: Their Finest Hour* (Boston: Houghton Mifflin, 1949), p. 391. Reprinted by permission of the publisher.

that way long enough for someone to count to five, and suddenly they are in front of him again, clenched this time, knuckles white against the even tan. The right fist moves up and down; the left fist opens, and the fingers spread out in supplication. When Billy Graham is good, he is very good, and no one else in the room says a word. "We're moving through dangerous waters," he says, and it is much the same thing he has been saying since that time twenty years ago when he knocked them dead in Los Angeles, a bouncing young evangelist, newly discovered by the Hearst papers, not yet a confidant of Presidents, or the world's best-known Protestant preacher, but mostly a curiosity, soon to be called by people who did not like him "The Barrymore of the Bible" or "Gabriel in Gabardine," his draped suits like as not being white or maybe even a bright green.

2 Now, however, he is in Memphis, in a fine, dark-blue suit, speaking at a prayer breakfast to the people who run Holiday Inns all over America. There are radio and TV, of course, and behind Billy Graham are three plainclothesmen, one of whom has hard, slit eyes that he never for a moment takes off the audience. Minutes before Graham arrived in Memphis the Reverend Ralph David Abernathy left, the city gratefully surrendered its spiritual care from a black to a white Baptist, and the cops are worried that a militant, remembering this is where Martin Luther King was killed, will take a shot at Billy. No one does, and so Billy Graham speaks, moving his listeners without embarrassing them, preaching both the Gospel and those sensible virtues that appeal to both Holiday Innkeepers and Presidents of the United States. Moreover, he is nice. Warmth and good fellowship are very deep in the room, and even old Slit Eyes is smiling. Anita Bryant has appeared, courtesy of Coca-Cola, for which she travels to and fro, and has sung and given a testimony. Miss Bryant was fetching in a Pucci creation about three inches above the knee, and when she sang she held a red Bible. When she was at *her* best she was singing in the lower register, her Bible clutched to her bosom, her eyes closed, and this had led a lady in the audience who wore a mink jacket and a big bouffant to dab at her eyes.

3 When Billy Graham comes on he tells jokes—one about Winston Churchill and George Bernard Shaw, one about Churchill and a moustache he once decided to grow, and one about politics, which is really a throwaway line. Billy Graham needs a great many jokes because he speaks to a great many people, and when he finds one he can use he gets it down just right. He had told the stories the week before in New York, and then passed them on to his brother-in-law, who is also a fine preacher, and the brother-in-law had used them when he spoke before a large group of ministers the next day. No matter, the stories work very well, and when Billy Graham gets down to the serious business he is about in Memphis his audience is with him.

4 "There are singers of siren songs in our times," he says, and then he talks about the siren songs. The first is that the United Nations can bring peace. Jesus said there will be wars and rumors of wars, and it is no good to think that anyone or anything other than Jesus can bring peace. Then, he says, there is the siren song saying that the politics of confrontation will soon end. But don't you know, he says, there are people saying," 'Let's go out and fight.' So guerrilla warfare is now being planned by the anarchists." He mentions Berkeley and Columbia,

and he says that Grayson Kirk, who was the president of Columbia during its late unpleasantness, was "one of the leading liberals on American campuses." Clearly, he is implying, liberalism is not enough. "The only thing that can save our country," he says, "is an awakening."

5 "The third siren song," he says, "is that democracy can survive without morality." He speaks of this for a while, and for the first time he is angry. It is startling. Garbo speaks, Graham rages. Sin has become a personal affront. He says that when his son visited him in New York he sought out the movie pages of the newspaper to find suitable entertainment for him, but found none, which was probably true, advertisements now being nearly unspeakable, and he asks why no one is making more things like *The Sound of Music.* An answer not forthcoming, he talks of the fourth siren song, this one the promise of an "economic Utopia." He says that the country has had the New Deal, the Fair Deal, the New Frontier, and now, referring to Hubert Humphrey's acceptance speech at the Democratic National Convention, the New Day. He says he is just back from Sweden, where they have sex grottoes, but there are unhappy faces on the street and a high suicide rate. The other night he was in Paris, where Sargent Shriver asked him to talk to some students. They were unhappy too. He says he has a friend, a movie star, whose son dropped out to become a hippie. He says he was invited to an island in the Caribbean by one of the world's richest men ("You all know his name") and the rich man said that a poor Baptist preacher on the island had everything, while he had nothing. He says he has a friend who will be the next Governor of Puerto Rico, and that the friend, although he was young and handsome and had a Ph.D. from Harvard, had nothing until he had Jesus.

6 Then Billy Graham crouches; his voice drops ever so slightly from jubilation to sadness, and he says very slowly and very quietly, "Is Jesus yours?" The innkeepers and their ladies suck in their breaths. So do I. Billy is so good and so certain and he knows so many famous people that we are all a little ashamed. "For I want to tell you something," he says, and now his eyes are *flashing,* "we're in trouble." Then it is over, and Billy is saying, "God bless you and thank you, and God bless the Holiday Inns."

7 "Too much work done in the name of Christ is rundown, baggy-trousers stuff," says T. W. Wilson, Billy Graham's old friend and current traveling companion. "Billy believes in going first-class." Indeed, there is general agreement among the members of the Graham organization that class tells and that one reason for their success, aside from God, is their flair. When Billy Graham was ordained in Florida in 1939 evangelism had fallen on hard times, its practitioners being mostly itinerant Southerners who worked the sawdust trail out of canvas cathedrals or, at best, timber tabernacles. Billy—Billy Francis to his family—has had very little of this since his early days as a barnstormer with Youth for Christ, when he traveled to a different city every night aboard an old DC-3, and spread the Word with considerably more hints of fire and brimstone than he does now. His apprenticeship, however, had begun in the late 1930s when, as a student at Florida Bible College, he practiced sermons before the bullfrogs and squirrels, or so the legend

goes, and later tried them while standing in the doorways of gin mills in Tampa. Once he so annoyed a bartender the man rushed out and dumped him.

8 That was only the briefest of setbacks, however, and in 1940, at the age of twenty-one, Billy Graham enrolled at Wheaton College in Illinois, where he won both a degree and a wife by 1943. Then he became the pastor of a small church in Western Springs, Illinois, appeared on a radio program in Chicago called "Songs in the Night," preached around the country, with a quick trip to Britain, and in 1947 became the president of Northwestern Schools in Minneapolis, this being the former Northwestern Bible Training Institute, a responsibility he relinquished in 1951. However, the move into the really big time did not come until Los Angeles in 1949, when he preached before 350,000 persons in eight weeks and 3,000 of them made inquiries, or decisions, for Christ. What was most helpful in all this, besides the blessing of Hearst, was that three of the inquirers were celebrities of a sort—a wiretapper for The Mob, an old Olympics miler, who had gone downhill ever since, and a cowboy radio star, who was also a boozer and a gambling man. They stepped forward when Billy gave the altar call and said that henceforth they were Jesus's men and not their own.

9 Making a decision for Christ means that you say you have made one, and while the appurtenances that surround decision-making in a Graham Crusade have changed over the years, the essentials have not. When Graham finished a sermon at a stadium in Pittsburgh not long ago, he looked at his audience and said, "You can meet Jesus tonight. Jesus is passing by in Pittsburgh. The busses will wait. It will take you only three or four minutes to walk here." Then, as his 2,000, or whatever, voice choir sang "Just as I am," thin lines of people drifted onto the stadium infield, where they were joined by counselors, the counselors choosing someone of the same sex and approximately the same age, color, and general station in life as their own. Then they all gathered around Graham's raised pulpit while he prayed over them, and then the counselors led their charges away, talked briefly with them, got their names, addresses, and phone numbers and promised to get in touch with them again. They had, in fact, just decided for Christ.

10 No one really knows how many will stay decided, or why the folks decided in the first place, or if Los Angeles is a better place in 1969 because Billy Graham preached there in 1949. Nonetheless, it was after that Crusade that he took off, becoming the most successful evangelist of all time and one of the most widely admired Americans too. This is fitting because he is the most American of men, the grandson of two Confederate soldiers, both of whom were well shot up, and the son of a lady who is related to both President James K. Polk and a man named Ezra Alexander, who signed the Declaration of Independence. Moreover, Billy Graham is tall and fair and blue-eyed, and he looks as if he could be the basketball coach of a small Midwestern college, or a movie actor who never made it big because someone like Ronald Reagan or maybe Sonny Tufts got the role instead. The general impression is that you have seen him before, and you have if you recall those snapshots of themselves that soldiers sent home in World War II, the ones in which they wore khaki, put their arms at parade rest, and looked smilingly and invincibly into the sun. Still, Graham's is a good face, handsome

without being pretty, and superbly suited to the business of evangelism, which, as his people will tell you instantly, has to do with selling a product.

11 Graham himself lives in Montreat, North Carolina, and although there are Billy Graham offices in, among other places, Paris, London, Frankfurt, Sydney, Buenos Aires, Atlanta, and Burbank, California, his true headquarters are in Minneapolis, which is the home of the Billy Graham Evangelical Association. This is the corporate part of the organization, where the money is kept, and where the actual, as opposed to the symbolic, selling is done. It is found in an old red-brick building, next to a faded hotel and across the street from a car dealer, and it is run by a man called George Wilson. Mr. Wilson is short, cheerful, and mildly plump, and if he were not associated with Billy Graham he would almost certainly be a captain of industry. "We believe the greatest message in the world should be spread by the most effective means and with the greatest haste," he says, and to these ends he has mustered about 450 people, a bank of computers, and a mailroom that works in three shifts.

12 When it all began, just after the Los Angeles triumph, Mr. Wilson operated with one girl and 600 square feet of office space. Now there are perhaps 160,000 square feet of space, and Mr. Wilson has just bought sixteen acres near the Minneapolis airport for more. (Statistics virtually leap out at you in the headquarters.) Furthermore, the computers use ten miles of eighteen-inch paper every month, Billy Graham is heard on 900 radio stations each week, and the mailroom sends out eighty million pieces of mail a year (this being significant enough to have led pros from both the Republican and Democratic National Committees to Minneapolis to find out how God's mailing techniques can serve their Caesars).

13 Billy Graham, or at least the Billy Graham Evangelical Association, will also get nearly 50,000 letters a week, a good many of which will be sent by people who say they have problems and a good many of which will contain contributions. There are about forty kinds of problems, mostly dealing with matters of faith and morals, and they are assorted and answered accordingly. The average contribution is $6, and talk about how much this might mean in round, annual figures tends to make the Graham people nervous, since it might appear that they are shaking the money tree too hard, and this could discourage further contributions.

14 For years, in fact, snoopy reporters have tried to find evidence that someone in the Graham organization was stealing money, or at least making too much of it. No one found the evidence, and it is just as well to let the thought die. There is a great deal of money around, but there are a great many expenses, too. In a year the Billy Graham Evangelical Association will spend, say, $1.5 million on radio time and more than $3 million on television time. (When Graham appears on TV he is seen on more stations than anyone except the President, and even then only when the President is making a major address.) There is also *Decision,* Billy Graham's monthly magazine, which is tabloid size, about sixteen pages, and has a circulation of four million, including the editions in French, German, Spanish, and Japanese. The annual subscription price is $2. There are also nearly three million sermons that are distributed each year at cost, and the movies that come out of the studios in Burbank. The first, done in 1950 for only $25,000, was called *Mr. Texas,* and it was about a wiseacre cowpoke who made his decision while

listening to Graham on the radio. ("All my life," he says at the denouement, "I've been riding on the wrong trail. I'm turning back. I'm going God's way. I think it's going to be a wonderful ride.")

15 Since then there have been many other movies, and their worth is measured not by what the critics say, since they generally say nothing about them at all, but by numbers. For example, it was recently noted on a sign in the Minneapolis office that *For Pete's Sake* had now been seen in 440 places by 1,284,025 persons, who made 52,478 decisions, while *The Restless Ones,* one of their greatest hits, had been seen in 1,701 places by 4,022,035 persons, who made 305,022 decisions. "We're not trying to be the biggest, the greatest, or anything else," Mr. Wilson says, but it is the biggest and greatest evangelical outfit ever, and it got this way mostly because the rallies and Crusades that Mr. Graham has been conducting have been bigger and greater than anyone else's. From 1947, when they first began counting, through the end of last year, and with no figures included for the times the turnstiles and pocket counters didn't work, the Graham organization says its man has faced 39,525,522 persons and that 1,188,638 of them have come forth to make decisions for Christ.

16 The man who has stirred so many others is himself the most engaging of men. It is probable that there are those who have met Billy Graham and disliked him, but there is little record of it, and the people around him sometimes speak of him the way others speak of Him, only more affectionately. "There's one particular thing we feel," says George Wilson, "that God has given us through the ages a spokesman for His Church, Billy Sunday, Dwight Moody, the Wesley brothers, and now Billy Graham." "I really believe that deep down in his heart he loves his enemies," says T. W. Wilson. "And in airplane terminals he carries old ladies' suitcases and never tells who he is, and he never passes up the needy when he sees them on the street." "The thrilling thing is that he's still as humble as he was at Wheaton," says Walter Smyth, who has known and worked with Billy since about then. "I can't explain the humility. I've never known him to be jealous of any other human being. Such a sincere individual. He believes with every fiber of his being, and when he speaks he speaks with authority—of God."

17 Billy Graham, in fact, is a happy man, who knows what he knows, and for that matter knows who he knows. "I've never felt a moment of despair," he said not long ago, thereby contradicting the experience of most of his species. He was in New York, where he had taken Richard Nixon to church, visited Archbishop Terence Cooke, conferred with the editors of *Reader's Digest,* and had been put to bed with a virus. ("Billy said to me," T. W. recalled the next day, "T, can you think of anything that I've done in my life, anything at all, to deserve these sicknesses?") A visit by Billy Graham is a carefully orchestrated affair in which there is no room for a virus, and this one, just before the November election, had begun with a press conference. He was asked about politics, as he always is, and he had spoken about the Crusade he will hold in New York in June. He also said that he considered New York a second home, although he was appalled by it, and he guessed that it "has had more social experimentation than any other city in the world." (Later, at a luncheon attended by businessmen he repeated

this, and when he got to Memphis a few days later he said that he had just left a city that "has had more social experimentation than any other city in the world.")

18 Despite this, he said, there are "all kinds of muggings, robbery taking place, even in the churches." There is "culture against culture." There is "confusion and frustration." Mayor Lindsay had said that "nobody can instill affection in the hearts of others," meaning that legislation can go just so far, and Billy said he certainly agreed with him. He said New York was ripe for a Crusade, and that this one would use thousands and thousands of volunteers, 25,000 of whom would do follow-up work, checking on those who made inquiries during the Crusade and seeing to it that they found a home in a New York church. As always, he said, he would accept no money for the Crusade. The money for it, $924,000, would be raised in New York, and at the end the books would be audited and the results released to the churches and the press.

19 In all this he was smooth without being oily, and he hardly ever stopped smiling, the smile having once been helped by cosmetic dental surgery, and although he saw ruination all about him, he found reasons to rejoice, too. For one thing, there were hippie boots, which hippies, he said, call "Jesus boots." "Many psychologists," he insisted, "say this reflects a longing for Jesus." For another thing, there were the young people who were concerned, involved, longing to get the country right again. "I don't have much sympathy for the tactics of civil disobedience and confrontation," he said, "but the people I'm talking about are that wonderful group of idealists." The reporters, however, wanted to talk about Mr. Nixon. Would he endorse him? He would not, really, although he allowed they had been friends twenty years, and that he had preached not long before at the funeral of Mr. Nixon's mother. The reporters, who had pretty much abandoned the Crusade by then, wanted to know where Billy Graham *really* stood on the issues. "My message is so intensely personal," he said, "that people miss the overwhelming social content." Did he think the people had lost confidence in their elected leaders? Well, maybe, he said. Vietnam? He just didn't know enough about it, but he was certain the United States wasn't over there murdering people the way the Nazis did. "People concerned about the Vietnam war don't seem as concerned about Biafra and the Arab-Israel war," he said, and soon he was noting that his Pittsburgh Crusade had attracted a larger percentage of Negroes than any other Crusade. A little after that he thanked the reporters for coming, stayed around long enough for a camera crew to make a special tape, and then shook hands with old friends all the way to the door.

20 On the road, which is where he is most of the time, Billy Graham arises at precisely 6:45 (he is the most punctual of men), prays, eats breakfast, and reads newspapers. As he reads he clips out articles, most often ones that tell of national peril or moral decline, and later he stuffs them into the pocket of his suit jacket, which is a 43 Long, along with an old wallet full of credit cards and an honorary police badge. Since he is called on for written or spoken words nearly every day of his life, he must find many topics, or at least the semblance of them, and he finds them in the clippings and in the Bible, the verse quite often being John 3:16. Billy Graham spends a great deal of his time in hotel rooms, dining

in his room most of the time, and all the rooms are checked out beforehand by an advance man. The underside of a celebrated evangelist's life is that he does not live like you or me, but, dealing as he does in goodness, must worry about fanatics, assassins, hysterics, drunks, Christian bores, pagan boors, and the great legion of enterprising women who would claim him as their own if they could and thereby win headlines, fleeting fame, and a part in a dirty French movie. It is a life like no one else's, other than a Presidential candidate's, and the evangelist does more of it than the candidate, his consolation being that while neither one is truly his own man, he at least has God, while the other has only Mammon.

21 "Just the loss of privacy is difficult," Graham was saying in one of the hotels. "People may not know who you are, but they're always whispering." He had just won over an audience of businessmen, and now he was sitting, absolutely at ease, in a big leather armchair. His friends say that Billy Graham has found his natural home in a pulpit, but it is possible that he is even better when he confronts just one other person. Artlessness envelops him, sincerity is palpable, and good humor is nearly a weapon.

22 "When fame first came," he said, "*Time* and Henry Luce began to promote me. That frightened me. I just wish I could pull back some of the things I said. I'm worried that I brought disrepute to the name of Christ." Those were the days when Billy Graham spoke more explicitly than he does now about things like the United Nations and the Supreme Court, wore hand-painted ties, and sometimes appeared with Roy Rogers' horse at children's services. "I had read about the big evangelists, and I knew they were famous only two years, and I thought I'd be famous only two years. But the Lord sent my key men to me. I've never had a disagreement with them, and if nothing else happened the fellowship would still make it worthwhile."

23 Oddly, for an old country boy, much of the fellowship has been conducted in the council halls of the mighty, which includes that room in Miami Beach where Richard Nixon settled on Spiro T. Agnew. The question is why, and the answer may be that Billy Graham confirms for our kings and rulers what they believe to be the contours of their lives and the nation's. He does this, I think, without raising his voice, which is the voice of old country boys and Middle Americans everywhere, and without forcing our kings and rulers to any commitment other than to goodness, and goodness, of course, he passes on by osmosis. This makes them feel nice. "I've tried to limit my contact with Presidents to moral and spiritual questions," he said. "One President asked my advice on a political question—we were seated around a dinner table—and my wife kicked me under the table and said aloud, 'You keep your counsel.' I think the next President will face the greatest crisis of any President in history, greater than Lincoln's. [This, remember, was just before the election.] You have today the superweapons. You have this growing polarization with the New Left and the New Right. I foresee by 1972 four major political parties. The President will have to unify the country, and this will be at a time of rising crime, of the politics of confrontation, at a time of rising affluence. We're seeing the failure of many of our social experiments. We're seeing a major revolution. We may come out of it a stronger nation or a dictatorship. No, I don't know if the dictatorship would be from the right or the left."

24 The threat, however, would seem to be from the left. There is much in Billy Graham's preaching of the specter of Antichrist, the great antagonist who will conquer and be conquered, which will lead to the risen Christ. "Antichrist may be a person or a system," Billy Graham said. "If it is a person then it will be someone out of a Godless society. The coming of Christ is relatively near. We all thought Russia was changing, but it isn't. I was recently given a briefing in Washington, and it was frightening." I did not stop to ask him why he had been given a briefing, and he went on to talk of other things. "Some people in our society," he said, "have been promised more than the politicians can deliver and they're frustrated." It is a terrible time, he was saying, and our next President will need all the support we can give him.

25 Would he stand for public office? No. "People have always wanted me to lead a crusade against Communism," he said, "and there are pressures from the right and the left. I've been approached by both major parties, too. When? Oh, I forget when, but the first time was when Willis Smith died and the North Carolina Democrats wanted to have me agree to have the Governor appoint me to the Senate. At least two Presidents have asked me about major jobs, but the Gospel is more important to me than anything else. NBC wanted me to appear opposite Arthur Godfrey at one time, at one million dollars a year, and I turned that down, too."

26 Through all this Billy Graham is smiling, not piercingly, like Mandrake the Magician, the way Bishop Sheehan did on television, and not a smarmy smirk, either. It is pleasant and manly. Billy Graham once wrote to a friend that "I have seen so many pictures of Jesus as a weakling that I am sick of it. He was no sissie and He was no weakling." He must have been, Graham concluded, "straight, strong, big, handsome, tender, gracious, courteous." It is a description of an athletic Eagle Scout, or of Graham himself, certainly not of a short, swarthy Semite, and it is absolutely no good knocking it. Billy knows what he knows. Jesus looked the way he did because "no sin and mar had come near His body," and Graham frets over his own ailments, wondering if a virus is not a visitation.

27 "I try to think of myself as an Ambassador for Christ," he was saying now, and this time he was walking through midtown Manhattan behind a pair of great dark glasses and under a deerstalker hat. "Some of the extreme fundamentalists are among my most vocal critics and extreme liberals think I'm too fundamentalist. But I think the vast majority of church people support me." He stopped at a crowded street corner, waiting for a light to change, and was jostled by some ladies with lumpy shopping bags. He smiled from behind his glasses at none of them in particular and looked pleased with himself. Midway across the intersection he said that he first met Hubert Humphrey in 1949 when they were skinny-dipping in the pool at the YMCA in Minneapolis, but that they have never had much to say to each other. "But Nixon, I guess, is one of my ten best friends," he said. "I first met him in the Senate cafeteria when I was having lunch with Clyde Hoey, the Senator from North Carolina. He was an old-fashioned man with long flowing hair, and he called Nixon over and said to me, 'I want you to meet him. He's an outstanding young man and he's going places.' Actually, I had met Nixon's parents before that because they had attended some evangelical conferences that I had, too."

28 A blind Negro stood motionless in the middle of the street, rattling a tin cup. Graham stepped over, dropped some coins in, and slipped his arm around the man's shoulders. He whispered something, and as he drew away he said, "God bless you." Then he began talking about all the "confusion and frustration" in the city, which was what he had been talking about for the last few days, and he said that New Yorkers seemed to think they lived in the center of the universe. "But when I was in the Fijis," he said, "everyone there believed that was the center of the universe." There was a thought here, but it got lost on the crowded street.

29 Billy Graham is walking through bright, shining Kennedy Airport, carrying three newsmagazines and the New York *Post,* and resuming a conversation left over from the day before. "Niebuhr is an economic theologian," he says, "Tillich is more of a philosopher, and Barth, we need more men like him. The trend now is toward an evangelical theology. Too many ministers think they're social engineers. They even want to get into the business of deciding where highways should go. You must remember that the worst part of history was in the Dark Ages, when the Church ran everything." For himself, he says, he wants no part of it, and sometimes he thinks his wife has something when she says he should take it easy and just write. Still, he says, there are things to do. Last year he sent George Wilson over to the Cunard Line to buy the *Queen Mary.* Imagine! The *Queen Mary!* He wanted to hold conferences on it. There is also talk that he may found a university. He allows that he may.

30 When he gets on the plane, carefully taking a window seat, while posting T. W. Wilson on the aisle, no one recognizes him. Then he slips off the dark glasses and another passenger says, "For Christ's sake, Doc, that's Billy Graham." Graham never blinks. When we are aloft, the stewardesses, both of whom have champagne hair, approach him. One says her mother adores him. The other asks for his autograph. All during the flight he is in and out of the dark glasses, chewing gum, skimming through his magazines, and looking gracious every time someone stops by. When I order a bloody mary I hope he will think it is tomato juice. When it comes I say to hell with it and start toying with the swizzle stick. A moment later I stop and move the whole thing to a corner of the tray where he can't see it. Soon, T. W. corks off. The magazine in the seat pocket in front of Billy Graham is called *The American Way.* I stare at him. A lady with a beaded hat and a gold lorgnette stares at him. He stares out the window. There is nothing out there but clouds. I wonder if he knows something we don't.

Distinguishing Types
of Words Semantically

THE PROCESS OF ABSTRACTING

The most famous explanation of the process of abstracting is found in S. I. Hayakawa's *Language in Thought and Action.* Hayakawa did not originate the ideas upon which the explanation is based; as he acknowledges in a footnote in the chapter treating this process, he was indebted to Alfred Korzybski's *Science and Sanity* (1933). But Hayakawa uses in his explanation a more effective image to represent the idea than Korzybski had used, and his style is more appealing than Korzybski's. The following excerpt from *Language in Thought and Action* presents the image of the abstraction ladder to you in Hayakawa's words, with his diagram of the image. The dialog that follows the excerpt builds upon the ideas in the excerpt.

Bessie, the Cow

The universe is in a perpetual state of flux. The stars are growing, cooling, exploding. The earth itself is not unchanging; mountains are being worn away, rivers are altering their channels, valleys are deepening. All life is also a process of change, through birth, growth, decay, and death. Even what we used to call "inert matter"—chairs and tables and stones—is not inert, as we now know, for, at the submicroscopic level, it is a whirl of electrons. If a table looks today very much as it did yesterday or as it did a hundred years ago, it is not because it has not changed, but because the changes have been too minute for our coarse perceptions. To modern science there is no "solid matter." If matter looks "solid" to us, it does so only because its motion is too rapid or too minute to be felt. It is "solid" only in the sense that a rapidly rotating color chart is "white" or a rapidly spinning top is "standing still." Our senses are extremely limited, so that we constantly have to use instruments, such as microscopes, telescopes, speed-ometers, stethoscopes, and seismographs, to detect and record occurrences which our senses are not able to record directly. The way in which we happen to see and feel things is the result of the peculiarities of our nervous systems. There are "sights" we cannot see, and, as even children know today with their high-frequency dog whistles, "sounds" that we cannot hear. It is absurd, therefore, to imagine that we ever perceive anything "as it really is."

Inadequate as our senses are, with the help of instruments they tell us a great deal. The discovery of microörganisms with the use of the microscope has given us a measure of control over bacteria; we cannot see, hear, or feel electromagnetic waves, but we can create and transform them to useful purpose. Most of our conquest of the external world, in engineering, in chemistry, and in medicine, is due to our use of mechanical contrivances of one kind or another to increase the capacity of our nervous systems. In modern life, our unaided senses are not half enough to get us about in the world. We cannot even obey speed laws or compute our gas and electric bills without mechanical aids to perception.

To return, then, to the relations between words and what they stand for, let us say that there is before us "Bessie," a cow. Bessie is a living organism, constantly changing, constantly ingesting food and air, transforming it, getting rid of it again. Her blood is circulating, her nerves are sending messages. Viewed microscopically, she is a mass of variegated corpuscles, cells, and bacterial organisms; viewed from the point of view of modern physics, she is a perpetual dance of electrons. What she is in her entirety, we can never know; even if we could at any precise moment say what she was, at the next moment she would have changed enough so that our description would no longer be accurate. It is impossible to say completely what Bessie or anything else really *is*. Bessie is not a static "object," but a dynamic process.

The Bessie that we experience, however, is something else again. We experience only a small fraction of the total Bessie: the lights and shadows of her exterior, her motions, her general configuration, the noises she makes, and the sensations she presents to our sense of touch. *And because of our previous experience, we observe resemblances in her to certain other animals to which, in the past, we have applied the word "cow."*

The Process of Abstracting

The "object" of our experience, then, is not the "thing in itself," but *an interaction between our nervous systems* (*with all their imperfections*) *and something outside them.* Bessie is unique—there is nothing else in the universe exactly like her in all respects. But we automatically *abstract* or select from the process-Bessie those features of hers in which she resembles other animals of like shape, functions, and habits, and we *classify* her as "cow."

When we say, then, that "Bessie is a cow," we are only noting the process-Bessie's resemblances to other "cows" and *ignoring differences*. What is more, we are leaping a huge chasm: from the dynamic process-Bessie, a whirl of electro-chemico-neural eventfulness, to a relatively static "idea," "concept," or *word*, "cow." In this connection, the reader is referred to the diagram entitled "The Abstraction Ladder," on page 36.

As the diagram illustrates, the "object" we see is an abstraction of the lowest level; but it is still an abstraction, since it leaves out characteristics of the process that is the real Bessie. The *word* "Bessie" (cow_1) is the lowest *verbal* level of abstraction, leaving out further characteristics—the differences between Bessie yesterday and Bessie today, between Bessie today and Bessie tomorrow—and selecting only the similarities. The word "cow" selects only the similarities between Bessie (cow_1), Daisy (cow_2), Rosie (cow_3), and so on, and therefore leaves out still more about Bessie. The word "livestock" selects or abstracts only the features that Bessie has in common with pigs, chickens, goats, and sheep. The term "farm asset" abstracts only the features Bessie has in common with barns, fences, livestock, furniture, generating plants, and tractors, and is therefore on a very high level of abstraction.

Our concern here with the process of abstracting may seem strange since the study of language is all too often restricted to matters of pronunciation, spelling, vocabulary, grammar, and sentence structure. The methods by which composition and oratory are taught in old-fashioned school systems seem to be largely responsible for this widespread notion that the way to study words is to concentrate one's attention exclusively on words.

But as we know from everyday experience, learning language is not simply a matter of learning words; it is a matter of correctly relating our words to the things and happenings for which they stand. We learn the language of baseball by playing or watching the game *and studying what goes on.* It is not enough for a child to learn to *say* "cookie" or "dog"; he must be able to use these words in their proper relationship to nonverbal cookies and nonverbal dogs before we can grant that he is learning the language. As Wendell Johnson has said, "The study of language begins properly with a study of what language is about."

Once we begin to concern ourselves with what language is about, we are at once thrown into a consideration of how the human nervous system works. When we call Beau (the Boston terrier), Pedro (the chihuahua), Snuffles (the English bulldog), and Shane (the Irish wolfhound)—creatures that differ greatly in size, shape, appearance, and behavior—by the same name, "dog," our nervous system has obviously gone to work *abstracting* what is common to them all, ignoring for the time being the differences among them.

DIALOG 2

The Abstraction Ladder

1. Please refer to the abstraction ladder. Look at the man on stairs, not yet on the ladder, holding a tray loaded with objects. What do these objects represent?	Characteristics of Bessie as the observer sees her.

ABSTRACTION LADDER

Start reading from the bottom *UP*

8. "wealth"

8. The word "wealth" is at an extremely high level of abstraction, omitting *almost* all reference to the characteristics of Bessie.

7. "asset"

7. When Bessie is referred to as an "asset," still more of her characteristics are left out.

6. "farm assets"

6. When Bessie is included among "farm assets," reference is made only to what she has in common with all other salable items on the farm.

5. "livestock"

5. When Bessie is referred to as "livestock," only those characteristics she has in common with pigs, chickens, goats, etc., are referred to.

4. "cow"

4. The word "cow" stands for the characteristics we have abstracted as common to cow_1, cow_2, cow_3 . . . cow_n. Characteristics peculiar to specific cows are left out.

3. "Bessie"

3. The word "Bessie" (cow_1) is the *name* we give to the object of perception of level 2. The name *is not* the object; it merely *stands for* the object and omits reference to many of the characteristics of the object.

2.

2. The cow we perceive is not the word, but the object of experience, that which our nervous system abstracts (selects) from the totality that constitutes the process-cow. Many of the characteristics of the process-cow are left out.

1. The cow known to science ultimately consists of atoms, electrons, etc., according to present-day scientific inference. Characteristics (represented by circles) are infinite at this level and ever-changing. This is the *process level*.

2. Hayakawa states in the entry beside this picture that many of the characteristics of the process-cow are left out. What does *process-cow* mean?	A particular cow as it actually exists, not as it is perceived.
3. In your own words, explain what the second step is.	It is the image or picture of the object in the mind of the observer.
4. What are some of the characteristics included in the process-cow that are not included in the perception of the cow?	Characteristics like details of digestion, lactation, and circulation of the blood; cell structure; and the structure of the individual hairs in the hide.
5. Is this image an abstraction?	Hayakawa says it is an abstraction, because the eye has automatically selected some of the details in the process-cow without seeing, or being able to see, the other details. In this technical sense the perception is an abstraction.
6. Technically, Hayakawa is correct, but in this course we will use *abstraction* in the usual sense of conscious abstraction and say therefore that abstraction begins on the fourth level. We will call the third-level term the specific term. Why are quotation marks used around "Bessie," the specific term?	To show that "Bessie" is a word, a symbol for an object, not the object itself.
7. How does "cow" differ from "Bessie"?	It is a class term rather than a specific term, because it has no specific referent.
8. Why is the man on the ladder beside the fourth entry holding fewer objects than the man below him is holding?	The objects stand for the characteristics all cows have in common, and these are fewer than the individual characteristics any observer can perceive when looking at a specific cow.
9. What are some of the characteristics not symbolized by *cow*?[9]	Characteristics like a certain color and weight, an exact shape, and exact markings.

[9] We are italicizing the terms instead of setting them in quotation marks as Hayakawa does, since that is our practice in this book.

10. We can say that as a term *cow* is an abstract term. What is a synonym for *abstract* in this context?	*General.*
11. What happens to the objects on the tray as the man climbs higher?	They become fewer.
12. And what does this symbolize?	That fewer characteristics of any specific object are signified by the terms in the lefthand column as they go up.
13. What, then, does *to abstract* mean?	To overlook differences in order to relate things that have characteristics in common.
14. What is a synonym for *to abstract?*	*To generalize.*
15. In an abstraction ladder, where is the most general term?	At the top.
16. Where is the specific term?	On the third level.
17. Are there any terms below the third level?	No, the two bottom levels are nonverbal.

18. Complete the abstraction ladder below to represent the automobile shown in the advertisement on the right.
   6. *automobile*
   5.
   4.
   3.
     2.
     1.
	6. *automobile*
	5. *Continental*
	4. *Continental Mark III*
	3. *Continental Mark III$_{649}$*
	  2. perception of Continental Mark III$_{649}$
	  1. process–Continental Mark III$_{649}$
	On the third level one might have Wilson J. Cartwright's Continental Mark III, or the serial number, or any index number from 1 to *n;* but there must be something to indicate that this is a specific Continental Mark III.

19. Is this a correct abstraction ladder?
   7. *Plymouth*
   6. *Fury*
   5. *Red Fury*
   4. *1970 Fury*
   3. *Fury$_1$*
     2. perception of Fury$_1$
     1. process-Fury$_1$
	No.

The Continental Mark III.

What makes this the most authoritatively styled, decisively individual motorcar of this generation?

Even small details like the clock are handled distinctively. In fact, it's not just a clock but a true chronometer from the famous jeweler, Cartier.

The engine is the most advanced V-8 in the automotive industry. It features 365 horsepower, 460 cubic inches in a great new, deep-breathing design.

Ask your Continental dealer about Sure-Track braking, the safest, straightest way to stop a car. Computer technology has made it the most advanced automotive braking system in the world.

Your Continental dealer will be pleased to demonstrate this most distinguished motorcar.

LINCOLN·MERCURY

20. If not, why not?	The fourth and fifth levels are wrong.
21. They are wrong because the term on the fifth level must completely contain the term on the fourth level. Since not all 1970 Furys are red, the fifth level here does not contain the fourth. For the ladder to be correct all the way up, we must be able to say that the term on level 3 stands for an example of the class symbolized on level 4, which is a type of the class symbolized on level 5, which is a type of the class symbolized on level 6, and so forth. Can this be done with the ladder on *Continental Mark III?*	Yes. *Continental Mark III*$_{649}$ stands for an example of a Continental Mark III, which is a type of Continental, which is a type of automobile.
22. Does *Continental Mark III*$_{649}$ represent an example of each of the higher classes as well as an example of a Continental Mark III?	Yes, an example of a Continental and an example of an automobile.

23. Make a correct abstraction ladder with *Fury*$_1$ as the third-level term.	6. *automobile*
	5. *Plymouth*
	4. *Fury*
	3. *Fury*$_1$
	  2. perception of Fury$_1$
	  1. process-Fury$_1$

24. Do the terms listed below form an abstraction ladder?
    7. *United States*
    6. *state*
    5. *county*
    4. *city*
    3. *Austin*
      2. perception of Austin
      1. process-Austin
	No. (If you answered, "Yes," read the next three questions. If you answered correctly, go on to number 28.)

25. Austin is an example of a city. Is a city a type of county?	No.
26. Is a county a type of state?	No.
27. Is any one of the fifty states a type of United States?	No.

28. What is the relationship of a city to a county, a county to a state, and one of the fifty states to the United States?	A city is a part of a county, a county is a part of a state, and one of the fifty states is a part of the United States.
29. Is Fury$_1$ part of a Fury?	No, it *is* a Fury.
30. Is the relationship of the specific to the general the same as the relationship of the part to the whole?	No, the specific term does not symbolize a part of a general class; it symbolizes a whole thing, that is, an example of any class on its abstraction ladder.
31. What makes the specific thing, like Fury$_1$, an example of a class, a larger class, and still larger classes?	It has in it all of the characteristics abstracted to define the class, however large it is.
32. To summarize the lesson, define the process of abstraction.	The process of abstraction consists in overlooking differences in specific things in order to classify them according to characteristics they have in common.

DIALOG 3

Semantical Classification of Words

The relation of specific terms to general terms is not difficult to understand when there is no question about whether a term is either specific or general. Difficulties arise, however, when one tries to see *specific* and *general* in the full extension of their meanings because some specific terms cover composite referents and others refer to invisible referents, and because general, or class, terms overlap another type of abstract term. The following dialog attempts to define the range of specific and general terms by distinguishing these terms from similar and overlapping terms.

1. What type of meaning does a specific word express?	It refers to or calls to mind one thing in the objective world, such as Bessie or Continental Mark III$_{649}$. This thing is called its referent.

2. What is a class word?	It is a word that stands for the characteristics that several specific things have in common.
3. Name three class words.	*Cow, man, house.*
4. Does a class word have just one referent?	No, not in itself. For example, *house* can refer to a cabin by a river or a mansion on a hill, among other things.
5. In a written context, does a class word like *house* ever have a specific referent?	Yes. If the specific house has been described, it can later be referred to as *the house.* The reader will know because of the context which house the class word refers to.
6. Can you think of another example of a class word made specific by context?	If a person is being described, one knows that an expression like *his head* refers to a specific head, even though *head* is a class word.
7. Then a specific word has one referent, and a class word, though it has no referent by itself, may have any number of referents, depending upon the context. A class word may also be called a ——————— word or an ——————— word.	general, abstract
8. Are *copper, water,* and *oxygen* class words?	Yes, they stand for characteristics that all specimens of copper, water, and oxygen have in common.
9. The word *specimen* in your answer is significant. What is the difference between a specimen and an example?	A specimen does not have the form of an entity as an example does. One has to separate the specimen from a larger amount of the substance.
10. For this reason one does not speak of *a* water in the way one speaks of *a* man. Since *copper, water,* and *oxygen* are class words, are all terms that refer to solid substances, liquids, and gases class words?	Yes.
11. Is *United States of America* a specific term?	I suppose so, since it refers to one nation, but no one has a real perception of the whole.

12. Though no one can perceive its full referent, it has a referent in the objective world, and this referent can be classified. Consequently, we must call it a specific term. Can you name other specific terms that refer to composite referents?	*The American Federation of Labor, Twentieth-Century Fox, Harcourt, Brace & World, American Air Lines,* the *National Education Association, Denver University,* the *Senate of the United States,* and so forth.
13. Can you think of a term for anything so all inclusive that it cannot be classified?	*Nature.*
14. This word is so comprehensive in its primary definition, the sum of all existing things, that it cannot be classified. In addition to being composite, it is unique. Is *humanity* a unique term?	Yes, since individual men are examples of man, not of humanity.
15. All of the specific and general terms we have discussed have symbolized specific visual impressions and what visual impressions have in common. Are there specific and general terms for other types of sense impressions?	We speak of a *taste,* a *sound,* an *odor* —these seem to be class terms.

16. Can you make an abstraction ladder with the class word *odor?*	7. *sense perception*
	6. *odor*
	5. *fragrance*
	4. *rose fragrance*
	3. *rose fragrance$_3$*
	  2. perception of rose fragrance$_3$
	  1. process–rose fragrance$_3$

17. It seems that people have not been so creative in naming natural olfactory sensations on the fourth level as in naming visual sensations. To make the fourth-level term, one modifies the fifth-level term by the name of the source. Have people been more creative in naming manufactured fragrances?	Yes—for example, *My Sin, Evening in Paris, Hypnotique, Hai Karate.*
18. Are these names fourth-level terms or third-level terms?	They have proper names like third-level terms and are names of specific perfumes, but since each perfume is put into bottles at various times and places, it must vary from bottle to bottle. This makes me feel that we should say *My Sin$_{1,2, \ldots n}$.*

19. The abstraction ladder is not adequate to represent all that you have said. We have done enough, however, to show that there are specific fragrances from physical sources in the objective world and that these can be named. Which term, according to our study so far, means the opposite of *general* or *abstract?*	Specific.
20. You have probably read in some English textbooks that the opposite of *abstract* is *concrete.* A typical list of concrete terms is *flower, fish, book,* and *cow.* If one of these concrete words were put on an abstraction ladder, which level would it be on?	Probably the fourth or the fifth. It could not be on the third, which is reserved for specific words.
21. Is *Jonathan C. Bricker* concrete?	Yes.
22. Is *Jonathan C. Bricker* specific?	Yes.
23. Is *man* concrete?	Yes.
24. Is *man* specific?	No.
25. Do *concrete* and *specific* have overlapping meanings?	Yes.
26. Are they synonyms?	No.
27. How would you define *concrete term?*	A concrete term may be a specific term or a class name covering specific terms.
28. A concrete term like *cow* or *man* is an abstract term in the context of the abstraction ladder. Yet *concrete* is sometimes the opposite of *abstract.* Try to state two meanings of *abstract* as the term relates to both *specific* and *concrete.*	*Abstract* means not concrete, and *abstract* means not specific, even though *concrete* and *specific* are not synonyms.
29. A typical list of abstract (nonconcrete) terms is *love, honor, beauty, courage, intelligence,* and *refinement.* Can words like these ever have referents in the objective world? In other words, do they name impressions conveyed by the physical senses?	No. (If you answered, "Yes," read numbers 30 and 31.)

30. Suppose you see a man and a woman embracing, and you say, "This is love." Are you really seeing love?	No, I see a man and a woman, and I infer that they are in love.
31. *Love* denotes an inference, an interpretation of a situation perceived, not the situation itself. If you see a man rushing into a burning building to rescue a child, are you seeing courage?	No, I see a man rushing into a burning building, and I judge the man to be courageous.
32. Can we set up a ladder from specific to general for inferential and judgmental terms like *love* and *courage?*	There could not be any nonverbal levels. This is about as close as we could come to an abstraction ladder: 4. *emotion* 3. *love* 2. *romantic love* 1. Mary Henderson's love for Bill Simmons
33. Your level 1 is an inference that interprets one situation, and we can say that if we are talking about romantic love we are thinking of something more general than Mary's love for Bill. Do we have a full range of terms to signify different degrees of generality in inferences (and judgments)?	No, words like *love, hate,* and *anger* can be classified as emotions, and there are terms to represent these concepts, but of these, only love has standard subclasses with names, and even these subclasses of love do not cover specific inferences (inferences on specific situations) with names of their own.
34. In other words, we can only speak of abstract (nonconcrete) terms and more general abstract terms.	[See page 46 for a summary classification of semantical types of words.]

EXERCISE 2

Semantical Classification of Words

The sentences in the following exercise are quotations from readings found in this book. Rewrite the sentences, classifying the boldface words and word groups as follows: Put nonconcrete words in parentheses. Circle specific, concrete words (both those with single referents and those with composite referents). Underline class words. Draw rectangles around class words made specific by context. Put unique words in brackets. Treat plural words as you would if they were singular.

Semantical Classification of Words

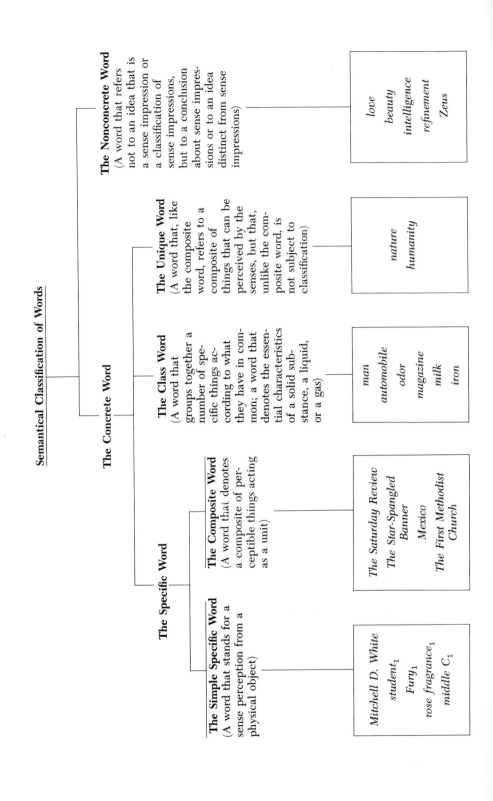

The Concrete Word

The Specific Word

The Simple Specific Word
(A word that stands for a sense perception from a physical object)

Mitchell D. White
student₁
Fury₁
rose fragrance₁
middle C₁

The Composite Word
(A word that denotes a composite of perceptible things acting as a unit)

The Saturday Review
The Star-Spangled Banner
Mexico
The First Methodist Church

The Class Word
(A word that groups together a number of specific things according to what they have in common; a word that denotes the essential characteristics of a solid substance, a liquid, or a gas)

man
automobile
odor
magazine
milk
iron

The Unique Word
(A word that, like the composite word, refers to a composite of things that can be perceived by the senses, but that, unlike the composite word, is not subject to classification)

nature
humanity

The Nonconcrete Word
(A word that refers not to an idea that is a sense impression or a classification of sense impressions, but to a conclusion about sense impressions or to an idea distinct from sense impressions)

love
beauty
intelligence
refinement
Zeus

1. Hastily, **Oliver** drove the **tractor** back the way he had come.
2. In physical **science man** has to an impressive degree learned to control and direct the **forces** and **materials** supplied by **nature**. . . .
3. Even now, many **politicians** think that the most devastating **insult** you can apply to an **opponent** is to call him a "**planner.**"
4. They riot against the **inattention, intransigence,** and **condescension** of **administrators** with which they have lost patience.
5. Around five o'clock on **Friday** morning, June 4, 1954, an Upton, Massachusetts, garage **mechanic** whom I'll call Alfred Edison—a married man and the **father** of a three-year-old **daughter**—was wrenched from **sleep** by a grinding **pain** in the **stomach.**
6. Biomedical **engineering,** particularly its **possibilities** of organ **transplant,** genetic **modification,** and control of **disease,** promises substantial increase in human **longevity.**
7. Among them is a new **book** called **What Every Woman Should Know About Investing Her Money,** by **H. H. Levy** (Dartnell, **$6.95**), which, the **Wall Street Journal** reports, is "selling very, very well" to "**housewives, secretaries** and female **executives.**"
8. In **Selma, Montgomery,** and **Birmingham, students** learned first-hand the **necessity** and **effectiveness** of civil **disobedience.**
9. Only a square **viewer** wants to know where the black **monolith** came from and where it is going.
10. By now, obviously, the **horse**—without losing its identity as **horse**—has also become a **symbol.**

HOW SEMANTICAL DISTINCTIONS RELATE
TO PURPOSE IN WRITING

Writers who wish to arouse emotions in the interest of a cause without giving any reasons use very general concrete and nonconcrete terms, mentioning no specific name that does not carry with it an aura of appropriate emotion. In *The Tyranny of Words*, Stuart Chase quotes the following statement by Will Hays, whom he calls a czar of Hollywood, as a "horrible example" of abstract writing:

> Listen for a moment, listen with eyes aloft, listen to the voice of experience and the call of inspiration from the spirit of America which was Washington and Lincoln and Roosevelt [Teddy]—listen and hear them call: Carry on! Carry on now against the foes of our household as you fought at Valley Forge, at Argonne and at Château-Thierry. Carry on! Carry on! Find dishonesty if there be dishonesty and crush it; find the right and cleave to it.[10]

[10]New York: Harcourt, Brace & World, 1938, pp. 379–80.

Like many other emotional appeals that depend upon abstract language, this passage gives no information at all about the action it urges. It could be used to inspire a customarily law-abiding person to set fire to a public building, or it could be used to inspire a policeman to protect the same building. A writer may have reason to arouse emotion when describing a starving child he has seen, when describing the killing of an elderly man by a hit-and-run driver, or when reporting in detail how a court of law has exempted a young man from punishment apparently because he is the son of wealthy and influential parents. But to turn emotion on and off by using abstract language unrelated to specific contexts is unscrupulous.

Writers—propagandists—who wish to promote ends that to them seem desirable, even though the means to these ends may be reprehensible, may use nonemotive general and composite terms to make their subjects palatable. George Orwell described this technique effectively in 1945, in an essay called "Politics and the English Language." In the following excerpt from this essay, he is talking about propagandistic techniques of Russian Communists and their supporters, but the techniques can be used by anyone dedicated to a cause that requires inhumane, destructive means for its realization.

> Defenceless villages are bombarded from the air, the inhabitants driven out into the countryside, the cattle machine-gunned, the huts set on fire with incendiary bullets; this is called *pacification*. Millions of peasants are robbed of their farms and sent trudging along the roads with no more than they can carry: this is called *transfer of population* or *rectification of frontiers*. People are imprisoned for years without trial or shot in the back of the neck or sent to die of scurvy in Arctic lumber camps: this is called *elimination of unreliable elements*. Such phraseology is needed if one wants to name things without calling up mental pictures of them. Consider for instance some comfortable English professor defending Russian totalitarianism. He cannot say outright, "I believe in killing off your opponents when you can get good results by doing so." Probably, therefore, he will say something like this:
>
> "While freely conceding that the Soviet regime exhibits certain features which the humanitarian may be inclined to deplore, we must, I think, agree that a certain curtailment of the right to political opposition is an unavoidable concomitant of transitional periods, and that the rigors which the Russian people have been called upon to undergo have been amply justified in the sphere of concrete achievement."
>
> The inflated style is itself a kind of euphemism. A mass of Latin words falls upon the facts like soft snow, blurring the outlines and covering up all the details.[11]

Writers who wish to give exact information and call precise images to their

---

[11]In *Shooting an Elephant and Other Essays* (New York: Harcourt, Brace & World, 1945), pp. 88–89.

readers' minds use many concrete terms with referents that one person can perceive. Notice the precision and the concreteness of the key terms in the following paragraphs quoted from the beginning of a report by Kenneth Weaver, assistant editor of the *National Geographic:*

> In the dark of the moon, a deer mouse scurries softly across a forest floor. Virtually invisible and soundless, he seems safe from danger—but the unerring strike of a rattlesnake brings his journey to an abrupt end. Faint radiations of heat from the mouse, reaching two sensitive pits in the viper's head, have betrayed the exact location of the tiny mammal's warm body.
>
> In a desert cavern, bats returning from a night's feeding swirl in apparently chaotic swarms. They seem doomed to collisions on a massive scale, yet miraculously they avoid hitting one another or the cavern walls. Each bat utters streams of ultrasonic squeaks that echo from obstacles and warn it to change course.
>
> The rattlesnake, with its sensitivity to infrared radiation, and the bat, with its skill at echo-location (comparable to sonar and radar), are natural examples of what scientists call remote sensing. Simply defined, that means getting information about things at a distance, or about things one cannot touch.[12]

When precise, informative writers treat a composite subject that does not lend itself to illustration, as a general subject like remote sensing does, they break it down into parts, describing in detail those aspects that they know best.

Some people would set out more confidently to write on the University of North Carolina, American culture, education, communication, or humanity than on such aspects of these large subjects as the process by which a course is normally added to the curriculum in the College of Arts and Sciences at the University of North Carolina, how one hundred families on the other side of town actually live, what John Dewey's schools were really like, how a transistor works, or how their great-great grandfathers earned their livings. The reason is that when writing on a composite or a general subject, they can use abstract terms, repeating ideas that they have read or heard, ideas that are in the public domain, so to speak. It would take much more time and effort for them to use specific, concrete terms or describe aspects in detail, because it would be necessary for them to have firsthand knowledge of a limited subject and to form their own ideas.

Most young people today are bent upon "telling it like it is." In the process of "telling it like it is," which means in our jargon, we suppose, "interpreting real situations convincingly," no skill is more important than the knowledgeable use of specific words and concrete class words.

Of course, such words can be used to excess, just as any other good thing can

---

[12]"Remote Sensing: New Eyes to See the World," *National Geographic*, Vol. CXXXV, No. 1 (January 1969), p. 48.

be used to excess. A writer who continually uses terms from the third or the fourth level of the abstraction ladder without ever summarizing or interpreting in more general terms is exasperating, and a writer who gives minute descriptions of narrow subjects without ever relating these subjects to a broader context is unreadable. Few readers, for example, would want to read page after page of precise descriptions of the habits of deer mice and bats if the author had no intention of making a point, sooner or later. The important thing to remember, though, is that abstract terms, however necessary, go a long way. A few will summarize or interpret several paragraphs of precise details.

Distinguishing Basic Sentence Elements from Modifiers

The skeleton of almost every declarative sentence in English is one of five basic grammatical patterns or one of their transformations, or a combination of two or more of these patterns and transformations. The skeletons of sentences, like other skeletons, are rarely seen except when they are being studied, and they would be quite uninteresting if they were studied for themselves alone. They are not studied for themselves alone, however, but for their significance within sentences that are given body and color by modifiers. It is also important for a student of writing to study modifiers, since they make sentences appealing, as flesh and color make a person appealing; but one can hardly do that without understanding first the homely skeletal structures that modifiers adorn. If you know these structures, you are ready to study the sections on sentence structure in Part I of this book. If you do not, the following exercises should prove helpful.

This explanation will include questions that you might ask when reading the sentence patterns and examples, with answers stated below the questions. At the end of the treatment of each variation of each pattern, a sentence based on that variation will be given for you to write and mark. You can check your marking of these sentences by turning to pages 63–64.

The sentences used in this explanation are quoted from three of the articles that you may read later in this course: "The TV Generation," "The Secret of Nancy Drew," by Arthur Prager, and "Robert Frost: The Way to the Poem," by John Ciardi. The sentences for you to write and mark are taken from various selections in this book.

BASIC SENTENCE PATTERNS

Pattern 1:   S–InV (Subject–Intransitive Verb) or N–V
Example:
>   S(N)   InV(V)
>   Frost, (like every good poet), began (by playing a game with himself).

What is an intransitive verb? It is a verb that does not take an object or a complement, that is, a verb that does not need a noun, a noun equivalent, or an adjective to complete its meaning.

Why are you using both S and N? S shows how the structure functions; N shows what the structure is. The distinction is important because N's can function in positions besides the subject position.

Does N mean noun? Yes, but not only *noun;* it can mean any structure that can be used as a noun may be used. The various structures that can be labeled N will be used in the examples in this explanation and will be listed together in a summary at the end.

Is *game* not a noun? Yes, but it completes the meaning of *playing,* not *began,* the predicate verb. Consequently, since it is not part of the basic sentence pattern, we have not labeled it.

Does S stand for simple subject or complete subject? It stands for the essential structural elements in the complete subject. The complete subject is S + *modifiers,* if there are modifiers. When there are no modifiers, S is the complete subject.

Why are *like every good poet* and *by playing a game with himself* set in parentheses? They are modifiers. Throughout this explanation modifiers and appositives will be set in parentheses.

Which kinds of modifiers are they? *Like every good poet* is a prepositional phrase used as the adjectival modifier of *Frost; by playing a game with himself* is a prepositional phrase used as the adverbial modifier of *began.* Since you will be studying modifiers in detail later, however, you can call all types of modifiers just modifiers. Our purpose now is to distinguish modifiers from the essential structures in the patterns.

How can I recognize a modifier? A modifier is a word, a phrase (a group of related words not having a subject and a predicate verb), or a clause (a group of related words having a subject and its predicate verb) that qualifies some word outside itself in the sentence but that is not essential to the structure of the sentence and/or the sense of the predicate verb. *Frost began* is structurally complete, and the sense in which *began* is used is not different from the sense in which it is used in the original sentence; thus the modifiers are not essential to the basic pattern.

Example:
>   S(N)   InV(V)
>   (Clearly), the man stopped (because the beauty of the scene moved him). . . .

Why did you not set off *of the scene?* **It is a modifier.** We are setting off only whole modifiers of essential structures. The whole clause *because the beauty of the scene moved him* modifies *stopped.* Since *of the scene* is a modifier within a modifier, we did not set it off.

Why did you underline *the* **instead of putting it into parentheses? Is it not a modifier?** Since we have defined modifiers as unessential structures, we cannot call *the* a modifier. A native speaker of English will never say, "Man stopped." He will say, "John stopped," "He stopped," "Men stopped"; but if he uses *man,* he will put *the, a, this, many a, such a,* or some other such expression, in front of it. Many grammarians now call such words determiners. (Some grammarians call them limiting adjectives.) Sometimes N means *determiner + noun,* not just *noun:* thus *the man* is underlined and N written above it.

Are all determiners essential? No, only determiners that come before singular count-nouns, that is, nouns that represent things that can be counted, like boys, classes, ideas, and cities.

Sentence to write and mark: Rules for limiting time will vary for different families and different children.

Pattern 2: S–LV–SC (Subject–Linking Verb–Subject Complement) or N_1–V–N_1 and N–V–Adj

Example (with N):

S(N_1)	LV(V)	SC(N_1)

Negroes (in the earlier books) were   (minstrel-show) stereotypes (with names like Mandy and Beulah).

Why have you used the subscripts after the N's this time? When two N's have the same subscripts the second N identifies or classifies the first; it does not refer to a different referent. If you are trying to decide whether a noun is a subject complement, ask yourself whether the second N refers to an entirely different referent. If it does, the N is not a subject complement. If the N is used as a subject complement, it refers either to the same referent as the first N or to a class including the referent of the first.

How can one tell a linking verb from an intransitive verb? The easiest way to begin is to memorize a list of linking verbs: such as, *be* (and all its forms, including *am, is, are, was, were, have been, has been, had been, will be, will have been, may be, can be*), and all the forms of the verbs *taste, sound, smell, remain, seem, appear, become,* and *mean.* Memorizing a list does not completely solve the problem, however, because some of these verbs can be used as intransitive verbs also. Notice the *is* in the following sentence, where it means

INV(V) S(N)

exists, or *has being:* "(At the opposite pole) is   the ('catharsis') school, (based on the psychiatric theory that TV violence offers a healthy outlet for a child's hostilities and aggressions)." If is does not mean *exists* or *has being,* but merely shows a relationship between the subject and a noun or an adjective, it is a linking verb.

Example (with N):

S(N$_1$)   LV(V) SC(N$_1$)

Another (early) fear (that proved invalid) was   that television would lower (school) grades [and] lessen (book) reading.

Why is *and* set in brackets? It will be our practice throughout this explanation to set connectors and transitional words in brackets to distinguish them from essential structures and modifiers.

What does N$_1$ stand for in the subject complement? A noun clause.

How can you tell that *that proved invalid* is a modifier and *that television would lower grades and lessen reading* is used as a noun? The easiest way is to look at the structures of the two clauses. In the modifying clause, as in all modifying clauses beginning with *that*, *that* functions as a noun (in this case it is the subject of the clause). In the clause used as a noun, as in all noun clauses beginning with *that*, *that* simply introduces the clause; it does not function as a noun.

Example (with N):

S(N$_1$)   LV(V)   SC(N$_1$)

To read any (one) poem (carefully) is   (the) (ideal) preparation (for reading another).

What is the first N$_1$ called? It is an infinitive phrase. The essential parts of the phrase are the infinitive, *to read*, and its object, *any poem*.

What does *carefully* modify? It modifies *to read*. It is, like *one*, a modifier within the infinitive phrase; the whole phrase acts as the complete subject of the sentence.

Example (with N):

S(N$_1$) LV(V)   SC(N$_1$)

That does(n't) mean watching (with the kids) (every day).

What is the second N$_1$? It is a gerund, or a verb used as a noun. The gerund can take an object, as the infinitive can take an object: for example, if the gerund phrase above were *watching television with the kids every day*, then *television* would be the object of *watching*. As the phrase actually is stated, it has only the gerund and two unessential modifiers.

Sentence to write and mark: It does mean offering alternative values and opinions to ones that children get from TV.

Example (with Adj):

S(N)   LV(V) SC(Adj)

(Indeed), (the) statistics are   fearsome.

Why have you not called *fearsome* **a modifier?** It tells something about *statistics*, but since it is essential, it is not a modifier by the definition that we are using. It is called a predicate adjective.

Why is *fearsome* **essential?** The verb, *are*, would mean only *exist* without it; therefore the sense of the verb depends upon the predicate adjective.

Example (with Adj):

       S(N)   LV(V) SC(Adj)

(The) characters (who support Nancy in her adventures) seem   pallid (compared to their heroine).

Is *who support Nancy in her adventures* **a clause or a phrase?** A clause, with *who* as the subject.

Example (with Adj):

         S(N)   LV(V)   SC(Adj)

(The) (dire) predictions (of harm) remain unproved.

Is *unproved* **an adjective? It looks like a verb.** It is a verbal adjective (verb used as an adjective), as the past participle form of a verb always is in a sentence unless it has an auxiliary verb in front of it.

Example (with Adj):

         S(N)   LV(V)   SC(Adj)

(Such) questions will have to remain unanswered (until there's more adequate research on TV violence with less contradictory results).

Is *will have to remain* **all one verb?** Yes. Certain verbs—like *use, have, go, be, be about,* and *ought*—sometimes combine with infinitives to make predicate verbs: as in, "I used to sing," "I have to sing," "I am going to sing," "He is to sing," "She is about to sing," and "You ought to sing."

Example (with Adj.):

                                                                        S(N)

(By 1957), (although they still drop their consonants), (Negro) characters

LV(V)   SC(Adj)   SC(Adj)

have become articulate [and] informative.

In this sentence there is a compound adjective. Can one have compound N's and V's also, without changing a pattern? Yes.

Is *Negro* **not essential? Are you not using** *characters* **in a different sense without it?** *Negro*, like any other modifier, qualifies the word that it modifies, but it does not give *characters* a different sense, so that *characters* would be found in a dictionary under the third definition instead of the second. The linking *is* is really a different word from the intransitive *is* of existence. *Characters* does not become a different word when *Negro* is placed before it.

Sentence to write and mark: The biological revolutionaries of today are not antireligious but simply unreligious.

Pattern 3:   S–TrV–DO (Subject–Transitive Verb–Direct Object) or N_1–V–N_2

Example:

$\quad\quad\quad\quad$ S(N_1) $\quad\quad\quad\quad\quad\quad\quad\quad\quad\quad\quad\quad$ TrV(V) $\quad\quad$ DO(N_2)
[But] (few) <u>children</u> (born in the last 15 years) <u>can remember</u> <u>a time</u> (without television).

What is a transitive verb? A transitive verb is a verb that takes at least one object, that is, a verb that requires at least one N whose referent is different from the subject's to determine the sense in which it is used.

How can one tell that *a time* is not a subject complement? As the subscript 2 indicates, *a time* refers to a different referent from that which *children* refers to.

Is it always true that an N referring to a second referent will be a direct object? There are three conditions under which it is *not* true:

1. If there is a third N referring to a third referent, as in Pattern 4 (page 57).

$\quad\quad\quad\quad\quad\quad\quad\quad\quad\quad\quad\quad\quad\quad\quad\quad\quad\quad\quad\quad\quad\quad\quad\quad$ N $\;$ V
2. If the second N is a reflexive pronoun, as in "I cut <u>myself</u>"; in "I <u>cut</u>

$\quad$ N
<u>myself</u>" the second N refers to the same referent as *I* does, even though *myself* is a direct object.
3. If the subject and the direct object are inverted, so that the direct object

$\quad\quad\quad\quad\quad\quad\quad\quad\quad\quad$ DO(N_1) $\quad\quad\quad\quad$ S(N_2) TrV(V)
$\quad$ precedes the subject, as in "<u>The ceremony,</u> <u>he</u> $\quad$ <u>hated.</u>"

Under other conditions where there are two N's (in other words, most of the time) the second N is a direct object. You should remember as you look for direct objects, though, that a noun introduced by a preposition or a verbal is not marked N.

Example:

(In a local bookstore), (mixed among out-of-date Little Golden Books and

$\quad\quad\quad\quad\quad\quad\quad\quad\quad\quad\quad\quad\quad\quad\quad\quad\quad$ S(N_1) $\quad\quad\quad\quad$ TrV(V) $\quad\quad$ DO(N_2)
the misadventures of improbable animals), <u>my daughter</u> <u>had found</u> <u>a row</u>
(of blue-jacketed volumes), (each bearing in a printed medallion of the intrepid girl detective's seductively *nice* face).

Do you mean that *a row* is essential and *volumes* is not? *A row* is sufficient to give sense to *has found*. If you feel that *volumes* is the object of *has found* and *a row of* is a determiner, you have strong support from some grammarians, and we must admit that it is mainly for the sake of convenience that we reject this interpretation. Suppose we have this sentence: "A row of blue-jacketed volumes (was, were) standing on the top shelf when I was last in the library."

In English usage *was* is the correct choice, because *row* controls the number of the verb. To say that verbs sometimes agree with determiners would increase the difficulty of teaching agreement. We therefore hold to the older interpretation that *row* is a noun used as the direct object and *of blue-jacketed volumes* is a prepositional phrase modifying *row* by telling the kind of row.

Example:

$$S(N_1) \quad TrV(V) \quad DO(N_2)$$
[But] (recent) <u>research</u> <u>indicates</u> <u>that</u> (such) <u>influence</u> <u>is</u> <u>slight</u>.

Why did you underline *is* and *slight?* They are essential elements in the noun clause *such influence is slight.* The only modifier in this clause is *such. Slight* is a predicate adjective within the clause.

You have marked the noun clause N_2. Does the clause have a referent? Strictly speaking, no. We will use N_2 with noun clauses in this pattern to emphasize that the clause does not identify or classify the first N.

Is it unusual to find a noun clause used as a direct object? No, Pattern 3 with a noun clause as the direct object is probably used more frequently in nonfiction prose than any other construction. Here are two more examples of this construction. The direct object is compound in the first.

$$S(N_1) \hspace{4cm} TrV(V) \quad DO(N_2)$$
1. <u>The</u> (third) [and] (now most popular) <u>school</u> <u>contends</u> <u>that</u> <u>TV</u> (itself)

$$\hspace{5cm} DO(N_2)$$
(rarely) <u>causes</u> <u>crime</u> [or] <u>aggression</u> [but] <u>that</u> <u>it</u> <u>can</u> <u>be</u> <u>a</u> (contributing)

<u>factor</u>.

$$\hspace{3cm} S(N_1)TrV(V) \hspace{3cm} DO(N_2)$$
2. (If you're over 21), <u>you</u> <u>can</u> (probably) <u>remember</u> <u>when</u> <u>your</u> <u>family</u> <u>got</u>

<u>its</u> (first) (TV) <u>set</u>.

Are you sure a noun clause can begin with *when?* Some grammarians say that the reader understands *the time* before *when your family got its first TV set* and that *time* is therefore the direct object, modified adjectivally by the clause beginning with *when.* But we will follow other grammarians in calling the clause simply a noun clause; therefore, the answer is "Yes."

Example:

$$\hspace{5cm} S(N_1) \hspace{1cm} TrV(V)$$
(When I asked my daughter why she had loved Nancy), <u>she</u> . . . <u>said</u>

$$\hspace{1cm} DO(N_2)$$
(simply), "<u>You</u> <u>can</u> <u>identify</u> (with her)."

Do you mean that the direct quotation is a direct object? Yes. Something must follow verbs like *said, replied,* and *remarked* in constructions where they are predicate verbs following subjects. Without a statement, directly or indirectly given, such a verb, in this position, has no meaning.

Are direct quotations usually direct objects? They are direct objects when they give meaning to verbs, as the direct quotation does in the example above. When they are not controlled by verbs, quotations are generally appositives. In the following example, the direct quotation is an appositive to *the first,*

$$DO(N_1) \quad S(N_2) \; TrV(V)$$

which is itself the direct object: "The first, he   has stated (himself) (in 'The Mowing'): '(Anything more than truth would have seemed too weak).'"

In the first direct quotation, *You can identify with her,* **does** *identify* **not need an object?** Yes, the reader must understand *identify yourself with her.*

In the sentence of which this quotation is a part, is *Nancy* **not a direct object?** Yes, but it is in a noun clause within an adverb clause, a modifier. We are marking direct objects in the basic patterns only.

Sentence to write and mark: But even here we must not forget that some identities are intolerable to their distracted possessors.

Pattern 4:   S–TrV–IO–DO (Subject–Transitive Verb–Indirect Object–Direct Object) or N_1–V–N_2–N_3

Example:

$$S(N_1) \quad TrV(V) \; IO(N_2) \qquad DO(N_3)$$

(Many) (other) critics give   broadcasters the benefit (of the doubt) (on motives).

How can one identify indirect objects? If it takes two objects to complete the meaning of the verb, if those two objects do not refer to the same referent, and if the second object is not an infinitive, the first object is an indirect object. Another test is to place *to* or *for* in front of the first object, in this way: "Many other critics give *to* broadcasters the benefit of the doubt on motives." If the sense is not changed, even though the wording may sound awkward, the first object is an indirect object. It is useful, further, to know that certain verbs often are followed by indirect objects, which of course are followed by direct objects. Some of these verbs are *give, tell, do, read, ask, deny, write, offer,* and *find.* A few simple examples of indirect objects used with these verbs are the following: "He gave *me* a ring," "He told *her* a lie," "He did *Jim* a favor," "He read *the audience* a poem," "He asked *coaches* their opinions," "He denied *everyone* entrance," "He wrote *whoever was concerned* a letter," "He offered *me* his coat," "He found *the orchestra* a good selection to play."

Example:

$$S(N_1) \; TrV(V) \qquad\qquad\qquad IO(N_2) \; DO(N_3)$$

He   might (just as well) have told us   that he was going (to the general store), [or] returning (from it) (with a jug of molasses he had promised to bring Aunt Harriet and two suits of long underwear he had promised to bring the hired man).

Is the direct object a noun clause? Yes.

Where does the complete noun clause end? At the end of the sentence.

Why have you marked modifiers within the noun clause? Because the noun clause is part of the basic structure, not a modifier. We always mark modifiers of essential elements of basic structures.

Why have you marked the last twenty-six words as one modifier? They constitute a prepositional phrase modifying *was returning*, an essential half of the verb in the noun clause, and though there are many modifiers within this prepositional phrase, none modifies anything outside of the phrase.

Is *he had promised to bring Aunt Harriet* a modifier? Yes, it is a subordinate clause telling which jug of molasses, even though the relative pronoun that introduces the clause, *that* or *which* (acting as the direct object), is unexpressed.

Sentence to write and mark: I asked him what seemed to be the trouble.

Pattern 5: S–TrV–DO–OC (Subject–Transitive Verb–Direct Object–Objective Complement) or N_1–V–N_2–N_2, N_1–V–N_2–Adj, and N_1–V–N_2–Inf (Infinitive)

Example (with N):

$$S(N_1)\ TrV(V)\ DO(N_2)\ OC(N_2)$$

(From the pre-teen point of view), this makes him a (perfect) Daddy.

How does Pattern 5 with the N differ from Pattern 4? In Pattern 4 the N used as the indirect object always has an entirely different referent from the N used as the direct object. In Pattern 5, the N used as the objective complement identifies or classifies the referent of the N used as the direct object, as, in the sentence above, *Daddy* (in spite of the capital letter used by the author) classifies *him*. As when learning Pattern 4, it is useful here to look closely at verbs. Some of the verbs that ordinarily appear in sentences based on Pattern 5 are *make, elect, think, appoint, consider, believe, choose,* and *find.* The following sentences illustrate the use of these verbs in Pattern 5: "We thought (or believed, or considered) her *the* best *dancer* at the party," "We chose (or appointed, or elected) him *Man-of-the-Year,*" "You may find this *the* best *solution* to your problem."

Example (with N):

$$S(N_1) \hspace{3cm} TrV(V)\ DO(N_2)$$

(Some) parents [and] teachers find the (NABB's) (evaluation) publica-

$$OC(N_2)$$

tion/to be/ a (valuable) aid.

What do the slash marks mean? By a popular interpretation of sentences like the one above, the *to be* is superfluous. The slash marks are intended to indicate that *to be* is superfluous, since the relationship between *publication* and *aid* is clear without it.

Sentence to write and mark: Robertson called his ship the *Titan.*

Example (with Adj):

$$S(N_1) \ TrV(V) \quad DO(N_2) \ OC(Adj)$$

(One evening) I   observed her   curled   (up) (in a ball) (on the sofa), (shoes off), (face unusually serious and preoccupied).

Example (with Adj):

$$S(N_1) \hspace{10cm} TrV(V) \quad DO(N_2) \hspace{2cm} TrV(V)$$

Mothers (who have never read the series) examine it   [and] find

$$DO(N_2) \ OC(Adj)$$

it   harmless (if not downright wholesome).

I see that *harmless* is the objective complement modifying the object of the second verb in the compound transitive verb, but isn't *wholesome* also an adjective used as an objective complement? Yes, but it is in an elliptical subordinate clause beginning with *if*, not in the basic pattern.

Sentence to write and mark: But those students who have reached this stage of impatience and disaffection are suddenly making themselves heard with frightening clarity.

Example (with Inf):

$$S(N_1) \hspace{3cm} TrV(V) \hspace{1.5cm} DO(N_2) \ OC(Inf)$$

(A few karmas ago), circumstances compelled me   to raise a (small) daughter, (without benefit of wife and mother), (in the insecure atmosphere of a large hotel).

Example (with Inf):

$$S(N_1) \hspace{1.5cm} TrV(V) \ DO(N_2) \ OC(Inf)$$

(This) boldness makes Nancy blush   (to her fingertips) (a frequent habit

$$OC(Inf)$$

of hers) [and] change the subject (to "something less personal").

Do you mean that *blush* and *change* are infinitives without *to*? Yes.

Is it unusual to have an infinitive without *to*? It is not very unusual when the infinitive is used as an objective complement. Here are some simple examples of this usage: "Don't make me *laugh*," "This makes Sammy *run*," "Let her *cry*," "Watch him *jump*," "We have heard him *play* the piano."

Sentence to write and mark: By presenting a different point of view or an opposed set of motives, the foil moves the more important character to react in ways that might not have found expression without such opposition.

PASSIVE TRANSFORMATIONS

Transformation of Pattern 3

Example:
S(N)
The possibility (that television would work great physical harm on children,
Passive Verb
particularly on their sight and posture), was (much) feared (in the early 1950's).

Why have you called this a transformation? Because, according to transformational grammarians, it is derived from "_____ feared the possibility." The subject might be *parents* or *responsible adults in the United States*, or some other similar expression. One cannot say that anything is feared without implying that it is feared by someone or some group of persons or animals. Sometimes the context explains who this someone or group is. At other times, the author chooses to be vague, but the reader knows that logically the fear was experienced by someone or some group. Since passive constructions always state or imply agents who were responsible for the action in the verb, every passive construction may be considered a transformation of an active construction in which someone or a group is the subject of the verb. We can use the example above to illustrate the process of transformation.

$S(N_1)$ TrV(V) DO(N_2)
Pattern 3: _____ feared the possibility. (active verb)

To transform this into the passive construction:
1. Move the direct object to subject position.
2. As the verb, use the appropriate form of *be* + the past participle form of the stated verb. The form of *be* is appropriate if it is the same tense as the active verb being replaced. (If the stated verb were *saw*, the passive verb would be *was seen. Feared* is both the past form and the past participle form.)
3. State or imply *by someone* after the verb.
   Illustrations of this process:

Active Verb
Pattern 3: Geoffrey pays the family's hospital bills.
Passive Verb
T: The family's hospital bills are paid by Geoffrey.
Active Verb
Pattern 3: Effie milks all of the cows.
Passive Verb
T: All of the cows are milked by Effie.
Active Verb
Pattern 3: Helen asked the most provocative question.

Passive Verb

T: The most provocative question <u>was asked</u> by Helen.

Active Verb

Pattern 3: Someone <u>has found</u> the billfold that Mr. Thomas lost at the foot-ball game.

Passive Verb

T: The billfold that Mr. Thomas lost at the football game <u>has been found</u>.

Examples:

S(N) Passive Verb

<u>He</u> <u>is</u> (roundly) <u>punished</u> (for his transgressions).

S(N) Passive Verb

(Occasionally), <u>a child</u> <u>will be fatigued</u> (by lack of sleep).

Sentence to write and mark: Quality-control is maintained by checking the output and replacing defective parts.

Transformation of Pattern 5
Example:

S(N) Passive Verb Retained Object

(Moral) <u>judgments</u> <u>are</u> (simply) <u>regarded/as/expressions</u> (of one's personal decisions) . . . .

S(N) TrV(V) DO(N$_2$) OC(N$_2$)

[**Pattern 5:** ——————— <u>regard</u> (moral) <u>judgments/as/expressions</u> (of one's per-sonal decisions).]

Is a retained object a direct object? An object retained from a Pattern 5 is like a direct object in one respect: it follows an action verb. But it is like a subject complement in another respect: it renames or classifies the subject.

Sentence to write and mark: Superstition is defined in some school text-books as any belief which cannot be scientifically verified.

EXPLETIVE TRANSFORMATIONS

There Transformation (from Pattern 1)
Example:

InV(V) S(N)

(Apparently) /there/ <u>is</u> <u>a</u> (rock-ribbed) <u>streak</u> (of conservatism) (in the nine-to-eleven group).

S(N) InV(V)

[**Pattern 1:** (Apparently), <u>a</u> (rock-ribbed) <u>streak</u> (of conservatism) <u>is</u> (in the nine-to-eleven group).]

What is *there* **called?** It is called an expletive. All it does is allow the speaker to invert the subject and its verb.

Sentence to write and mark: There are about forty kinds of problems, mostly dealing with matters of faith and morals . . . .

It *Transformation (from Pattern 2)*

Example:

      LV(V)   SC(Adj) S(N)
/It/ <u>was</u> also <u>clear</u>   <u>that I had gone</u> (as far as I could go alone).

                 S(N)   LV(V) SC(Adj)
[**Pattern 2:** <u>That I had gone</u> (as far as I could go alone) <u>was</u>   <u>clear</u>.]

Are there other transformations? Yes, many. Modifiers are themselves transformations of basic patterns. We are studying only these, because they are the ones that you might confuse with basic sentence patterns.

Sentence to write and mark: It is virtually certain that the moral sanctions of birth control are going to be transformed.

COMPOUNDED PATTERNS

Two or more of any of the patterns above can be joined together in one sentence with connectors like *and, but, so, however, nevertheless,* and *for this reason.*

Examples:

                              S(N)   LV(V) SC(Adj)   SC(Adj)
Pattern 2 + Pattern 3: <u>My daughter</u> <u>is</u>   <u>grown</u> (now), [and] <u>oriented</u>
                                                $S(N_1)$ TrV(V)
(toward more sophisticated pleasures), [but] (Nancy's) <u>magic</u> (still) <u>galva-</u>
    DO(N2)
<u>nizes</u> <u>the</u>   (nine-to-eleven-year-old) <u>set</u> (in the same wonderful way).
                                               S(N)   InV(V)
Pattern 1 + Expletive T. of Pattern 1: <u>Hannah</u> [and] <u>Nancy</u> (never) <u>depart</u>
                                                InV(V)   S(N)
(from their servant-mistress relationship), [and] /there/<u>is</u>   (no) <u>doubt</u>
(about who is boss).
                                                 S(N)   Passive Verb
Passive T. of Pattern 3 + Pattern 2: (Sometimes) <u>the girls</u> <u>are joined</u> (by
                       $S(N_1)$ LV(V) $SC(N_1)$ SC(Adj)
Helen Corning), [but] <u>she</u>   <u>is</u>   a <u>weakling</u>, [and] (too) <u>lah-de-dah</u> (to
contribute anything to the excitement).

I know that the comma is used before *but* **to separate the two sentence patterns. Why is the comma used before** *and?* *Weakling,* a noun, and *lah-de-dah,* an adjective, do not make a good compound subjective complement; nevertheless, the author does not want to repeat *she is* (*she is a weakling, and she is too lah-de-dah*). When he uses the comma, he expects the reader to understand *and she was too lah-de-dah.*

Sentence to write and mark: Then the hills gradually close, and while they do not grow higher they become steeper.

SENTENCES THAT YOU HAVE MARKED

Answers

1. Pattern 1
S(N)   Inv(V)
<u>Rules</u> (for limiting time) <u>will vary</u> (for different families and different children).

2. Pattern 2
S(N₁) LV(V)   SC(N₁)
<u>It</u>   <u>does mean</u> <u>offering</u> (alternative) <u>values</u> [and] <u>opinions</u> (to ones that children get from TV).

3. Pattern 2
                    S(N)   LV(V)   SC(Adj)
(The) (biological) <u>revolutionaries</u> (of today) <u>are</u>   (not) <u>antireligious</u> [but]
        SC(Adj)
(simply) <u>unreligious.</u>

4. Pattern 3
                    S(N₁) TrV(V)   DO(N₂)
[But] (even here) <u>we</u>   <u>must</u>   (not) <u>forget</u> <u>that</u>   (some) <u>identities are intoler-</u><u>able</u> (to their distracted possessors).

5. Pattern 4
S(N₁) TrV(V) IO(N₂) DO(N₃)
<u>I</u>   <u>asked</u>   <u>him</u>   <u>what seemed to be the trouble.</u>

6. Pattern 5
S(N₁)   TrV(V) DO(N₂) OC(N₂)
<u>Robertson</u> <u>called</u> <u>his ship</u> <u>the Titan.</u>

7. Pattern 5
            S(N₁)
[But] (those) <u>students</u> (who have reached this stage of impatience and disaffec-
    TrV(V)   DO(N₂)   OC(Adj)
tion) <u>are</u>   (suddenly) <u>making</u> <u>themselves</u> <u>heard</u>   (with frightening clarity).

8. Pattern 5
                                                S(N₁)
(By presenting a different point of view or an opposed set of motives), <u>the foil</u>

TrV(V) DO(N$_2$)   OC(Inf)
<u>moves</u> <u>the</u> (more important) <u>character</u> <u>to react</u> (in ways that might not have found expression without such opposition).
9. Passive T
S(N)   Passive Verb
<u>Quality-control</u> <u>is maintained</u> (by checking the output and replacing defective parts).
10. Passive T
S(N)   Passive Verb   Retained Object
<u>Superstition</u> <u>is defined</u> (in some school textbooks)/as/<u>any belief</u> (which cannot be scientifically verified).
11. Expletive T
        InV(V)   S(N)
/There/ <u>are</u>   (about forty) <u>kinds</u> (of problems, mostly dealing with matters of faith and morals) . . . .
12. Expletive T
        LV(V)   SC(Adj) S(N)
/It/ <u>is</u>   (virtually) <u>certain</u> <u>that</u> (the moral) <u>sanctions</u> (of birth control) <u>are</u> <u>going to be transformed.</u>
13. Compound
          S(N)   InV(V)
(Then) (the) <u>hills</u> (gradually) <u>close,</u> [and] (while they do not grow higher)
S(N) LV(V)   SC(Adj)
<u>they</u> <u>become</u> <u>steeper.</u>

SUMMARY OF THE CONSTITUENTS
OF THE SINGLE-PATTERN DECLARATIVE SENTENCE
WITH A VERB IN ACTIVE VOICE

This type of sentence consists of a complete subject and a complete predicate. A complete subject consists of N, with or without modifiers. N may be any of the following:

A proper noun, like *Willis Howard, Idaho,* or *Magna Carta* (a noun that is semantically a specific word)
A mass noun, like *beauty, courage, iron,* or *water* (a noun that is semantically either a nonconcrete word or a concrete class word denoting a solid substance, a liquid, or a gas)
A determiner plus a count noun, like *the band, an apple,* or *a girl* (a count noun is semantically a concrete class word that groups specifics)
A personal pronoun, like *I, we, you, he, she, it,* or *they*
An indefinite pronoun, like *someone, anyone,* or *something*
An infinitive, like *to walk, to remain,* or *to rejoice*

An infinitive plus its object, like *to seek the truth* or *to conquer nature*

A gerund, like *walking, remaining,* or *rejoicing*

A gerund plus its object, like *seeking the truth* or *conquering nature*

The essential part of a noun clause, like *that I knew him, that he was rich,* or *what it meant*

A complete predicate consists of one of the following, with or without modifiers:

An intransitive verb

A linking verb followed by a predicate noun or a predicate adjective used as a subjective complement

A transitive verb followed by one of these:

    a noun used as a direct object

    a noun used as an indirect object followed by a noun used as a direct object

    a noun used as a direct object followed by a noun used as an objective complement, an adjective used as an objective complement, or an infinitive used as an objective complement

---

EXERCISE 3

Discerning Basic Patterns in Sentences

Write the following sentences, labeling and underlining the essential elements in the patterns and enclosing modifiers by using the method illustrated in the examples in the preceding explanation. Above each sentence, write the number of the basic pattern or write *Passive T, Expletive T,* or *Compound.* The sentences in this exercise are taken from readings in this book.

1. They could not in good conscience forcibly resist respected authority.
2. In our culture we have come, for the most part, to regard the empirical scientific method /as/ the only way to get at truth about reality.
3. Many readers are forever unable to accept the poet's essential duplicity.
4. Kosterin had repeatedly charged that Stalinism was returning to the Soviet Union.
5. The proletariat is not the main social group likely to produce the New Prometheans of the 1970's and 1980's.
6. Indeed, one of the most plausible constructions to be put upon it was that nothing much *could* be done except to submit patiently to the winnowing processes of nature.
7. Work in this vein has just begun.
8. And in folklore the dragon is credited with the creation of Taiwan.
9. Breakfast was completely innocuous.
10. She gave me a very odd look.
11. There is a great deal of money around, but there are a great many expenses, too.
12. Yet mere prophets of gloom can never make a revolution.

13. There are of course many individuals of a naturally cheerful or feckless temperament, today as always, but groups of men with an articulated hope for the future of the entire race are much rarer.
14. Helen and I found Taiwan, like so many developing nations, torn between the two worlds of transition and tradition.
15. A poet's pleasure is to withhold a little of his meaning.
16. "As long as the Communists occupy the mainland, there will be no end to the disturbances in Southeast Asia . . . ."
17. The man ends scene two with all these forces working upon him simultaneously.
18. Even now, many politicians think that the most devastating insult you can apply to an opponent is to call him a "planner."
19. Yet in the teeth of this observable fact, we go on trying to settle disputes by diplomacy as if we were still living in the days of Machiavelli or Metternich.
20. This somehow showed the futility of everything, and in fact, the book was called *Futility* when it appeared that year, published by the firm of M. F. Mansfield.
21. The problems brought into focus are threatening and staggering, but perhaps they would be manageable in time if they were our basic problems.
22. That is dinner, and it will keep him moving for several more hours and keep his stomach working and his heart pumping.
23. We found him feeding his ducks beside a pond stocked with fish.
24. Thus when the barbarians finally came, civilized by now, it was an easy matter to make them Chinese . . . .
25. These words were written before the Great Wall was built.

PART I
Factual Detail

"... it is only the roughness of the eye that makes any two persons, things, situations, seem alike."

Walter Pater, the Conclusion to *The Renaissance*

Perception

Our atmosphere is full of impulses—technically photons—that we cannot perceive with our unaided senses. We cannot perceive bone beneath skin and muscle without the aid of a machine, as we could if we were sensitive to X-rays. We cannot perceive radioactive ores beneath layers of earth without the aid of a machine, as we could if we were sensitive to gamma rays. As some rays, like X-rays and gamma rays, are too short for our senses, others, like infrared rays, are too long. We never see the New York skyline as it is depicted facing page 238, but we would if we were sensitive to infrared rays. This "heat picture" was taken by a thermograph, an instrument sensitive to the infrared rays that all physical objects emit. The hotter the object, the more electromagnetic radiation it gives off. The thermograph records radiation as colors—red for the hottest temperature, yellow for cooler, green for still cooler, black for coolest. Detectors of heat, or infrared rays, can locate all sorts of things that light waves do not reveal—from a small fire hidden in a forest to a blocked carotid artery in the head of a man.[1] Our sense of hearing and our sense of smell are as limited as our sight, and for the same reason—our senses are capable of receiving waves of certain lengths and only these.

Yet, we have more perceptive power than we use. Many impulses escape us, not because we are incapable of receiving them, but because we do not *will* to receive them. Human vision is such that a person with normal vision cannot help perceiving mass, color, and general outline when his eyes are open and there is sufficient light, but he does not see details unless he tries, and he generally does not try unless he has a reason.

In childhood the pleasure of seeing may be reason enough to concentrate

---

[1]Such a blockage is illustrated in Kenneth F. Weaver's "Remote Sensing, New Eyes to See the World," *National Geographic*, Vol. CXXXV, No. 1 (January 1969), p. 57. All of the scientific facts in the paragraph above are derived from Weaver's article.

intently upon objects and scenes; even to adults in a new situation, the pleasure of seeing may be enough reason to observe closely. In the following excerpt from *Life on the Mississippi*, Mark Twain describes a sunset that he witnessed with pleasure early in his training as a riverboat pilot:

> A broad expanse of the river was turned to blood; in the middle distance the red hue brightened into gold, through which a solitary log came floating, black and conspicuous; in one place a long, slanting mark lay sparkling upon the water; in another the surface was broken by boiling, tumbling rings, that were as many-tinted as an opal; where the ruddy flush was faintest, was a smooth spot that was covered with graceful circles and radiating lines, ever so delicately traced; the shore on our left was densely wooded, and the somber shadow that fell from this forest was broken in one place by a long, ruffled trail that shone like silver; and high above the forest wall a clean-stemmed dead tree waved a single leafy bough that glowed like a flame in the unobstructed splendor that was flowing from the sun. There were graceful curves, reflected images, woody heights, soft distances; and over the whole scene, far and near, the dissolving lights drifted steadily, enriching it every passing moment with new marvels of coloring.[2]

After he had become an experienced pilot Mark Twain would have observed this scene as closely, but not for the pleasure of seeing. At that time he would have observed because it was his business to observe, and every detail would have had a practical significance, as he explains in the following passage:

> Then, if that sunset scene had been repeated, I should have looked upon it without rapture, and should have commented upon it, inwardly, after this fashion: "This sun means that we are going to have wind tomorrow; that floating log means that the river is rising, small thanks to it; that slanting mark on the water refers to a bluff reef which is going to kill somebody's steamboat one of these nights, if it keeps on stretching out like that; those tumbling 'boils' show a dissolving bar and a changing channel there; the lines and circles in the slick water over yonder are a warning that that troublesome place is shoaling up dangerously; that silver streak in the shadow of the forest is the 'break' from a new snag, and he has located himself in the very best place he could have found to fish for steamboats; that tall dead tree, with a single living branch, is not going to last long, and then how is a body ever going to get through this blind place at night without the friendly old landmark?"[3]

As a riverboat pilot, Mark Twain had to be observant to be efficient, as orthopedists, surgeons, artists, stock judges, copy readers, mechanics, pilots of airplanes,

---

[2]New York: Harper & Row, 1923, pp. 78–79.
[3]*Ibid*, pp. 79–80.

interior decorators, photographers, and detectives must be observant to be efficient.

It is to be expected that a person at his work will see more details in his surroundings than a layman will, because he has trained himself to look for certain things at certain times and to be alert to all signs of change. How one's general background and education—training in a broader sense—condition all of one's seeing is not, however, so obvious. See what you can learn about your own perception by answering the following questions.

1. What do you read below?

2. How many *F*'s are there in the following statement?
   THESE FOLDERS OF FILES DO NOT FURNISH THE FULL
   REPORT OF FACTUAL INFORMATION THAT WE NEED.
3. How many *than*'s do you see?
   than, than, than, than, than, than, then, than
4. Can you find a three-letter word in the first figure on page 72?
5. Can you see a star in the second figure on page 72?
6. What is the most interesting thing in the photograph on page 73?
7. Which President's head is engraved on the quarter? the dime? the nickel?
8. Do these signs look official?

Answers

1. bird in the *the* hand
2. eight *F*'s (Did you count the *F*'s in the two *OF*'s?)

3. seven *than*'s; one *then*
4. FLY (spelled by the spaces)
5. The star is in the lower righthand corner, with one of the points touching the bottom edge.
6. If you saw the boy in the lower lefthand corner picking a pocket, you probably thought his action was the most interesting feature.
7. George Washington, on the quarter; Franklin D. Roosevelt, on the dime; Thomas Jefferson, on the nickel.
8. No word but STOP should appear on an octagonal sign; speed limit signs are rectangular.

Most of us see not everything in front of us but what our training, specialized and unspecialized, has predisposed us to see. We also tend to see in a given situation what we are looking for, while being almost oblivious of everything else, as the following series of photographs illustrates:

A young man "on the town"   A person needing to cash a check

Someone who is late for an appointment

To see many things well, one must have many kinds of knowledge, but must not be so conditioned by his knowledge that he can see things in only one way—see the black lines but not the spaces, for example. And he must have a reason to concentrate on details. The same combination of knowledge plus concentration is necessary for sharp distinctions of sounds, scents, and tastes.

What it is that prompts a man of wide knowledge to make almost a vocation of perceiving so-called commonplace impressions we cannot say, but such a man was Henry David Thoreau. And he thought that other persons could enrich their lives, as he had enriched his, by observing ordinary, natural scenes. The following quotation from his journal, written on April 9, 1841, expresses his passion for seeing:

> How much virtue there is in simply seeing! We may almost say that the hero has striven in vain for his preeminency, if the student oversees him. The woman who sits in the house and sees is a match for a stirring captain . . . . We are as much as we see.[4]

Thoreau's proficiency in observing is attested to in the following passage from the *American Notebook* of Nathaniel Hawthorne:

> [Thursday, September 1, 1842] Mr. Thoreau dined with us yesterday.... He is a keen and delicate observer of nature,—a genuine observer,— which, I suspect, is almost as rare a character as even an original poet; and Nature, in return for his love, seems to adopt him as her especial child, and shows him secrets which few others are allowed to witness. He is familiar with beast, fish, fowl, and reptile, and has strange stories to tell of adventures and friendly passages with these lower brethren of mortality. Herb and flower, likewise, wherever they grow, whether in garden or wildwood, are his familiar friends. He is also on intimate terms with the clouds, and can tell the portents of storms. It is a characteristic trait, that he has a great regard for the memory of the Indian tribes whose wild life would have suited him so well; and, strange to say, he seldom walks over a ploughed field without picking up an arrow-point, spear- head, or other relic of the red man, as if their spirits willed him to be the inheritor of their simple wealth.[5]

Thoreau was convinced that he did not need to travel from the environs of Concord, his home town, because he could find there enough impressions to challenge his perception. The following excerpt from his journal, dated July 11, 1851, will give you a taste of his description, and you will see how fundamental his acute senses were to his talent as a writer:

[4]Bradford Torrey, ed., *Journal 1837–1846, The Writings of Henry David Thoreau*, Vol. VII (Boston: Houghton Mifflin, 1906), pp. 247–48.
[5]Boston: Houghton Mifflin, 1892, pp. 318–19.

We go toward Bear Garden Hill. The sun is setting. The meadow-sweet has bloomed. These dry hills and pastures are the places to walk by moonlight. The moon is silvery still, not yet inaugurated. The tree-tops are seen against the amber west. I seem to see the outlines of one spruce among them, distinguishable afar. My thoughts expand and flourish most on this barren hill, where in the twilight I see the moss spreading in rings and prevailing over the short, thin grass, carpeting the earth, adding a few inches of green to its circle annually while it dies within.

As we round the sandy promontory, we try the sand and rocks with our hands. The sand is cool on the surface but warmer a few inches beneath, though the contrast is not so great as it was in May. The larger rocks are preceptibly warm. I pluck the blossom of the milkweed in the twilight and find how sweet it smells. The white blossoms of the Jersey tea dot the hillside, with the yarrow everywhere. Some woods are black as clouds; if we knew not they were green by day, they would appear blacker still. When we sit, we hear the mosquitoes hum. The woodland paths are not the same by night as by day, if they are a little grown up, the eye cannot find them, but must give the reins to the feet, as the traveller to his horse. So we went through the aspens at the base of the Cliffs, their round leaves reflecting the lingering twilight on the one side, the waxing moonlight on the other. Always the path was unexpectedly open.

In Baker's orchard the thick grass looks like a sea of mowing in this weird moonlight, a bottomless sea of grass. Our feet must be imaginative, must know the earth in imagination only, as well as our heads. We sit on the fence, and, where it is broken and interrupted, the fallen and slanting rails are lost in the grass (really thin and wiry) as in water. We even see our tracks a long way behind, where we have brushed off the dew. The clouds are peculiarly wispy tonight, somewhat like fine flames, not massed and dark nor downy, not thick, but slight, thin wisps of mist.

I hear the sound of Heywood's Brook falling into Fair Haven Pond, inexpressibly refreshing to my senses. It seems to flow through my very bones. I hear it with insatiable thirst. It allays some sandy heat in me. It affects my circulations; methinks my arteries have sympathy with it. What is it I hear but the pure waterfalls within me, in the circulation of my blood, the streams that fall into my heart?[6]

The coolness of surface sand, the sight of one's own tracks in the dew-covered grass, the sound of a distant waterfall—these are all simple impressions; but when reading Thoreau we feel that they are worth the concentration that it takes to share them.

---

[6]Bradford Torrey, ed., *Journal 1850–September 15, 1851, The Writings of Henry David Thoreau,* Vol. VIII, pp. 297–98, 300.

SUGGESTED WRITING ASSIGNMENT

Descriptive Journal Entries

All good firsthand reporting begins in sharp perception. Begin today to keep a journal of on-the-spot, at-the-moment impressions of specific sights, sounds, scents, and tastes. Write only two or three sentences a day, unless you wish to write more, rigorously omitting all inferences and value judgments to insure direct rendering of perceptions. After you have studied diction, arrangement, and sentence structure in description, you will be asked to expand some of your journal entries into paragraphs that you can submit for evaluation.

Diction in Description

TWO WAR REPORTS

Only concrete words with specific referents or referents made specific by context stir the senses; nonconcrete words and very general concrete words cannot create images. The two brief reports that follow, by Ernie Pyle and John Steinbeck, were both written during World War II. Ernie Pyle wanted to show his readers why to him an air raid shelter was the most dispiriting of war scenes. John Steinbeck wanted to show his readers that the war reports in their newspapers did not describe the war as a correspondent experienced it. Which of these writers describes scenes more vividly? Where is each writer most effective?

FROM **Ernie Pyle in England**

London,
February, 1941

1 . . . I got my first view of an underground shelter crowd at the big Liverpool Street tube station.

2 It was around eight o'clock on a raidless night. A policeman in the upper vestibule told us just to go down the escalator and take a look—as though it were a zoo. So we did.

ERNIE PYLE IN ENGLAND   New York: Robert M. McBride and Company, 1941, pp. 113–15.

3 Somehow I must have thought that there'd be nobody down there that night, or that if there were they'd be invisible or something, because I wasn't emotionally ready at all to see people lying around by the thousands on cold concrete.

4 In my first days in England I had seen terrible bomb damage. I had seen multitudinous preparations for war. I had talked with wounded soldiers. I had gone through London's great night of fire-bombing. I had listened for hours to the crack of guns and the crunch of bombs. And although I didn't especially know it at the time, none of these things went clear down deep inside and made me hurt.

5 It was not until I went down seventy feet into the bowels of the Liverpool Street tube and saw humanity sprawled there in childlike helplessness that my heart first jumped and my throat caught. I know I must have stopped suddenly and drawn back. I know I must have said to myself, "Oh my God!"

6 We hunted up the shelter marshal, and talked to him for a long time. He was immensely proud of his shelter, and I suppose he had a right to be, for they say it is paradise now compared to what it was in the beginning. He told us to take a walk through the shelter and then meet him at the back entrance.

7 This is a new section of the tunnel, not yet used by trains. The tube is narrower than most of New York's subway excavations, and it is elliptical in shape. It is walled with steel casing.

8 We walked to the far end, about an eighth of a mile, through one tube, and then back in the parallel tube. On benches on each side, as though sitting and lying on a long street-car seat, were the people, hundreds of them. And as we walked on they stretched into thousands. In addition, there was a row of sleeping forms on the wooden floor of the tube, stretched crosswise. Their bodies took up the whole space, so we had to watch closely when we put our feet down between the sleepers.

9 Many of these people were old—wretched and worn old people, people who had never known many of the good things of life and who were now winding up their days on this earth in desperate discomfort. They were the bundled-up, patched-up people with lined faces that we have seen sitting dumbly in waiting lines at our own relief offices at home.

10 There were children too, some asleep and some playing. There were youngsters in groups, laughing and talking and even singing. There were smart-alecks and there were quiet ones. There were hard-working people of middle age who had to rise at five o'clock and go to work. Some people sat knitting or playing cards or talking. But mostly they just sat. And though it was only eight o'clock, many of the old people were already asleep.

11 It was the old people who seemed so tragic. Think of yourself at seventy or eighty, full of pain and of dim memories of a lifetime that has probably all been bleak. And then think of yourself traveling at dusk every night to a subway station, wrapping your ragged overcoat about your old shoulders and sitting on a wooden bench with your back against a curved steel wall. Sitting there all night, in nodding and fitful sleep. Think of that as your destiny—every night, every night from now on.

12 People looked up as we came along in our good clothes and our

obviously American hats. I had a terrible feeling of guilt as I walked through there—the same feeling that I have had when going through penitentiaries, staring at the prisoners. I couldn't look people in the face; consequently I didn't see very much of the human visage that night, for I looked mostly at the floor. But I saw all I could bear. I saw enough.

13 Since that first night I have seen so much of it I no longer feel that way about the shelterers in mass. Repetition makes the unusual become commonplace. Enough of anything dulls the emotions. But I still think my first impression was a valid one. I still think it speaks the frightening poverty of character in this world more forcibly than do the bombs that cause it.

14 A bombed building looks like something you have seen before—it looks as though a hurricane had struck. But the sight of thousands of poor, opportunityless people lying in weird positions against cold steel, with all their clothes on, hunched up in blankets, lights shining in their eyes, breathing fetid air—lying there far underground like rabbits, not fighting, not even angry; just helpless, scourged, weakly waiting for the release of another dawn—that, I tell you, is life without redemption.

FROM **Once There Was a War**

John Steinbeck

Mediterranean Theatre
October 6, 1943

1 You can't see much of a battle. Those paintings reproduced in history books which show long lines of advancing troops are either idealized or else times and battles have changed. The account in the morning papers of the battle of yesterday was not seen by the correspondent, but was put together from reports.

2 What the correspondent really saw was dust and the nasty burst of shells, low bushes and slit trenches. He lay on his stomach, if he had any sense, and watched ants crawling among the little sticks on the sand dune, and his nose was so close to the ants that their progress was interfered with by it.

3 Then he saw an advance. Not straight lines of men marching into cannon fire, but little groups scuttling like crabs from bits of cover to other cover, while the high chatter of machine guns sounded, and the deep proom of shellfire.

4 Perhaps the correspondent scuttled with them and hit the ground again. His report will be of battle plan and tactics, of taken ground or lost terrain, of attack and counterattack. But these are some of the things he probably really saw:

5 He might have seen the splash of dirt and dust that is a shell burst, and a small Italian girl in the street with her stomach blown out, and he might

have seen an American soldier standing over a twitching body, crying. He probably saw many dead mules, lying on their sides, reduced to pulp. He saw the wreckage of houses, with torn beds hanging like shreds out of the spilled hole in a plaster wall. There were red carts and the stalled vehicles of refugees who did not get away. . . .

6 He would have smelled the sharp cordite in the air and the hot reek of blood if the going has been rough. The burning odor of dust will be in his nose and the stench of men and animals killed yesterday and the day before. Then a whole building is blown up and an earthy, sour smell comes from its walls. He will smell his own sweat and the accumulated sweat of an army. When his throat is dry, he will drink warm water from his canteen, which tastes of disinfectant.

7 While the correspondent is writing for you of advances and retreats, his skin will be raw from the woolen clothes he has not taken off for three days, and his feet will be hot and dirty and swollen from not having taken off his shoes for days. He will itch from last night's mosquito bites and from today's sand-fly bites. Perhaps he will have a little sand-fly fever, so that his head pulses and a red rim comes into his vision. His head may ache from the heat and his eyes burn with the dust. The knee that was sprained when he leaped ashore will grow stiff and painful, but it is no wound and cannot be treated.

8 "The 5th Army advanced two kilometers," he will write, while the lines of trucks churn the road to deep dust and truck drivers hunch over their wheels. And off to the right the burial squads are scooping slits in the sandy earth. Their charges lie huddled on the ground and before they are laid in the sand, the second of the two dog tags is detached so that you know that that man with that Army serial number is dead and out of it.

9 These are the things he sees while he writes of tactics and strategy and names generals and in print decorates heroes. He takes a heavily waxed box from his pocket. That is his dinner. Inside there are two little packets of hard cake which have the flavor of dog biscuits. There is a tin can of cheese and a roll of vitamin-charged candy, an envelope of lemon powder to make the canteen water taste less bad, and a tiny package of four cigarettes.

10 That is dinner, and it will keep him moving for several more hours and keep his stomach working and his heart pumping. And if the line has advanced beyond him while he eats, dirty, buglike children will sidle up to him, cringing and sniffling, their noses ringed with flies, and these children will whine for one of the hard biscuits and some of the vitamin candy. They will cry for candy: "*Caramela—caramela—caramela*—okay, okay, shank you, good-by." And if he gives the candy to one, the ground will spew up more dirty, buglike children, and they will scream shrilly, "*Caramela—caramela*." The correspondent will get the communiqué and will write your morning dispatch on his creaking, dust-filled portable: "General Clark's 5th Army advanced two kilometers against heavy artillery fire yesterday."

---

1. Ernie Pyle closes his report with a value judgment on shelter life as a whole. What is his judgment?

2. State at least two less comprehensive value judgments expressed in Pyle's report, and quote the description of a subjective reaction implying a value judgment.
3. Does Pyle use any specific terms in his report, terms that could be placed on the third level of an abstraction ladder?
4. Cite three instances in which Pyle uses the very general term *people* to refer to the shelter dwellers, without specifying a particular person.
5. Pyle divides the people in the shelter according to their ages, speaking of old people, children, youngsters, and middle-aged working people. Where would terms referring to these groups probably be placed on an abstraction ladder?
6. Do Pyle's modifying words make any representative of any of these groups specific enough to be visualized? If so, do his images support the value judgments referred to in answers to questions 1 and 2?
7. Are there any sharp images in Pyle's report?
8. How many value judgments do you see in Steinbeck's report?
9. Are there any specific terms in Steinbeck's report, terms that could be placed on the third level of an abstraction ladder?
10. Cite some passages in which fourth- and fifth-level terms are transformed by modifiers into visual, auditory, olfactory, gustatory, and tactile images.
11. Are the images in Steinbeck's report more stirring to the senses than those in Pyle's last paragraph—the restrictive clothes, the light in the eyes, and the fetid air?
12. Does Steinbeck need to say, "This was a paltry dinner," or "A correspondent may be terribly uncomfortable when writing the report that you will take so much for granted," or "War is hell," or "Oh, my God"?
13. Examine the words in the correspondent's official report: "General Clark's 5th Army advanced two kilometers against heavy artillery fire yesterday." This statement refers to a specific advance on a specific day that covered a measurable distance. It is a more specific statement, for example, than "The United States Forces are doing well in Italy now." But it is misleading. Why?
14. Which report is more effective—Pyle's or Steinbeck's?

DICTION IN JOURNAL ENTRIES

You have probably written at least one journal entry by now. Examine the words in it. Which word names the central subject? Is it a concrete term that refers to an object you have actually perceived? Have you used the *most* specific term for it that you know? Do your descriptive modifiers create images that stir the senses?

Objectivity in Description

Ernie Pyle's description of the London air raid shelter, with its value judgments and its references to the author's personal reactions, is obviously subjective. John Steinbeck's description of a battle from one correspondent's point of view is less subjective, because it abounds in objective detail and includes only a few value judgments; but it is not completely objective. By selecting only inglorious, painful, and revolting details, Steinbeck implies a repugnance to war; also, by selection and careful organization of details, he supports an inference that the usual report of a battle, far from describing the battle as any reporter has experienced it, treats a composite subject derived from battle plans and reports of various individuals, mainly military officers.

Completely objective description, which not only excludes value judgments and inferences, but in which also the objective details seem not to have been selected to convey an attitude or support an idea, is rare. It may seem paradoxical that to illustrate it best we must turn to the work of a novelist. Since a novelist creates his characters and situations, he does not simply describe what he perceives, and in this sense his statements cannot be objective reports. It is possible, however, for a novelist to limit himself in his presentation to what an observer could perceive, demanding of himself that every motion and every object he describes be true to life, and in that sense be objective. Further, he may be intent upon rendering the object itself, without trying to arouse an emotion or express an idea. Alain Robbe-Grillet, a contemporary French novelist, writes what he calls " 'fiction' of 'strictly material reality,' "[7] without psychological analyses, interior monologs, or any other introspective device. Roland Barthes, an interpreter of Robbe-Grillet's novels, has explained the purpose of Robbe-Grillet's work:

> Robbe-Grillet's purpose, like that of some of his contemporaries— Cayrol and Pinget, for example, though in another direction—is to establish the novel on the surface: once you can set its inner nature, its "interiority," between parentheses, then objects in space, and the circulation of men among them, are promoted to the rank of subjects. The novel becomes man's direct experience of what surrounds him without his being able to shield himself with a psychology, a metaphysic, or a psychoanalytic method in his combat with the objective world he discovers. The novel is no longer a chthonian revelation, the book of hell, but of the earth—requiring that we no longer look at the world with the eyes of a confessor, of a doctor, or of God himself (all significant hypos-

---

[7]In Bruce Morrissette, "Surfaces and Structures in Robbe-Grillet's Novels," tr. by Richard Howard, *Two Novels by Robbe-Grillet* (New York: Grove Press, 1965), p. 8.

tases of the classical novelist), but with the eyes of a man walking in his city with no other horizon than the scene before him, no other power than that of his own eyes.[8]

The excerpts from *Jealousy* that follow illustrate Robbe-Grillet's objective style. The narrator, the husband of A. . . , reports only what could be perceived by a real observer if the situation were real, without interpreting and without referring to himself.

FROM **Jealousy**

Alain Robbe-Grillet

1 On the log bridge that crosses the stream at the bottom edge of this patch, there is a man crouching: a native, wearing blue trousers and a colorless undershirt that leaves his shoulders bare. He is leaning toward the liquid surface, as if he were trying to see something at the bottom, which is scarcely possible, the water never being transparent enough despite its extreme shallowness. (pp. 52–53)

.   .   .

2 The man is still motionless, bending over the muddy water on the earth-covered log bridge. He has not moved an inch: crouching, head lowered, forearms resting on his thighs, hands hanging between his knees.

In front of him, in the patch along the opposite bank of the little stream, several stems look ripe for harvesting. Several boles have already been cut in this sector. Their empty places appear with perfect distinctness in the series of geometrical alignments. But on closer inspection it is possible to distinguish the sizeable shoot that will replace the severed banana tree a few inches away from the old stump, already beginning to spoil the perfect regularity of the alternate planting. (p. 54)

.   .   .

3 The brush descends the length of the loose hair with a faint noise something between the sound of a breath and a crackle. No sooner has it reached the bottom than it quickly rises again toward the head, where the whole surface of its bristles sinks in before gliding down over the black mass again. The brush is a bone-colored oval whose short handle disappears almost entirely in the hand firmly gripping it.

Half of the hair hangs down the back, the other hand pulls the other

[8]"Objective Literature: Alain Robbe-Grillet," tr. by Richard Howard, *Two Novels by Robbe-Grillet*, p. 25.

half over one shoulder. The head leans to the right, offering the hair more readily to the brush. Each time the latter lands at the top of its cycle behind the nape of the neck, the head leans farther to the right and then rises again with an effort, while the right hand, holding the brush, moves away in the opposite direction. The left hand, which loosely confines the hair between the wrist, the palm and the fingers, releases it for a second and then closes on it again, gathering the strands together with a firm, mechanical gesture, while the brush continues its course to the extreme tips of the hair. The sound, which gradually varies from one end to the other, is at this point nothing more than a dry, faint crackling, whose last sputters occur once the brush, leaving the longest hair, is already moving up the ascending part of the cycle, describing a swift curve in the air which brings it above the neck, where the hair lies flat on the back of the head and reveals the white streak of a part.

To the left of this part, the other half of the black hair hangs loosely to the waist in supple waves. Still further to the left the face shows only a faint profile. But beyond is the surface of the mirror, which reflects the image of the whole face from the front, the eyes—doubtless unnecessary for brushing—directed straight ahead, as is natural.

Thus A. . .'s eyes should meet the wide-open window which overlooks the west gable-end. Facing in this direction she is brushing her hair in front of the dressing table provided especially with a vertical mirror which reflects her gaze behind her, toward the bedroom's third window, the central portion of the veranda and the slope of the valley.

The second window, which looks south like this third one, is nearer the southwest corner of the house; it too is wide open. Through it can be seen the side of the dressing-table, the edge of the mirror, the left profile of the face, the loose hair which hangs over the shoulder, and the left arm which is bent back to reach the right half of the hair.

Since the nape of the neck is bent diagonally to the right, the face is slightly turned toward the window. On the gray-streaked marble table-top are arranged jars and bottles of various sizes and shapes; nearer the front lies a large tortoise-shell comb and another brush, this one of wood with a longer handle, which is lying with its black bristles facing up.

A. . . must have just washed her hair, otherwise she would not be bothering to brush it in the middle of the day. She has interrupted her movements, having finished this side perhaps. Nevertheless she does not change the position of her arms or move the upper part of her body as she turns her face all the way around toward the window at her left to look out at the veranda, the open-work balustrade and the opposite slope of the valley. (pp. 66–67)

.   .   .

4 A. . . is lying fully dressed on the bed. One of her legs rests on the satin spread; the other, bent at the knee, hangs half over the edge. The arm on this side is bent toward the head lying on the bolster. Stretched across the wide bed, the other arm lies out from the body at approximately a forty-five degree angle. Her face is turned upward toward the ceiling. Her eyes are made still larger by the darkness. (p. 92)

. . .

5 Between the remaining gray paint, faded by time, and the wood grayed by the action of humidity, appear tiny areas of reddish brown—the natural color of the wood—where the wood has been left exposed by the recent flaking off of new scales of paint. Inside her bedroom, A. . . is standing in front of the window and looking out between one of the chinks in the blinds.

The man is still motionless, leaning toward the muddy water, on the earth-covered log bridge. He has not moved an inch: crouching, head down, forearms resting on his thighs, hands hanging between his knees. He seems to be looking at something at the bottom of the little stream—an animal, a reflection, a lost object.

In front of him, in the patch along the other bank, several stems look ripe for cutting, although the harvest has not yet been started in this sector. The sound of a truck shifting gears on the highway on the other side of the house is answered here by the creak of a window-lock. The first bedroom window opens. (p. 121)

. . .

6 "When do you think you'll be going down?" A. . . asks.

"I don't know. . . ." They look at each other, their glances meeting above the platter Franck is holding in one hand six inches above the table top. "Maybe next week."

"I have to go to town too," A. . . says; "I have a lot of shopping to do."

"Well, I'll be glad to take you. If we leave early, we can be back the same night."

He sets the platter down on his left and begins helping himself. A. . . turns back so that she is looking straight ahead.

"A centipede!" she says in a more restrained voice, in the silence that has just fallen.

Franck looks up again. Following the direction of A. . . 's motionless gaze, he turns his head to the other side, toward his right.

On the light-colored paint of the partition opposite A. . . , a common Scutigera of average size (about as long as a finger) has appeared, easily seen despite the dim light. It is not moving, for the moment, but the orientation of its body indicates a path which cuts across the panel diagonally: coming from the baseboard on the hallway side and heading toward the corner of the ceiling. The creature is easy to identify thanks to the development of its legs, especially on the posterior portion. On closer examination the swaying movement of the antennae at the other end can be discerned.

A. . . has not moved since her discovery: sitting very straight in her chair, her hands resting flat on the cloth on either side of her plate. Her eyes are wide, staring at the wall. Her mouth is not quite closed, and may be quivering imperceptibly.

It is not unusual to encounter different kinds of centipedes after dark in this already old wooden house. And this kind is not one of the largest; it is far from being one of the most venomous. A. . . does her best, but does not manage to look away, nor to smile at the joke about her aversion to centipedes.

Franck, who has said nothing, is looking at A. . . again. Then he stands up, noiselessly, holding his napkin in his hand. He wads it into a ball and approaches the wall.

A. . . seems to be breathing a little faster, but this may be an illusion. Her left hand gradually closes over her knife. The delicate antennae accelerate their alternate swaying.

Suddenly the creature hunches its body and begins descending diagonally toward the ground as fast as its long legs can go, while the wadded napkin falls on it, faster still.

The hand with the tapering fingers has clenched around the knife handle; but the features of the face have lost none of their rigidity. Franck lifts the napkin away from the wall and with his foot continues to squash something on the tiles, against the baseboard.

About a yard higher, the paint is marked with a dark shape, a tiny arc twisted into a question mark, blurred on one side, in places surrounded by more tenuous signs, from which A. . . has still not taken her eyes. (pp. 64–65)

---

1. Please look again at the fourth excerpt. This is an exact description of what?
2. In the first, second, and fifth excerpts, are complete details of the man's appearance given?
3. Is the third excerpt a full description of A. . .'s brushing of her hair? Can you see the movement of both hands, in time with the movement of the head? Can you hear the movement of the brush?
4. Can the objects on the dressing table be visualized?
5. Notice the italicized words in the following sentences from the third excerpt: "A. . . *must have* just washed her hair, otherwise she would not be bothering to brush it in the middle of the day. She has interrupted her movements, having finished this side *perhaps*." Why does Robbe-Grillet not say simply that A. . . has washed her hair and that she has finished brushing the right side?
6. In the last excerpt, a narrative incident, which objects and positions are exactly described?
7. Which types of words (by semantical classification) does Robbe-Grillet use in these excerpts from *Jealousy?*

OBJECTIVITY IN JOURNAL ENTRIES

Your journal entries will consist mainly of objective details, that is, details that you have observed directly, rendered in concrete nouns and sensuous modifiers. These reports may, however, be either subjective or objective in intention. You may, like Steinbeck, select details to express an attitude or an idea, depending upon the reader to derive the attitude or the idea from reading the details. Or, you may write entries objective in intention as well as in technique, which do not lead the reader to derive an attitude or an idea. In these entries you may wish to begin with details as Robbe-Grillet does in the description of A. . . 's hair brushing, letting the full subject become clear to your reader gradually; or you may wish to give a general description of the subject first and then describe details. It would be best for you to try your hand at all of these types of description, consciously adjusting your techniques to your aim.

OBJECTIVITY IN DESCRIPTIVE PARAGRAPHS
WRITTEN BY STUDENTS

The following paragraphs were written by freshman students at the University of Arizona when asked in a composition class to be completely objective in describing an object or an action. They are reproduced here by permission.

Have these students succeeded in being objective and in creating clear images? Which do you think is the best description?

1.

It sits on the table, contained in a metal case of light tan color. On the front face are four rows of flat, round disks with distinctive symbols slightly indented in the top. Above, and set back further in the center of the object, a thin sheet of white material extends up and curves limply backward over a cylinder. The sheet jerks unevenly toward the left at a rapid pace. It stops for a short time and then continues again. At the left, the sheet is lined with black figures, the number of which increases as it jerks to the left. In the middle of the object there is a semi-circular opening from which an arm extends and slaps the white sheet in a lightning fast motion, leaving an imprint on the white material. After a while the black figures run in a horizontal line. Then, the cylinder slides back to the right and rolls upward, revealing clean, unmarked white, the previous line of black marks above it. It continues with the jerking, slapping, rolling and clackity-clack noises just as before, leaving marks in a line parallel to the one above.

STEPHANIE KNOWLES

2.

In the well-lit corridor between the Student Union game room and Louie's Lower Level sit nine small card tables, each surrounded by four folding chairs. On one particular table, covered with a tweedy brown plastic cloth, sits a clear square ashtray. Flaring up in the center of the tray is a crumpled Twinkie wrapper under which lies half a lime, most of the juice gone, with several of the seeds lying in the ash-covered bottom of the receptacle. One Marlboro cigaret butt and a twisted Juicy Fruit gum wrapper complete the inventory of the ashtray. Standing to the left are two identical water glasses, short, squatty, and a third full. Beyond the glasses sits a white card covered with pencil marks. Just beyond the card and lying at the very edge of the chrome-ringed table is another ashtray with traces of both burned and unburned tobacco and one small wooden match, half burned, and two paper matches, the tips charred, one upturned reading "On the Campus." Adjacent to the second ashtray is a crinkled matchbook, stripped of its contents, which says in white letters on a red background, "Associated Students' Bookstore, close cover before striking."

RICHARD DUCOTE

3.

As the squad passed in front of me, the order rang out, "By the right flank . . . march!" The first man in the squad took one more step, planted his left foot, dusting his shoe with chalk from a yard marker. The trailing foot, the right, stepped out to the right, perpendicular to the original line of march, paralleling the yard marker. Meanwhile he pivoted on the ball of his left foot, body turning, brass flashing. His right foot then landed. His well-starched pants rustled with the maneuver, as did his shirt. He now marched off in a straight line, arms swinging, clothes rustling, shoes and brass flashing.

PETER A. KAUTH

Arrangement of Details in Description

BASIC SPATIAL PATTERNS

When one sets out to describe an object or a scene, he must decide not only whether he will begin with a general description or with a detail, but also how he will proceed from detail to detail. Why should a certain detail be described first and another next? His decision will depend on the shape of the subject, the position from which he is viewing the subject, and his purpose in describing the subject. Let us assume that in the instances to be considered first the purpose is simply to transmit to the mental eye of the reader an image of the subject, as much as possible like the image the writer actually sees. If the subject is a clown on stilts seen in full view from a seat in a circus tent, the writer will probably begin with the stilts and proceed upward, or begin at the head and proceed downward to the stilts. In describing any subject in which the main line is vertical—a skyscraper, the Eiffel Tower, Michelangelo's statue of David—one will be likely to present the details in order from top to bottom or from bottom to top. If the main line is horizontal, as in a football field, a dashboard on an automobile, or a large, conventional stage, he will begin (perhaps after a general description) with a detail on the left side and move to the right side, or *vice versa*—if he can see the whole horizontal line in a sweep of the eye, as when seated in a side stand looking down at a football field or in an auditorium looking at a stage. If one enters at the end of a long room the main line of which is horizontal, however, he will not observe details from right to left or from left to right, but from near to far or from far to near. A guide leading viewers through a cave will have a similar point of vision, and if he pauses to direct attention to curiously formed stalactites and stalagmites to be seen in the next thirty yards, he will probably mention the closest detail first and proceed to the farthest detail. If a writer wants to describe the landscaping of his front yard as seen from the front entry or describe any expanse of open country, he will probably begin with a detail on his left or his right side and sweep around in a circular motion to the other side.

The following diagrams illustrate the simple patterns discussed above for ordering details in description so as to represent certain movements of the eye over a subject from a specified point of vision (PV). D stands for *detail,* and the details are numbered in the order that they would appear on paper in a description; their relative positions indicate the visual pattern that the writer would be creating for the movement of the reader's mental eye. Each pattern is based on the principle of addition: $D_1 + D_2 + D_3 + D_4 + D_5 =$ the Whole.

I. Bottom-to-top or top-to-bottom order of visualization

$$D_5 \qquad D_1$$
$$D_4 \qquad D_2$$
$$D_3 \qquad D_3$$
$$D_2 \qquad D_4$$
$$D_1 \qquad D_5$$

PV   PV

II. Horizontal order of visualization; right-to-left or left-to-right

$$D_4\ D_3\ D_2\ D_1$$

$$D_1\ D_2\ D_3\ D_4$$

PV

III. Far-to-near or near-to-far order of visualization

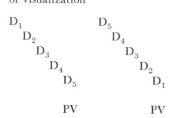

PV   PV

IV. Clockwise (or counterclockwise) order of visualization

$$D_3 \qquad D_4$$
$$D_2 \qquad\qquad D_5$$
$$D_1 \qquad\qquad D_6$$
$$\qquad PV$$

In the following paragraph a student has arranged details in one of the patterns diagramed above. See whether you can diagram the pattern, naming the details themselves instead of calling them D_1, D_2, and so forth.

> Sitting on the cool green cement by the edge of our oval-shaped pool, I feel a breeze arising, at first gently, lifting my paper from my lap and returning it again. At the end of the pool, on my right, leaves begin to move soundlessly in the unripened tangerine tree, and above it butterflies flutter, as if uncertain where to light. Upon the creamy flesh-colored wall, at a left oblique from the tree, two green, pear-shaped vases tremble slightly. The pale oleander leaning toward them straightens and droops again. Directly across the pool from me, to the left of the oleander, is a grayish-brown wooden gate leading out to the back alley. The paint on the latch is chipped, and the dull gray metal shows through. Above the latch is a dark rectangular-shaped hole where another latch appears to have been. A jasmine shrub, about a foot taller than the wall, casts a shadow over the left three-fourths of the gate. To the left of the jasmine, tall mulberry trees on the other side of the wall create dancing shadows on the sunlit surface of the pool. The water, disturbed lightly by the breeze, ripples in soft mounds. Suddenly, a cloud covers the sun, the wind rises—and the scene before me is changed.

THE BOTTOM-TO-TOP PATTERN OF ARRANGEMENT
IN TWO CONTEXTS

Read the following description, observing the deliberation with which James selects a point of vision from which to observe Chartres Cathedral and the order in which he describes details of the façade.

[Description of Chartres Cathedral]

Henry James

1 I spent a long time looking at Chartres Cathedral. 2 I revolved around it, like a moth around a candle; I went away and I came back; I chose twenty different standpoints; I observed it during the different hours of the day, and saw it in the moonlight as well as the sunshine. 3 I gained, in a word, a certain sense of familiarity with it; and yet I despair of giving any very coherent account of

it. 4 Like most French cathedrals, it rises straight out of the street, and is without that setting of turf and trees and deaneries and canonries which contribute so largely to the impressiveness of the great English churches. 5 Thirty years ago a row of old houses was glued to its base and made their back walls of its sculptured sides. 6 These have been plucked away, and, relatively speaking, the church is fairly isolated. 7 But the little square that surrounds it is regretfully narrow, and you flatten your back against the opposite houses in the vain attempt to stand off and survey the towers. 8 The proper way to look at the towers would be to go up in a balloon and hang poised, face to face with them, in the blue air. 9 There is, however, perhaps an advantage in being forced to stand so directly under them, for this position gives you an overwhelming impression of their height. 10 I have seen, I suppose, churches as beautiful as this one, but I do not remember ever to have been so touched and fascinated by architectural beauty. 11 The endless upward reach of the great west front, the clear, silvery tone of its surface, the way a few magnificent features are made to occupy its vast serene expanse, its simplicity, majesty, and dignity—these things crowd upon one's sense with a force that makes the act of vision seem for the moment almost all of life. 12 The impressions produced by architecture lend themselves as little to interpretation by another medium as those produced by music. 13 Certainly there is something of the beauty of music in the sublime proportions of the façade of Chartres.

14 The doors are rather low, as those of the English cathedral are apt to be, but (standing three together) are set in a deep framework of sculpture—rows of arching grooves, filled with admirable little images, standing with their heels on each other's heads. 15 The church, as it now exists, except the northern tower, dates from the middle of the thirteenth century, and these closely packed figures are full of the grotesqueness of the period. 16 Above the triple portals is a vast round-topped window, in three divisions, of the grandest dimensions and the stateliest effect. 17 Above this window is a circular aperture, of huge circumference, with a double row of sculptured spokes radiating from its centre and looking on its lofty field of stone as expansive and symbolic as if it were the wheel of Time itself. 18 Higher still is a little gallery with a delicate balustrade, supported on a beautiful cornice and stretching across the front from tower to tower; and above this is a range of niched statues of kings—fifteen, I believe, in number. 19 Above the statues is a gable, with an image of the Virgin and Child on its front, and another of Christ on its apex. 20 In the relation of all these parts there is such a spaciousness and harmony that while on the one side the eye rests on a great many broad stretches of naked stone there is no approach on the other to over profusion of detail. . . .

21 The inside of the cathedral corresponds in vastness and grandeur to the outside—it is the perfection of Gothic in its prime. 22 But I looked at it rapidly, the place was so intolerably cold. 23 It seemed to answer one's query of what becomes of the Winter when the Spring chases it away.

---

1. James's purpose is not only to describe Chartres Cathedral as an object, but also to convey to the reader a sense of the grandeur and majesty that

he thinks characteristic of it. Cite five or six passages in which he expresses
value judgments.

2. What two problems does James encounter in trying to describe Chartres?
3. Does he solve the first problem?
4. How does establishing a point of vision help an author organize details in
   space?
5. How does a clear point of vision in a description help a reader?
6. Which sentences constitute the actual description of the facade of the
   cathedral?
7. List or sketch the details in the order given by James, beginning at the
   bottom of your page and going up.
8. What transitional terms has James used to indicate the spatial relationship
   of the parts of the building to one another? What are some expressions that
   help place decorations?
9. What is the importance of such terms in descriptive writing?

FROM **In the Labyrinth**

Alain Robbe-Grillet

1 It is the same filament again, that of a similar or slightly larger lamp,
which glows so uselessly at the crossroads, enclosed in its glass cage on top of
a cast-iron pedestal, a gas light with old-fashioned ornaments that has been con-
verted into an electric street light.

2 Around the conical base of the cast-iron pedestal that widens toward
the bottom and is ringed by several more or less prominent moldings, are em-
bossed the slender stems of a stylized spray of ivy: curling tendrils; pointed,
five-lobed, palmate leaves, their five veins very prominent where the scaling black
point reveals the rusted metal. Slightly higher a hip, an arm, a shoulder are leaning
against the shaft of the lamppost. The man is wearing a faded military overcoat
of no particular color, perhaps once green or khaki. His face is grayish; his features
are drawn and give the impression of extreme fatigue, but perhaps a beard more
than a day old is largely responsible for this impression. Prolonged waiting, prolonged immobility in the cold may also have drained the color from his cheeks,
forehead, and lips.

3 The eyelids are gray, like the rest of the face; they are lowered. The
head is bowed. The eyes are looking at the ground, that is, at the edge of the
snow-covered sidewalk in front of the base of the street light and the two heavy
marching boots with rounded toes whose coarse leather shows scratches and other

IN THE LABYRINTH   Translated by Richard Howard. Reprinted by permission of Grove Press, Inc.
Copyright © 1965 by Grove Press, Inc.

signs of wear and tear, more or less covered by the black polish. The layer of snow is not thick enough to yield visibly underfoot, so that the soles of the boots are resting—or virtually resting—on the level of the white snow extending around them. At the edge of the sidewalk, this surface is completely unmarked, not shining but smooth, even, delicately stippled with its original granulation. A little snow has accumulated on the upper edge of the last projecting ring that encircles the widening base of the lamppost, forming a white circle above the black circle by which the latter rests on the ground. Higher up, some flakes have also stuck to other asperities of the cone, accenting the successive rings and the upper edges of the ivy leaves with a white line, as well as all the fragments of stems and veins that are horizontal or only slightly inclined.

4 But the bottom of the overcoat has swept away several of these tiny agglomerations, just as the boots, changing position several times, have trampled the snow in their immediate vicinity, leaving in places yellower areas, hardened, half-raised pieces and the deep marks of hobnails arranged in alternate rows.

1. What is the relation of the first paragraph in this excerpt to the other paragraphs?
2. What is the order of the details?
3. List the details in the second paragraph in Robbe-Grillet's order, beginning at the bottom of your page and going up.
4. Which transitional expression in the second paragraph points upward?
5. How is the reader's eye directed downward from the man's head to the ground?
6. Where is the observer?
7. Which details in the description are most vivid?
8. In the last paragraph there is a logical rather than a spatial transition. Upon which type of logical relationship is the transition based? Which words mark this transition?

EXERCISE 4

Spatial Patterns of Arrangement

More than one answer can be given to the questions in this exercise. You are therefore asked to give reasons for some of your answers.

1. What is the point of vision in the photograph on page 94? In other words, where would an observer be standing if he had exactly the view shown in the photograph? Which spatial pattern would you use to order details if you were describing this scene? Why would you use this pattern? Would you describe the general scene before describing the first detail?

2. Which patterns would you combine to describe the scene in this photograph (or in the photograph on page 95)? Do you think this photograph evokes a mood or expresses an idea? If you think so, how could you convey the mood or idea most effectively to a reader?

3. Where is the point of vision in the photograph above? Which spatial pattern seems best suited to a description of the details? Which detail would you mention last if you were describing the scene depicted?

SUGGESTED WRITING ASSIGNMENT

Description of a Scene

Select a scene or an object on campus, and observe it closely from a definite point of vision. Give a general description of the subject or mention its name; then describe details, organized according to a spatial pattern. Be objective when describing the details, and as key words use concrete words that are as specific in significance as you can make them.

STUDENT RESPONSES TO A SIMILAR ASSIGNMENT

Below are three paragraphs written by freshman students in response to an assignment similar to that above. Evaluate these paragraphs by the following criteria:

Has each student chosen a subject worth describing?

Does each give a general description before beginning to describe details?

Is each subject observed from a point of vision?

Can you discern a spatial pattern of organization in each description? If so, which pattern?

Are the details objectively described?

Are the words concrete?

Are there any specific images?

1.

A 1961 Corvair sits solidly in the middle of the gray, dirt-packed, parking lot. The body of the car leans heavily to the right side with two flat tires, its candy-apple red exterior blanketed by a heavy layer of dust, its tinted windshield covered with a film of grime. In the rear of the car the grill and bumper are bent in a folding vertical line, the hub caps crumpling inward, with the rust covered muffler hanging loosely to the ground. The chrome on the hood of the Corvair is covered by tiny hairlike scratches and a few pebble sized dents. From the twisted aerial hangs a tired looking red and blue banner stirring gently when the breeze stirs.

JUDY SAMSEL

2.

I am sitting on the ground before a building. The building has a rectangular front and is one story high with the width being approximately thirty feet. There is a door shown on the front of the building. It is placed approximately in the center of the "rectangle," having equidistant space on each side of the door. There are two windows showing. There is a window on the left of the front of the building, being approximately centered between the door and the left edge of the building. The other window is approximately centered between the door and the right edge of the building. There are flower beds or boxes directly beneath the windows, having the same width as the windows.

JOSE REYNOSO

3.

From a distance it is seen located between the Education Building, on its left, and the Psychology Building, on its right. It has eight sides, stretching upward to a rounded dome which revolves slowly. On opposite sides are extensions, jutting out from the flat surface, and forming five-sided walls, their tops slightly slanted toward the sides of the octagon. Directly in front is the door, set back in a deep arch of engravings and rows of radiating spokes. Above the door are three windows, close together, set back slightly in the brick of the walls. The windows are long, their panes tinted red and surrounded by blue frames. Still higher and on the top rim of the side of the octagon are the words *Steward Observatory,* engraved in the wall. On top of the octagon rests the dome, sparkling white, with rays extending downward from the top. A section is open in the dome, exposing a large telescope, peering out the opening, pointing in the direction of the sun. The dome revolves as the sun moves across the sky. It just moved slightly to the right.

CHARLOTTE LUCE

EMPHASIS UPON SELECTED DETAILS IN DESCRIPTION

We have assumed that in each of the descriptions considered so far the author's purpose has been to create for the reader a full image of a scene or an object. An author may wish, however, to emphasize certain details or to show in the order of the details an order of importance. In reading the following passage from Herman Melville's *Moby Dick,* one can observe that the narrator's point of vision is a point just inside the entrance to the public room, but he can see that it is not the author's intention to describe the whole room. Melville evokes a general mood by referring to the duskiness of the atmosphere and the roughness and oldness of the floor and by suggesting the oppressiveness of the ceiling. Then he directs the reader's mental eye from near to far along one of the walls to the most important feature of the room, in a far corner—the bar in the whale's jaw. As he moves toward this most significant part of the room he describes only one object—a "shelf-like table" and its contents.

> Crossing this dusky entry, and on through yon low-arched way—cut through what in old times must have been a great central chimney with fireplaces all round—you enter the public room. A still duskier place is this, with such low ponderous beams above, and such old wrinkled planks beneath, that you would almost fancy you trod some old craft's cockpits, especially of such a howling night, when this corner-anchored old ark rocked so furiously. On one side stood a long, low, shelf-like table covered with cracked glass-cases, filled with dusty rarities gathered from this wide world's remotest nooks. Projecting from the further angle of the room stands a dark-looking den—the bar—a rude attempt at a right whale's head. Be that how it may, there stands the vast arched bone of the whale's jaw, so wide, a coach might almost drive beneath it. Within are shabby shelves, ranged round with old decanters, bottles, flasks; and in those jaws of swift destruction, like another cursed Jonah (by which

indeed they called him), bustles a little withered old man, who, for their money, dearly sells the sailors deliriums and death.[9]

Thus Melville creates the proper background for a comment on alcoholic "poisons," which will follow in his next paragraph.

Winston Churchill's subject in the following passage is a very different kind of room from the public room in Melville's Spouter Inn, and he describes it more fully than Melville describes his room; but, clearly, one feature of the room is the most important.

> The Group Operations Room was like a small theatre, about sixty feet across, and with two storeys. We took our seats in the dress circle. Below us was the large-scale map-table, around which perhaps twenty highly trained young men and women, with their telephone assistants, were assembled. Opposite to us, covering the entire wall, where the theatre curtain would be, was a gigantic blackboard divided into six columns with electric bulbs, for the six fighter stations, each of their squadrons having a sub-column of its own, and also divided by lateral lines. Thus, the lowest row of bulbs showed as they were lighted the squadrons which were "Standing By" at two minutes' notice, the next row those "At Readiness," five minutes, then "At Available," twenty minutes, then those which had taken off, the next row those which had reported having seen the enemy, the next—with red lights—those which were in action, and the top row those which were returning home. On the left-hand side, in a kind of glass stage-box, were the four or five officers whose duty it was to weigh and measure the information received from our Observer Corps, which at this time numbered upwards of fifty thousand men, women, and youths. Radar was still in its infancy, but it gave warning of raids approaching our coast, and the observers, with field-glasses and portable telephones, were our main source of information about raiders flying overland. Thousands of messages were therefore received during an action. Several roomfuls of experienced people in other parts of the underground headquarters sifted them with great rapidity, and transmitted the results from minute to minute directly to the plotters seated around the table on the floor and to the officer supervising from the glass stage-box.
>
> On the right hand was another glass stage-box containing Army officers who reported the action of our anti-aircraft batteries, of which at this time in the Command there were two hundred. At night it was of vital importance to stop these batteries firing over certain areas in which our fighters would be closing with the enemy.[10]

If Churchill's purpose had been to describe the setting for the sake of the setting, he could have used the clockwise or counterclockwise order, but such was not his purpose. On this day all of the planes of the Royal Air Force were to be

[9]Boston: L. C. Page, 1892, pp. 17–18.

[10]Sir Winston Churchill, *The Second World War: Their Finest Hour* (Boston: Houghton Mifflin Company, 1949), pp. 333–34. Reprinted by permission of the publisher.

engaged in air battles with the Luftwaffe, and after describing the room, Churchill would explain to the reader how he received reports on the air men's activity from the lights on the gigantic blackboard. The blackboard with its six rows of lights is the most important feature of the room; it is therefore described before anything else on its level of the building. In his description of it, Churchill moves row by row, from bottom to top; then he turns left to the glass "stage-box" where officers are receiving information from the Observer Corps, and then right to the glass "stage-box" where officers are receiving reports on anti-aircraft batteries. The room is fully enough described, with the aid of an apt comparison between this room and a theater, for the reader to understand the action that will be reported. Churchill, thus, has satisfied his purpose.

To summarize: the purpose of the author is as important in determining the order of details as the point of vision and the shape of the subject.

EXERCISE 5

Selecting Details to Emphasize in Descriptions

1. Please look at the photograph on page 100. Imagine standing where you could see the whole scene pictured here. If you were to describe this scene, would you give a general description of the pueblo before describing details? Why? Do you think the dimensions of the pueblo are important? Would you, instead of describing all objects in the room with equal emphasis, emphasize the man, describing him first and then moving to his left and to his right? Which is more impressive in relation to the man—the objects in the pueblo or the empty space? Explain.

2. Explain why it is evident in the photograph above that the photographer has selected the monument as the center of interest. Why would a general description of the fence, the clothes line, and the building in the background be sufficient to give meaning to a detailed description of the monument?

SUGGESTED WRITING ASSIGNMENT

A Description with a Central Subject

Select an interior or another location in which there is a center of interest. Before beginning to describe this location, decide which pattern of arrangement will be appropriate to a detailed description of the central subject. Then consider how much you will need to say about the surrounding objects to give the central subject an appropriate setting. Finally, decide whether you will give a general description before describing the first detail and how you will organize the details in the entire description.

After you have written the description, write a note to the reader stating your intention and explaining your method of development.

TIME ORDER AND THE MOVING POINT OF VISION

Suppose that instead of observing the scene depicted on page 96 from a stationary point of vision, an observer walks from the cross to the refuse, then to the cars, and then toward the house. Suppose that as he slides down the rise at the back corner of the house, he sees the elderly man approaching him on the path and stops to converse with him. If the observer later described what he had seen as he walked, he would use a moving point of vision, or, more precisely, a chronological sequence of different points of vision. Such a description might appear in a narrative, but it could also appear in a nonfiction report.

The moving point of vision, with an implied chronological order, is often necessary to an observer who is describing a very large object, as well as to an observer who is moving from place to place. The observer will perhaps walk around the object or get on top of it. In the following selection, Alberto Moravia, an Italian novelist, describes the Great Wall of China as it looked to him and his wife in 1968. The whole context of the description is given in the selection. The Moravias—who have driven from Peking with Mr. Li, a guide—approach the wall from the China side.

A few facts about the Great Wall that the author does not include may be useful. According to *Collier's Encyclopedia*, the Wall is twenty to fifty feet high, from fifteen to twenty-five feet thick at the base, and about twelve feet thick at the top.

FROM **Lobster Land: A Traveler in China**

Alberto Moravia

1 The road runs along the bottom of a narrow valley, green and flourishing. The stony river bed with shallow limpid water is visible between the bushes. Then the hills gradually close, and while they do not grow higher they become steeper. And the valley becomes a gorge.

2 We arrived at a small group of peasant houses, low yellow constructions with dried-mud walls and straw roofs. The car stopped and we saw a kind of arch or bridge of white marble, a massive and elaborate structure, a veritable work of art planted there in the middle of the unchanging countryside. It was one of the gates of the Great Wall, and soldiers and excise officers probably once stood guard there. It must have been an inner gate, part of a system of lesser walls that defended the nearby capital. The authentic Great Wall is much farther away.

3 We got out of the car and looked at the gate. Like all Chinese monuments, it was both massive and ornamental. The idea of solidity was oddly blended with that of refinement. The gate was covered with fine low-relief sculptures on both sides. The subject was exactly what one would have expected, given the place and function of the monument: this was civilization, as represented by heroes, sages and emperors, bending the neck of barbarism, depicted in the form of dragons, serpents and monsters. Anyone entering China would have understood at once. He was leaving the void of barbarism and entering the realm of civilization. Albeit this realm consisted only of ceremony and etiquette; that is, a void like any other.

4 We climbed to the top of the gate. It had been abandoned, like so many artistic creations in China today. Weeds were growing between the bricks, there were cracks in the marble, and the sculptures were scratched, darkened and defaced. The gate ought to be restored, but there is slight chance that it can be done in the near future. Mr. Li's tone was dry and slightly bored as he explained what this gate was. The Chinese today are not interested in the Great Wall, for it no longer serves any purpose. Other times, other Great Walls. The most one can hope for is the restoration of some section of the fortifications, designed in harmony with the times, to be educational and scientific. But the marble arch is too beautiful to be restored.

FROM LOBSTER LAND: A TRAVELER IN CHINA   Reprinted with the permission of Farrar, Straus & Giroux, Inc., from *The Red Book and The Great Wall* by Alberto Moravia. Copyright © 1968 by Farrar, Straus & Giroux, Inc. Italian edition copyright © 1967 Casa editrice Valentino Bompiani. By permission of Martin Secker & Warburg Limited.

5 We returned to the automobile and drove on through the valley, or rather the gorge. Finally, at the point where the gorge is narrowest, we saw the Great Wall, the real one, the one that traverses 3,000 miles of mountains. I recognized the presence, the efficacy, the power of the myth in the emotion that suddenly took hold of me. It is true, of course, that the place itself is indescribably evocative. On both sides of the gorge, the mountains seem to withdraw, as if they were fleeing from the gorge from one peak to another. And along the edge of these two continuous ridges, standing out against the blue sky, the huge gray stone serpent, sinuous and soft, embracing the tortuous turns of the mountain range, also takes flight.

6 The beauty of the Great Wall is in its faithful pursuit of the meandering mountains. A squared-up wall in the middle of a plain, like the Escorial, for example, has something dismal, abstract and lifeless about it. But to look at the Great Wall is to experience a serpentine vitality. The reptile may be decrepit but it is alive. One is almost surprised that it does not move, slithering off, curl around the mountains, and finally disappear on the horizon. Its vitality is subtle, insinuating, resilient, sly, tenacious, parasitic and symbiotic. There is a kind of marriage between ivy and the tree trunk around which it twines. And this marriage is also very Chinese; it is designed to endure because it is bound to nature, a natural fact, a natural situation.

7 We walked up to the wall. The way in which the Chinese military engineers went about constructing the Great Wall is clear. The wall winds up and down the mountains like an amusement park roller coaster. Where the mountain forms a peak there is a guard tower, and between one peak and another, i.e., between one tower and another, the wall descends and rises again over a distance that is never too great to prevent a clear view of anything that might happen along that particular section of wall. In other words, one has a clear view of the wall from one tower to the next. Thus the barbarians were effectively held at bay. As soon as they would appear, the soldiers stationed in the towers at the ends of the threatened section of the wall would leap to the defense. And a system of signals from tower to tower could warn Peking of an imminent attack.

8 Probably the greater part of the Great Wall has been abandoned, as have so many monuments in China. Overrun with weeds, its battlements crumbling, its parapets fallen down and its towers mutilated, the Great Wall must be merely a shapeless ruin of stone and brick in many places. But in that gorge so near Peking, the Great Wall has been restored with the greatest attention. There is even a restaurant. And in the open area before the restaurant several tourist buses and many cars were parked. Dense groups of Chinese tourists were climbing up the wall, toward the towers. They climbed slowly, looking as small as ants in the distance. They carried picnic lunches and bottles of beer wrapped in handkerchiefs. The Great Wall seemed to move them and delight them more than any other monument in Peking. It is "their" monument, the only Chinese monument that has something universal to say—a myth of mankind in general.

9 We picked out what seemed the shortest and least steep section of the wall and started to climb ourselves. One can go up the wall by broad steps or by extremely steep inclines. These ramps are so steep that one must crawl up

them, and to come down again one must lean far back. It was a calm clear day, but oddly enough a wild cold wind was blowing on top of the wall—evidently the wind that whirls in the void beyond the wall. And there was the void: we looked out at it between the battlements. Beyond the gorge, past a kind of ridge of shrubs, was an immense green plain, bright, golden in the sun, mysterious and thriving. And the idea came back of the void from which the wall was intended to protect China. All it was was something different and perhaps, who knows, something better. Perhaps the Great Wall was not only intended to defend and to protect but to prevent comparisons and confrontations.

10 Moreover the revolution that has renovated China came from there, from that immense plain, mysterious, green and golden in the sun. Over there, in a straight line running thousands of miles, is Lenin's Russia and Marx's Europe. Over there is the homeland of the barbarian ideas that have rejuvenated the decrepit old lady with her tiny feet and age-old etiquette. But the danger now is that these barbarian ideas will be bound up, like ladies' feet, in orthodox dogma, that they too will become matters of etiquette, ceremony and ritual.

11 We climbed several steps and then began to clamber up a tremendously steep ramp. We climbed into the wind that struck from all sides and seemed to want to hurl us down. We finally reached a guard tower. It was three stories high, with rooms and stairs and passageways. There were crenels for shooting arrows, and projectiles and small windows for the mouths of culverins. Everything had been marvelously restored. Everything was brand-new and dead. I turned to our guide. "I suppose the Great Wall at least served some purpose."

12 "It protected the empire for centuries against barbarian invasions."

13 "But what happened in China during all those centuries?"

14 "Well, it's clear what happened. First the empire grew and prospered, and then it went into decline."

15 "So the Great Wall at some point no longer managed to protect China from its own decadence and corruption."

16 He shrugged his shoulders, and inside me I knew he was not wrong to do so. My remark was a sophism. "There is no relation between the two. On the one hand, the empire built the Great Wall for purely military reasons. And on the other, China went into decline."

17 "Let's have a closer look at this. Try to understand me. If China had not built the Great Wall and had remained open to foreign influences and ideas and innovations, perhaps it would not have gone into decline."

18 "There was no chance of beneficial ideas or influences or innovations coming from Mongolia. Just armed warriors on horseback."

19 "I haven't made myself clear. For the Great Wall is chiefly a symbol."

20 "A symbol of what?"

21 "The symbol of invincible Chinese conservatism."

22 "There's nothing invincible. China today is a revolutionary country, the most revolutionary country in the world. And the Great Wall is a great work of Chinese military engineering."

23 When our visit was ended and we returned to the car that was to take us back to Peking, I couldn't resist quoting Lao Tzu's words of the Tao. "The court is corrupt, The fields are overgrown with weeds, The granaries are empty;

Yet there are those dressed in fineries, With swords at their sides, Filled with food and drink, And possessed of too much wealth. This is known as taking the lead in robbery. Far indeed is this from the way."

24 These words were written before the Great Wall was built. What can Great Walls protect except that which should not be protected? Life, at its fullest and most mature, has no need of Great Walls.

---

1. What type of basic organization does this selection have?
2. What purpose is served by the action statements—like "We returned to the automobile and drove through the valley, or rather the gorge"?
3. How does Moravia give the reader a general impression of the shape and "movement" of the Wall?
4. Which sentence in paragraph 6 gives the Wall a personality, or rather shows Moravia's subjective impression of the Wall's character?
5. Which features of the Wall and its immediate surroundings does Moravia emphasize?

Sentence Structure in Description

MODIFIERS

The following analysis of modifiers has in it information that you will need in order to understand the lessons on sentence structure that follow in Part I and the lessons on sentence structure in Part IV.

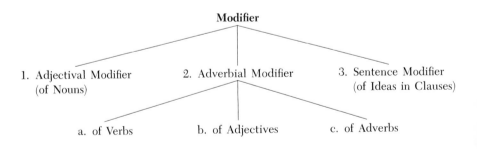

Modifier

1. Adjectival Modifier (of Nouns)   2. Adverbial Modifier   3. Sentence Modifier (of Ideas in Clauses)

a. of Verbs   b. of Adjectives   c. of Adverbs

Detail 1: Adjectival Modifier (of Nouns)

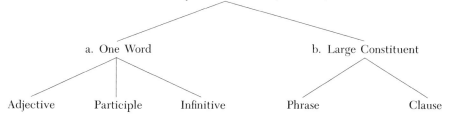

a. One Word

Adjective   Participle   Infinitive

b. Large Constituent

Phrase   Clause

Detail 1a: One-Word Adjectival Modifier

Adjective

Color: He wore a pink shirt.
Size: It was a gigantic building.
Number: He spoke four times.
Kind: She is a pretty girl.
　　　They were compulsive gamblers.

Infinitive

Which one: The road to take
is outlined in red.
The lawyer to see has an office
on the fifth floor of this
building.

Participle

Present Participle
(*ing* form of verb)

Action: The turning clock amused us.
Condition: The remaining work
　　beckoned us.

Past Participle
(*ed, en, t, n* form of verb)

Condition: A hardened criminal
　　escaped.
Object of action: The hunted
　　man appeared.
　　The shorn lamb looked miserable.

Detail lb: Large-Constituent Adjectival Modifier

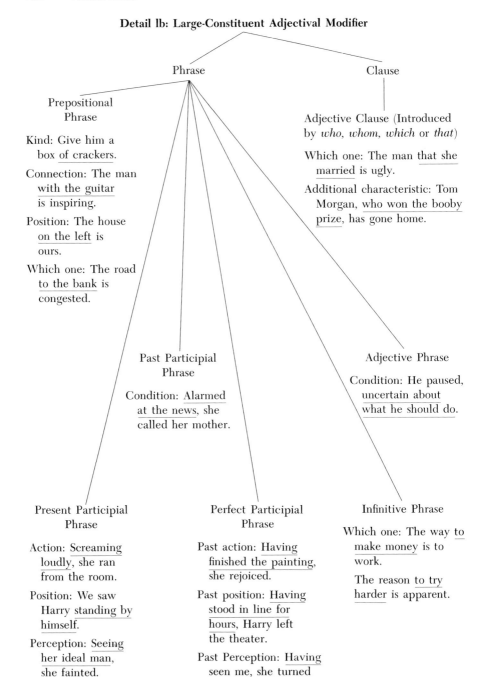

Phrase

Clause

Prepositional Phrase

Kind: Give him a box of crackers.

Connection: The man with the guitar is inspiring.

Position: The house on the left is ours.

Which one: The road to the bank is congested.

Adjective Clause (Introduced by *who, whom, which* **or** *that*)

Which one: The man that she married is ugly.

Additional characteristic: Tom Morgan, who won the booby prize, has gone home.

Past Participial Phrase

Condition: Alarmed at the news, she called her mother.

Adjective Phrase

Condition: He paused, uncertain about what he should do.

Present Participial Phrase

Action: Screaming loudly, she ran from the room.

Position: We saw Harry standing by himself.

Perception: Seeing her ideal man, she fainted.

Perfect Participial Phrase

Past action: Having finished the painting, she rejoiced.

Past position: Having stood in line for hours, Harry left the theater.

Past Perception: Having seen me, she turned around.

Infinitive Phrase

Which one: The way to make money is to work.

The reason to try harder is apparent.

Detail 2a: Adverbial Modifier of Verbs

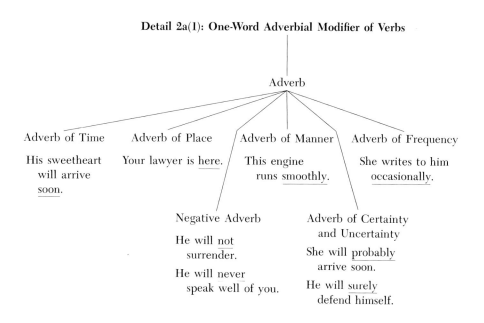

Detail 2a(1): One-Word Adverbial Modifier of Verbs

Detail 2a(2): Large-Constituent Adverbial Modifier of Verbs

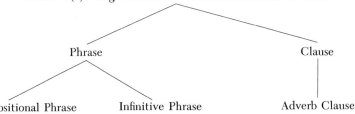

Phrase   Clause

Prepositional Phrase   Infinitive Phrase   Adverb Clause

Means: He cracked the
nuts <u>with his teeth</u>.

Connection: She walked
with <u>me</u> to the
hospital.

Direction: She walked
with me <u>to the hos-
pital</u>.

Place: We found the
stolen money <u>in his
locker</u>.

Time: The sun will rise
<u>in a few minutes</u>.

Manner: She read <u>with
speed and efficiency</u>.

Source: The report came
<u>from Mr. Henderson's
office</u>.

Comparison: She ambled
<u>like an elephant</u>.

Amount: Eggs are cheaper
<u>by the dozen</u>.

Reason: They spoke
<u>to convince
their opponents</u>.

They ran fast
<u>to prove their
speed</u>.

Time: The sun rose <u>before we
arrived home</u>.

Place: I will go <u>wherever
you go</u>.

Manner: I will do this <u>as
I please</u>.

Condition: <u>If he calls</u>,
tell him to bring the
check.

Do not pay him <u>unless
he finishes cutting the
weeds</u>.

Reason: I spoke in his defense <u>because I believed
his story</u>.

Concession: <u>Although he
was frightened</u>, he fought
bravely.

Purpose: We delayed the trip
<u>so that you could go along</u>.

Detail 2b: Adverbial Modifier of Adjectives

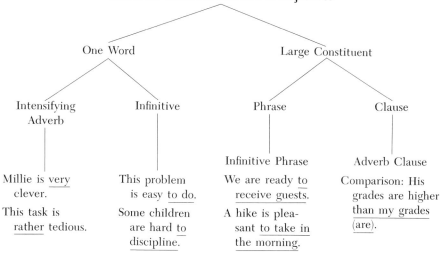

One Word

Large Constituent

Intensifying Adverb

Infinitive

Phrase

Clause

Infinitive Phrase

Adverb Clause

Millie is <u>very</u> clever.

This task is <u>rather</u> tedious.

This problem is easy <u>to do</u>.

Some children are hard <u>to discipline</u>.

We are ready <u>to receive guests</u>.

A hike is pleasant <u>to take in the morning</u>.

Comparison: His grades are higher <u>than my grades</u> (are).

Detail 2c: Adverbial Modifier of Adverbs

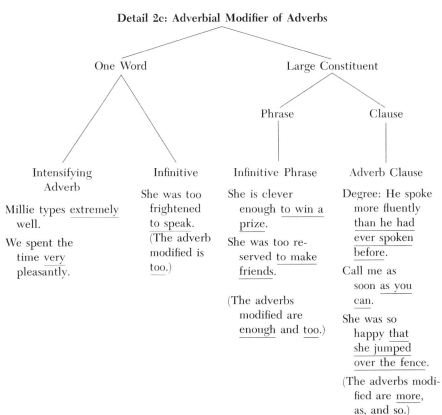

One Word

Large Constituent

Phrase

Clause

Intensifying Adverb

Infinitive

Infinitive Phrase

Adverb Clause

Millie types <u>extremely</u> well.

We spent the time <u>very</u> pleasantly.

She was too frightened <u>to speak</u>. (The adverb modified is <u>too</u>.)

She is clever <u>enough to win a prize</u>.

She was too re- served <u>to make friends</u>.

(The adverbs modified are <u>enough</u> and <u>too</u>.)

Degree: He spoke more fluently <u>than he had ever spoken before</u>.

Call me as soon <u>as you can</u>.

She was so happy <u>that she jumped over the fence</u>.

(The adverbs modi- fied are <u>more</u>, <u>as</u>, and <u>so</u>.)

Detail 3: Sentence Modifiers of Ideas in Clauses

Nominative Absolute Phrase

He took her ice skates from her closet, a mischievous
gleam in his eye.

Her eyes flashing, she pushed her way through the crowd.

(The nominative absolute phrase does not modify a word outside its own structure, but it is related by idea to an idea
in an independent clause.)

ADJECTIVAL MODIFIERS IN CONTEXT

In the excerpts below, from Alberto Moravia's "Lobster Land: A
Traveler in China," each adjectival modifier is underlined. The name of the
modifier and word modified are indicated above each modifier. Predicate adjectives are not underlined, since they are essential to sentence patterns. The following abbreviations are used in the notations:

Adj—Adjective
C Adj—Compound Adjective
Adj Ph—Adjective Phrase
Prep—Prepositional Phrase
Pres P Ph—Present Participial Phrase
Past P Ph—Past Participial Phrase
Adj Cl—Adjective Clause

                Adj:day Adj:day   Adj:wind Adj:wind
It was a calm   clear   day, but oddly enough a wild   cold   wind
                      Prep:top   Adj Cl:wind
was blowing on top of the wall—evidently the wind that whirls in the void
Prep:void
beyond the wall. And there was the void: we looked out at it between the
                                          Prep:kind Prep:ridge
battlements. Beyond the gorge, past a kind of ridge   of shrubs, was an

Adj: plain Adj: plain   Adj: plain Adj Ph: plain   C Adj: plain
immense   green   plain, bright,   golden in the sun, mysterious and
thriving.

                                          Past P Ph:one
The subject was exactly what one would have expected, given the place and
            Prep:place [and] function   Past P Ph:
function of the monument: this was civilization, /as/ represented

civilization   Pres P Ph:heroes, sages, emperors   Prep:
by heroes, sages and emperors, bending the neck   of

neck   Past P Ph:barbarism
barbarism, depicted in the form of dragons, serpents and monsters. Anyone

Pres P Ph:Anyone
entering China   would have understood at once. He was leaving the void

Prep:void   Prep:realm
of barbarism and entering the realm of civilization.

ADVERBIAL MODIFIERS IN CONTEXT

In the following excerpt, also from "Lobster Land: A Traveler in China,"
each adverbial modifier is underlined. The name of the modifier and word modified are indicated above the modifier. The following abbreviations are used in
the notations:

Adv—Adverb
Prep—Prepositional Phrase
C Prep—Compound Prepositional Phrase
Inf Ph—Infinitive Phrase
Adv Cl—Adverb Clause

<pre>
                   C Prep: winds   Prep: winds
The wall winds up and down the mountain like an amusement park roller
             Adv Cl: is
coaster. Where the mountain forms a peak there is a guard tower, and
Prep: descends [and] rises   Prep: descends [and] rises
between one peak and another, i.e., between one tower and another, the
                       Adv: descends [and] rises Prep: descends [and] rises
wall descends and rises again   over a distance
           Adv: is Adv: great   Inf Ph: too
that is never   too   great to prevent a clear view of anything that might
           Prep: might happen
happen along that particular section of wall.
</pre>

LARGE-CONSTITUENT ADJECTIVAL MODIFIERS
EMPHASIZED IN THIS COURSE

The Adjective Phrase

The adjective phrase consists of an adjective that is usually modified
by an adverb, a prepositional phrase, or an infinitive phrase, or a combination
of these.

Examples:

We waited for the last play of the game, certain of defeat. (Here the adjective certain is modified by the prepositional phrase of defeat. The adjective phrase modifies we.)

Finally awake to the truth, he told us the whole story. (Here the adjective awake is modified by the adverb finally and the prepositional phrase to the truth. The adjective phrase modifies he.)

Eager to win the game, he forgot the rules of good sportsmanship. (Here the adjective eager is modified by the infinitive phrase to win the game. The adjective phrase modifies he.)

The Past Participial Phrase

The past participle (for example, *walked, played, seen, torn*) in the past participial phrase functions in just the way an adjective does in the adjective phrase, and it also may be modified by an adverb, a prepositional phrase, or an infinitive phrase.

Examples:

These biscuits, burned on the bottom and unbaked on the top, are impossible to eat.

Wilson Baker, always haunted by fear of failure, pushed himself to success.

Determined to make the team, Brian worked out six hours a day.

The Present Participial Phrase

The present participial phrase may consist of a present participle with its modifiers; but, unlike the past participle in a phrase, it may also take an object. In other words, it has retained some of the characteristics of a verb while taking on some of the characteristics of an adjective.

Examples:

Timidly raising his hand, Ralph formed in his mind an answer to Mr. Sigler's question. (Here raising, the present participle, is modified by the adverb timidly, and it takes the object his hand. The present participial phrase modifies Ralph.)

Lillian walked casually toward home, humming contentedly, not anticipating the catastrophe that she would have to face. (Here Lillian is modified by two present participial phrases. In the first, the participle humming is modified by the adverb contentedly; in the second, the participle anticipating is modified by the adverb not, and it takes the object the catastrophe, which is modified by the adjective clause that she would have to face.)

The Adjective Clause

The adjective clause consists of a relative pronoun (*who, which, that*) used as a subject, plus a predicate verb with its possible object or complement;

or, of a relative pronoun (*whom, which,* or *that*) used as an object, plus a subject and a verb. It may have in it any kind of adjectival or adverbial modifier. A restrictive adjective clause ordinarily makes the noun it modifies less general.

Examples:

Ministers who practice what they preach are respected by their congregations. (Ministers who practice what they preach is less general than ministers.)

The students who led the riot must be questioned. (The students who led the riot is less general than the students.)

Occasionally, a restrictive clause will distinguish the referent of one noun from the referent of another without making it less general. Such a noun is almost always preceded by the.

Examples:

The five students who led the riot must be questioned. (But: These five students, who led the riot, must be questioned.)

The Bob Wilson who lives on Maple Avenue is the one I am talking about.

A nonrestrictive adjective clause gives information about the noun it modifies, but it does not make it less general or distinguish its referent from another that would be easily confused with it.

Example:

Reverend William McDowell, who practices what he preaches, is respected by his congregation. (Since Reverend William McDowell is specific, it cannot be made less general, and there is no question here of confusing this minister with another whose name is the same.)

APPOSITIVES

Though most grammarians do not classify appositives as modifiers, it is appropriate to consider them now, because like modifiers, they can be used to expand basic sentence patterns. The appositive consists of a noun, modified or not modified, that refers to the same referent as another noun in the sentence, which it normally follows. In the following excerpt from "Lobster Land: A Traveler in China," the appositives, with all of their modifiers, are underlined.

> We arrived at a small group of peasant houses, low yellow constructions with dried-mud walls and straw roofs. The car stopped and we saw a kind of arch or bridge of white marble, a massive and elaborate structure, a veritable work of art planted there in the middle of the unchanging countryside.

In the first sentence, the appositive <u>constructions</u> refers to the same referent as <u>houses</u>. In the second sentence, both of the appositives, <u>structure</u> and <u>work</u>, refer to the same referent as <u>arch or bridge</u>.

EXERCISE 6

Modifiers

1. What are three general classes of modifiers?
2. Which class of words (part of speech) is modified by adjectival modifiers?
3. Which classes of words are modified by adverbial modifiers?
4. Are there more types of phrases or clauses?
5. Which types of phrases may modify either nouns or verbs?
6. Which types of phrases may modify only nouns?
7. Why is a nominative absolute phrase called a sentence modifier?
8. Which words may introduce an adjective clause?
9. How does a restrictive adjective clause differ from a nonrestrictive adjective clause?
10. Name the modifiers numbered below and the word each modifies.
    a. But the (1) <u>little</u> square (2) <u>that surrounds it</u> is (3) <u>deplorably</u> narrow, and you flatten your back (4) <u>against the opposite houses</u> in the (5) <u>vain</u> attempt (6) <u>to stand off and survey the towers</u>.
    b. (7) <u>Above this window</u> is a circular aperture, (8) <u>of huge circumference</u>, (9) <u>with a double row</u> of (10) <u>sculptured</u> spokes (11) <u>radiating from its centre</u> and looking on its (12) <u>lofty</u> field (13) <u>of stone</u> as expansive and symbolic (14) <u>as if it were the wheel of Time itself</u>.

DIALOG 4

The Cumulative Sentence

In one of his most famous essays, "The Study of Poetry," Matthew Arnold, a Victorian poet and critic, praises the prose style of John Dryden, a seventeenth-century poet, critic, and playwright. After quoting a sentence written by Dryden, Arnold exclaims, " . . . here at last we have the true English prose, a prose such as we would all gladly use if we only knew how."[11] The sentence that excited Arnold's admiration is this: "What Virgil wrote in the vigour of his age, in plenty and at ease, I have undertaken to translate in my declining years; struggling with wants, oppressed with sickness, curbed in my genius, liable to be misconstrued in all I write."[12] Arnold's comment

[11]In *Essays in Criticism: Second Series* (New York: Macmillan, 1924), p. 88.
[12]*Ibid.*

on this sentence implies that he did not understand why it was effective or how other sentences of the same type could be written. Yet it is a sentence that a student with your grammatical knowledge can analyze, and it belongs to a type of sentence that through understanding and imitation you can learn to write. The basic pattern of Dryden's sentence is $S(N_1)$–$TrV(V)$–$DO(N_2)$, though the direct object comes before the subject and verb:

DO   S TrV
What Virgil wrote in the vigour of his age, in plenty and at ease, I have undertaken to translate in my declining years.

The reason for this inversion (placing the object before the subject) is that Dryden wanted the sentence to end with a description of his own situation and did not want the description to be very far removed from the pronoun it would modify (*I*). Since inversions are often awkward, they should not be used except for good reasons, and the inversion is not the structure in this sentence that we want to recommend here. The most effective part of the sentence is the series of modifiers after the base structure, which describes the writer's situation. The technique of stating the main idea and then adding large-constituent modifiers to give details is one which has been used since the time of Dryden but which has seldom been described by grammarians. Most readers were not aware of it as an effective type of sentence until Francis Christensen of the University of Southern California described it in an article in 1963, naming it the cumulative sentence. Christensen, in this article, calls it "the typical sentence of modern English."[13] Even if one does not agree that it is the typical sentence, one must recognize that it is common to good prose, especially to description. An example of the cumulative sentence in modern prose is this sentence from Thomas Wolfe's "A Portrait of Bascom Hawke":

Poverty, fanatical study, the sexual meagerness of his surroundings, had made of him a gaunt zealot: at thirty he was a lean fanatic, a true Yankee madman, high-boned, with gray thirsty eyes and a thick flaring sheaf of oaken hair—six feet three inches of gangling and ludicrous height, gesticulating madly and obviously before a grinning world.

This type of sentence, the cumulative sentence, states the main idea and then adds modifiers and appositives to give details, generally on a lower level of abstraction. This is an especially appropriate type of sentence for a student of descriptive writing to master, since one cannot write it without thinking of details. The structure does, as Francis Christensen has maintained, generate thought.

    This lesson is not an exhaustive treatment of the cumulative sentence. It concentrates on the sentence in which the modifiers are adjective phrases, participial phrases, and/or nominative absolute phrases, though occasionally other structures do appear.

---

[13]Francis Christensen, "A Generative Rhetoric of the Sentence," *College Composition and Communication*, Vol. XIV, No. 3 (October 1963), p. 156.

1. Read this sentence: "Before today Jody had been a boy, dressed in overalls and a blue shirt—quieter than most, even suspected of being a little cowardly." [John Steinbeck, "The Red Pony"] What is the base structure?	Jody had been a boy.
2. What is the pattern of the base structure?	S(N_1) LV(V) SC(N_1) Jody had been a boy.
3. What is before today?	Prepositional phrase.
4. Is the sentence a cumulative sentence?	Yes.
5. What reasons can you give for the preceding answer?	It has large-constituent modifiers after the base structure.

6. In the diagram below, label the modifiers after the base structure:
     ² Before today (adverbial modifier)
   ¹ Jody had been a boy (base structure)
     ² dressed in overalls and a blue shirt
     ² quieter than most
     ² even suspected of being a little cowardly
	(past participial phrase)
	 (adjective phrase)
	 (past participial phrase)

7. In a diagram of a cumulative sentence the base structure is always marked 1 (for the first layer); every modifier of a word in the base structure is marked 2 (for the second layer). Why is even suspected of being cowardly marked 2?	It modifies Jody, not one of the phrases between it and Jody.

8. How do the adjective phrase and the past participial phrases function notionally, that is, as far as meaning is concerned?	They describe Jody and suggest the impression he made on people.
9. Suppose Steinbeck had expressed his meaning this way: "Before today Jody had been a boy who had dressed in overalls and a blue shirt. He had been quieter than most, and he had been suspected of being a little cowardly." Is this better than his actual sentence?	No.
10. What reasons can you give for the preceding answer?	It contains several unnecessary words. Turning the adjective phrases into clauses and placing two of the clauses in a second sentence makes the description less concise: the reader does not get the total impression of Jody as readily as he does when reading Steinbeck's version.

11. Transform sentences b, c, d, and e below into adjectives or adjective phrases.
 	
    a. During the war Seegar had thought of him as a natural soldier.
    b. He was tireless.
    c. He was fanatic about detail.
    d. He was aggressive.
    e. He was severely anxious to kill Germans.
	b. tireless
	c. fanatic about detail
	d. aggressive
	e. severely anxious to kill Germans

12. What is the adjective in the second adjective phrase (answer 11,e)?	anxious

13. This is the way Irwin Shaw combined the five ideas in 11, in "Act of Faith": "During the war Seegar had thought of him as a natural soldier, tireless, fanatic about detail, aggressive, severely anxious to kill Germans." Diagram this sentence, marking and labeling the base structure and the layers of modification. (The base structure consists of the basic elements of the sentence pattern with, in sentences where they appear, the immediate modifiers of these elements. Immediate modifiers include adjectives, adverbs, prepositional phrases, and infinitive phrases in natural positions, as well as restrictive adjective phrases, restrictive participial phrases, and restrictive subordinate clauses. The term *base structure* is used here instead of *main clause*, Christensen's term, because in grammar *main clause* means every unsubordinated clause, even one that contains modifiers that are out of natural order and nonrestrictive phrases; it of course excludes all subordinate clauses, even restrictive ones. The sentence you are being asked to diagram is grammatically a main clause, though only part of it is a base structure. "He is the man who spoke to me," which could be a base structure in a cumulative sentence, is not grammatically a main clause, but a main clause plus a subordinate clause.)

[2] During the war (prepositional phrase)
[1] Seegar had thought of him as a natural soldier (base structure)
  [2] tireless (adjective)
  [2] fanatic about detail (adjective phrase)
  [2] aggressive (adjective)
  [2] severely anxious to kill Germans (adjective phrase)

---

14. Fill in the grammatical labels in the diagram of the following sentence: "The sun was coming over the ridge now, glaring on the whitewash of the houses and barns, making the wet grass blaze softly." [John Steinbeck, "The Red Pony"]

[1] The sun was coming over the ridge now   (base structure)
  [2] glaring on the whitewash of the houses and barns   (present participial phrase)
  [2] making the wet grass blaze softly   (present participial phrase)

15. Diagram the following sentence, noting that there are two base structures: "He would come up to meet them from some lower cellar-depth, swearing, muttering, and banging doors; and he would come toward them howling greetings, buttoned to his chin in the frayed and faded sweater, gnarled, stooped and frosty looking, clutching his great hands together at the waist." [Thomas Wolfe, "A Portrait of Bascom Hawke"]	[1]He would come up to meet them from some lower cellar-depth (base structure) 　[2]swearing (present participle) 　[2]muttering (present participle) 　[2]banging doors (present participial phrase) [1]he would come toward them (base structure) 　[2]howling greetings (present participial phrase) 　[2]buttoned to his chin in the frayed and faded sweater (past participial phrase) 　[2]gnarled (past participle) 　[2]stooped (past participle) 　[2]frosty looking (present participial phrase) 　[2]clutching his great hands together at the waist (present participial phrase)
16. How do the first three modifiers function notionally?	They show simultaneous actions of the man who is modified.
17. How many kinds of adjectival modifiers have we set off so far in this dialog?	Adjectives, adjective phrases, participles (present and past), and participial phrases (present and past).
18. Now we will add nominative absolute phrases to the types of modifiers in the lesson. Nominative absolute phrases are formed in the following ways: 　　noun + participle or participial phrase 　　noun + adjective or adjective phrase 　　noun + appositive 　　noun + prepositional phrase 　　noun + adverb The noun may have a modifier in front of it. Diagram the following sentence and label the constituents of each nominative absolute phrase: "Six boys came over the hill half an hour early that afternoon, running hard, their heads down, their forearms working, their breath whistling." [John Steinbeck, "The Red Pony"]	[1]Six boys came over the hill half an hour early that afternoon (base structure) 　[2]running hard (present participial phrase) 　　　　noun + adverb 　[2]their heads down (absolute) 　　　noun + present participle 　[2]their forearms working (absolute) 　　　noun + present participle 　[2]their breath whistling (absolute)

19. What notional function do the three nominative absolute phrases perform?	They focus attention on separate parts of the subject modified, the boys.

20. Diagram the following sentence by the same method, labeling the constituents in the nominative absolute phrase: "Once well into the country, Paul dismissed the carriage and walked, floundering along the tracks, his mind a medley of irrelevant things." [Willa Cather, "Paul's Case"]	[2] Once well into the country (elliptical adverbial clause)
	
	[1] Paul dismissed the carriage and walked (base structure)
	   [2] floundering along the tracks (present participial phrase)
	
	     noun + appositive
	   [2] his mind a medley of irrelevant things (absolute)

21. Do the same with this sentence: "William Howland sat alone on the front porch and mended traces, a glass of bourbon and water by his side." [Shirley Ann Grau, *The Keepers of the House*]	[1] William Howland sat alone and mended traces (base structure)
	
	   noun + prepositional phrase
	  [2] a glass of bourbon and water by his side (absolute)

22. And this: "He stood watching the approaching locomotive, his teeth chattering, his lips drawn away from them in a frightened smile . . . ." [Willa Cather, "Paul's Case"]	[1] He stood (base structure)
	   [2] watching the approaching locomotive (present participial phrase)
	
	   noun + present participle
	  [2] his teeth chattering (absolute)
	
	   noun + past participial phrase
	  [2] his lips drawn away from them in a frightened smile (absolute)

23. What is the notional function of the nominative absolute phrases in the preceding sentence?	They focus attention upon parts of the subject.

24. As you diagram the following sentence and label the constituents of the absolute phrases, note that these phrases perform the same notional function as those in 23: "The professor spoke for ninety minutes, his elbows resting on the lectern, his eyes glassy, his voice a monotone."

> [1] The professor spoke for ninety minutes (base structure)
>
> noun + present participial phrase
> [2] his elbows resting on the lectern (absolute)
>
> noun + adjective
> [2] his eyes glassy (absolute)
>
> noun + appositive
> [2] his voice a monotone (absolute)

25. State the simple sentence from which each of the absolute phrases in 24 was derived.

> His elbows were resting on the lectern.
> His eyes were glassy.
> His voice was a monotone.

26. What was left out of each sentence to form the nominative absolute phrase?

> A form of the verb *be*.

27. The following sentence has three nominative absolute phrases, but it is diagramed somewhat differently from any that you have done. See if you can discern the difference before you look at the diagram: "John fell through the door and into the room, his feet wildly stumbling for stability, his hands thrusting outward, each finger reaching for support."

> [1] John fell through the door and into the room (base structure)
>
> noun + present participial phrase
> [2] his feet wildly stumbling for stability (absolute)
>
> noun + present participial phrase
> [2] his hands thrusting outward (absolute)
>
> noun + present participial phrase
> [3] each finger reaching for support (absolute)

28. Why is each finger reaching for support labeled 3?

> This phrase does not refer directly to John's falling; that is, it does not refer to the base structure. It refers to the hands thrusting outward, the preceding phrase, which is labeled 2.

29. It is possible to go even beyond the third layer of modification. Try to diagram the following sentence from John Ruskin's description of J. M. W. Turner's painting *The Slave Ship:* "Purple and blue, the lurid shadows of the hollow breakers are cast upon the mist of night, which gathers cold and low, advancing like the shadow of death upon the guilty ship as it labors amidst the lightning of the sea, its thin masts written upon the sky in lines of blood, girded with condemnation in that fearful hue which signs the sky with horror, and mixes its flaming flood with the sunlight, and, cast far along the desolate heave of the sepulchral waves, incarnadines the multitudinous sea."

> [2] purple and blue (compound adjective)
> [1] the lurid shadows of the hollow breakers are cast upon the mist of the night (base structure)
>> [2] which gathers cold and low (adjective clause)
>> [2] advancing like the shadow of death upon the guilty ship (present participial phrase)
>>> [3] as it [the ship] labors amidst the lightning of the sea (adverbial clause)
>>> [3] its [the ship's] thin masts written upon the sky in lines of blood (absolute)
>>>> [4] girded [the masts girded] with condemnation in that fearful hue (past participial phrase)
>>>>> [5] which signs the night with horror (adjective clause)
>>>>> [5] [which] mixes its flaming flood with sunlight (elliptical adjective clause)
>>>>> [5] [which] // incarnadines the multitudinous sea (elliptical adjective clause)
>>>>>> [6] cast far along the desolate heave of the sepulchral waves (past participial phrase)

30. Most modification in cumulative sentences, however, does not go beyond the third layer. You should have no difficulty diagraming the following sentence: "María Rosa ran, dodging between beehives, parting two stunted bushes as she came, lifting her knees in swift leaps, looking over her shoulder and laughing in a quivering, excited way." [Katherine Anne Porter, "María Conception"]

> [1] María Rosa ran (base structure)
>> [2] dodging between beehives (present participial phrase)
>> [2] parting two stunted bushes (present participial phrase)
>>> [3] as she came (adverbial clause)
>> [2] lifting her knees in swift leaps (present participial phrase)
>> [2] looking over her shoulder (present participial phrase)
>> [2] laughing in a quivering, excited way (present participial phrase)

31. Why do you think Katherine Anne Porter used a series of present participial phrases instead of a series of short sentences to describe María Rosa's running?	If each action were put into a separate sentence, each action would seem separate from the others. Using the series of phrases creates the impression that the actions occur in quick succession or simultaneously.
32. So that you will not think that large-constituent modifiers belong to cumulative sentences only, consider the following sentence: "And then, gripping their greasy little wads of money, as if the knowledge that all rewards below these fierce and cruel skies must be wrenched painfully and minutely from a stony earth, they went in to pay my uncle." [Thomas Wolfe, "A Portrait of Bascom Hawke"] Why is this *not* a cumulative sentence?	The base structure (they went in to pay my uncle) comes at the end of the sentence. It is preceded by modifiers. In the cumulative sentence the base structure comes first, and it is followed by modifiers.

33. The sentence in 32 is called *periodic* instead of *cumulative.* Try to diagram this periodic sentence: "And as he stands, tall, misshapen, lonely in his lonely and illkept kitchen, holding in his hand an iron skillet in which yesterday's old grease is bleakly caked, there goes through him a glow, a surge of something almost hot, almost triumphant." [William Faulkner, *Light in August*]	2 as he stands (adverbial clause)
	    3 tall (adjective)
	    3 misshapen (adjective)
	    3 lonely (adjective)
	    3 in his lonely and illkept kitchen (prepositional phrase)
	    3 holding in his hand an iron skillet (present participial phrase)
	        4 in which yesterday's old grease is bleakly caked (adjective clause)
	1 there goes through him a glow (base structure)
	    2 a surge of something almost hot, almost triumphant (appositive)

34. Periodic sentences are of course acceptable in your descriptions, though you will be trying consciously to learn to use cumulative sentences. What is the cumulative sentence?	The type of sentence in which the base structure, which comes first, is followed by large-constituent modifiers, usually on a lower level of abstraction than that of the base structure.
35. What types of modifiers have we emphasized in this dialog?	Adjective phrases, participial phrases (present and past), and nominative absolute phrases.

36. What is a nominative absolute phrase?	A phrase composed of a noun followed by a modifier. It is absolute grammatically (does not modify a word in another structure), but it functions as a notional modifier (refers to a preceding idea).
37. If you want to give the reader the impression that actions are happening in quick succession or simultaneously, what type of modifier will you probably use?	The present participial phrase.
38. If you want to focus attention on parts of a subject you have already introduced, what type of modifier will you use?	The nominative absolute phrase.

EXERCISE 7

Composing Cumulative Sentences to Describe Position, Action, and Appearance

Throughout this exercise *diagram* means *write the base structure and arrange large constituent modifiers below it as in Dialog 4, numbering the modifiers according to the layer of modification and writing their grammatical names in parentheses after them.* If you are not sure how to punctuate the sentences you compose, observe the punctuation of the sentences given in the exercise, and study the punctuation patterns that follow the exercise.

1. Diagram this sentence describing a golfer's position: **The golfer was at the top of the backswing, his weight entirely on the right side, his left shoulder under his chin, his club horizontal to the ground, his hands under the shaft.**
2. Please look at the photograph on page 127, concentrating on the position of the boy, who is playing marbles. Observe the position of each hand and arm, the position of each foot and leg, the position of the head, and the set of the gaze. Write one cumulative sentence about the boy: state in general terms in the base structure what the boy is doing, and then in a series of nominative absolute phrases, describe the details of his position, beginning with the position of his right leg. Do not describe the clothes,

the hair, or other details of appearance that would take the reader's attention off the position. After you have written the sentence, diagram it.

3. Diagram the following sentence describing action: **The drum major, marking time while facing the front rank of the band, signaled *Halt*, raising his baton horizontally with both hands to arm's length over his head while blowing a long shrill blast on his whistle, then quickly lowering the baton to the waist, raising it over the head, and lowering it again with finality, punctuating each swift movement with a short blast of the whistle.** (The first present participial phrase interrupts the base structure. At the point where the interruption occurs, place two slanted parallel lines (//); write the phrase under the base structure.)

4. Using mainly present participial phrases as large-constituent modifiers, construct a cumulative sentence to describe the action implied in the photograph on page 128. Diagram your sentence.

5. Diagram the following sentence describing, primarily, appearance: **The professor, a graying, hawk-nosed little man in a blue business suit, stood behind the lectern, almost hidden, gathering his thoughts to answer a question just asked him, his head tipped to the right, vertical lines cut deeply between his squinting eyes, his lips parted and pursed slightly as if he would begin by saying *whew*, softly.**

6. Select either the photograph on page 129 or that on page 130, and look closely at the details of appearance. In a cumulative sentence, use various kinds of large-constituent modifiers, and possibly an appositive, to describe either the seated woman or one of the women on the beach. Diagram your sentence.

7. a. What kind of meaning does one generally convey with an adjective phrase or a past participial phrase? Illustrate.

   b. What kind of meaning does one generally convey with a present participial phrase? Illustrate.

   c. What kind of meaning does one generally convey with a nominative absolute phrase? Illustrate.

8. Observe details in the photograph of the coal miner above. Write, in two or three sentences, a description of the miner's position and appearance. Use one cumulative sentence in the description.

PUNCTUATION PATTERNS RELATING
TO LARGE-CONSTITUENT ADJECTIVAL MODIFIERS
AND TO APPOSITIVES

Adjective Phrase

1. Sentence pattern, adjective phrase.
   Example:
   He remained in the bombed city, certain that he would be rescued.
2. Adjective phrase, sentence pattern.
   Example:
   Happy to be home, the Merediths began to unpack.
3. Subject, adjective phrase, complete predicate.
   Example:
   This story, remarkably superior to your others, is sure to be published.

Past Participial Phrase

1. Sentence pattern, past participial phrase.
   Example:
   He left his office late that evening, demoralized by the reports he had
   received during the day.
2. Past participial phrase, sentence pattern.
   Example:
   Weakly supported and badly administered, the project was sure to fail.
3. Subject, past participial phrase, complete predicate.
   Example:
   The project, weakly supported and badly administered, was sure to fail.

Present Participial Phrase

1. Sentence pattern, present participial phrase (not modifying the noun that
   immediately precedes it).
   Example:
   He faltered suddenly in his stride, remembering another task to be done.
2. Sentence pattern   present participial phrase (restrictive modifier of the
   noun immediately preceding).
   Example:
   We saw the water standing by the road. (Note how the meaning would
   change if a comma were placed after <u>water</u>.)
3. Present participial phrase, sentence pattern.
   Example:
   Remembering another task to be done, he faltered suddenly in his stride.
4. Subject, nonrestrictive present participial phrase, complete predicate.
   Example:
   My mother, waiting at the airport, became impatient.
5. Subject   restrictive participial phrase   complete predicate.
   Example:
   The passengers waiting at the station became impatient. (This implies
   that there were other passengers who were not waiting at the station.)

Prepositional Phrase

Long prepositional phrase, sentence pattern.
Example:
> In the interest of those who could not attend, we postponed the voting.

Infinitive Phrase

Infinitive phrase, sentence pattern.
Example:
> To prevent further pollution of the air, all carbon black plants in this area are converting to smokeless systems.

Absolute Phrase

1. Sentence pattern, absolute phrase.
   Examples:
   > He returned home, his spirits high.
   > The child turned around and around, his hands clasped together on top of his head.
   > The motorist stood by his stalled car, his eyes searching the long prairie road for an approaching vehicle.
2. Absolute phrase, sentence pattern.
   Example:
   > The war having ended, the men returned home.

Adjective Clause

1. Sentence pattern restrictive adjective clause.
   Example:
   > We missed the boy who had been our guide on the last hike.
2. Sentence pattern, nonrestrictive adjective clause.
   Example:
   > We missed Quentin, who had been our guide on the last hike.
3. Subject   restrictive adjective clause   complete predicate.
   Example:
   > The boy who had been our guide on the last hike never wanted to see us again.
4. Subject, nonrestrictive adjective clause, complete predicate.
   Example:
   > Quentin, who had been our guide on the last hike, never wanted to see us again.

Appositive

1. Sentence pattern, nonrestrictive appositive.
   Example:
   > I left the key with Mrs. Grantly, a thoroughly dependable neighbor.
2. Subject, nonrestrictive appositive, complete predicate.
   Examples:
   > Mrs. Grantly, a thoroughly dependable neighbor, has offered to take care of our pets while we are away.

His latest dream, to have a yacht like President Nixon's *Julie*, probably will not be realized.

(Restrictive appositives, like the following, are not set off by commas. Notice that the noun preceding the appositive is an introduction to it.

The word "<u>therefore</u>" should not be used in this text.
The geologist <u>Harold Williams</u> will speak at the Liberal Arts Auditorium tonight.
The proposal <u>that we admit twelve new members to our club</u> passed without opposition.)

PUNCTUATION IN CUMULATIVE SENTENCES

As a general rule, the first large-constituent modifier following the base structure in a cumulative sentence is set off by a comma from the base structure, and every adjective phrase, participial phrase, nominative absolute phrase, appositive, or nonrestrictive adjective clause following the first modifier is set off by a comma.

A prepositional phrase or an infinitive phrase is generally not set off if it modifies the word immediately preceding it.

The restrictive adjective clause is not set off.

The adverbial clause is usually not set off unless it indicates reason, concession, or purpose.

The punctuation in the following sentence from Robbe-Grillet's *In the Labyrinth* is typical.

In the window recesses the snow has formed an uneven layer, very shallow on the sill but deeper toward the back, making an already considerable drift that fills the right corner and reaches as high as the pane.

In this sentence a comma sets off the adjective phrase <u>very shallow on the sill but deeper toward the back</u> from the base structure; a comma sets off the present participial phrase <u>making an already considerable drift that fills the right corner and reaches as high as the pane</u>; a comma is not used to set off the restrictive adjective clause <u>that fills the right corner and reaches as high as the pane</u> within the present participial phrase.

Robbe-Grillet sometimes uses a colon between the base structure and the first modifier, as in this description of the man on the log bridge, from *Jealousy:* "He has not moved an inch: crouching, head lowered, forearms on his thighs, hands hanging between his knees." A colon used in this way is effective, but unusual. The commas used to set off the three nominative absolute phrases are typical.

EXERCISE 8

Appreciating Cumulative Sentences in Context

A. Read the following excerpt from "A Sound of Thunder," by Ray Bradbury.[14]

1 Out of the mist, one hundred yards away, came *Tyrannosaurus rex.*

.   .   .

2 It came on great oiled, resilient, striding legs. 3 It towered thirty feet above half of the trees, a great evil god, folding its delicate watch-maker's claws close to its oily reptilian chest. 4 Each lower leg was a piston, a thousand pounds of white bone, sunk in thick ropes of muscle, sheathed over in a gleam of pebbled skin like the mail of a terrible warrior. 5 Each thigh was a ton of meat, ivory, and steel mesh. 6 And from the great breathing cage of the upper body those two delicate arms dangled out front, arms with hands which might pick up and examine men like toys, while the snake neck coiled. 7 And the head itself, a ton of sculptured stone, lifted easily upon the sky. 8 Its mouth gaped, exposing a fence of teeth like daggers. 9 Its eyes rolled, ostrich eggs, empty of all expression save hunger. 10 It closed its mouth in a death grin. 11 It ran, its pelvic bones crushing aside trees and bushes, its taloned feet clawing damp earth, leaving prints six inches deep wherever it settled its weight. 12 It ran with a gliding ballet step, far too poised and balanced for its ten tons. 13 It moved into a sunlit arena warily, its beautifully reptile [sic] hands feeling the air.

1. Which sentences in this passage are cumulative?
2. Diagram sentence 3.
3. Diagram sentence 4.
4. Name the large-constituent modifier in sentence 12 (far too poised and balanced for its ten tons).
5. Name the large-constituent modifier in sentence 13.
6. List the present participles in the passage. What is the effect of so many present participles?
7. Rewrite sentence 11 as four sentences, converting each large-constituent modifier into a sentence. What happens to the effect when the sentence is broken into four sentences?

B. Read the following excerpt from *The Keepers of the House*, Shirley Ann Grau's Pulitzer-prize-winning novel.[15]

---

[14]From "A Sound of Thunder," copyright 1952 by The Crowell-Collier Publishing Company, from *The Golden Apples of the Sun* by Ray Bradbury. Reprinted by permission of Doubleday & Company, Inc.

[15]From *The Keepers of the House*, by Shirley Ann Grau. © Copyright 1964 by Shirley Ann Grau. Reprinted by permission of Alfred A. Knopf, Inc.

1 It was jabbering like that when we finished and went to the upper side of the field to spread the last gas there. 2 I took off my splashed and splattered coat. 3 We both rubbed our hands with mud to clean them. 4 Then we set the fire. 5 Oliver's match lit at once. 6 My first two went out in the wind. 7 I knelt and sheltered the third match with my body the way I might do an infant, and burned my hand with the cupping protection I gave it—but I got my grass alight. 8 We stood a moment or two and watched the flame grow. 9 A patch, a blob of light, pushed forward like spume by the wind. 10 Then the two blobs, Oliver's and mine, joined and spread into a line, and the line grew from a flat thing on the ground like a child's mark, to a thing with height and width, and a crackling voice.

11 Hastily, Oliver drove the tractor back the way he had come. 12 I followed, stopping only once to light the grass by the roadside cars. 13 I scrambled up the Indian mound, panting, with the singing of gasoline-fed flames in my ears. 14 I stumbled and fell full length, the breath jarred out of me, my tired body aching and resisting and wanting to stay huddled against an earth that seemed so warm on the chill windy night. 15 But I got up—just a moment to rest—and ran through the sheltering woods, circling back to the house. 16 And all the way, the pistons of my legs pushing me up and down, the pressure of my lungs bursting my ribs, I kept worrying: Will it be there? 17 Will they have gotten to it in the little while it was left alone?

18 When, through the last fringe of trees, I could see that the house stood white and untouched, I stopped and felt sick with relief. 19 I leaned against a thin pine and rested my head on its bark. 20 Oliver popped out of the dark, on foot this time; he had left the tractor hidden in the trees. 21 I asked: "How long before they can't put out the fire back there? 22 How long will that take?"

23 "I never done nothing like that before."

1. In which paragraph do you find several cumulative sentences? List the numbers of the sentences.
2. How does the incident in the paragraph just named differ from the incidents in the other two paragraphs?
3. Do you see any relationship between the incident described in this paragraph and the use of the cumulative sentence?

C. Read the following excerpt from "Young Man Axelbrod," by Sinclair Lewis.[16]

1 In Joralemon we call Knute Axelbrod "Old Cottonwood." 2 As a matter of fact, the name was derived not so much from the quality of the man

---

[16] From *Selected Short Stories of Sinclair Lewis* (New York: The Literary Guild, 1935), 281–82, excerpt from "Young Man Axelbrod." Copyright 1917 Century Company; Copyright renewed 1945 Sinclair Lewis. Reprinted by permission.

as from the wide grove about his gaunt white house and red barn. 3 He made a comely row of trees on each side of the country road, so that a humble, daily sort of a man, driving beneath them in his lumber wagon, might fancy himself lord of a private avenue.

4 And at sixty-five Knute was like one of his own cottonwoods, his roots deep in the soil, his trunk weathered by rain and blizzard and baking August noons, his crown spread to the wide horizon of day and the enormous sky of a prairie night.

5 This immigrant was an American even in speech. 6 Save for a weakness about his j's and w's, he spoke the twangy Yankee English of the land. 7 He was the more American because in his native Scandinavia he had dreamed of America as a land of light. 8 Always through disillusion and weariness he beheld America as the world's nursery for justice, for broad, fair towns, and eager talk; and always he kept a young soul that dared to desire beauty.

1. What is the one striking cumulative sentence in this passage? Diagram it.
2. What is the purpose of this cumulative sentence? Is it descriptive?
3. Why is the cumulative form appropriate to the idea expressed in the sentence?

PROBLEMS IN THE CONSTRUCTION AND THE USE OF CUMULATIVE SENTENCES

Used correctly, cumulative sentences add precision and depth to one's style. But misused, they only confuse or amuse the reader. Some problems that students have had in constructing and using cumulative sentences are discussed below. In every instance, a sentence labeled *original* is the composition of a student, and every revision is his instructor's. The conclusions reached after considering these students' problems can be guidelines for you as you try to improve your style through an effective use of the cumulative sentence.

I. Problems relating to the placement of modifying phrases

A. Writers are sometimes uncertain where to place participial phrases and nominative absolute phrases in a sentence when these phrases refer to the same subject. Consider this sentence:

Original
The old car chugged slowly along, its wheels wobbling, its doors rattling, its exhaust pipe spewing out clouds of black smoke, fogging up the countryside, leaving the crowded city behind.

Revision

The old car chugged slowly along, leaving the crowded city behind, its wheels wobbling, its doors rattling, its exhaust pipe spewing out clouds of black smoke, fogging up the countryside.

The fault in the original sentence is that the participial phrase <u>leaving the crowded city behind</u> is placed too far from the word it modifies, <u>car</u>. Vagueness in the modification has been removed in revision by placing the participial phrase closer to <u>car</u>. The subjects in the nominative absolute phrases, <u>wheels</u>, <u>doors</u>, and <u>exhaust pipe</u>, clearly show in their meaning that they refer to <u>car</u>; they do not depend upon close placement for clarity.

> Conclusion: To insure clarity in a sentence that ends with a combination of nominative absolute phrases and participial phrases, place the participial phrases as close as possible to the words they modify. An absolute phrase will refer clearly to the subject of the base structure even when a participial phrase intervenes.

B. The principle of the conclusion above applies to the placing of adjective phrases and prepositional phrases as well as to the placing of participial phrases. Note how moving the adjective phrases (underlined) improves the first sentence below and how moving the prepositional phrase (also underlined) improves the second. Note also that the nominative absolute phrases are quite clear in the revisions, even though other phrases separate them from the subject of the sentence, to which they refer in meaning.

1. Original

Jim stretched out to rest, his head aching from the ear-splitting sound of the machinery, his eyes smarting from the blowing dust, <u>thirsty for a cool drink</u>, <u>tired from the day's work.</u>

Revision

Jim stretched out to rest, <u>thirsty for a cool drink</u>, <u>tired from the day's work</u>, his eyes smarting from the blowing dust, his head aching from the ear-splitting sound of the machinery.

2. Original

Richard quietly watched the pigeon, its feathers ruffled for warmth, its body squatting down over its feet, its head tucked under one wing, <u>on the park bench.</u>

Revision

Richard quietly watched the pigeon <u>on the park bench,</u> its feathers ruffled for warmth, its body squatting down over its feet, its head tucked under one wing.

II. Problems relating to tense

A. Writers who have learned that they should not shift tenses unnecessarily are sometimes afraid to use both present participles and past participles in a series of nominative absolute phrases. But so using them does not necessarily constitute an error. In the following correct sentence the main verb is in the past tense, and the modifiers include one past participle and two present participles: <u>John looked up,</u> <u>his fists clenched,</u> <u>his lips quivering,</u> <u>his tear-filled eyes staring off into the distance.</u> The time of action in this sentence is controlled by the main verb, not by the participles.

> Conclusion: Nominative absolute phrases using past participles and nominative absolute phrases using present participles may be combined in a series in the same sentence. The form of the participle is determined by the meaning the writer wishes to express. The present participle expresses action happening at the same time as the time of the verb in the base structure and also describes a noun or a pronoun. The past participle describes without expressing action. The only participle that expresses action prior to that of the verb in the base structure is the perfect participle. In the following sentence closing the door occurs before walking into the room: <u>John walked softly into the room,</u> <u>having closed the door gently.</u> <u>Having closed</u> is a perfect participle.

B. Writers are sometimes reluctant to use a series of present participles to express actions that are not simultaneous, but the English language sometimes permits such usage. Consider this sentence: <u>When the bottom of the bag ripped open, the walnuts spilled on the table, exciting the cat as they clattered loudly, rolling in all directions and tumbling off the edges of the table to the floor.</u> One can assume that the actions suggested in this sentence occurred in sequence: some of the walnuts hit the table, the cat jumped, the walnuts spread toward the edges, some of the walnuts fell off. But the actions occurred so quickly as to be almost simultaneous.

> Conclusion: If an emphasis on progressive movement is desired, the chronology of action can be shown by placement of various

present participial phrases, as in the preceding sentence. Participial phrases representing actions that occur before the action of the other participial phrases are placed before those phrases. This arrangement is effective only when the actions represented happen very close together in time.

III. Problems relating to the appropriateness of using cumulative sentences
   A. Writers sometimes use the cumulative sentence when it is inappropriate to the meaning being stated. Consider the following sentence:

> Original
> He calculated the momentum, force, and strength that he would need, his mind cooperating easily.

> Revision
> He calculated the momentum, force, and strength that he would need.

In the original sentence <u>his mind cooperating easily</u> adds nothing to the sense.

> Conclusion: One should not form a cumulative sentence just for the sake of varying the sentence structure; one should be sure that the modification after the base structure strengthens the meaning of the sentence.

   B. Sometimes writers use cumulative sentences when other forms would express the intended meaning more effectively.

> Original
> The couple on the roller-coaster were sick at their stomachs, jerking around with the quick descents and the sharp curves.

> Revision
> Jerking around with the quick descents and the sharp curves, the couple on the roller-coaster were sick at their stomachs.

Because <u>jerking</u> might be associated with <u>stomachs</u> instead of <u>couple</u>, to ludicrous effect, it is much better to use the periodic sentence of the revision than the original cumulative sentence.

> Original
> John moved toward Bob, clenching his fists, biting his lip, squinting his eyes.

Revision

Clenching his fists, biting his lip, and squinting his eyes, John moved toward Bob.

Here, placing the modification before the base structure clarifies the ambiguity of the first sentence by making it completely clear to whom the modification refers.

Original

Mr. Jones handed his wife the wallet, emptied of its contents.

Revision

Mr. Jones handed his wife the empty wallet.

If the context called for a humorous emphasis on a recent emptying of the contents, the original sentence would be effective. But in a context where the meaning centers in the action of the verb, the revision is much more effective.

Conclusion: Cumulative sentences should not be used when other structures will express the intended meaning more effectively.

SUGGESTED WRITING ASSIGNMENT

A Full Description from a Photograph

Select a photograph from the three following pages to describe from the photographer's point of vision. Before beginning to write, decide what your purpose is. Do you wish to describe the whole scene without giving any feature central importance? (The time limit or word limit set by your instructor, as well as the complexity of the photograph you have chosen, will influence your decision.) Do you wish to be entirely objective, or do you wish to express a value judgment while describing enough details objectively to allow the reader to form a different value judgment if his values differ from yours? After you have set your purpose, decide how you will begin (with a general description or with a detail), how you will explain your point of vision, and what your pattern of spatial organization will be.

As you write, try to apply all that you know about sentence structure, punctuation, and diction, including transitional words that make your pattern of organization clear.

When you have finished, write a note to the reader, explaining your purpose, the extent to which you have been objective, and your plan of organization.

SUGGESTED WRITING ASSIGNMENT

Expansion of Journal Entries

Select two of your journal entries for additional development. Evaluate each of these entries in the light of your knowledge of purpose, point of vision, spatial patterns of organization, sentence structure, and diction in descriptive writing. Then expand and revise each entry to make it as effective as you can.

The Report on a Composite Subject

The subjects of your descriptions have been specific objects, persons, or scenes that you have been able to perceive in one place at one time. The subject of your next composition will be a specific composite entity that can be observed only in part in one place at one time. Reporting on such a subject consists mainly of describing parts, listing statistics and other statements of fact, narrating events in chronological order, explaining operations step by step, and quoting informed persons. The only one of these processes that is not easy to execute is description. You will not be asked, therefore, to practice the other processes individually. It will be sufficient, before you write your report, to observe the interplay of these processes in a professional report of this type and to consider the sources of information pertinent to the various processes.

The selection that follows has been extracted from "Taiwan: the Watchful Dragon," a report by Helen and Frank Schreider on Taiwan today. It is only about three-fifths the length of the original report, but it illustrates all of the processes of reporting mentioned above except a detailed explanation of an operation.

The subjects that comprise the full report, interesting aspects of life in Taiwan today, are numerous: land reform, eating habits, religious festivals, the ship-building industry, damage caused by Typhoon Gilda, highways, exports, lures to investors, the ancient customs of aborigines and the encroachment of new ideas into even the most primitive sections of the island, rice harvesting, tourist attractions, military defense, and Premier and Madame Chiang Kai-shek. The authors arrange these subjects in a loose geographical and chronological pattern based on the itinerary of a tour they have made of Taiwan and the smaller islands under its control.

The first city they visit is Taipei, the busy capital of Taiwan. Taipei is a good opening subject, because by describing the material contrasts they observe there, the authors can evoke contrasting tendencies in what they feel to be the spirit of Taiwan as a whole. On the one hand, they see fast-moving motor traffic and lively trade in luxuries and modern appliances manufactured on the island. On the other hand, they see a huge papier-mâché dragon, ancient symbol "of power and good," as it is being carried down a street in the traditional celebration of the birthday of Dr. Sun Yat-sen. Frank Schreider generalizes upon the strangely incongruous but harmonious strains of old and new in the culture: "Helen and I found Taiwan, like so many developing nations, torn between the two worlds of transition and tradition. But unlike those that abandon the old to embrace the new, Taiwan embraces both."

Following the order of the itinerary, the authors describe first their visit to the Northern port of Chilung, where they admire a shipbuilding industry, and then their encounter with Typhoon Gilda at Yehliu, a coastal town northeast of Taipei. They next describe a trip by automobile from the northern end of the island down the East Coast Highway to the southern tip and then back north about fifty miles to Daladalai, a village in the interior, and then to Sun Moon Lake, a resort center in the middle of the island. They then abandon the automobile tour as an organizational device, reporting how they flew to Quemoy to observe the military defenses there. They violate their geographical and chronological order at the end of the report to present last what they know will be to many readers the most interesting aspect of the report—an account of their visit with President and Madame Chiang Kai-shek in Tapei.

The structure of this report—a loose chronological structure that allows discrete development of various topics—is a practical and popular type of structure for a report on a composite subject. In fact, if the report is long, any other type of structure tends to become too restrictive.

Like all other reporters, the Schreiders are dependent for their information upon only a few types of sources—their own observations, oral statements of informants, and written reports. When they are working from their own observations, as when recounting their experiences in the aboriginal village of Daladalai, they are the most descriptive. Their primary method of presenting material from informants, a typical method, is the direct quotation. The list of informants for their report is long: James Wei, Director of Information Services; Dr. T. H. Shen, Chairman of the Chinese American Commission on Rural Reconstruction; Chen-fu Koo, president of a cement corporation; Y. T. Pan, a new landowner; Thomas Hsueh, a Chinese American engineer; Christopher H. P. Yen, a shipbuilder; Chang, a cab driver; James Yu, manager of a marble works; Thomas

T. C. Kuan, an executive in the Koahsiung Export Processing Zone; Lorain Tinnes, an executive in the General Micro-Electronics Company; an aboriginal woman; Lieutenant Commander Lollington Cheng, chief officer in Quemoy; Major General Richard G. Cirrolella, Chief of the United States Military Assistance and Advisory Group; and Lieutenant Colonel James Chen, a fighter pilot. Each of these experts on an aspect of Taiwanese life is identified when introduced, but they all remain unobtrusive, the emphasis throughout being on the information itself.

The Schreiders are not precise in crediting their written sources, perhaps because their reputations as reporters are established and because the facts they use from written sources are common knowledge among educated Taiwanese. If they should be questioned on a statement of fact, however, they would be expected to give its source. Students learning to report should name all sources of statistics and other facts that they have not observed, and this is not a bad practice for experienced reporters like the Schreiders, who could have named their written sources as unobtrusively as they named their informants. One can assume that their sources were newspapers, recently written history books, government surveys and reports of various kinds, and reports by American agencies. A passage composed from such sources is the following:

> But I doubt that even an exhausted dragon could sleep through the frenzy of Taiwan's economic boom, maintained, says the Bank of America in a special report, at one of the highest rates in the world.
>
> With six years of compulsory education, Taiwan's literacy rate exceeds 90 percent. With more than 40 percent of the people under 15, one out of four persons is in school. The young population has helped create what the Bank of America calls "Taiwan's most important and least expensive resource . . . its supply of diligent and intelligent working people."

The reference above to the Bank of America's "special report" is the Schreiders' most precise acknowledgment of a written source.

As you read the selection from "Taiwan: the Watchful Dragon," stop occasionally to ask how the Schreiders got the particular bit of information being reported—whether from direct observation, observation enlightened by comments of informants, statements of informants altogether, or a written source. Observe how the informants are introduced and identified, how quotations are punctuated, and how statistics are listed. Examine the diction and sentence structure in the descriptive passages.

FROM **Taiwan: the Watchful Dragon**

Helen and Frank Schreider

The incredible thing is that it exists. It lies in the Pacific, a brave speck in the shadow of a colossus, only 100 miles from its implacable enemy—the world's most populous country, 700 million strong. For nearly 20 years the Communists on mainland China and the Nationalists on Taiwan have waged their quiet war.

Taiwan must be as tightly run as a battleship, I thought as we flew into Taipei. In a continual state of war, the island must be an austere place to live.

Austere? Hardly, though to judge by the machine-gun-like explosions reverberating through Taipei's streets, the quiet war had erupted into a shooting one.

"Firecrackers," laughed Chang, our driver. "Big holiday. Birthday of Dr. Sun Yat-sen, father of China. Big dragon dance at City Hall."

Chang raced the hired car away from the palatial Grand Hotel and penetrated the bedlam of traffic along Chungshan North Road. Exhaust fumes clouded the air. Cars, buses, and taxis clogged the four-lane boulevard. Taipei was suffering the pangs of progress.

"Few years ago only rice fields here," Chang said, waving toward the new high-rise hotels and office buildings. "Now too much cars. Too much motorcycles. Terrible, sir."

A taxi tried a left turn from the right lane. Chang cut him off with a glare. A motorcycle, all but hidden under its passengers, darted from a cross street, father, mother, two babies, dog in box on fender, all blissfully oblivious to the outraged horns.

A broom vendor halted his bristling pushcart and haggled in the middle of the street with a customer. Chang swerved and sped across the new overpass into the old Japanese-built section of town.

Pedicabs scurried like spiders through shop-lined alleys (they have been banned since last June as traffic hazards). Wares overflowed onto the sidewalks —refrigerators, rice cookers, television sets, textiles, a bewildering array of plastic toys and utensils, all Taiwan-made. Restaurants advertised the typical food of every province of mainland China. Medicine shops prescribed dried sea horses for virility and snake glands for the eyes.

We arrived in City Hall square with the dragon. Drums, cymbals, and a shattering blast of firecrackers announced him, a 100-foot-long, 30-manpower dragon of red-and-gold silk and papier-mâché. He postured coyly and slyly, fearsomely playful, turning his awesome head, prancing toward each new flash of firecrackers, and frequently breathing fire. There were tributes to Dr. Sun, and flowers for his statue in the square. At last the gala day ended, the crowds scattered, and the magnificent dragon went into storage until the next celebration.

Symbol of power and good, old as China, the dragon is as much a part of Taiwan life as firecrackers, food, and frivolity; as much a part of the Taiwan scene as buffalo-drawn plows and the skeletons of hastily rising apartments. He roosts on temples and adorns jetliners. And in folklore the dragon is credited with the creation of Taiwan.

Long ago, says the legend, when mists still wreathed the earth and serpents swam the seas, dragons played off the coast of China. They played hard, as dragons do, so hard that their tails stirred the ocean bottom and an island rose. Here the dragons rested and slept, and here they reside still.

Old natives of Taiwan tell this tale and are convinced that it is true, for, in the northernmost part of the island, dragons' breath still colors the air with sulphur fumes, and from fissures and caves comes the rumble of their snores.

But I doubt that even an exhausted dragon could sleep through the frenzy of Taiwan's economic boom, maintained, says the Bank of America in a special report, at one of the highest rates in the world.

With six years of compulsory education, Taiwan's literacy rate exceeds 90 percent. With more than 40 percent of the people under 15, one out of four persons is in school. The young population has helped create what the Bank of America calls "Taiwan's most important and least expensive resource . . . its supply of diligent and intelligent working people."

Japanese, American, Overseas Chinese, and European firms are investing in Taiwan at a record rate. The value of industrial exports now exceeds that of agricultural exports. The increased production of electronics components, plastics, paper, cement, handicrafts, textiles, and canned goods spurred a 13 percent rise in the gross national product for 1967.

While much of the continent wallowed in war and revolution, hunger and discontent, how did tiny Taiwan achieve a standard of living surpassed in Asia only by Japan and Hong Kong, an economy so stable that the United States has ended all but military aid?

Historically and racially Chinese, Taiwan had been a part of China for more than 200 years when Japan occupied it after the first Sino-Japanese War in 1895. Liberated by Japan's defeat in World War II, the island became part of the Nationalist China of Chiang Kai-shek. But his newly appointed governor abused his position and brutally suppressed an uprising by the people. Great numbers of Taiwanese died in the disorders. Many more were executed.

Another governor was appointed. In 1949, Chiang lost the mainland to the Communists and moved his regime to Taipei. With him came more than half a million officers and enlisted men and a million civilians—teachers, students, businessmen, industrialists, and artists.

Humiliated by Communist victories in the homeland, fearing an invasion of Taiwan itself, and smarting under the concerted attack of world opinion, the Nationalists were very close to extinction. But Communist China's intervention in the Korean War helped save them.

Aware that a take-over of Taiwan by the Communists would pose a grave threat to Allied efforts in Korea, the United States assumed defense of the island. With increased economic aid from the U.S.—almost $1,500,000,000 over 15 years —President Chiang Kai-shek set out to build a new China on Taiwan.

The Nationalists still claim to be the legal government of all China. In their lawmaking body, called the Legislative Yuan, elderly representatives deliberate, but cannot act, on the responsibilities delegated to them when they were elected in provinces of mainland China 20 years ago. Only on Taiwan do the people remain free to elect new provincial representatives. Today, of the 115 countries that maintain diplomatic ties with either of the two Chinas, 67 recognize the Nationalists, 48 the Communists.

Helen and I found Taiwan, like so many developing nations, torn between the two worlds of transition and tradition. But unlike those that abandon the old to embrace the new, Taiwan embraces both.

Veteran journalist James Wei, who directs the government's information services, explained Taiwan's plans for her future by introducing us to her past. We were on a first-name basis soon after meeting him at Taipei's new National Palace Museum, repository of the largest collection of Chinese art in the world.

"Only here," he told us, moving his hand to encompass the treasures around us, "do we preserve China's heritage. On the mainland the Communists with their Cultural Revolution and their Red Guards are destroying the past.

"But we believe that no country can survive without respect for the arts. Men died to save these treasures. They were moved across China for decades, buried in caves, carried on sampans, hidden from the Japanese and then the Communists. More than 240,000 pieces finally reached Taiwan.

"They must be preserved at all costs—not only because they stand for 4,000 years of China's evolution, but also because we can learn from them for the future."

• • •

"Yes, the past speaks to us of many things—trial and error, moderation, perseverance. On the mainland we made many mistakes. But we learned that the past alone was not enough. Now the Communists have found that the new ways alone won't work either.

"The only way to beat an idea or a system is with a better one. Here on Taiwan we must preserve our culture, but we must make it better by adding something new."

The first "something new" that the Nationalists added was land reform. The provincial government, with the assistance of the Chinese-American Joint Commission on Rural Reconstruction, administered the program. Dr. T. H. Shen, Chairman of JCRR, described it to us with enthusiasm:

"When Taiwan was freed from Japan in 1945 and returned to China, 80 percent of the people were farmers. Most of the land was owned by big landlords. The farmers were just tenants. Today, more than 90 percent of the farms on Taiwan are operated by their owners.

"The results speak for themselves. Since 1945 Taiwan's population has doubled—to more than 13 million people. Yet we're self-sufficient in food and have plenty left to export. Production of rice, sugar cane, sweet potatoes, and other crops has doubled, tripled, and in some cases quadrupled.

"JCRR helped farmers set up cooperatives and develop better seeds and irrigation methods and more efficient land use. We encouraged fishing, livestock raising, and health programs. Today, according to the World Health Organization, Taiwan is one of the healthiest, best-fed countries in Asia.

"Now we're sharing what we've learned with other nations in Asia, Latin America, and Africa by sending teams there and inviting their people here.

"With many countries we share a basic problem—limited land. Only about 25 percent of Taiwan is arable. But we learned that asparagus does well in the marginal land along rivers and seashore. And mushrooms can grow in layers, on trays in darkened sheds, in effect multiplying the land area. We're among the world's largest exporters of these two foods."

"But what's happened to the landlords whose property was taken for land reform?" I asked.

Dr. Shen smiled. "Why not talk to a few and find out?"

Mr. Chen-fu Koo, a Taiwan-born former landlord, greeted us in his plush, paneled office in Taipei. In his blue-silk mandarin robe he looked very much the country squire, Chinese style, but the modern desk with its futuristic telephones and the production chart on the wall were all business—as befitted the president of Taiwan Cement Corporation, one of the country's largest industries. I asked how he felt about land reform.

"I used to have 14,820 acres of good land and thousands of tenants. Now I have seven acres and no tenants. And I'm much better off. The government paid for the land. They did not confiscate it as in Communist China.

"But they did not pay in money—there wasn't much money then. I was paid in stock in Japanese-owned industries that had become government property when Taiwan was returned to China. One of those industries was cement. Others were mining, lumber, and paper.

"In effect the exchange turned landlords into industrialists and tenants into landowners. With both land and industry in private hands, the economy prospered."

Mr. Y. T. Pan is one of those new landowners. We found him feeding his ducks beside a pond stocked with fish. Lacy bamboo and papaya trees and thriving banana plants dotted the hill behind his 12 acres of prime rice terraces.

With quiet pride Mr. Pan led us across a concrete threshing floor, past a motorcycle and several bicycles, into the sitting room of his sprawling brick house. Dominating one wall was the family altar, like a massive sideboard of carved wood surmounted by paintings and images of the gods that the Taoist Chinese revere.

As we sat on a sofa between a television set and a hi-fi, Mr. Pan told us how land reform had affected him.

"My family has farmed here for generations. We used to live in a mud house. We paid half our crop to the landlord. If we had a bad year, we had to pay anyway.

"Then the government bought the land and sold it to us. We paid in rice, and in ten years the land was ours—for less than we had been paying in rent. For the first time we could save money. We tore down the old house and built this one.

"But most important, I can educate my sons. I didn't go to school, and I was too poor to spare my number-one son from work in the fields. But numbers two and three finished primary school and number four went to high school. Number five finished college and number six is still studying—that's his guitar—he likes your music. Me? I like Taiwanese opera."

Mr. Pan glanced toward the altar. "The gods have been good. Each year I offer a pig at the *pai-pai.*"

. . .

Though bountifully blessed with food, Taiwan has few natural resources for industry. It must import most of its raw materials. Chilung, northern Taiwan's major port, is rapidly expanding its facilities. We drove there with Thomas Hsueh, a young Chinese-American engineer whose Taiwan Argonaut Corporation is building boats for export.

"If I didn't think the investment climate was good, I wouldn't be here," he said as we rolled along the new MacArthur Highway linking Taipei and Chilung.

"Taiwan is moving from the bicycle stage to motorcycles, and that's a good sign. But when a country begins to have more cars than motorcycles, labor costs are usually getting too high for industries that need little skilled labor and a minimum of capital equipment, and they sometimes feel forced to move on to a cheaper labor area.

"We won't be moving on. Our business requires years of costly training to develop a variety of skills. We simply cannot afford to move on when labor gets a little higher."

We saw those skills exemplified in sleek fiberglass sloops and other craft in various stages of completion.

"Our quality control is the same as in the U.S.," Tom said. "And all our materials come from the States too. Yet we can produce below Stateside costs. We can compete despite high transportation costs because our labor cost is low. How long can we do it? With the quality of labor we have, we can compete indefinitely despite the fact that labor costs will increase. We are also using the latest production techniques to stay ahead of our competition. Taiwan is like Japan 15 years ago, and Japan today is certainly still doing well despite tremendous increases in labor costs."

Chilung's fledgling shipbuilding industry is gearing for competition too.

"We're building 90,000-ton ships now, and we're planning even bigger ones," Mr. Christopher H. P. Yen of Taiwan Shipbuilding Corporation told us. "When Taiwan's new steel mill is completed, we hope to compete with Japan."

Optimistic though this may be, Chilung has its sights set high. The big news was containerization, the advanced concept in shipping that is reducing cargo-handling costs and loading times in major ports of the world.

Tom explained how it works: Massive 200,000-ton ships—specially built to handle cargo in sealed standard-size containers—would leave European and American ports bound for Asia. But instead of stopping at each Asian port along the way, they would head for Taiwan and transfer their cargo to smaller ships.

"By using small ships for the shorter runs, the huge container ships with their high overhead costs would lose less time in port. With the cargo in sealed containers, pilferage and breakage would be minimized. Insurance costs would go down.

"And Taiwan is geographically ideal to serve as a feeder station. We're only 380 miles from Hong Kong, 550 miles from Manila, 725 miles from Nagasaki."

Taiwan's location has its drawbacks too; for three months of the year typhoons pose a continuing threat. Chang's usual good humor was noticeably lacking when we discussed a drive along the East Coast Highway.

"Maybe so you find other driver?" he suggested hopefully.

"But this is November," Helen assured him. "The typhoon season is over."

Season or no, Typhoon Gilda caught us at Yehliu, a small fishing port near Chilung. Sweeping out of the east, rain charged in horizontal sheets. Lightning slashed the sky. Like sheep in a storm, boats huddled forlornly in the narrow harbor. Gray spindrift fogged the air, tugging at slickered fishermen as they fought to secure their craft. We raced back to Taipei in a raging thunderstorm that flooded east coast towns, leaving two dead, hundreds of homes destroyed, and crop damage totaling millions of dollars.

The debris of Gilda's wrath still littered the graveled East Coast Highway when it was reopened to traffic. Workers—men and women—scooped fallen rock from the narrow track scratched along cliffs rising in places to a thousand feet.

Formerly the most dangerous road on the island—Taipei's streets today claim that dubious distinction—the East Coast Highway is now one way. Moving alternately north and south in timed convoys, traffic detours the old sheer-drop bends and runs instead through new hand-cut tunnels. Forbidden to stop along the road, we caught only glimpses of the soaring mountains to our right and the pounding, rock-studded sea below. We were as relieved as Chang when the road dipped down to Hualien, east Taiwan's largest town and only deepwater port.

Hualien is near the eastern end of the East-West Cross-Island Highway. Intended to open inaccessible timber and farm lands of central Taiwan, the road passes through dramatic Taroko Gorge, a river-cut canyon in a mountain of marble.

James Yu, manager of Hualien's largest marble works, showed us through his plant. Chips were flying from lathes turning out lamp bases, vases, and ashtrays for the growing number of tourists. More important economically, multibladed saws rasped through truck-size chunks to produce slabs of green, rust, black, or white marble for buildings and monuments.

"Marble is one of Taiwan's few exportable raw materials," Mr. Yu said. "We estimate there are billions of tons in these mountains, much of it excellent quality. We even export to Italy."

South of Hualien the highway turns away from the sea to enter a long, narrow valley. We paralleled a narrow-gauge railway, sometimes driving across its revetment-protected trestles where highway bridges had been washed away by rain-swollen streams. Settlements were mere clusters of wood or cement buildings; farm houses were grass huts.

At Taitung ripening pineapples tinted convoluted hills—a successful use of marginal land. And then we were along the sea again. Sisal stripped from the sandy dunes lay drying like witches' white hair on the road. A fisherman surfed his bamboo raft through frothy breakers and unloaded his catch: three silvery, squirming scabbard fish, meager reward for a morning's work.

Taiwan has been compared in shape to a tobacco leaf. On the southern-most tip of the tapering stem, near Oluanpi, Helen and I stood braced in the wind that had followed us since we left Taipei. Like most of the east coast the country had an air of desolation, as though the typhoon-tired land could provide little more than sustenance, as though the winds of storm were winning out over the winds of progress sweeping the rest of Taiwan.

Now our road led northwestward toward Kaohsiung, Taiwan's southern industrial center, where the winds of progress blow strongly indeed. Still miles from the city, we passed the Chinese Petroleum Corporation's refinery. Then a silver snake of a pipeline paralleled our route, leading us to the harbor of a city white with the dust of cement plants, fragrant with the sawdust of plywood factories, acrid with the fumes of plastics industries.

On 170 acres of reclaimed land beside Kaohsiung's protected harbor, 123 investors from Japan, the United States, and Europe are erecting factories to produce items ranging from wigs to wire, pearl necklaces to paper containers, integrated circuits to umbrellas. Kaohsiung Export Processing Zone—KEPZ for short—is part of Taiwan's master plan for transforming an agricultural society into an industrial one.

By encouraging the development of "labor-intensive" industries—those where hand labor is more practical than machine—Taiwan is capitalizing on its most abundant resource, low-cost labor.

In the new Administration Building, Mr. Thomas T. C. Kuan, an executive of KEPZ, tallied for us the advantages it offers to Taiwan and to investors.

"Outside the zone foreign investors sometimes encounter archaic red tape. Here we minimize it. There's no import duty on machinery, equipment, or raw materials, no income tax for the first five years, no tax at all except for a small revenue-stamp tax to cover administrative costs.

"We also help the investor build his factory, guarantee plenty of water and electricity at low rates, and help him recruit labor."

"Sounds like a one-way street for the investor," I said. "How does Taiwan benefit?"

"It's Taiwan's low-cost labor that brings foreign investors here," Mr. Kuan replied. "But as our labor becomes more expensive, other countries—South Korea, for example—will be more attractive. In the meantime Taiwan's domestic industries are absorbing new techniques in management and production. We're developing a pool of trained workers with a high regard for quality control. As our wage scales rise to the point where foreign investors look elsewhere, we hope that our increased efficiency will keep us competitive in the world markets."

How productive are these workers? Lorain Tinnes of General Micro-Electronics, a subsidiary of Philco-Ford, was more than enthusiastic. He led us along lines of benches where blue-smocked ex-farm girls peered into microscopes and assembled Space Age electronics components. He stopped beside a shy Taiwanese girl who was bonding wires $\frac{1}{1000}$ of an inch in diameter to a circuit printed on a tiny piece of silicon.

"Theoretically, the maximum capacity of these bonding machines is 400 units a day. After three weeks of training this girl produced 340 units. We named her Worker of the Month. The very next day she produced 414 units. These girls just like to work. They make a game of it."

Most of the workers at KEPZ are Taiwan-born Chinese from the western plains. The lure of factory jobs has not yet penetrated the central mountain range where most of Taiwan's aborigines live.

Divided into nine tribal groups, the aborigines claim Malayan origin. During Japanese administration they were isolated in reservations, partly because of their inhospitable habit of hunting heads.

They are far less isolated now. Where the tourists have not reached, the missionaries have. With John Whitehorn, an English Presbyterian, we hiked into Daladalai, a Paiwan tribe village some three hours' climb from road's end at Santimen.

For much of the way we followed a foot trail over mountainsides covered with bamboo, juniper, and cedar. Few lances of light broke through, and we walked in gloom until the trail ended abruptly at a gorge crossed by a narrow suspension bridge. Hundreds of feet long, strung dizzily above rock-studded, milky-green streams, it spanned the abyss like a spider web. We walked with cautious steps, watching for rotten boards, clinging to trembling handrails, pausing briefly to glance down the valley at the crudely cultivated patches of Paiwan farms.

The few people we met—pipe-smoking, betel-nut-chewing men and women, heavily laden with firewood and medicinal herbs for lowland markets —nodded pleasantly as we passed. Those coming up the trail moved with springy stride, despite their massive loads of rice, salt, and bottled drinks from the plains.

A flight of stone steps led us the last hundred yards to Daladalai. Rows of houses stood on terraces cut in the hillside; on each terrace were elevated barns and rows of spindly betel-nut palms. Paths between the houses were paved with fine slate, and slate walls reached to the eaves of grass roofs, each roof weighted with stones against typhoon winds.

It was Sunday, and the small concrete church was full when we arrived. Men in shirts and trousers, some with ties, sat on one side of the aisle, women in shapeless cottons on the other. All were singing, and the Paiwan words seemed incongruous, set to the familiar hymn tunes played on a foot-pumped organ. The atmosphere was relaxed. Babies suckled, children played, and a dog strolled in.

We stayed that night in the house of a chieftain's family. The daughter, a kindergarten teacher, had "come up from the plains" for a visit, but she insisted we have her bed while she stayed with a friend.

In the large one-room house, the slate floor was swept clean, and the two sleeping areas were separated by sacks of onions that added their own character to the smoke from a wood fire smoldering in a corner. In contrast to the parents' simple sleeping platform, the daughter's end of the house was papered with Christmas cards and calendar pictures of Chinese movie stars. Enclosed with curtains, her platform boasted red-satin pillows and a pink puff spread over Japanese-style sleeping mats.

The old mother squirted a stream of red betel-nut juice out the window. Her stained lips cracked a smile like a sliced tomato.

"She brought those ideas up from the plains," she snorted with that mixture of pride and contempt the old reserve for the young.

We sat on low stools close to the fire and shared the family's bean-and-rice gruel. An oil lamp glowed orange on a beam overhead, throwing in bold relief crude carvings of snakes and human skulls, mark of a family that had once hunted heads.

The old mother grunted in pleasure at our interest. She pulled a basket from beneath her bed and unfolded a coarse black-cotton jacket embroidered and beaded with symbols like those on the beam. She showed us a headdress heavy with bells, cowrie shells, and boars' tusks: a bridal costume passed down through generations. She had been married in it, and—for all her new ways—so had her daughter.

We left Daladalai and turned north across the fertile plains that produce most of the island's food. Route 1, Taiwan's western artery, was the usual madcap race track.

Timber trucks contested the right of way with bullock carts teetering under high loads of sugar cane. Buses bullied automobiles, and tiny taxis with locomotive-size horns blasted bicycles and motorcycles off the road in a well-established pecking order. In a continuous stream of traffic, the highway pulsed with the press of people of one of the most densely populated lands in the world.

•   •   •

Perhaps nowhere is news of Asia watched more closely than on Taiwan. Headlines banner the war in Viet Nam and North Korea's growing belligerence; guerrilla raids in Laos, Cambodia, and Thailand; riots in Hong Kong; purges in Communist China. With each new upheaval editorials hint that the time is near for Nationalist China's return to the mainland.

In a rare audience, Chiang Kai-shek summed up Nationalist China's viewpoint:

"As long as the Communists occupy the mainland, there will be no end to the disturbances in Southeast Asia. The Republic of China here on Taiwan must return to the mainland to clear up the mess."

The President and Madame Chiang Kai-shek had received us in their Grass Mountain home on the outskirts of Taipei. Carpets the color of rubies accented an array of Ming dynasty oxblood porcelain. Roses glowed in the light of a fire, and Madame Chiang's own paintings graced the walls. Despite its large size, the reception room radiated warmth and friendliness.

Tea was served with sandwiches, cake, and dumplings. In the cultured English that reflects her Wellesley College background, Madame Chiang discussed Chinese painting with Helen; the President, speaking through an interpreter, asked me about our tour of Taiwan.

So relaxed was the atmosphere that more than an hour passed before we realized it. President and Madame Chiang Kai-shek rose to bid us goodbye, and at the door I looked back. The President was standing with hands on hips and an alert twinkle in his eyes. For all his 81 years he was still lean and straight, but I wondered how—or if—his lifelong dream of a united China would be realized.

Not even the most optimistic Nationalist Chinese believe that this goal can ever be achieved by military action alone. They point to the government's "70 percent political—30 percent military policy."

"First we must make Taiwan an example for all Asia of progress through free enterprise," a friend in Taipei told us. "We must capitalize on the broken promises of the Communists. Our intelligence reports indicate that many people on the mainland are already disillusioned. We must encourage revolt. When it comes, we will be ready."

And so the quiet war goes on, amid the rumble of factories on Taiwan and the roar of rockets from the mainland.

SUGGESTED WRITING ASSIGNMENT

A Report on a Composite Specific Subject

Observe an organization, a business, a church (one congregation), an experimental program, or another type of specific enterprise with a number of aspects. Select three to six aspects that you think will be interesting to readers, and gather facts about them. Before you write the report, consider whether a chronological pattern would be appropriate for ordering the aspects.

Include in your report a few quotations of informants' statements, and list statistics (if there are relevant statistics). Describe at least one person, object, or location in detail. In the description, arrange your details in a clear spatial pattern, use concrete nouns and vivid modifiers, and include at least one cumulative sentence.

Try to make your report as appealing as possible to the reader, especially at the beginning when you are trying to engage his attention. Open with a striking quotation, a brief narrative, an interesting description, a hypothetical situation involving the reader, or some other attractive device.

Do not use written sources for this report.

PART II

Exemplification

". . . the present age exhibits to the individual man who contemplates it the spectacle of a vast multitude of facts awaiting and inviting his comprehension. . . . intellectual deliverance begins when our mind begins to enter into possession of the general ideas which are the law of this vast multitude of facts."

Matthew Arnold, "On the Modern Element in Literature"

Classification

Though knowledge of factual details is essential to sound thinking, and reference to factual details essential to responsible writing, we would be overwhelmed by the multitudinousness of details if we could not relate them to one another by means additional to space and time—as we say, by logical means. While we realize with Walter Pater, an English essayist of the Victorian Age, that "it is only the roughness of the eye that makes any two persons, things, situations, seem alike"—that the individuality in everything must be appreciated—we realize also, with Matthew Arnold, that it is frustrating to be surrounded by disorganized facts. To be able to relate what one sees to what one has seen, to comprehend the general idea in a swarm of specific facts, is, as Arnold has said, a kind of "intellectual deliverance."

The most accessible of all logical relations is similarity, and the capacity of the human mind to see similarities is truly remarkable. A very small child can see the similarities between a real horse—a breathing, moving, brown-haired creature fifteen hands high, which he can sit upon—and a stylized, fancifully colored, painted "horse" on a flat sheet of paper—a painting so small that he can cover it with his hand. He can accept *horse* as the name of both, and he can identify a third horse that is not exactly like either of those he has seen.

We classify by seeing similarities and overlooking differences, and we tend to accept the classifications made by others, at least when we are children. But, as it does not follow that we can describe just because we can see, so it does not follow that we can write about classifications just because we can classify. This part of the book will show how the mental process of classification that we perform unconsciously can be carried forward into a consciously formed composition—in other words, how we explain a system of classification to others and how we call attention to a little-noticed similarity in a variety of specific facts. We shall first review the terminology of classification, in Dialog 5, and then examine some readings that illustrate the rationale of classification in writing.

DIALOG 5

The Terminology of Classification

Please refer to these sets when answering the questions that follow them.

Set A
6. *plant*
5. *cactus*
4. *saguaro*
3. *saguaro*$_1$
    2. perception of saguaro$_1$
    1. process-saguaro$_1$

Set B
6. *athlete*
5. *baseball player*
4. *pitcher*
3. *Don Drysdale*
    2. perception of Don Drysdale
    1. process–Don Drysdale

Set C
6. *automobile*
5.
4. *Caprice*
3. *Caprice*$_3$
    2. perception of Caprice$_3$
    1. process-Caprice$_3$

Set D
6.
5. *criminal*
4.
3.
    2.
    1.

1. What, earlier in this book, did we call such lists as those above?	Abstraction ladders.
2. What is a synonym for *abstraction* when it refers to terms on such lists?	*Generalization.*
3. In the list in Set A, which term is the specific term?	*Saguaro*$_1$.
4. The specific term is always on which level of the ladder?	The third.
5. From now on we shall often call the third level the example level. Why can we call it this?	Because the referent of the term on the third level is an example of the class represented by every term above it, as saguaro$_1$ is an example of a saguaro, of a cactus, and of a plant.
6. Is *saguaro* a term that represents an example of a cactus?	No. It represents a type of cactus, not an example of a cactus.

7. Strictly speaking, only terms on the _____ level of the abstraction ladder, or _____ terms, can be called examples.	third, specific
8. Which is the more general term—*saguaro* or *cactus?*	*Cactus.*
9. On an abstraction ladder the fourth level is more general than the _____, the fifth is more general than the _____, and the sixth is more general than the _____.	third, fourth, fifth
10. *Being more general* means *covering more specific terms,* or more _____.	*examples*
11. General words can also be called class words. If one class is less general than another it can be called a subclass. The saguaro is a _____ of the cactus.	subclass
12. A synonym for *class* is *type.* We can speak of classes and subclasses, of types and _____.	sub-types
13. In the abstraction ladder in Set B, Don Drysdale is an example of a _____, a _____, and an _____.	pitcher, baseball player, athlete
14. A pitcher is a _____ of baseball player; a baseball player is a _____ of athlete.	type, type
15. If *baseball player* is a class, *pitcher* is a _____.	subclass
16. Complete Set C by writing the appropriate word on the fifth level.	*Chevrolet*

17. Complete Set D.	One possibility:
	6. *wrong-doer*
	5. *criminal*
	4. *thief*
	3. *Bonnie Parker*
	   2. perception of Bonnie Parker
	   1. process–Bonnie Parker

ORGANIZING BY CLASSIFICATION

The main idea of some compositions is simply "There are four (or some other number) classes of _____ ." One division of the composition treats the first type; another, the second type; and so forth. In the brief article below, Sylvia Porter presents a straightforward division of a class, jobs for women, dividing it into six subclasses and each subclass into less general subclasses. The division begins in the fourth paragraph.

Jobs for Women

Sylvia Porter

Never has the job outlook been brighter for you, if you are a trained young college woman. Never has the warning to you been clearer to complete your basic training, to keep your special skills up-to-date, to stay in tune with the working world in which you live.

An obvious reason for the favorable job trend for women is the extremely low unemployment rate among skilled men today which translates into severe shortages in many job categories. Another obvious factor is the cumulative impact of the anti-discrimination laws affecting women workers: the Civil Rights Act of 1964, the Equal Pay Act of 1963.

Where are the most provocative opportunities for the college-trained American woman now? Here is the latest rundown from the Labor Dept.'s Women's Bureau:

Mathematics: Starting salaries are among the highest of any field, especially if you have a Master's Degree or a Ph.D. The most promising fields for female mathematicians are jobs in private industry (especially in the computer and aerospace industries); in colleges and universities (teaching or doing basic research) and in the federal government. Of special interest to women are the part-time job opportunities in consulting, teaching and programming.

Pharmacy: Indicative of the trend here is the fact that while women account for only 8 per cent of all U.S. pharmacists, they represent 14 per cent of all pharmacy students. Pharmacy covers much more than filling prescriptions; it may be research, sales, hospital work or a job at a university, government agency or corporation.

Optometry: Only one in 20 U.S. optometrists is a woman but the demand for vision specialists is now far outrunning the supply. The requirement is a total of six years of college and specialized optometry school and then an optometrist can go into private practice or work in private industry, a health clinic or the

JOBS FOR WOMEN   *Arizona Daily Star*, February 11, 1969, Editorial Page. Reprinted by permission of Publishers-Hall Syndicate.

military. Optometry specialities include children's reading problems, industrial optometry, research, contact lenses, vision and highway safety. There are excellent part-time job opportunities.

Public Relations: Building and improving the image of a corporation, foundation, individual, college, trade, profession, government agency, etc. may involve research, writing of speeches, press releases, financial reports. Today, one in four in this field is a woman and a Liberal Arts degree is generally sufficient.

Engineering: Women hold only a picayune number of the jobs but the opportunities are multiplying in fields ranging from bio-engineering to medical engineering to human engineering.

Technical writing: the fields of medicine and aerospace are the most fertile for qualified women technical writers but jobs are everywhere: hospitals, government agencies, universities, pharmaceutical and electronics companies, scientific magazines. Part-time opportunities are plentiful.

A classification may be more personal than Miss Porter's classification of jobs for women, and the individuality of thought will probably reflect itself in individuality of style, as in E. B. White's discussion of types of obscurity in poetry. Notice as you read this discussion that while classifying, White questions popular taste in poetry, satirizes people who think poets are set off from other mortals by superior madness, and satirizes poets who cannot resist using irrelevant phrases that sound pleasing.

FROM **Poetry**

E. B. White

"I wish poets could be clearer," shouted my wife angrily from the next room.

Hers is a universal longing. We would all like it if the bards would make themselves plain, or we think we would. The poets, however, are not easily diverted from their high mysterious ways. A poet dares be just so clear and no clearer; he approaches lucid ground warily, like a mariner who is determined not to scrape his bottom on anything solid. A poet's pleasure is to withhold a little of his meaning, to intensify by mystification. He unzips the veil from beauty, but does not remove it. A poet utterly clear is a trifle glaring.

The subject is a fascinating one. I think poetry is the greatest of the arts. It combines music and painting and story-telling and prophecy and the dance. It is religious in tone, scientific in attitude. A true poem contains the seed of wonder; but a bad poem, egg-fashion, stinks. I think there is no such thing as

From POETRY   From *One Man's Meat* by E. B. White. Copyright, 1939 by E. B. White. Reprinted by permission of Harper & Row, Publishers.

a long poem. If it is long it isn't a poem; it is something else. A book like *John Brown's Body,* for instance, is not a poem—it is a series of poems tied together with cord. Poetry is intensity, and nothing is intense for long.

Some poets are naturally clearer than others. To achieve great popularity or great fame it is of some advantage to be either extremely clear (like Edgar Guest) or thoroughly opaque (like Gertrude Stein). The first poet in the land—if I may use the word loosely—is Edgar Guest. He is the singer who, more than any other, gives to Americans the enjoyment of rhyme and meter. Whether he gives also to any of his satisfied readers that blinding, aching emotion which I get from reading certain verses by other writers is a question which interests me very much. Being democratic, I am content to have the majority rule in everything, it would seem, but literature.

There are many types of poetical obscurity. There is the obscurity which results from the poet's being mad. This is rare. Madness in poets is as uncommon as madness in dogs. A discouraging number of reputable poets are sane beyond recall. There is also the obscurity which is the result of the poet's wishing to appear mad, even if only a little mad. This is rather common and rather dreadful. I know of nothing more distasteful than the work of a poet who has taken leave of his reason deliberately, as a commuter might of his wife.

Then there is the unintentional obscurity or muddiness, which comes from the inability of some writers to express even a simple idea without stirring up the bottom. And there is the obscurity which results when a fairly large thought is crammed into a three- or four-foot line. The function of poetry is to concentrate; but sometimes over-concentration occurs, and there is no more comfort in such a poem than there is in the subway at the peak hour.

Sometimes a poet becomes so completely absorbed in the lyrical possibilities of certain combinations of sounds that he forgets what he started out to say, if anything, and here again a nasty tangle results. This type of obscurity is one which I have great sympathy for: I know that quite frequently in the course of delivering himself of a poem a poet will find himself in possession of a lyric bauble—a line as smooth as velvet to the ear, as pretty as a feather to the eye, yet a line definitely out of plumb with the frame of the poem. What to do with a trinket like this is always troubling to a poet, who is naturally grateful to his Muse for small favors. Usually he just drops the shining object into the body of the poem somewhere and hopes it won't look too giddy. (I sound as though I were contemptuous of poets; the fact is I am jealous of them. I would rather be one than anything.)

The subjectivity, the surprising use of words that are apt but unusual in such a context, like *unzips* and *bauble,* and the irony of some of the statements—for example, "A discouraging number of reputable poets are sane beyond recall"— brighten this discussion; but it is still basically a simple classification of admirable and contemptible classes of obscurity in poetry.

In the composition below, by a student, sensory experience in one kind of setting is divided into four subclasses: sights, sounds, scents, and tactile impressions.

A Student Composition Based on Classification

Bob Hartnack

A stroll along the beach during the early morning hours can provide a fantastic sensory experience for anyone willing to brave the cool air and loss of sleep.

One's sense of sight is treated to a great variety of scenes, all changing at a rapid pace. As the fog begins to lift off the ground and water, the first rays of the sun can be seen. The seagulls, in their never-ending search for food, circle overhead, often swooping down to the surface of the water. The waves end their journey across the sea by crashing on the shore. Great mounds of white foam are pushed shoreward by each wave.

An assortment of sounds constantly surrounds the beach walker on his early morning hike. Every few seconds the boom of a large wave crashing on shore penetrates the stillness of the morning. The screeching of the birds as they fight over a morsel of food often frightens the beach-walker until he has discovered the innocent source of the cry. The noise created by stepping on dry sand is often very similar to the bark of a seal. Hours can be passed listening to the noises of the shore.

The odor of the beach is something the beach-walker will never forget. The pungent odor of decaying seaweed fills his nostrils. The refreshing smell of salt air is probably the most rewarding experience that he has. The moist, cool air is an absolute delight to breathe.

One's feet, of course, receive numerous different sensations. The slimy feeling of seaweed as it slides under the feet is a rather strange experience. The cool ocean water swirling around the toes and ankles refreshes the feet after a long hike. Rocks occasionally cause pain as the beach-walker strolls along the shore. However, the pain is soon replaced by some new sensation.

A stroll along the shore can certainly be an unforgettable experience. The feelings, the scents, the sounds, and the sights all combine to form a truly exciting setting for a beach-walker.

Thus far, we have illustrated development by subclasses, without examples. Sylvia Porter does not in her discussion of jobs for women describe a specific position in pharmaceutical research being filled by a specific woman, nor does she give any other examples of specific jobs. E. B. White does not quote obscure lines from any poem. Bob Hartnack has not described a specific sunrise, a specific fright from hearing the screech of birds, or any other specific experience. All of these compositions, in our opinion, would have been better with examples. Though Sylvia Porter was working within a strict word limit, the fifty words she spent in the first paragraph giving advice could have been spent more effectively in giving an informative example. Though E. B. White was not writing a whole chapter on obscurity, there seems no reason for his not quoting a few lines in which a poet "unzips the veil from beauty" or not citing a few lyric baubles that got dropped into poems. If he had done this, the reader would know whether to agree with him or not. Bob Hartnack intended to evoke the typical sensations of a beach-walker, and this he did well; but he might have described some of these so vividly that they would have carried the force of immediate sensation.

The subjects treated in the three selections you have just read lend themselves to development by subclasses without examples better than most subjects, however. As you read the following article, think how useless it would be without reference to specific books. Also, as you read it, or when you have finished, fill in a classification diagram of it like the following, stating the general class of books treated, the three subclasses that provide the basic structure of the article, and all of the examples cited. Could one of the subclasses be divided into less general subclasses before examples are given?

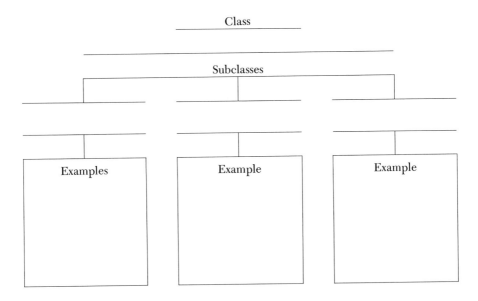

The Pecuniary Culture

Walter Guzzardi, Jr.

Next to making money, the favorite occupation of the affluent society seems to be writing about money. That may not be very surprising: we do live, after all, in what Veblen early on recognized as "the pecuniary culture"—a better if less catchy phrase than "the affluent society"—and it is probably predictable enough that its pecuniary peculiarities should be coming in for a fair amount of attention from writers and analysts these days. At the same time, though, the river of written words about money (fortunately, the number of words spoken on the subject will never be known) merits some observation and comment. Never before in history have so many writers devoted so much attention to one aspect or another of the money-making process, raising the question whether they are saying anything sensible, and, beyond that, whether money—even stacks and stacks of it—is all that engaging. There is also the question whether some of these writers are really interested in money or whether in fact they, like some of the people who make money, aren't really more interested in something else.

Generally, the money-writing genre breaks down into two main streams. One stream frankly appeals to the avarice of the reader. An example that appeared a few years ago bore, appositely enough, a green dustjacket emblazoned with pithy slogans that went right to the heart of the matter, and therefore command a certain amount of respect, regardless of how one may feel about the esthetics involved. "America's 100 Best Money-Making Ideas!" reads the slash across the top of the jacket. This is followed in larger type by the book's title, *Income Opportunities,* spelled out in large block capitals. Then, down the jacket's margin, run the punchy come-on phrases: "Mail Order Business!" "Success Stories—How They Did It, How YOU Can Too!" "Make Extra Money, and Keep Your Regular Job, Too!" In case all those jabs don't make the point clear the blurb drives it home with a sledge hammer: "This book will show you how you can make . . . undreamed-of profits," it says with assurance.

Within this how-to-get-it group all sorts of specialized approaches have been developed. (I speak now only of books, leaving out such publications as a new biweekly newspaper called *Physicians Financial Letter,* which appeals directly to the cupidity of doctors by offering them confidential appraisals of and advice about their portfolios.) Among them is a new book called *What Every Woman Should Know About Investing Her Money,* by H. H. Levy (Dartnell, $6.95), which, the *Wall Street Journal* reports, is "selling very, very well" to "housewives, secretaries and female executives." And it looks as though books about money—or, more exactly, about stock certificates, which are more intriguing—may eventually paper over the generation gap: Hawthorn's *The Bulls and the Bears,* by Adrian A. Paradis ($3.95), aimed at the ten-to-fourteen-year-olds, went into a second printing for the holiday season, while Harcourt, Brace & World is doing well with *Investing Money: The Facts About Stocks and Bonds,* by Ruth Brindze ($3.50), directed at the teen-age market.

On a somewhat more sophisticated level but making the same kind of appeal to adult audiences is a new edition of *Happiness Is a Stock that Doubles in a Year,* by Ira U. Cobleigh (Bernard Geis, $6.95). The fly-leaf makes perfectly clear the reason why a new edition is necessary: "In the first edition," it says, the author "offered forty-five stocks, of which 31 per cent actually doubled, or better, within a year." The author in this case is an economist and a financial editor who has written ten or so books about stocks. In *Happiness* (Part II) he rambles through

THE PECUNIARY CULTURE *Saturday Review,* January 11, 1969. Copyright 1969 Saturday Review, Inc. Reprinted by permission of the author.

some fairly general comments, accurate but not especially informative, about the national economy and the growth industries, and then finally arrives at the section that lists those happiness-making stocks, introducing it with the frank comment: "This is the chapter you've been waiting for, of course." By the time the reader has finished it, with visions of that 31 per cent of the earlier list glittering before his eyes, he is probably much too dazzled even to pause over the final paragraphs, one of which begins: "Nothing in this book is to be construed as a recommendation, endorsement, representation or offer to buy and sell any security at any time."

The other stream that makes up the money-writing genre eschews all promises of personal enrichment. One of its leading exponents is John Brooks, novelist and essayist, whose long, fine pieces about the business world have appeared often in the pages of *The New Yorker*. Brooks is a thoroughgoing reporter and a serious writer who digs into business situations and makes sure that he understands them in their complicated particulars before he discusses them. But it is fair to say that Brooks's main interest isn't business or money—it's people. He habitually turns a magnifying glass on the way people act in a business context, and that is what he has done very effectively in a new book called *Business Adventures: Twelve Classic Tales from the Worlds of Wall Street and the Modern American Corporation* (Weybright & Talley, $10).

Business Adventures, all of which has appeared over the years in *The New Yorker*, is full of clear, witty writing. It comprises a fascinating collection of tales about the foibles of businessmen. Among the best is a chapter called "The Impacted Philosophers," dealing with the famous anti-trust case involving General Electric a few years ago. That event was, of course, one of the most fully reported in the history of business, but John Brooks (like *Fortune* writer Richard Austin Smith, who entitled his two long pieces "The Great Electrical Conspiracy") has found something new and illuminating and entertaining to say about it.

That Brooks's interest, though, continues to center on people is revealed when he recalls a bit of dialogue between Arthur Vinson of G.E. and Senator Kefauver. In this exchange Vinson responded to Kefauver's suggestion that "You wouldn't be a vice president at $200,000 a year if you were naïve" by saying, "I think I could well get there by being naïve in this area. It might help." Quite rightly, Brooks bores in: "Was Vinson really saying to Kefauver what he seemed to be saying—that naïveté about anti-trust violations might be a help to a man in getting and holding a $200,000-a-year job at General Electric? It seems unlikely. And yet what else could he have meant?" Somehow, though, the curiosity stirred in the reader by Brooks's question—we really do want to know the answer—has more to do with Vinson and with Kefauver than with G.E. This takes nothing away from the fine job Brooks has done here, and in another outstanding chapter called "Xerox Xerox Xerox Xerox." But it does show where his preoccupation lies.

Inevitably, the most successful book of all is one that brings the two main streams together. The story of money and the promise of personal profit are present, but so are the people. The confluence of the two themes in *The Money Game*, by 'Adam Smith' (Random House, $6.95), has made it a best-seller for months, and must have made its author—a former *Fortune* writer whose real name is George Goodman—as rich as many of the people who flocked to buy the book would like to be.

The chapter headings of *The Money Game* show pretty clearly the way the focus shifts from money to people and back. The first one penetrates the reader like a dart with its heading "YOU," and then moves in closer by breaking "you" down into three abstractions: Identity, Anxiety, and Money. The second chapter reinforces the point: "Can Ink Blots Tell You Whether You Are the Type Who Will Make a Lot of Money in the Market?" it asks. At the end the author quotes Keynes: "The love of money as a possession . . . is a somewhat disgusting morbidity, one of those semi-criminal, semi-pathological propensities which one hands over with a shudder to the specialists in mental disease." 'Adam Smith' then asks the critical question "Do YOU want to take the money game, or leave it alone?" He enjoins the reader: "You have to make your own choice, and there are many other and more productive outlets for time and energy. Until daylight, I wish you the joys of the Game."

The Money Game richly deserves its success. It is written by a man who knows the Game, has played it, and has never lost his wit or his humor in the process. From the way combines are put together ("'Sell the company? You're crazy,' said Uncle Harry") to the reason why the little man can't be a successful trader ("I was out of town that day, and couldn't call my broker, and when I got back there were all those rumors . . .") to the horrors and complications of the commodity market ("How can cocoa go down?" said the great Winfield. "Cocoa is going to forty cents. *Minimum.* Six times your money."), 'Adam Smith' knows what he is talking about. And it's a pleasure to listen to him.

Like sex, money is never going to die out as a subject for writers. All the books about sex, though—all that very clear, very precise and very clinical descriptive material about copulation in its many manifestations—gets to be a bore after a while. It is too direct, and it needs garnishment. The same is true with books about money. Investment opportunities are losing their appeal, and they all begin to sound the same, especially the bit about "Nothing in this book is to be construed as an endorsement. . . ." But when you talk about people and the way they relate to money—that's a stream that will never dry up.

SUGGESTED WRITING ASSIGNMENT

The Classification Theme

In the selection above, Walter Guzzardi, Jr. develops the idea that there are three subclasses of popular financial books. Write a serious or a humorous essay on two, three, or four subclasses of a class of things that you are familiar with—possibly, ugly women, guitars, vacuum cleaners, athletic awards, social pressure, unwelcome criticism, campus slang, irritating mannerisms, or television commercials.

Use examples as support, and develop some of the examples with descriptive detail, using concrete words and precise modifiers to make your subject perceptible. Consider using the cumulative sentence to present the detail of one of the examples.

Turn in with your theme a classification diagram of the theme.

The two classification themes below are reproduced with the permissions of the students who wrote them, one of whom asked not to be named. Perhaps observing the strengths and the weaknesses of these themes, each of which is followed by an evaluation, will help you anticipate some of the possibilities and some of the problems that you will meet in writing your classification theme.

Offensive Attacks in Football

Ron Stanley

1 Dominance of the offense in college football has become increasingly apparent in recent years, and never has it been more a factor than in the present season, college football's centennial year. 2 Coaches are developing new and greatly diversified attacks, including innovations such as the "wishbone T" and "triple option." 3 Generally, there are three major types of offense from which a coach must choose one as suitable for his team—a passing attack, a combination of the pass and run, or a running attack.

4 A passing attack is obviously the most exciting of the three 5 Fans are usually attracted much more to a game in which the air is filled with footballs than to a three-yards-and-a-cloud-of-dust battle. 6 If a team is not blessed w th exceptional size or speed, it often turns to the passing game, placing its fortunes in the hands of an inexperienced sophomore quarterback and a crop of fast, talented receivers. 7 Such was the case of Southern Methodist University (S.M.U.) last season. 8 On the strength of a strong and accurate arm, unheralded nineteen-year-old Chuck Hixson led S.M.U. to an 8-2-1 season, including a post-season bowl game. 9 Thus S.M.U. became the "Cinderella team" of the Southwest Conference, narrowly losing the conference championship to Arkansas. 10 S.M.U. could be defeated only when its offense was plagued by interceptions.

11 A combination of the passing and running game is a second major type of offensive attack. 12 A team that emphasizes this means of offense is generally labeled "explosive," because it can break the game wide open by the run or pass in just a short time, which can be demoralizing to a team using a conservative "ball control" game plan. 13 Kansas State, a major surprise on the gridiron this season, bases its offense on this kind of attack. 14 Lynn Dickey's pinpoint passing, coupled with the brilliant running of wingback Abe Herron, has enabled the Wildcats to become a major contender for the Big Eight Conference championship. 15 Inconsistency has been Kansas State's only drawback.

16 The last, and perhaps the most successful, offense is that which relies primarily on the running game. 17 A team which consistently runs the ball is actually boldly challenging the opposing defense to stop it. 18 Whereas several interceptions will plague a passing team, and inconsistency often hampers a team that passes and runs equally, a running team will usually play a tough, solid game. 19 The University of Texas has long used the run as the primary basis for its offense, and few teams are able to keep the big, tough Longhorns from reaching the end zone. 20 Texas' short, consistent rushes also enable it to maintain control of the ball and therefore reduce the amount of time its opponent has to score. 21 This team's perfect 6–0 record and number two national ranking are ample support for its powerful method of offense.

Comments on "Offensive Attacks in Football"

Arrangement: Ron Stanley's theme follows a classification scheme, as this diagram shows:

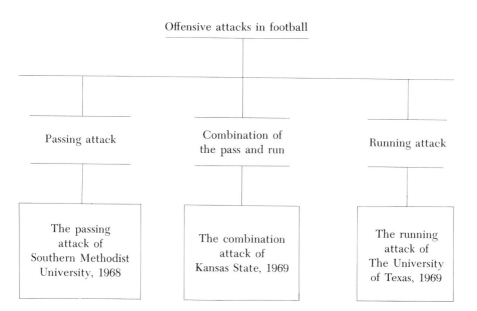

Content: The subject has a wide appeal and is suitable to the assignment. Sentence 3 states the unifying idea of the theme clearly. The first two sentences introduce the subject attractively; equally effective concluding sentences are needed. Mr. Stanley's comments in the body of the theme on the relative merits of the three types of offensive attacks are interesting and not inappropriate. His examples of the three attacks, however, are insufficiently developed: the running attack of the Longhorns of the University of Texas is described in only general terms, and there is no concrete description of a specific play involved in any of the three attacks.

Sentence structure: Good. The sentences throughout are correctly formed. The appositives in sentences 1 and 13 and the in-set past participial phrase in sentence 14 are effectively used. Short cumulative sentences ending with present participial phrases (sentences 2, 6, 8, 9) function perfectly. Short sentences 7 and 15 and the rather long periodic sentence in the last paragraph (sentence 18) provide pleasing variety.

Diction: On the whole, the diction is natural, precise, and economical, though *blessed* in sentence 6 sounds unnatural and *thereby* would be more precise in sentence 20 than *therefore.*

Mechanics: Excellent.

Injustice to Negroes

1 Negroes have been denied many rights throughout the history of the United States. 2 A poll tax, the act of charging a Negro to vote, was used very effectively until the Supreme Court declared it unconstitutional. 3 Sarah Jones, a middle-aged Negro, was denied the right to vote by means of the poll tax in the 1952 presidental election. 4 Mrs. Jones lived in the slums of Birmingham, Alabama, and was financially unable to pay money charged Negro citizens to vote.

5 Voting again has been denied by means of the grandfather's clause. 6 If a Negroes ancestors were qualified to vote before the Civil War, then he could vote. 7 A very large majority of Negroes were unable to vote because of this qualification. 8 James Berry, on his twenty-first birthday, went to register for the state primary in the nomination of the governor; he was denied the right to register because his great-grandfather had not voted before the Civil War.

9 The literacy test provided an effective means to disqualify a Negro from the privilege of voting; only in recent years has this been declared unconstitutional.

10 William Sloan, a sixty-five year old, a member of the middle income class, was asked to state the Bill of Rights as it was written by our forefathers. 11 Mr. Sloan failed the literacy test and was unable to vote; but Mrs. Clark, a white woman, was granted the privilege of voting without a literacy test.

12 The denial of education to Negro children has played a major role in the history of the United States. 13 The Supreme Court upheld for many years the separate but equal theory derived from the case of Plessey vs. White Schools, but the government failed to meet the provision that the schools with Negro children attending would have the same facilities as the schools with white children attending. 14 A young Negro man applied to enroll at a College of Law. 15 He was denied admittance because the state had built an old building, dilapidated and quite small, for him to attend college in.

16 Brown vs. Board of Education ruled that Negroes have to be admitted to white schools, however behind the scene practices continue to take place. 17 Very few Negroes today attend colleges or universities.

18 Many instances occur and reoccur through the history of the United States showing that Negroes have been denied the right to vote and the right to equal education. 19 Devices to get around the law will probably always occur. 20 John Doe, a Negro, can still be denied the right to vote today.

Comments on "Injustice to Negroes"

Arrangement: Two subclasses of injustice are discussed—unfair voting rules and inferior schools. The second subclass, the development of which begins in the fourth paragraph, comes as a surprise, however, because after naming the general class, injustice, in sentence 1, the writer immediately refers to the poll tax as a subclass. Before the poll tax is mentioned, the more general subclass that covers it, voting rules, should be established. The reader would then anticipate a second subclass. The organization, on the whole, is good, the two major subclasses being clearly divided from each other and the examples being well arranged.

Content: The content is interesting and important, but some of the examples are imprecise and some of the details inaccurate. The reference to the grandfather's clause is vague. Where was the restriction described here as the grandfather's clause imposed, and when? City and year are not given in the example here (in sentence 8) as they are in sentence 3. In sentences 3, 4, 8, 10, and 11 the writer's sources of information for the examples are not specified. Has she known the persons to whom she refers and witnessed their difficulties, or is she using a source in which an author states that he has known the persons and has witnessed their difficulties? If she has not known them or is not using a factual source, they are not examples, even though they may represent typical practices. An example is needed in sentence 14, but the reference to "a young Negro man" is too general to serve as an example. In sentence 2 the poll tax is incorrectly defined. In the seven states where the poll tax was imposed, it had the effect of barring more Negroes than whites from voting, but it was a tax that everyone who voted in those states had to pay. The precise name of the case referred to in sentence 13 is *Plessy vs. Ferguson* (1896).

Sentence Structure: Good, especially in the handling of appositives, as in sentences 2, 3, and 11, and compound sentences, such as sentences 8, 9, 11, and 13.

Diction: There are no errors in diction.

Mechanics:

Sentence 3: *Presidential* is misspelled.

Sentence 6: *Negroes,* a plural form is misused for the singular possessive form, *Negro's.*

Sentence 16: The comma before *however* is incorrect. When *however* joins sentence patterns, a semicolon should be placed before it and a comma after it.

Sentence 18: A comma should be placed after *States* to set off the present participial phrase following it.

CLASSIFICATION WITH PROGRESSION

A writer organizing by classification will sometimes see in the subclasses a progression in time, importance, quality, or degree. If one is discussing the subclasses of municipal taxes a ,family in a given area has to pay, for example, he may arrange the subclasses according to the dates when the taxes were imposed or according to their importance (from the most expensive to the least, or *vice versa*). If he is discussing types of fur coats available for men, he may organize the subclasses according to quality, as suggested by price. If he is discussing childhood diseases, he may organize the subclasses according to degrees of seriousness.

The structure of the following essay by James Thurber is a classification with progression.

The Lady on the Bookcase

James Thurber

One day twelve years ago an outraged cartoonist, four of whose drawings had been rejected in a clump by *The New Yorker,* stormed into the office of the late Harold Ross, editor of the magazine. 'Why is it,' demanded the cartoonist, 'that you reject my work and publish drawings by a fifth-rate artist like Thurber?' Ross came quickly to my defence like the true friend and devoted employer he was. 'You mean third-rate,' he said quietly, but there was a warning glint in his steady grey eyes that caused the discomfited cartoonist to beat a hasty retreat.

With the exception of Ross, the interest of editors in what I draw has been rather more journalistic than critical. They want to know if it is true that I draw by moonlight, or under water, and when I say no, they lose interest until they hear the rumour that I found the drawings in an old trunk or that I do the captions while my nephew makes the sketches.

The other day I was shoving some of my originals around on the floor (I do not draw on the floor; I was just shoving the originals around) and they fell, or perhaps I pushed them, into five separate and indistinct categories. I have never wanted to write about my drawings, and I still don't want to, but it occurred to me that it might be a good idea to do it now, when everybody is busy with something else, and get it over quietly.

Category No. 1, then, which may be called the Unconscious or Stream of Nervousness category, is represented by 'With you I have known peace, Lida, and now you say you're going crazy' and the drawing entitled with simple dignity, 'Home.' These drawings were done while the artist was thinking of something else (or so he has been assured by experts) and hence his hand was guided by the Unconscious which, in turn, was more or less influenced by the Subconscious.

Students of Jung have instructed me that Lida and the House-Woman are representations of the *anima,* the female essence or directive which floats around in the ageless universal Subconscious of Man like a tadpole in a cistern. Less intellectual critics insist that the two ladies are actual persons I have consciously known. Between these two schools of thought lies a discouragingly large space of time extending roughly from 1,000,000 B.C. to the middle nineteen thirties.

Whenever I try to trace the true identity of the House-Woman, I get to thinking of Mr. Jones. He appeared in my office one day twelve years ago, said he was Mr. Jones, and asked me to lend him 'Home' for reproduction in an art magazine. I never saw the drawing again. Tall, well-dressed, kind of sad-looking chap, and as well spoken a gentleman as you would want to meet.

Category No. 2 brings us to Freud and another one of those discouragingly large spaces—namely, the space between the Concept of the Purely Accidental

"With you I have known peace, Lida, and now you say you're going crazy."

Home.

"All right, have it your way—you heard a seal bark!"

and the Theory of Haphazard Determination. Whether chance is capricious or we are all prisoners of pattern is too long and cloudy a subject to go into here. I shall consider each of the drawings in Category No. 2, explaining what happened and leaving the definition of the forces involved up to you. The seal on top of the bed, then ('All right, have it your way—you heard a seal bark'), started out to be a seal on a rock. The rock, in the process of being drawn, began to look like the head of a bed, so I made a bed out of it, put a man and wife in the bed, and stumbled onto the caption as easily and unexpectedly as the seal stumbled into the bedroom.

The woman on top of the bookcase ('That's my first wife up there, and this is the *present* Mrs. Harris') was originally designed to be a woman crouched on the top step of a staircase, but since the tricks and conventions of perspective and planes sometimes fail me, the staircase assumed the shape of a bookcase and was finished as such, to the surprise and embarrassment of the first Mrs. Harris, the present Mrs. Harris, the lady visitor, Mr. Harris and me. Before *The New Yorker* would print the drawing, they phoned me long distance to inquire whether the first Mrs. Harris was alive or dead or stuffed. I replied that my taxidermist had advised me that you cannot stuff a woman, and that my physician had informed

"That's my first wife up there, and this is the *present* Mrs. Harris."

"For the last time—you and your horsie get away from me and stay away!"

"The father belonged to some people who were driving through in a Packard."

me that a dead lady cannot support herself on all fours. This meant, I said, that the first Mrs. Harris was unquestionably alive.

The man riding on the other man's shoulders in the bar ('For the last time, you and your horsie get away from me and stay away!') was intended to be standing alongside the irate speaker, but I started his head up too high and made it too small, so that he would have been nine feet tall if I had completed his body that way. It was but the work of thirty-two seconds to put him on another man's shoulders. As simple or, if you like, as complicated as that. The psychological factors which may be present here are, as I have indicated, elaborate and confused. Personally, I like Dr. Claude Thornway's theory of the Deliberate Accident or Conditioned Mistake.

Category No. 3 is perhaps a variant of Category No. 2; indeed, they may even be identical. The dogs in 'The father belonged to some people who were driving through in a Packard' were drawn as a captionless spot, and the interior with figures just sort of grew up around them. The hippopotamus in 'What have you done with Dr. Millmoss?' was drawn to amuse my small daughter. Something about the creature's expression when he was completed convinced me that he had recently eaten a man. I added the hat and pipe and Mrs. Millmoss, and the caption followed easily enough. Incidentally, my daughter, who was two years old at the time, identified the beast immediately. 'That's a hippotomanus,' she said. *The New Yorker* was not so smart. They described the drawing for their files as follows: 'Woman with strange animal.' *The New Yorker* was nine years old at the time.

Category No. 4 is represented by perhaps the best known of some fifteen

"What have you done with Dr. Millmoss?"

"Touché!"

"Well, I'm disenchanted, too. We're *all* disenchanted."

drawings belonging to this special grouping, which may be called the Contributed Idea Category. This drawing ('Touché!') was originally done for *The New Yorker* by Carl Rose, caption and all. Mr. Rose is a realistic artist, and his gory scene distressed the editors, who hate violence. They asked Rose if he would let me have the idea, since there is obviously no blood to speak of in the people I draw. Rose graciously consented. No one who looks at 'Touché!' believes that the man whose head is in the air is really dead. His opponent will hand it back to him with profuse apologies, and the discommoded fencer will replace it on his shoulders and say, 'No harm done, forget it.' Thus the old controversy as to whether death can be made funny is left just where it was before Carl Rose came along with his wonderful idea.

    Category No. 5, our final one, can be called, believe it or not, the Intentional or Thought-Up Category. The idea for each of these two drawings just came to me and I sat down and made a sketch to fit the prepared caption. Perhaps, in the case of 'Well, I'm disenchanted, too. We're *all* disenchanted,' another one of those Outside Forces played a part. That is, I may have overheard a husband say to his wife, on the street or at a party, 'I'm disenchanted.' I do not think this is true, however, in the case of the rabbit-headed doctor and his woman patient. I believe that scene and its caption came to me one night in bed. I may have got the idea in a doctor's office or a rabbit hutch, but I don't think so.

    As my eyesight grew dimmer, the paper I drew on grew larger, and even though I used a heavy black crayon, the fine Ohio clarity of my work diminished. In one of my last drawings I had to make the eyes of a young lady so large that it was easy to arrive at the caption: 'Where did you get those big brown eyes and that tiny mind?' Seven years ago I shifted to luminous white crayon on dead black paper, and then finally gave up drawing altogether for writing, meditation, and drinking.

"You said a moment ago that everybody you look at seems to be a rabbit. Now just what do you mean by that, Mrs. Sprague?"

Most of my originals have disappeared, mysteriously or otherwise. Thirty were never heard of again after a show in Los Angeles. Several pretty girls with big brown eyes and minds of various sizes have swiped a dozen or so of the scrawls, and a man I loved, now dead, told me one day he had taken seven drawings from my office desk to give to some friends of his in California. That is what became of Dr. Millmoss, among others. My favourite loss, however, occurred at the varnishing, or vanishing, of a show of my drawings in London in 1937. Seems that someone eased a portfolio of two dog drawings. I'm mighty proud of that, and I like to think that Scotland Yard was duly informed of the incident. Theft is an even higher form of praise than emulation, for it carries with it the risk of fine and imprisonment, or, in the case of my 'work,' at least a mild dressing down by the authorities.

If you should ever run across 'Home' or 'What have you done with Dr. Millmoss?' write to me, not to J. Edgar Hoover. We are equally busy, but he would only be puzzled, and possibly irked. So much for my drawings, wherever they are.

1. Consider the names of the five subclasses (categories) in this essay. The progression in these subclasses is from what to what?
2. What is the class name that covers the five subclasses?

Classification with Progression

Select a subject that can be divided into three (or, at the most, four) subclasses. Make a classification diagram, including examples, before you begin to write. Use a climactic order in the arrangement of the subclasses, placing the most recently developed, the most important, the best, or the most appealing subclass last. Be sure to develop the last subclass at least as fully as the others.

Develop one example of each subclass in detail, using concrete nouns and precise, vivid modifiers. Use at least one cumulative sentence in the development of the examples.

Turn in your classification diagram with your theme.

A STUDENT CLASSIFICATION WITH PROGRESSION

Can you discern a principle of progression in the following theme? The theme is well organized, according to a classification scheme. Is the development of the subclasses well proportioned? Are any examples developed? Can you improve the wording at any point?

From Bubblegum to the Beatles

Rollah A. Aston

1 While the majority of groups that perform today's popular music are classified under the heading of *rock,* there are at least four distinct and separate categories within this large framework, each one having its own particular characteristics and audience appeal. 2 The first and simplest of these categories consists of the Bubblegum rock groups, so called because they appeal largely to teen-agers in the thirteen- to sixteen-year-old age bracket. 3 These groups play music that is simple in every aspect. 4 There are no complicated passages of lead guitar present, and the beat is often a basic one first used in the mid and late fifties. 5 The words usually express love in a very simple manner. 6 Two of the most successful Bubblegum groups are the Ohio Express, noted for their hit records "Yummy, Yummy, Yummy," and "Chewy, Chewy"; and the 1910 Fruitgum Company, with their hits "Simple Simon Says," and "1, 2, 3 Red Light."

FROM BUBBLEGUM TO THE BEATLES   Reprinted by permission.

7 The Blues, Psychedelic, and Acid rock groups make up the second main category. 8 A whining lead guitar, a strong beat that can be either fast or slow, and voices singing and screaming at a high level of intensity are characteristics of the music performed by these groups. 9 The age of the audience to which this music appeals is usually between seventeen and twenty-four. 10 The Jimmy Hendrix Experience, whose hit records include "Purple Haze" and "Fire," is perhaps the most widely followed of these groups. 11 Other groups are the Doors, the Grateful Dead, and Jefferson Airplane.

12 The third category consists of the Motown and soul groups. These groups, including the Temptations and the Four Tops, are usually comprised of blacks; they specialize in vocals. 13 A variety of instruments, ranging from saxophones to violins, are used as back-ups for these singers. 14 These groups have perhaps the widest range of audience appeal of all the four categories. 15 One of the Motown groups, Diana Ross and the Supremes, is followed by nine-year olds and adults as well. 16 The last main category is the "Good Music" rock group, including the Beatles and the Buffalo Springfield. 17 This kind of group performs music that has in it elements of classical, jazz, country-western, and just about every other type of music that has been in existence over a long period of time. 18 Many college professors and budding young composers are now discovering the magic present in many of the compositions played by these groups, such as the Beatles' "Yesterday" and "Michelle."

Definition

DIALOG 6

The Relation of Classification and Example to Definition

1. Suppose that on a rainy day when nothing's happening, you open *Webster's Seventh New Collegiate Dictionary* to read for an hour or two. It may be that you will come upon the word *crucible* and see that it is defined as "a pot of very refractory material used for melting and calcining a substance that requires a high degree of heat." Why should this definition remind you of the classification diagram?	The first thing I am told is that *crucible* is a subclass that belongs to the class *pot*. I see before me: pot crucible

2. Why are you given the second part of the definition, "of a very refractory material used for melting and calcining a substance that requires a high degree of heat"?	So that I will not confuse a crucible with some other kind of pot, like a crock or a flower pot.
3. What kind of information are you given that will help you distinguish it from another kind of pot?	The kind of material it is made of and the use to which it is put.
4. The dictionary definition does what, in the terms of a classification diagram?	It relates the word to a larger class and distinguishes it from other words in the same class.
5. Ever since Aristotle, the great classifier among ancient Greek philosophers, introduced the classification form for definitions, it has been the most common form. He used these terms to describe it: *Definition of term = genus + differentia.* Can you translate this into words that we have been using?	Definition of term = class to which the thing belongs (*genus*) + characteristics that distinguish this thing from others in its class (*differentia*).
6. Can you picture a crucible from having read an Aristotelian type of definition of *crucible?*	No.
7. What does it leave out that you are accustomed to seeing in a classification diagram?	Examples.
8. How could you be given examples of *crucible?*	I could be given detailed descriptions of specific crucibles, I could be shown pictures of specific crucibles, or I could be taken to a steel plant and shown some crucibles at blast furnaces.
9. Suppose that before being shown the blast furnaces you had not seen a dictionary definition of *crucible* and had not heard crucibles discussed. Suppose, further, that you were shown fifteen specific crucibles. Would you be entirely satisfied with your understanding of *crucible?*	If I had seen fifteen crucibles *being used*, I might be satisfied with my understanding of *crucible*, but I would find it difficult to talk about crucibles if I had not heard them discussed.

10. Classifying words and distinguishing words in the same class—that is, relating a specific image to a system of thought—is essential to communication. A comprehensive definition of a word like *crucible* will combine the Aristotelian form with at least one example. Can you describe a comprehensive definition in an equation?	Definition of term = *genus + differentia + example.*
11. Of the types of words that we classified in Preliminary Distinctions—simple specific words, composite specific words, class words, unique words, and nonconcrete words—which type is best suited to definition by the equation stated above?	Class words are best suited to definition by this equation.
12. · Why is definition by this equation not suitable to the definition of specific words—either simple or composite?	Because though one can give the genus and differentia of a specific word, one cannot give an example, since the term itself stands for an example.
13. To define a specific term one would have to add a description or a picture to the Aristotelian definition or show the object being defined. If the specific word were a composite word like *Taiwan, The Atlantic Monthly,* or *Phi Beta Kappa,* how would you proceed in writing the description?	I would divide the referent into parts or aspects.
14. Is there any difference between a subclass and an aspect or a part?	Yes, a subclass has in it all of the characteristics of the class, but a part or an aspect does not.
15. To illustrate: *crucible* is a subclass of *pot* because it stands for "a rounded metal or earthen container"; but *education in Taiwan* is not a subclass of Taiwan, because it does not stand for an island off the southeast coast of China, ruled by Nationalist Chinese. Why does a unique term not lend itself to the Aristotelian form of definition?	It is too comprehensive to be classified.
16. The nonconcrete term *love* is defined in *Webster's Seventh* as an "affection based on admiration or benevolence." Is this the Aristotelian form of definition?	Yes.

17. Can you give an example of *love?*	No, since *love* is nonconcrete and judgmental, I cannot give an example of it as I can give an example of *crucible,* but I can describe a specific situation in which I think love is being expressed.
18. If one assumes that other nonconcrete words behave as *love* does, what can one generalize about defining nonconcrete words?	One can give this formula: Definition of term = *genus + differentia + description of a situation judged to express the idea in terms of specific persons, places, or objects.*
19. Please summarize this dialog by explaining how to define a class word, a specific composite word, and a nonconcrete word.	To define a class word, state the *genus* (larger class to which the word belongs) + the *differentia* (characteristics that distinguish this word from others in the same class) + an *example* (the term that refers to a specific object in the subclass, a description of a specific object in the subclass, a picture of the specific object, or the specific object itself). To define a specific composite word, give the *genus + differentia +* an *analysis* (description of parts or aspects). To define a nonconcrete word, give the *genus + differentia +* a *specific situation* (a situation judged to express the idea in terms of specific persons, places, or objects).

EXERCISE 9

Writing Definitions

A. Describe the type of definition you would use for each of the following terms:

1. *bolt* (noun)   4. *shrimp*
2. *absurdity*   5. *loneliness*
3. *Encyclopædia Britannica*   6. *joke* (noun)

B. Select two of the terms above and write a definition of each, using the method you have described as appropriate.

DIFFICULTIES IN DEFINING GENERAL NONCONCRETE WORDS

The inclination to give short, pat definitions of very general nonconcrete words is a symptom of superficial thinking, and superficiality of thought in regard to such words is quite serious, since it influences one's behavior and one's judgments of other people. We can see how strong that tendency is in most of our minds when we stop to think how seldom we use subclass words of general value words like *freedom, imperialism, oppression, justice,* and *morality.* When we make a judgment of a specific situation, we often do it in very general terms. There must be as many possible subclasses of justice and other very general nonconcrete concepts as there are subclasses of automobiles, but the names for these subclasses are not in common use. If we can judge thinking from words used to express thoughts, we must conclude that we speakers of the English language tend to be more discriminating in our discussions of material objects than we are in our discussions of values.

In the following essay, Richard Peters discusses at length the definition of *morality* (in paragraphs 3–10). Does he ever define *morality?* Are the questions he raises and the distinctions he makes in types of morality more instructive than a brief definition would be?

Rules with Reasons: The Bases of Moral Education

Richard Peters

1 To the question—why do problems of moral education loom so large nowadays?—an obvious answer is that standards are no longer stable. A moral code cannot be taken for granted as it could, say, fifty years ago. Not that people now tend to fall short more frequently of the standards which they set themselves; rather there is much more dispute about what such standards should be. Older people are often shocked, not because the young have no standards but because they seem to have different ones.

2 There is something to this thesis, but not, I would suggest, quite as much as is often claimed. Perhaps in more settled and stable times parents were able to pass on a code, the details of which could be adequate for their children. When such conditions no longer obtained, after World War I, it is true that some of the younger generation did revolt on certain matters, proclaiming defiantly that morals were merely a matter of private feeling or of individual decision. But both

RULES WITH REASONS: THE BASES OF MORAL EDUCATION   From *The Nation,* January 13, 1969. Reprinted with permission of *The Nation.*

their subjective stance and the reliance of the older generation on a tradition seem equally inadequate at this time. For, on the one hand, it sounds pretty thin to suggest that telling lies and being cruel are wrong just because of one's private feelings or personal decisions; and on the other hand, established traditions palpably cannot deal adequately with such an issue as sexual morality. The task of this generation is to work out a morality that does justice both to the "Victorian" view and to the progressive protest against it. My present purpose is to mark out such a middle road.

3 The first task is to identify what we are talking about when we speak of morals. What *is* a moral matter as distinct from a legal or religious one? The question is not as simple as it sounds, for moral rules cannot be identified simply by their content. Theft, murder and incest, for instance, are against the law; they are also religious sins and defy custom. And they are thought immoral. On the other hand there are some rules like those against lying and the breaking of promises that are generally matters of morality, and matters of law only under very special circumstances. Still other practices, like spitting, are highly indeterminate. Is it immoral to spit in the street? It is against the law in the subway, but in some homes it is quite customary when near a fire. What makes some say that it is an immoral practice and not just a filthy habit? What lies behind the conviction that some rules are matters of morality and others not?

4 It is surely the suggestion that *reasons* support such concepts as *good, right, wrong* and *ought* which gives them the status of moral rules. Such reasons mark out their importance. A rule is a rule of law if, roughly speaking, it has issued from a determinate source such as a king, a parliament or a judge. It may or may not be backed by what we would deem a sufficient reason, or deal with a matter of moral importance. If, on the other hand, we call something like shaking hands a matter of *custom,* we suggest that there's no such determinate source. Heaven knows where it came from and there may or may not be some point to it. If we were to speak of it as a moral rule, however, that would imply a reason, however limited.

5 To say that moral rules are those which have some backing in reasons does not, of course, go far enough; for reasons may be very peculiar. Imagine, for instance, a discussion about corporal punishment in which one person is against it because it gives rise to bruises. "What is wrong with a few bruises?" asks the other. "They turn blue," replies the opponent of such drastic measures, "and our bounden duty is to minimize the amount of blueness in the world. It's such a horrible color." We would think such a man morally mad, even though he gave reasons for his policies. And this would be because his fundamental principle, which made reasons relevant to him, was "Minimize the blueness in the world" instead of our commonly accepted principle of "Minimize suffering."

6 I've introduced this rather grotesque example merely to indicate the crucial point that fundamental principles are needed to make reasons relevant, and to confer *importance* on the moral rules which they support. The task of the moral philosopher is to show why a principle such as "Minimize suffering" is defensible, whereas a principle such as "Maximize suffering" or "Minimize blueness" is not. I cannot pursue the crucial task of justifying fundamental principles

any further in this article.* I shall have to assume a general agreement that some fundamental principles—such as those of fairness, freedom, respect for persons and the like—are justifiable and that others are not. Such abstract higher order principles lie behind the conviction that matters like theft and the breaking of promises are wrong, and other things like holding a fork in the left hand, rather than in the right, are merely conventions. When, too, we wonder about the morality of such acts as spitting or extramarital sex relations we are looking at them through peepholes provided by such principles. The principles make us take account of some aspects of these practices rather than others.

7 My example, too, brings out the further point that there are different *levels* of morality. A small number of fundamental higher order principles are appealed to for justification of other lower order moral rules. Our duty, for instance, to obey the government obviously derives from more abstract principles such as the protection of the general welfare. But these lower-order rules are not all of a piece. Some rules, like those relating to spitting, depend very much on time and place; others, like those concerned with contracts or with noninjury to the person, are not as relative. Indeed it is difficult to conceive of a society of men in which some such rules did not obtain.

8 This, I think, is where one of the widespread muddles about morality creeps in; people do not distinguish among the different types of rules within a moral system. They will think that because some rules, say about gambling or sex, are relative and depend very much on time, place and circumstances, *all* moral rules are similarly relative. In parts of Africa, it is said, men are encouraged to have more than one wife; in Europe only one; in the United States only one at a time. Therefore, all morals as to marriage are relative. And fraud, murder, rape and theft are then presumably just as "culture-bound" as spitting in the street!

9 It should not be thought, either, that any simple appeal to a lack of consensus about moral rules necessarily establishes anything of ultimate significance about their validity. If consensus were the acid test of validity, science would also be in an insecure position; for the scientific view of the world is accepted by only a minority of the human race. If there are good reasons for moral or scientific beliefs, the fact that many cannot grasp them is irrelevant. There are probably many in the Trobriand Islands—or in England—who cannot grasp Newton's laws. Is our estimate of their truth affected by this deficiency?

10 Those who attack "absolute" moral principles often develop another type of argument. They say that such principles cannot be absolute because there are circumstances in which they must be bent a bit. What about "white lies"? What about breaking a promise to save someone's life? This is really a very feeble objection, because most people who believe that there are fundamental principles of morality also claim that these principles are subject to an "other things being equal" clause. If there is more than one fundamental principle, it must sometimes be the case that there is a conflict of principle. A person must nevertheless act in such cases, and whatever he does, *one* of his principles is infringed. A "white lie" is not told out of inclination or for gain or glory. It is told when the truth

---

° See my *Ethics and Education* (Allen and Unwin, 1966).

might cause needless suffering. In such a case other things are *not* equal. But because there are *some* cases where a principle must be infringed, nothing follows about the general duties involved. The general duty to tell the truth is not undermined by the fact that on rare occasions other duties are more urgent.

11 I have spent so much time on the refinements of morality before mentioning anything about moral *education* because I believe that efforts at moral education on the part of well-meaning parents and teachers are often hamstrung by confusions of the sort that I have indicated. The realization that some moral matters are far from straightforward leads to a generalized agnosticism about morality and to a lack of firmness in handing on rules to children. Children, it is proclaimed, must decide such issues for themselves. As if anyone—let alone a child—ever decided for himself that lying and cruelty are wrong!

12 Actually a child is well along to maturity before he can assess the rules which structure his life, can work out a code "of his own." This parallels the history of the race; for morality, as a code distinct from religion, custom and law, took a very long time to emerge. A small child lacks the subtlety of discrimination required to distinguish matters of morality from matters of law and custom, let alone to decide "for himself" on his moral principles.

13 How then can this process get started? Obviously this child must learn to use concepts such as "right," "wrong," and "ought." How can he do so except by being initiated into the code of a community, into a tradition? Much is picked up by imitation and identification—especially in the sphere of attitudes to others. But morality is not a skill like swimming, to be learned purely by imitation; it involves learning a whole family of concepts, which cannot be acquired without a great deal of instruction and explanation. Parents often think that they are teaching children not to steal by scolding or punishing them when they take what belongs to somebody else. They do not ask themselves whether the child has yet the concept of property, of people having rights to things, and of distinctions like that between lending and giving. Without a grasp of this family of concepts, a child cannot properly understand what stealing is. Moral education must always take account of where children are, and that requires considerable imagination. Because of his limited conceptual apparatus, a child's actions look quite different to him and to the adults who are judging him.

14 But learning to be moral is not just a matter of learning to apply concepts correctly to certain situations; it is also a matter of learning to behave consistently in the required way. Rules must regulate something and what they regulate are human inclinations. Children must develop early the habit of regulating their inclinations. They will usually learn to do this gradually if there is a steady and predictable pressure from their parents; for one of the most valid generalizations about human behavior is that people behave overwhelmingly in accordance with their understanding of what is expected and approved. That is why *consistency* on the part of parents is so important. If a child is brought up within a firm framework of rules, and is consistently approved of when he conforms to them, he will gradually take the rules into his own mind. In this way a firm basis of habits can be laid down. Without that start, a later development of an autonomous code is most unlikely. For how can children learn to adopt rules of their own

and also learn to apply them intelligently to varying situations if they have not learned from the inside what constitutes a moral rule?

15 Very young children do not properly understand moral concepts. By that I mean that, though they can learn to regulate their inclinations with the consciousness that certain things are right and wrong, their grasp of the *grounds* for such judgments is very hazy. They regard rules, so Piaget argues, as more or less transcendentally laid down. The notion of the validity of rules, and that they are grounded in principles, takes much longer to dawn. So it is pointless to expect very young children to do what they should because they see the reasons for it. That will come later as their understanding increases and their sympathies and loyalties begin to extend to their contemporaries. In the early stages they have to learn to do what is right without properly understanding why.

16 Many readers may be shocked by such a suggestion. If so, it is perhaps because their view of learning is modeled too much on "discovery methods" in, say, mathematics whereby children can be induced, through appropriate questioning, to grasp principles, to have "insight," etc. That is one very important way of learning, but it obviously has little application to such things as mechanical skills or historical facts. The beginning of wisdom in understanding human learning is to realize that there are many ways of learning and many different *types* of things that have to be learned. And one of the palpable facts is that most things in life must be learned *before* they are properly understood. In any case, understanding is usually a matter of degree. Young children learn that bodies fall to the ground if you drop them; but they cannot possibly understand why. Indeed, how many educated adults can explain gravity? In the learning of skills, such as golf or cooking, great proficiency can be attained by a mixture of practice and imitation, without the slightest understanding of the underlying principles. Morality is not just a body of beliefs; nor is it merely a system of skills. But it is like both in that during the early stages traditions must be accepted on trust from those with more experience and wisdom. Trust is essential, for without that relationship between parent or teacher and child the basic body of rules cannot be imparted with firmness and without fear.

17 What should form the content of a basic body of rules to provide the substance for a tradition? It would obviously include either fundamental principles themselves, such as the consideration of people's interests; or such rules as those relating to respect for persons, for property and for the keeping of contracts, that fall under the fundamental principles. A few such rules can be insisted on, without constantly correcting children over trivialities. Many conscientious parents seem to me to lack discrimination in this respect. They make as much fuss over table manners and tidiness as they do over lying and stealing. If children are hemmed in by rules, they have trouble developing a sense of what is morally important and what is not. I often doubt that parents are clear about this themselves!

18 Children vary greatly in the pace of their development, and no hard and fast rules can be laid down as to when the giving of reasons will begin to bite on a child's behavior. But one thing is apparent—reasons will be ineffective until the child's psychological development has reached the point where they

awaken some response in him. A good reason for keeping a promise is the inconvenience caused to others if it is broken. But what does that mean to a boy who cares nothing about others? How can he even be moved by respect for persons if he has not gained the sympathy out of which such an attitude arises? How the psychological underpinning for morality emerges is a matter for psychologists, but I suspect that children largely learn to care if they are brought up by those whose own sympathy spreads like a contagion.

19 If all goes well, as the child begins to develop interests and companions outside the home, his capacity for moral reasoning will also develop—that is, if he is *encouraged* to discuss different points of view. In our highly differentiated society he will find that he has much need for such a capacity, because on many matters he will find that standards conflict. He may find, too, that social changes make some of his parents' views seem a bit old-fashioned—at least on matters that do not fall under basic moral rules. At that point there is some justification for saying that he must decide for himself where he stands. He will, however, be able to do so only if his early training has given him the necessary equipment. It is most unlikely that he will find that his parents have been mistaken on basic rules such as those relating to injury to the person and to property and to the keeping of contracts. On more relative matters, such as thrift, business ethics or sex relations, he may come to think that they are mistaken. It would be surprising nowadays if an adolescent of any spirit accepted all his parents' standards! But at least he should learn to accept or reject elements in the tradition into which he has been initiated by seeing how they square with fundamental principles. A solid basis of rules has to be passed on in such a way that a sane and sensitive morality can grow out of it. Reason must have an inheritance of traditions to work upon.

20 The view of morality I have here advanced assigns a crucial role to the authority of parents and teachers, both in laying down a foundation of moral rules and in encouraging children, as they develop, to strike out on their own. So I must end by saying a bit about authority, for I think that on this matter, also, there are many muddles. Our society has staged a successful revolt against the *traditional* concept of authority which gave unlimited prerogatives to men over women, to parents over children, to employers over employees. But in overthrowing this patriarchal type of authority we have tended to go too far, concluding that there is no place at all for authority—save, of course, in the sphere of law and state action. This all-or-none reaction overlooks the fact that in school and home, as well as in the state, there is a paramount need for authority—provided that it is *rationalized* and carefully related to the tasks at hand and the individuals concerned.

21 Authority is what bridges the gap between the generations, for unless authority figures are identified and accepted, knowledge and skill can be handed on only by coercion or bribery. In the old days children were often driven to learning things that were difficult. Progressive teachers in revolt against this approach appealed to the methods of the supermarket, where a premium is placed on appetite. The treatment of children fell in with the tendency of modern industrial societies to gear everything to consumer wants. Progressive therapists tended

to forget the extreme plasticity of children's desires and the enormous part played by identification with others. This oversight is relevant both to the formation of wants and to the taking in of rules to control and channel them. Authority enters here as an intermediary between bribery and coercion. It should not be used, of course, to keep children in subservience but to bring about identification with the elements of a society that must be transmitted. A child may become interested in learning something like metal work because he admires his teacher; he may take into himself the code of a beloved parent. But unless he comes to sense what there is of value in the cherished pursuit, unless he comes to feel subjectively the rightness of a course of action, the teacher and parent have failed. Their task is to use their authority so that another generation will eventually grasp what there is of merit for itself in a style of life. They must work hard, in other words, to do themselves out of a job.

22 As children get older, self-discipline should take the place of imposed discipline. Constraints become internalized and children begin to weigh from within the validity of their promptings. But their tendency to be self-critical, to develop a code of their own, depends on the extent to which they must have kept critical company. The dialogue within reflects the dialogue without; that is why discussion is so important during adolescence. Those in authority over children will, therefore, attempt to get children to do what is sensible by appealing to their common sense instead of ordering them around or appealing to their own status. They will not say, "I'm your father and I'm telling you not to smoke," but will point out the dangers involved. It is a further question, however, whether a child's acceptance of good reasons should be the final criterion for his action. If a parent explains to a child why it is stupid and wrong to put objects on railway lines, and yet sees him doing so, will he stand aside and reflect that the boy is learning to choose? Parents must weigh their own fundamental principles against what is instructive for their children.

23 Example, of course, is crucial. Parents and others must provide a pattern out of which the child can eventually develop his own style of self-regulation. This is not likely to happen unless exercise of authority is rationalized and sensitively adapted to age, to persons, and to the tasks in hand. For the young will rightly rebel against the irrational expression of a traditional status. In brief, teachers and parents must learn to be in authority without being authoritarian.

---

1. When Richard Peters asks, "What *is* a moral matter as distinct from a legal or religious one?" which part of the definition of *a moral matter*—genus, differentia, or specific situation—is he considering?
2. When he asks the following question, which part of the definition seems uncertain? "What lies behind the conviction that some rules are matters of morality and others not?" (paragraph 3, the last sentence)
3. What is the point of the anecdote about minimizing the amount of blueness in the world?
4. Restate in your own words the main idea of paragraph 8.
5. In paragraphs 9 and 10 Peters tries to refute two assumptions about absolute moral rules. What are these assumptions?

6. If absoluteness does not rest on consensus, what does it rest on? Does Peters explain the basis for his assumption that some moral rules are absolute?

SUGGESTED WRITING ASSIGNMENT

Definition of a Subclass of a General Nonconcrete Word

Richard Peters assumes that moral rules fall into two big subclasses, absolute rules and relative rules. Do you agree? If you do not, what would you call subclasses of *moral rule?* Select one of Peters' subclasses or one of yours and list less general subclasses under it. Then write a definition of one of these less general subclasses, and illustrate it by descriptions of two specific situations that in your opinion express the essential characteristics of the less general subclass.

Generalization

DIALOG 7

The Anatomy of the Generalization

Please refer to these sets of statements as you read the questions following. The statements are arranged on levels, like terms in an abstraction ladder, though the nonverbal levels are omitted.

Set A
6. Plants grow in most parts of the world.
5. Cacti (or cactuses) grow in Arizona.
4. Saguaros grow in Tucson and its environs.
3. A six-foot saguaro with no arms is growing in the southeast corner of my front yard.

Set B
6.
5. Some elderly men drive even new automobiles slowly.
4. Elderly men who live in our neighborhood drive their Chevrolets slowly.
3. Frederick C. Hendricks, my seventy-five-year-old neighbor, never drives his 1970 Caprice faster than thirty-five miles an hour.

Set C
6. Some athletes excel.
5. Some baseball players have set records.
4.
3.

1. In Set A, which of the four statements is specific?	A six-foot saguaro with no arms is growing in the southeast corner of my front yard.
2. What makes it a specific statement?	It has a specific subject (*a six-foot saguaro with no arms*, which is roughly equivalent to $saguaro_1$).
3. Is this specific statement a report of a perception?	Yes.
4. Is statement 4 more general than statement 3?	Yes.
5. Why?	It is more general because its subject, *saguaros*, is more general than the subject of statement 3 (*a six-foot saguaro with no arms*).
6. Why is statement 6 the most general of the four?	It is the most general because its subject, *plants*, is more general than *cacti*, which is more general than *saguaros*.
7. What is essential to a general statement?	A general term is essential.
8. What is essential to a specific statement?	A specific term or a class term made specific by description is essential.
9. Is statement 3 in Set A an example?	Yes.
10. What is the saguaro growing in my front yard an example of?	It is an example of a saguaro growing in Tucson (statement 4), of a cactus growing in Arizona (statement 5), and of a plant growing in the world (statement 6).

11. Is statement 4 in Set A an example?	No.
12. Is it less general than statement 5?	Yes, but it is not specific and is therefore not an example.
13. Study Set B, thinking of the relationship of each statement to each of the others. Write a very general statement for the sixth level.	Some elderly people drive their automobiles slowly.
14. Study Set C. For the fourth level, write a statement less general than statement 5. Write an example for the third level.	One possibility: 4. Some pitchers have set records by pitching scoreless innings. 3. Don Drysdale set a world's record by pitching $58\frac{2}{3}$ scoreless innings.
15. Can you state another example of statement 4 in Set C?	Walter Johnson once set a record by pitching 56 scoreless innings.
16. Is it easier to think of examples of statement 5?	Yes.
17. Why?	The more general a statement is, the more examples it covers.
18. Write a set of four statements with an example on the third level, a related general statement on the fourth, a more general related statement on the fifth, and a still more general related statement on the sixth.	Individual answer.
19. Consider the structure of the type of general statement we have been writing. In "Some baseball players have set records," what is the complete subject?	The complete subject is *some baseball players*.
20. What is the complete predicate?	The complete predicate is *have set records*.
21. Is there a general term in the complete subject?	Yes, *baseball players*.
22. Is there a general term in the complete predicate?	Yes, *records*.

23. How does the following set of statements differ from Sets A, B, and C?

Set D

6. Clarence Wilson is thoughtful of others.
5. Clarence Wilson is generous.
4. Clarence Wilson gives money to charitable organizations.
3. Clarence Wilson gave $350.00 to the Salvation Army on December 16, 1969.

A term in the complete predicate goes from very general to specific, but the subject is specific in all four statements.

---

24. Complete this ladder of statements.

Set E

6.
5.
4. Clara Louise Walters eats chocolates.
3. Clara Louise Walters is eating a Russell Stover's chocolate bon-bon.

6. Clara Louise Walters eats sweets.
5. Clara Louise Walters eats candy.

---

25. Is "Clara Louise Walters is eating a Russell Stover's chocolate bon-bon" an example of "Clara Louise Walters eats candy"?

Yes.

---

26. Can we conclude from what we have said so far that a statement is general when there is a general term in the complete subject and a general term in the complete predicate and that a statement is general when there is a general term in the complete predicate, even if the subject is specific?

Yes.

---

27. How does the following set of statements differ from Sets A, B, C, D, and E?

Set F

6. Insects have six legs.
5. Flies have six legs.
4. Horse flies have six legs.
3. The horse fly that just landed on your hand has six legs.

In Set F the general term in the predicate remains on the same high general level; in all of the others the term in the predicate has become less general, less general, less general, and finally specific.

28. What three types of general statements have been illustrated in this dialog?	1. The general statement in which there is a general term in both the complete subject and the complete predicate. 2. The general statement in which there is a general term in the complete predicate but not in the complete subject. 3. The general statement in which there is a general term in the complete subject but not in the complete predicate.
29. We shall call all three of these types of general statements generalizations. Write these sentences and mark the grammatical patterns with the symbols you used in marking the examples of basic sentence patterns (S(N), LV(V), and so forth). 　a. Insects have six legs. 　b. Clarence Wilson is generous. 　c. Some athletes excel. 　d. Plants grow in most parts of the world.	$\quad$ S(N$_1$)　TrV(V)　DO(N$_2$) a. Insects have　(six) legs. $\quad$ S(N)$\qquad\qquad$ LV(V) SC(Adj) b. Clarence Wilson is $\qquad$ generous. $\qquad\quad$ S(N)　InV(V) c. (Some) athletes excel. $\quad$ (SN)　InV(V) d. Plants grow (in most parts of the world).
30. Write and mark this classifying statement: There are three general types of poetry.	$\qquad$ InV(V)$\qquad\qquad\qquad$ S(N) /There/ are $\quad$ (three)(general) types (of poetry).
31. A classifying statement will be an expletive (*there*) transformation of S(N)–InV(V) or it will consist of wording that can be translated into a pattern of this kind. The classifying statement says only that certain types of something *are*, or *exist*. It does not predicate a characteristic of the types, except existence. How does a generalization differ from a classifying statement?	The classifying statement predicates only existence; the generalization predicates a characteristic of the subject besides existence.
32. The classifying statement and the generalization are two types of general statements. There are other types, but we are not concerned about them now. When we use the term *generalization*, will we be talking about a classifying statement?	No.

HOW GENERALIZATION RELATES TO FACT, VALUE JUDGMENT, AND INFERENCE

All of the statements in the sets in Dialog 7 are statements of fact. The following statements from this dialog are specific facts:

Don Drysdale set a world's record by pitching $58\frac{2}{3}$ scoreless innings.

Clarence Wilson gave $350.00 to the Salvation Army on December 16, 1969.

The horse fly that just landed on your hand has six legs.

The following statements from Dialog 7 are factual generalizations:

Some pitchers have set records by pitching scoreless innings.

Clarence gives money to charitable organizations.

Insects have six legs.

Factual generalizations are based on many observations of the same kind of detail, plus knowledge of a noncontroversial system of classification.

Generalizations may also be value judgments, as in this ladder of statements:

6. Economic conditions are getting worse.
5. The cost of living, unfortunately, is rising.
4. Food costs, unfortunately, are rising.
3. Unfortunately, the cost of a quart of milk went up three cents at Cane's Market last Thursday.

We can speak of specific judgments and judgmental generalizations.

Generalizations may be inferences, as in this ladder of statements:

6. The cost of living will continue to rise next year.
5. Food costs will rise next year.
4. The cost of dairy products will rise next year.
3. The price of milk will probably go up at Cane's Market again next year.

We can speak of specific inferences and inferential generalizations.

When you use generalizations as topic sentences of paragraphs or thesis statements of essays, you may be dealing with facts, inferences, or value judgments; but in all such papers you will be using specific statements as support.

EXERCISE 10

Writing Sets of Generalizations

1. Write a set of four factual generalizations on levels 3 through 6.
2. Write a set of four judgmental generalizations on levels 3 through 6.
3. Write a set of four inferential generalizations on levels 3 through 6.

DIALOG 8

Generalizations That Are Effective as Topic Sentences or Thesis Statements

1. Suppose that a fifteen-year-old girl who lives next door to Mrs. Filmore brushed by her in front of her house one morning without speaking, and a fourteen-year-old boy who lives down the street walked through her living room one day with mud on his boots and a cap on his head. Suppose that after these incidents, Mrs. Filmore concludes, "Teen-agers these days have bad manners." Why is her generalization not reliable?	*Teen-agers*, since it is unqualified, means *all teen-agers*, and Mrs. Filmore cannot judge all teen-agers from the behavior of two.
2. If she had said, "Many teen-agers these days have bad manners," would her generalization have been reliable?	No. This statement, with *many* as the qualifier, could not have been drawn responsibly from two examples.
3. Would "Some teen-agers these days have bad manners" be reliable?	Yes, because *some* can mean *a few.*
4. How does one determine whether a generalization is reliable?	One determines whether a generalization is reliable by considering whether the speaker or writer could have derived the generalization from examples that he has observed or read about in reports based on observations. If his generalization goes beyond his examples, he is overgeneralizing, or making an unreliable generalization.
5. Is "People are sometimes late" an interesting generalization?	No.
6. If not, why not?	It states an idea that everyone is familiar with; everyone can state examples from his observations.
7. Is "Worldwide, this year has been the year of student power" more interesting? (This statement was made in *Time*, June 7, 1968.)	Yes.

8. If so, why?	That student power is a worldwide force is a new, interesting idea, and though anyone can give some examples of student power, few persons can speak of student power around the world.
9. Generalizations used as topic sentences in paragraphs or as thesis statements for themes should be _____ and _____ .	reliable, interesting
10. If you are writing a paragraph or a short theme, how can you assure your reader that your generalization is reliable?	By using a generalization that would appear on the fourth level (at the highest, the fifth level) of the abstraction ladder. Statements that are more general cannot be adequately supported in a short paper.
11. What is the only way to support a fourth-level generalization adequately?	To give examples based on observation or on secondary reports.
12. Can generalizations be supported adequately without examples?	No. Examples must be given or must be clearly implied in less general statements about classes. There is no way to support a generalization except by reference to the specifics.
13. What will insure that your generalization is interesting?	Stating a common characteristic that the reader has not thought about, or giving examples the reader has not had an opportunity to observe.

A PATTERN OF ARRANGEMENT FOR EXAMPLES
DEVELOPING A GENERALIZATION

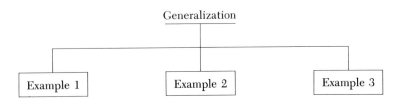

Generalization

In Hawthorne's stories unsophisticated characters
often have instinctive insight into reality hidden
beneath deceptive appearances.

Example 1	Example 2	Example 3
In *The Scarlet Letter,* the hypocritical Mr. Dimmesdale is shunned by children, even though adults believe him to be the perfect man that he appears to be.	In "Feathertop: A Moralized Legend," a little child is the only person who is not deceived by the scarecrow's impersonation of a man.	In *The House of the Seven Gables,* Phoebe Pyncheon, an unsophisticated young woman, shrinks from the touch of the hypocritical Judge Pyncheon, a cousin, even though he appears to be a benevolent man.

This pattern is similar to a classification diagram, but the generalization is stated as a complete sentence, and each example is stated as a complete sentence. A generalization is never just a subject, but always a subject with a predication.

SUGGESTED WRITING ASSIGNMENT

A Generalization Developed by Detailed Examples

Write a composition of two or three paragraphs in which you use two or three detailed examples or illustrations to develop a generalization that you have formed. Examples from reading are admissible, but examples from real life are preferred. Be sure that the generalization is a conclusion that *you* have formed.
    An example of this type of composition follows.

Special Insight

Dramatic irony occurs in real life as well as on stage. One afternoon I was sitting at the end of an 18-foot wooden bench in a narrow corridor of the basement of a university library, facing a row of five or six soft drink machines—

drinking a Coca-Cola that had cost me thirty cents. After having lost a dime in the first machine and another in the second, I had gratefully accepted a Coke from the third. Before sitting down, I had torn a sheet of paper in half, had written "Out of Order" on both halves, and had stuck my two "signs" up on the useless machines. In a moment, a tired-looking, bespectacled young man in a seersucker suit approached the first machine, read the sign, moved to the second machine, read the sign, and then put a dime in the third, taking his Coke without special gratitude. While I was drinking my Coke, reading, as usual, I saved four people twenty cents each, though none of them was aware of me.

The second example of special insight is more serious. On a sunny day when I was driving past the main gate of a university, I saw two young men directly in front of me in a red convertible with the top rolled down. My attention went immediately to the rider, because he had been much in my thoughts for a few days and it seemed a remarkable coincidence that I should see him at this time. I recognized him from having seen his picture in an annual. He was about twenty years old, his bare shoulders bronze beneath the sun, his brown hair cropped close, as was the fashion then, his eyes lost behind sun glasses. He looked completely carefree as he sat with his head turned left toward his companion, talking nonchalantly, a tennis racket standing up in the seat beside him. His name was on the roll of one of my classes, but he had never seen me, as far as I knew. A friend of his, using his name, had been attending class for him, especially on exam days. This young man did not know at this time, as I knew, that in a day or two he would receive a summons from the Dean.

DEVELOPING A GENERALIZATION
WITH SUBGENERALIZATIONS AND EXAMPLES

When it is your purpose to use at least five or six examples to develop a generalization, the pattern of arrangement described above may be too simple. If the examples fall into subclasses, it is necessary to form a subgeneralization to cover each subclass and to arrange the subgeneralizations so that they clearly support the generalization.

Below, step by step, is a process that you might enact after receiving an assignment to develop a generalization with five or six examples.

1. Suppose you decide that your subject will be *violence on television*, but you do not have a predication in mind. You cannot develop the idea that there are six kinds of violence on television and start listing the types, since a mere classification would not satisfy the assignment.
2. You begin to think about violent acts you have seen on television, visualizing them in as much detail as possible.
   a. You remember that while watching *The Avengers* one evening you saw Emma Peel discover that a common house cat had been transformed

by the remote control of a villain into a tigerish (still small, but vicious) man-killer. This discovery explained what terrified victims had seen earlier as they had turned toward the camera, thrown their arms up crosswise in front of their faces, and screamed. The villains had learned how to regress the cat to an earlier stage of evolutionary development.

b. While watching *The Man from U.N.C.L.E.*, you saw some agents of T.H.R.U.S.H. lead an apprehensive Arabian (the larger setting was an Arabian desert) into a room and chain him to a pole facing a glass wall behind which some other agents were ready to operate a machine. The first group of agents left the room, and the other group activated the machine. From pipes in the wall a white foam rolled out, enveloping the victim. When the air cleared, the victim had vanished; evidently the foam had caused his body to disintegrate.

c. While watching *Mannix*, you saw Mannix and his girlfriend, who was carrying a black briefcase with a million dollars in it, running across a golf course, trying to escape from a helicopter overhead that was descending toward them. As the copter bore in, its landing runner swiped the girl and knocked her to the ground, killing her. Mannix fired at the pilot of the helicopter; the pilot slumped over, and the copter crashed into the side of a mountain.

At this point it occurs to you that the instruments of lawless violence in these incidents have not been guns, knives, or other conventional weapons. You remember reading an article in the *Saturday Review* in which Richard L. Tobin had listed the types of weapons he had seen in eight hours of watching for violence on television: "seven different kinds of pistols and revolvers, three varieties of rifle, three distinct brands of shotgun, half a dozen assorted daggers and stilettos, two types of machete, one butcher's cleaver, a broadaxe, rapiers galore, an ancient broadsword, a posse of sabers, an electric prodder, and a guillotine."[1] Maybe it would be worth pointing out that the instruments of violence are sometimes not conventional kinds like those listed by Tobin, but scientific and pseudoscientific inventions not normally used in the real world as weapons.

3. Now that you have an idea, you try to think of other incidents to support it.

a. You remember that while watching *Peyton Place*, you saw Rodney and Norman Harrington on a motorcycle, riding up a narrow mountain road. An automobile approached whose driver was obviously determined to

---

[1]"On the Hour Every Hour," *Saturday Review*, Vol. LI, No. 23 (June 7, 1968), p. 63.

hit the motorcycle. The motorcycle, swerving to the left to miss the automobile, rolled over the side of the mountain.

b. You remember seeing on *The Avengers* a scientist who had created a gun that shot a beam that could shrink a human being to the height of about one inch. He had intended this weapon to be used defensively in war, but some villains had stolen it and had been using it for their own purposes. They used the beam on Stead, but even in his diminished state, he was not powerless. At a crucial moment, when the villain needed all of his powers of concentration, Stead managed to divert his attention by taking a common fountain pen, shouldering it as if it were a huge spear, and jabbing it into the villain's leg.

4. You stop to consider what you could do with these incidents. You have a helicopter, an automobile, and a fountain pen—scientific inventions not intended to be used as weapons. You have a device for regressing a house cat, a foam that causes a body to disappear, and a gun that shrinks human beings. So, you predicate: **Violence on television is often executed by unconventional means.**

5. You know that the automobile, the helicopter, and the fountain pen are real inventions created for purposes other than violence. You know that the regressed cat, the foam, and shrinking gun are fantastic "scientific" inventions. And you write your subgeneralizations: **Some of these means are realistic scientific inventions not created to be destructive. Other means are fantastic weapons invented by fictional "scientists."** The only incident hard to classify is the last one you thought of, since it has both fantasy and the fountain pen. You decide to place it under fantasy, because in this context, even the fountain pen, being oversized in comparison with the people, is fantastic.

6. You write your generalization diagram.

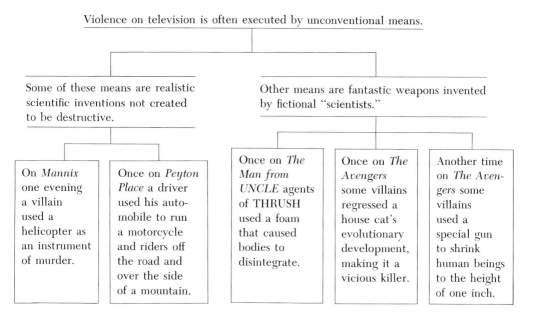

Violence on television is often executed by unconventional means.

Some of these means are realistic scientific inventions not created to be destructive.

Other means are fantastic weapons invented by fictional "scientists."

On *Mannix* one evening a villain used a helicopter as an instrument of murder.

Once on *Peyton Place* a driver used his automobile to run a motorcycle and riders off the road and over the side of a mountain.

Once on *The Man from UNCLE* agents of THRUSH used a foam that caused bodies to disintegrate.

Once on *The Avengers* some villains regressed a house cat's evolutionary development, making it a vicious killer.

Another time on *The Avengers* some villains used a special gun to shrink human beings to the height of one inch.

7. You write the theme, making whatever changes in wording seem appropriate to the developing context and adding transitional expressions.

An introductory concession that relates the thesis to a familiar background.	Although it is customary for critics of violence on television to associate this violence with conventional weapons like guns and knives, which are within the reach of children, violence on television is often executed by unconventional means. Some of these means are realistic scientific inventions originally created to be useful, not
Transitional expression; summary statement on an example.	destructive. For example, a helicopter has been used as an instrument of murder on *Mannix*. In one show Mannix and his girlfriend, who is carrying a black briefcase with a million dollars in it, are running across a golf course, trying to escape from a helicopter overhead that is descending toward them. As the copter bears in, its landing runner swipes the girl, killing her. Mannix fires at the pilot, obviously a bad guy; the pilot slumps over, and the copter
Transition between examples, including classification of the examples (as spectacular).	crashes into the side of a mountain. Almost as spectacular an example of the conversion of a useful machine into a murder weapon is this: In *Peyton Place* Rodney and Norman Harrington are riding up a narrow mountain road on

a motorcycle. An automobile approaches whose driver is obviously determined to hit the motorcycle. The motorcycle, swerving to the left to miss the automobile, rolls over the side of the mountain.

Fantastic weapons invented by fictional "scientists" also become instruments of violence on television. In one show in *The Man from U.N.C.L.E.* series, <u>for example</u>, some agents of T.H.R.U.S.H. lead an apprehensive Arabian (the larger setting is an Arabian desert) into a room and chain him to a pole facing a glass wall behind which some other agents are ready to operate a machine. The first group of agents leaves the room, and the other group activates the machine. From pipes in the wall a white foam rolls out, enveloping the victim. When the air has cleared, the victim has vanished; evidently the foam has caused his body to disintegrate. <u>Equally fantastic is Emma Peel's discovery in *The Avengers* that a common house cat has been transformed by remote control of a villain into a tigerish (still small, but vicious) man-killer.</u> This discovery explains what terrified victims have seen earlier as they have turned toward the camera, thrown their arms up crosswise in front of their faces, and screamed. The villains have learned how to regress the cat to an earlier stage of evolutionary development. <u>*The Avengers* excels in pseudoscience. On another show in this series</u>, a scientist creates a gun that shoots a beam that can shrink a human being to the height of about one inch, intending that it be used in war as a defensive weapon. Some villains have stolen the gun, however, and are using it for selfish purposes. One of their victims is Stead, who even in his diminished state, is not powerless. At a crucial moment, when the villain needs all of his powers of concentration, Stead manages to divert his attention by taking a common fountain pen, shouldering it as if it were a huge spear, and jabbing it into the villain's leg.

<u>A helicopter swiping a victim on a golf course, an automobile running a motorcycle off the road and over a cliff— these are instruments of violence, but, more significantly, they are the chief "actors" in spectacles.</u> <u>A disintegrating foam, a regressed cat, and a gun for shrinking are instruments of violence, but it is their superficial ingenuity and the mild horror they create that attract the viewer, not their brutality.</u> Identifying unconventional means of violence on television is important because it may be an approach to identifying harmless violence.

Transitional expression.

Transition between examples, including classification of examples (as fantastic); summary statement on an example.

Transition between examples.

Summary of the two examples developing the first subgeneralization, with a judgment upon them.
Summary of the three examples developing the second subgeneralization with a judgment upon them.

---

8. You realize that in the concluding comment you have gone beyond your subject and that you will probably have to scratch the comment when you

correct the paper. But you are sure that your instincts are right: the development of a generalization like this would never stand alone in print. It would always be used as support of an inference or judgment. The development of the idea that violence on television is often executed by unconventional means would probably appear in an argument for a discriminating approach in the judgment of violence on television.

FROM GENERALIZATION DIAGRAM TO OUTLINE

If you write the parts of a generalization diagram in the order that they will appear in a theme, you will have written a sentence outline. All you will have to do to have a complete outline is to write in the proper symbols before the divisions and subdivisions.

Topic Sentence: Violence on television is often executed by unconventional means.

I. Some of these means are realistic scientific inventions not created to be destructive.
  A. On *Mannix* one evening a villain used a helicopter as an instrument of murder.
  B. Once on *Peyton Place* a driver used his automobile to run a motorcycle and riders off the road and over the side of a mountain.
II. Other means are fantastic weapons invented by fictional "scientists."
  A. Once on *The Man from U.N.C.L.E.* agents of T.H.R.U.S.H. used a foam that caused bodies to disintegrate.
  B. Once on *The Avengers* some villains regressed a house cat's evolutionary development, making it a vicious killer.
  C. Another time on *The Avengers* some villains used a special gun to shrink human beings to the height of one inch.

You see, below, how the abstract pattern of the generalization diagram relates to the abstract pattern of the outline.

The outline is not always as efficient in showing the organization of a composition that develops a generalization as the generalization diagram is. Suppose that you wanted to give only one example under a subgeneralization. You could show one example on a generalization diagram by drawing only one box under a subgeneralization. But the traditional outline, which works very well when there are at least two examples under a main division, cannot represent a composition effectively in which one of the main divisions is developed by one example. You

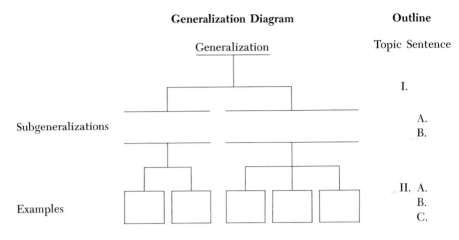

Generalization Diagram   **Outline**

Generalization   Topic Sentence

I.

Subgeneralizations   A.
B.

II. A.
Examples   B.
C.

cannot use just an A under I, a main division, without violating the conventional rule of outlining that there must be at least two subdivisions. The rule that outlaws an A without a B is based on the assumption that a main division cannot be subdivided into one part. It is true that nothing can be divided into one part, but *an example is not a part.* One example is sometimes sufficient to develop one idea. The generalization diagram can show development by one example or any number of examples. It should be remembered, however, that the generalization diagram pertains only to subjects developed by subgeneralizations and examples. It is not intended to be used as a type of "outline" for every kind of subject.

EXERCISE 11

Diagraming a Generalization, Subgeneralizations, and Examples

One rarely sees a whole essay developed according to the pattern in the generalization diagram, but one often sees such development as part of an essay. The following excerpt is structured on this pattern. It is about one-sixth of the whole essay, which is included in the final section of this book.

1. After reading the excerpt, make a generalization diagram of the development. (You may simplify the diagram by leaving out some of the lines, provided that you show clearly the relationships among the parts.) In the diagram, quote the generalization in Schillaci's words. In writing the sub-

generalizations and the examples, use the most concise wording (yours or Schillaci's), being sure, however, to make complete sentences. When you quote his words, use quotation marks.

2. Considering the structure of the development, why do you think we asked you to write a diagram instead of an outline?

FROM **The Now Movie: Film as Environment**

Anthony Schillaci

The new multisensory involvement with film as total environment has been primary in destroying literary values in film. Their decline is not merely farewell to an understandable but unwelcome dependency; it means the emergence of a new identity for film. The diminished role of dialogue is a case in point. The difference between *Star Trek* and *Mission: Impossible* marks the trend toward self-explanatory images that need no dialogue. Take an audio tape of these two popular TV shows, as we did in a recent study, and it will reveal that while *Mission: Impossible* is completely unintelligible without images, *Star Trek* is simply an illustrated radio serial, complete on the level of sound. It has all the characteristics of radio's golden age: actions explained, immediate identification of character by voice alone, and even organ music to squeeze the proper emotion or end the episode. Like *Star Trek,* the old film was frequently a talking picture (emphasis on the adjective), thereby confirming McLuhan's contention that technologically "radio married the movies." The marriage of dependence, however, has gone on the rocks, and not by a return to silent films but a turning to foreign ones. It was the films of Fellini and Bergman, with their subtitles, that convinced us there had been too many words. Approximately one-third of the dialogue is omitted in subtitled versions of these films, with no discernible damage—and some improvement—of the original.

More than dialogue, however, has been jettisoned. Other literary values, such as sequential narrative, dramatic choice, and plot are in a state of advanced atrophy, rapidly becoming vestigial organs of the body of film art as young people have their say. *Petulia* has no "story," unless one laboriously pieces together the interaction between the delightful arch-kook and the newly divorced surgeon, in which case it is nothing more than an encounter. The story line wouldn't make a ripple if it were not scrambled and fragmented into an experience that explodes from a free-floating present into both past and future simultaneously. *Petulia* is like some views of the universe which represent the ancient past of events whose light is just now reaching us simultaneously with the future of our galaxy, returning from the curve of outer space. Many films succeed by virtue of what they leave

From THE NOW MOVIE: FILM AS ENVIRONMENT From *Saturday Review,* December 28, 1968. Copyright 1968 Saturday Review, Inc. Reprinted by permission of the publisher and the author.

out. *2001: A Space Odyssey* is such a film, its muted understatement creating gaps in the action that invite our inquiry. Only a square viewer wants to know where the black monolith came from and where it is going. For most of the young viewers to whom I have spoken, it is just there. *Last Year at Marienbad* made the clock as limply shapeless as one of Salvador Dali's watches, while *8½* came to life on the strength of free associations eagerly grasped by young audiences. The effect of such films is a series of open-ended impressions, freely evoked and enjoyed, strongly inviting inquiry and involvement. In short, film is freed to work as environment, something which does not simply contain, but shapes people, tilting the balance of their faculties, radically altering their perceptions, and ultimately their views of self and all reality. Perhaps one sense of the symptomatic word "grooving," which applies to both sight and sound environments, is that a new mode of attention—multisensory, total, and simultaneous—has arrived. When you "groove," you do not analyze, follow an argument, or separate sensations; rather, you are massaged into a feeling of heightened life and consciousness.

SUGGESTED WRITING ASSIGNMENT

The Generalization Developed by Subgeneralizations and Examples

Drawing upon your own experience (including experience through reading and other artistic media, if you like), write a composition developing a generalization with subgeneralizations supported by examples. Try enacting the process by which the composition on television violence was written, to see whether it works for you. Turn in with your composition a generalization diagram or a sentence outline (if an outline is appropriate).

STUDENT COMPOSITIONS DEVELOPING
A GENERALIZATION BY SUBGENERALIZATIONS
AND EXAMPLES

Political Campaigns—Emphasis on the Negative

Mark Harrington

1 In many political campaigns candidates often concentrate more on their opponent's lack of qualifications than on their own positive qualities. 2 This modern day mud-slinging ranges from the skillful application of subtle crafts to

out and out name-calling, but regardless of the form it takes, it usually leaves one with the impression that a candidate, unable to think of something good to say about himself, finds it easier to point out his opponent's faults.

3 One way to show that an opponent is unfit for the job is to remind the public of his previous inefficiency in office. 4 In our recent contest for the governorship, Jack Williams used this method when he blamed Sam Goddard for many of the ills of state government when Mr. Goddard was governor.

5 Another good way to demonstrate to the public that an opponent is unfit for the office he seeks is to use an "exposé-type" of sensationalism. 6 Accusations of misconduct in office are hard to refute effectively, and the taint of scandal is difficult to remove once one's integrity has been publicly questioned. 7 "Rocky" Andresano used newspaper articles dating back fifteen years to illustrate dishonesty in the sheriff's office. 8 This was perhaps unfair, since Burr, the incumbent, had only been in office ten years.

9 Quoting your opponent out of context is one of the politicians' favorite stratagems. 10 A good example of this was Roy Elson's campaign against Barry Goldwater. 11 Mr. Elson came up with some quotations of Mr. Goldwater's that Mr. Goldwater could never have intended to stand alone. 12 After each quotation a voice dripping with sarcasm would say, "Now doesn't that sound great?"

13 Another effective means of discrediting an opponent is to associate him with undesirable elements or ideals. 14 The name "Wallace," for instance, is now almost synonomous with racism and bigotry. 15 A somewhat humorous example of this artifice occurred in Tucson when a man running for a local office paid a group of hippies to carry his opponent's signs.

Comments on "Political Campaigns—Emphasis on the Negative"

Arrangement: The structure of the theme is a clear generalization pattern. The generalization is stated in the first paragraph as the thesis sentence (sentence 1). Each of the succeeding paragraphs begins with a subgeneralization, each of which is followed by one example.

Content: The judgmental generalization developed here is appropriate and interesting. There is one flaw in its wording. The word *more* should not have been included, since there is really no attempt in the composition to compare the relative positive and negative emphases in campaigns.

Though each example is clear and specific, none is developed in detail. Descriptive detail would be especially appropriate to the last example, in which students recognized as hippies are said to have been hired by a candidate to march in support of his opponent.

The last paragraph is less effectively developed than the others, because the reference to Wallace obscures the relationship of the example to the subgeneralization in sentence 13. This reference is extraneous.

Sentence structure: There is faulty predication in sentences 10 and 15; the sentence structure is adequate otherwise.

Diction: The diction is precise; correct specific terms are used in all examples. Transitional words at the beginning of paragraphs emphasize the coherent structure of the composition.

Mechanics: Good, though *only* is misplaced in sentence 8 and *synonymous* is misspelled in sentence 14.

Black Actors and Actresses on Television

1 More and more black actors and actresses are being added to those already on TV programs. 2 These range from Bill Cosby to Nichelle Nichols and include Robert Hooks, Greg Morris, Otis Taylor, Diahann Carroll, and Gail Fisher.

3 Usually the black actors play opposite a white partner or partners. 4 Among the established actors Bill Cosby, Robert Hooks, and Greg Morris play these parts. 5 Bill Cosby is probably the most famous of these three having won three Emmies for his performances in *I Spy*. 6 In *I Spy* he plays the part of a trainer to tennis bum Robert Culp. 7 In actuality, however, both of them are United States agents abroad. 8 Cosby usually manages to play his various roles with humor whether he is about to be shot, blown up, or beaten.

9 Tall (6'2" or 3"), lanky, and usually dressed in a business suit, Robert Hooks plays the part of a New York detective on ABC's *NYPD*. 10 Like Cosby he has his white partners played by Jack Warden and Frank Converse. 11 In contrast to Bill Cosby, Hooks usually plays his role seriously, rarely ever joking in his routine assignments as a cop which might include the capture of a child molester or a homosexual blackmailer and the breaking of a prostitution ring.

12 The third and last of this group is Greg Morris, who stars in CBS's *Mission: Impossible*. 13 He plays opposite Martin Landau, Peter Graves, and Peter Lupus. 14 He will usually play more of an "intellectual" role than Lupus. 15 By this, I mean his jobs on the show require more intelligence than those of Lupus who is used primarily as a muscle man. 16 Among the recent black actors to arrive on the scene we find Otis Taylor. 17 He plays the part of Jemal, a former slave, on ABC's *The Outcasts*. 18 Like all of the others he has a white counterpart: Don Murray. 19 Neither of them have much love for each other, but do ride through the United States together. 20 Besides having his weekly episodal problems, Taylor has the major problem of his color and freedom. 21 This could be shown in his statement on one of the shows, "I'm free. 22 Nobody can tell me what to do."

23 The black actresses—established and new—also fit into a role category: they are women without husbands. 24 The only established black actress on TV of whom I can think is Nichelle Nichols who plays the part of Lt. Uhura, the

BLACK ACTORS AND ACTRESSES ON TELEVISION   Reprinted by permission.

communications operator on the *USS Enterprise,* on NBC's *Star Trek.* 25 Primarily, she is used as a supporting actress. 26 On occasion, however, she will have a major role. 27 Take, for example, the time she, Captain Kirk, Chief Medical Officer Bones, and Chekhov are transported to a planet on which they must fight for their lives as the gladiators of Rome did.

28 Of the new arrivals, Gail Fisher who plays Peggy on *Mannix* is another single girl who has never married. 29 I believe that she takes over where *Intertech* has left off. 30 Adding a coolness to the show and making Mike Connors resemble, to me at least, a Mike Hammer or Mike Shayne type, both having been private investigators with their own secretaries.

31 Diahann Carroll is the last of the new black actresses, and like the others she is single. 32 She has had a husband, but he has been killed in Viet Nam. 33 She has a young son, Corey. 34 In *Julia* she plays the part of a registered nurse to Lloyd Nolan. 35 Julia is unique in that she has as her neighbors and close friends a white couple. 36 Corey also has as his best friend a young white kid approximately the same age as he is.

37 As these examples show, there is a couple of role categories into which the black actor or actress fits: he is usually opposite a white partner and she is usually single.

Comments on "Black Actors and Actresses on Television"

Arrangement: The generalization in this composition is stated in the last paragraph rather than the first. This is not a bad arrangement, since the subgeneralizations introduce the examples related to them and are clearly separate from each other.

Content: The generalization (in sentence 37) is so ineffectively worded that it should be rewritten, but the idea of the generalization—that black actors are cast in similar roles and black actresses are cast in similar roles—is well supported in the preceding paragraphs. The many specific details in the examples make the composition informative and interesting.

Two unclear passages that should be improved are sentences 29–30 and sentence 34.

Sentence structure: Good use of relatively short cumulative sentences (5, 8, 11), but sentence 30 is fragmentary.

Diction: Good use of concrete class words and specific words throughout.

Sentence 8:   *Beaten* is anticlimactic.

Sentence 28:   *Single* and *never married* are redundant.

Sentence 31:   *Single* is misused.

Mechanics:

Sentence 2:   The reference of *these* is ambiguous. Does *these* refer to the black actors and actresses being added or to all of the black actors and actresses?

Sentence 5:   A comma should be used to set off the perfect participial phrase beginning with *having won.*

Sentence 8:   Again, a comma should be used to set off the large-constituent modifier (*whether he is about to be shot, blown up, or beaten*—an adverbial clause) from the base structure.

Sentence 10:   A comma should be used before *played. His white partners* does not need to be restricted; the past participial phrase modifying *partners* is therefore set off.

Sentence 11:   *Rarely ever* should be *rarely, if ever.* A comma should be used before *which* to set off the nonrestrictive adjective clause.

Sentence 15:   A comma should be used before *who* to set off the nonrestrictive adjective clause. This comment applies to sentences 24 and 28, also.

Sentence 19:   There is an error in agreement of subject and verb: *Neither of them have* should be *Neither of them has.*

SUGGESTED WRITING ASSIGNMENT

The Essay Examination

Write an essay examination for a course that you are taking or one that you have completed, asking at least one question that can be answered by arranging ideas in a classification of types and subtypes; one that can be answered by a definition; and one that can be answered by developing a generalization. For this course, for example, one could write:

    I. Discuss semantical types of statements.
   II. Define *abstracting.*
  III. Discuss how skill in description relates to development by examples.

A good essay written in answer to any of these directions would state examples, even though examples are not specifically called for in the wording.

    If you have an opportunity to exchange examinations with a classmate, write an answer to one of his questions while he writes an answer to one of yours. Grade each other's answer. If you cannot exchange examinations with another student, write an answer to one of your own questions. In writing your answer, apply what you have learned about supporting class statements with subclasses and examples; about classification, differentiation, and the use of examples in definitions; and about supporting a generalization with subgeneralizations and examples.

PART III
Comparison

It is impossible, if no more than one opinion is uttered, to make choice of the best: a man is forced then to follow whatever advice may have been given him; but if opposite speeches are delivered, then choice can be exercised. In like manner pure gold is not recognized by itself; but when we test it along with baser ore, we perceive which is the better.

Herodotus

Introduction

In the free, open society recommended by Herodotus and enjoyed by many peoples today, the ability to perceive and compare alternatives is essential. In our time of rapid change, we must "perceive which is the better" social and political alternative. In our personal lives we must compare and decide as we choose a career, a husband or wife, a way of life. As a scholarly tool, comparison again seems essential; we understand unfamiliar things or ideas more readily through comparing them to more familiar or concrete things or ideas. In essay examinations or other writing tasks, whether imposed by school, profession, or self, comparison is essential also as a means of discovering something to say about two or more subjects, as a means of organizing the details that have been discovered, and as a means of strengthening the total argument or interpretation being developed.

The tendency to compare things is common to man, as you will see if you attempt to avoid doing so for any length of time. But through study and practice one can develop this natural tendency into a conscious skill in thinking and writing. This is the purpose of Part III. As part of the process of learning to write comparisons, you will learn to distinguish the types of comparisons, to recognize and use standard patterns of comparison singly and in combination, to use balanced sentences to emphasize balance in thought, and to use appropriate transitional terms for comparisons. But the writing of comparisons can also be seen as one part of the whole process of composition comprising this book. Each part is like one box in a nest of boxes; exemplification can contain factual detail within it, and comparison can contain exemplification with factual detail inside. As the third of the four boxes that comprise this book, comparison does contain within it the patterns of thinking, of arranging, of sentence structure, and the diction of the types of development already discussed. Also, as the third box containing the first two, comparison can fit within the fourth box, explanation, in the writing you will do in Part IV of the book. Since comparison also necessarily deals with two or more subjects rather than one, and so, in a sense, with a double development, your essays for this part of the course will be more complex than were your earlier paragraphs and essays.

The word *comparison* is used throughout the text in the sense of "estimation of similarities and differences" (*Webster's New World Dictionary*)—that is, as a general term rather than as the similarity half of the term "comparison and contrast."

The Types of Comparisons

FROM **The Year 2000—The Trajectory of an Idea**

Daniel Bell

1 Time, said St. Augustine, is a three-fold present: the present as we experience it, the past as a present memory, and the future as a present expectation. By that criterion, the world of the year 2000 has already arrived, for in the decisions we make now, in the way we design our environment and thus sketch the lines of constraints, the future is committed. Just as the gridiron pattern of city streets in the nineteenth century shaped the linear growth of cities in the twentieth, so the new networks of radial highways, the location of new towns, the reordering of graduate-school curricula, the decision to create or not to create a computer utility as a single system, and the like will frame the tectonics of the twenty-first century. The future is not an overarching leap into the distance; it begins in the present.

2 This is the premise of the Commission on the Year 2000. It is an effort to indicate now the future consequences of present public-policy decisions, to anticipate future problems, and to begin the design of alternative solutions so that our society has more options and can make a moral choice, rather than be constrained, as is so often the case when problems descend upon us unnoticed and demand an immediate response.

3 But what began a few years ago as a serious academic enterprise—along with the Commission on the Year 2000, there is the *Futuribles* project in Paris, directed by Bertrand de Jouvenel, and the Committee on the Next Thirty Years (named with characteristic British understatement), of the English Social Science

From THE YEAR 2000—THE TRAJECTORY OF AN IDEA. Reprinted by permission from *Daedalus*, Journal of the American Academy of Arts and Sciences, Boston, Massachusetts, Vol. 96, No. 3, (Summer 1969).

Research Council, under Michael Young and Mark Abrams—has been seized, predictably, by the mass media and the popular imagination. The Columbia Broadcasting System has revamped its documentary program, "The Twentieth Century," into "The Twenty-First Century," to depict the marvels of the future. *The Wall Street Journal* has been running an intermittent series on expected social and technological changes. *Time* has published a compact essay on "The Futurists: Looking Toward A.D. 2000." The theme of the year 2000 now appears repeatedly on lecture circuits and in the feature pages of newspapers. Dr. Glenn T. Seaborg, chairman of the U.S. Atomic Energy Commission, in a speech to the Women's National Democratic Club, holds out a promising future for women. "By the year 2000, housewives . . . will probably have a robot 'maid' . . . shaped like a box [with] one large eye on the top, several arms and hands, and long narrow pads on each side for moving about." Dr. Isaac Asimov foretells in a Sunday-supplement interview in *The New York Post* that by the year 2000 man will be exploring the limits of the solar system and living underground. Even the beauty industry has clambered aboard. An article on *The New York Times* women's page carries the headline: "In the Year 2000: Push-Button Beauty." The article begins enchantingly: "The chic woman of the year 2000 may have live butterflies fluttering around her hairdo . . . attracted by a specially scented hair spray. The same woman, according to predictions made at a cosmetics industry luncheon, will control her body measurements by reclining on a chaise longue with electronic bubbles that massage away problem areas. . . . She will have available silicones for filling in frown lines and wrinkles on aging faces." . . . And most of the images of the future have concentrated on dazzling technological prospects. The possibility of prediction, the promise of technological wizardry, and the idea of a millennial turning point make an irresistible combination to a jaded press that constantly needs to ingest new sensations and novelties. The year 2000 has all the ingredients for becoming, if it has not already become, a hoola-hoop craze. . . .

    4 The simple point is that a complex society is not changed by a flick of the wrist. Considered from the viewpoint of gadgetry, the United States in the year 2000 will be more *like* the United States in the year 1967 than *different*. The basic framework of day-to-day life has been shaped in the last fifty years by the ways the automobile, the airplane, the telephone, and the television have brought people together and increased the networks and interactions among them. It is highly unlikely that in the next thirty-three years (if one takes the year 2000 literally, not symbolically) the impending changes in technology will radically alter this framework. Supersonic transport will "tighten" the network and bring the world more directly into the domestic frame. The major challenges and problems already confronting our society, however—a livable physical environment, effective urban planning, the expansion of post-graduate education, the pressures of density and the reduction of privacy, the fragility of political institutions beset by many pressure groups—will extend to the end of the century. Predicting the *social* future is relatively easy, for in the Augustinian sense it is already "present expectation," just as the expectations about urbanization, education, and medical care in the volume *Recent Social Trends*, written thirty-four years ago, are "present memory."

    5 This is not to say that substantial changes will not take place as they have been doing in the past thirty-three years. . . . In the next thirty-three years

we are likely to see great changes growing out of the new biomedical engineering, the computer, and, possibly, weather modification. Biomedical engineering, particularly its possibilities of organ transplant, genetic modification, and control of disease, promises a substantial increase in human longevity. Previous steps, principally the control of infant mortality, raised the average life expectancy; now the prolongation of life by the control of aging may be at hand. This may accentuate a tendency, already visible, in which the chief concern of a person (particularly in middle age) is not death from disease but staying young, thus strengthening the hedonistic elements in our culture. The impact of the computer will be vast. We will probably see a national information-computer-utility system, with tens of thousands of terminals in homes and offices "hooked" into giant central computers providing library and information services, retail ordering and billing services, and the like. . . . Weather modification, still only on the horizon, would shape a control of environment men have dreamed of for thousands of years, but the working out of the economic and social arrangements, if the technology were possible, would pose some difficult problems for human civilization. In all this, one should note that "technology" is itself changing, and this may be one of the more important kinds of change in the next thirty-three years. Technology is not simply a "machine," but a systematic, disciplined approach to objectives, using a calculus of precision and measurement and a concept of system that are quite at variance with traditional and customary religious, aesthetic, and intuitive modes. Instead of a machine technology, we will have, increasingly, an "intellectual technology" in which such techniques as simulation, model construction, linear programming, and operations research will be hitched to the computers and will become the new tools of decision-making.

.   .   .

6 We have begun to realize—and this is the positive side of the current interest in the year 2000—that it is possible to direct some of this change consciously, and because a normative commitment underlies any humanistic approach to social policy, we can try to widen the area of choice. Looking ahead, we realize that the rebuilding of American cities, for example, entails a thirty-five-year cycle, and one can rebuild cities only by making long-range commitments. In the process we are also forced to consider the adequacy of our political mechanisms, since Congress neither has a capital budget nor budgets money for long-range commitments. Furthermore, one must question whether a national society can sensibly be structured according to the present crazy-quilt pattern of fifty states and thousands of unwieldy municipalities.

7 In short, what matters most about the year 2000 are not the gadgets that might, on the serious side, introduce prosthesis in the human body or, on the lighter side, use silicones to lift wrinkles, but the kinds of social arrangements that can deal adequately with the problems we shall confront. More and more we are becoming a "communal society" in which the public sector has a greater importance and in which the goods and services of the society—those affecting cities, education, medical care, and the environment—will increasingly have to

be purchased jointly. Hence, the problem of social choice and individual values—the question of how to reconcile conflicting individual desires through the political mechanism rather than the market—becomes a potential source of discord. The relation of the individual to bureaucratic structures will be subject to even greater strain. The increasing centralization of government creates a need for new social forms that will allow the citizenry greater participation in making decisions. The growth of a large, educated professional and technical class, with its desire for greater autonomy in work, will force institutions to reorganize the older bureaucratic patterns of hierarchy and detailed specialization. The individual will live longer and face the problem of renewed education and new careers. The family as the source of primordial attachment may become less important for the child, in both his early schooling and his emotional reinforcement. This will be a more mobile and more crowded world, raising problems of privacy and stress. The new densities and "communications overload" may increase the potentiality for irrational outbursts in our society. Finally, there is the growing disjunction between the "culture" and the "social structure." Society becomes more functionally organized, geared to knowledge and the mastery of complex bodies of learning. The culture becomes more hedonistic, permissive, expressive, distrustful of authority and of the purposive, delayed-gratification of a bourgeois, achievement-oriented technological world. This tension between the "technocratic" and the "apocalyptic" modes, particularly among the intellectuals, may be one of the great ruptures in moral temper, especially in the universities.

8 The only prediction about the future that one can make with certainty is that public authorities will face more problems than they have at any previous time in history. . . . the society of the year 2000, so quickly and schematically outlined, will be more fragile, more susceptible to hostilities and to polarization along many different lines. Yet to say this is not to surrender to despair, for the power to deal with these problems is also present. It resides, first, in the marvelous productive capacity of our system to generate sufficient economic resources for meeting most of the country's social and economic needs. It is latent in the flexibility of the American political system, its adaptability to change, and its ability to create new social forms to meet these challenges—public corporations, regional compacts, nonprofit organizations, responsive municipalities, and the like. The problem of the future consists in defining one's priorities and making the necessary commitments. This is an intention of the Commission on the Year 2000.

DIALOG 9

The Types of Comparisons

Before beginning the dialog, read "The Year 2000—The Trajectory of an Idea."

1. The article you have just read contains the statement "Considered from the viewpoint of gadgetry, the United States in the year 2000 will be more *like* the United States in the year 1967 than *different*." This statement mentions the two major relationships treated in comparisons. What are they?	Likenesses and differences.
2. Differences can be of two types. The first three paragraphs of the article illustrate one type. Paragraphs 1 and 2 discuss scholarly study of the year 2000, study that is attempting to anticipate future problems in order to recognize and evaluate alternative solutions. The third paragraph discusses the popular and mass media view of the same year. Do these two views seem to be different *kinds* of interests in the future?	The popular view as shown by the mass media seems to be merely prediction of technological gadgets. This is a different kind of attitude toward the future from that of the Commission on the Year 2000.
3. Later in the article, Daniel Bell writes, "The relation of the individual to bureaucratic structures will be subject to even greater strain" (paragraph 7, page 225). Is this also a difference in kind?	It doesn't seem to be; Bell just says that there will be *more* of the same kind of thing.
4. *Difference in degree* is a matter of more or less or better or worse of some aspect of the subjects rather than of *difference in kind* of subjects. Locate in the Bell article other differences in degree following the statement quoted in question 3.	Some examples: greater centralization, greater need for citizen participation in policies, a larger professional and technical class and greater independence in work, longer life with more late education and second careers, less dependency on the family, more mobility, more crowding.
5. *Aspect* is defined as "the appearance of a thing as seen or considered from one point of view" (*Webster's New World Dictionary*). A comparison considers aspects, since objects can seldom be compared as wholes. Try, for instance, to compare the present and the year 2000 without mentioning any aspects of the two.	There cannot be any *detailed* comparison without mentioning aspects. Even "The present is inferior to the future" would imply "in every aspect" or "in most aspects" and would be meaningless unless it were developed by a consideration of many aspects, much as Bell does in his article.
6. Could you compare two small concrete objects such as eggs without discussing aspects?	You could say "The egg I just ate is superior to the one I ate at breakfast yesterday," and because the two subjects of your comparison belong to the

	same class, your listener would real- ize that they have most aspects in common. But at the same time, he would infer that you are probably talking about the particular aspects of such things as taste, firmness of white, and quality of preparation.
7. If you stated that a robot is superior to an egg or a man is superior to a broom, would another person know what aspects of the two objects were being compared?	No, and therefore the comparisons would not be valid.
8. Change the invalid comparison "A man is superior to a broom" into a valid comparison in degree by specifying the aspect being compared.	One example: Thadeus Wilson's hair is somewhat less coarse than the straw in this broom.
9. Any two subjects may be compared by either difference in kind or in degree. Decide whether the differences mentioned in the following statements are of kind or of degree: a. At the present time, you must use the library to obtain information; in the year 2000 you will be able to obtain the information in your home through connection with a central computer system. b. You will be able to obtain information much more quickly and efficiently than at present. c. Obtaining information electronically, however, will probably be more costly for the individual in the future. d. Obtaining information today involves being with other people, working with books, using physical activity on your part and possibly on the part of a reference librarian; obtaining information electronically, on the contrary, will involve no use of books and no dealings with other people.	a. kind b. degree c. degree d. kind
10. What words help to distinguish a statement of difference in degree from a statement of difference in kind?	"Degree terminology" such as *more* or *less*, *better* or *worse*, referring to any aspect—efficiency, wiseness, blonde-ness, greenness, skill in tennis, and so forth.

11. Observe again the sentences in question 9. What differences can you perceive in sentence structure between the statements of difference in kind and those in degree?	The statements of comparison in kind are stated in compound sentences; those in degree are not.
12. For students, summer is generally a time of leisure and recreation; winter, on the contrary, is a time of attending classes, carrying out research, and endless studying. Is this a statement of comparison?	Yes, one of difference in kind.
13. Is the statement in question 12 a significant comparison?	No, such a difference is taken for granted in our society.
14. Differences are always more significant if they are pointed out between two things that seem to be similar, and similarities if pointed out between things that seem to be different. Reread the first part of paragraph 4. Why do you suppose Bell wishes to stress similarities between the year 2000 and the present after pointing out that the popular view emphasizes spectacular changes or differences?	Probably precisely because most people and the mass media assume drastic differences, he develops a significant comparison by stressing what is not obvious—in this case, the similarities.
15. List the similarities between the present and the hypothetical future mentioned by Bell in paragraph 4.	The basic framework of day to day life will remain the same (although it will be "tightened"—a difference in degree is included), and both years will have the same problems and challenges in improving our environment, our higher education, and our political systems, and in coping with overpopulation and lack of privacy—all *literal* similarities.
16. *Literal similarity* is the first of the types of similarities. It is a similarity between subjects in the same order of being. The present and the near future are similar enough that comparisons of literal similarities between them can be made. Suppose, however, that you wished to note similarities between eggs and poetry. Could literal comparisons be drawn between them?	No, they do not belong to the same order of being.

17. A similarity between two subjects in different orders of being is called a *figurative similarity*. An analogy is one kind of figurative similarity. It is a comparison of similarities in relationships between objects of widely separated areas of being. The semanticist Hayakawa has said that "the verbal world ought to stand in relation to the extensional [objective, physical] world as a map does to the territory it is supposed to represent." In this analogy, is the verbal world being compared to the physical world or the map to the territory? If so, what similarity or difference is mentioned?	No similarities or differences between them are mentioned.
18. What *is* being compared?	The relationship between the verbal world and the physical world is being compared to the relationship between the map and the territory—a similarity in relationship. This is what makes it an analogy, a figurative comparison.
19. The process of drawing analogies is essential to learning. Why, for instance, ought a parent be proud of his young child for saying "tooths" shortly after learning the word "tooth"?	Because the child has gone through the intellectually sophisticated process of setting up an analogy comparing the relationship between "tooth" and "tooths" to a common relationship between singular and plural forms of nouns in the English language.
20. Complete the analogy that the child has almost unconsciously set up.	Tooth : tooths = dog : dogs (You could have used any of thousands of nouns, of course. Think how often the analogy would serve a child well. Indeed, similar analogies served each of us efficiently as we learned the complex formal and structural patterns of our language.)
21. Analogy is extremely useful in describing and explaining things because it can compare unfamiliar relationships to those familiar to the reader. How does the "verbal world : objective world = map : territory" analogy illustrate this use of analogy?	We are all familiar with using a map to guide us through unfamiliar territory, and this familiarity helps us to understand the relatively unfamiliar idea that our spoken and written language should have just as accurate a relationship to the physical world.

22. Try writing an analogy involving poetry and eggs.	One possibility: Poetry nourishes **the** mind and emotions as eggs nourish the body.
23. Explanatory analogies usually develop a series of similarities in relationships between things in different orders of being. George Orwell, for example, develops an unlikely analogy between language and a drunk in the following quotation from "Politics and the English Language": "A man may take to drink because he feels himself to be a failure, and then fail all the more completely because he drinks. It is rather the same thing that is happening to the English language. It becomes ugly and inaccurate because our thoughts are foolish, but the slovenliness of our language makes it easier for us to have foolish thoughts." How are the relationships of the two halves of Orwell's comparison similar?	Both halves of the analogy describe a circular relationship—the effect becomes a cause that then reinforces the original cause and so produces an intensified effect.
24. Is the following statement by E. B. White a literal or a figurative similarity? "The living language is like a cowpath: it is the creation of the cows themselves, who, having created it, follow it or depart from it according to their whims or needs."	It is figurative, since it implies a series of relationships between things in different orders of being (the cow and the cowpath and people and their language) in order to clarify what the relationship of people to their language really is—a combination of compliance and deviation from a tradition created by people themselves.
25. Figurative similarities may also be stated in the form of similes and metaphors. Semanticists, for example, are implying a type of similarity in the metaphor *abstraction ladder*. Why is this term a figurative similarity?	The concept that verbal symbols vary from specific to abstract is very different in kind from an actual ladder. It is the relationships that are similar as in a figurative similarity.
26. What is the value of using this metaphor to name the concept that symbols vary from specific to general?	It makes an abstract concept picturable, easier to understand and remember, by bringing it down the abstraction ladder to specific, vivid terms.
27. We have now discussed the types of similarities. As review, list them.	Literal similarity (in kind), figurative similarity (in relationship).

28. Sinclair Lewis wrote the following sentence in "Young Man Axelbrod." As you read it, decide which of the two types of similarities it is: "And at sixty-five Knute was like one of his own cottonwoods, his roots deep in the soil, his trunk weathered by rain and blizzard and baking August noons, his crown spread to the wide horizon of day and the enormous sky of a prairie night."

Figurative: it implies relationships between things different in kind—Knute and a tree.

29. Is the following sentence, also by Sinclair Lewis, literal similarity or figurative? "He saw himself as ridiculous, a ponderous, oldish man among clean-limbed youths, like a dusty cottonwood among silver birches."

Figurative (an analogy: he:cottonwood = youths:silver birches).

30. Which kind of comparison is this sentence? "Say, look here, Axelbrod; I've been thinking about you. . . . We ought to know each other. We two are the class scandal. We came here to dream. . . . You may not agree with me, but I've decided that you and I are precisely alike."

Literal similarity between two subjects of the same order of being.

31. Which is this cartoon?

"You individualists all look alike."

Literal.

32. And this?

Figurative.

The ability to see similarities in dissimilar objects is essential to a poet (and perhaps the poet's most distinguishing characteristic) and to writers in general, but it is also a sign of general intelligence—there are even books that claim to raise IQ's a number of points by presenting a series of pictures of dissimilar objects from which the reader is to abstract a common element. Consider how the demands of this course upon your ability to perceive have grown: first you were asked to perceive accurate and specific factual details in order to write reports; then you used perception combined with reasoning to discover what similar objects have in common (similarities) in order to form generalizations; and now you are asked to perceive significant similarities and differences between objects both similar and dissimilar.

33. When the differences between subjects to be compared are commonly accepted knowledge, what does a meaningful comparison stress?	Similarities that are not obvious, either in aspects or in relationships.
34. Conversely, when two subjects are similar, what will a meaningful comparison stress?	Differences.
35. List the two types of differences and the two types of similarities.	Differences in kind and differences in degree, similarities in kind (literal) and similarities in relationship (figurative).

Very often, of course, a careful comparison reveals *both* similarities *and* differences that are significant, as in Daniel Bell's article about the year 2000. You will face the problem of how to organize the results of your comparative thinking in the next area of study, where you will learn patterns for arranging comparisons.

Patterns for Arranging Comparisons

THE COMPARISON PATTERNS

There are a limited number of basic patterns for arranging the similarities and differences that you discern between any two objects, situations, attitudes, or ideas—the two subjects of your comparison. The similarities and differences discussed will be those between aspects of the subjects of comparison rather than between the whole subjects. You will not, for example, compare the two whole paintings following page 238, but several aspects of both paintings. As you look at the two paintings, "Distant Thunder" by Andrew Wyeth and "The Poet Reclining" by Marc Chagall, you probably notice the obvious similarities in the reclining figures, the grassy areas on which they lie, and the evergreen trees to the upper left of each figure. But the differences in treatment of these objects in the two paintings—differences in the use of perspective, detail, and color— seem more significant. The Wyeth painting, you realize, shows the reclining figure in perspective, from a point of vision to the front and slightly above; the Chagall figure is presented without perspective, as though viewed from directly above. The Wyeth painting shows almost infinite detail in the rendering of the blades of grass and occasional flowers; in contrast, the Chagall painting shows the grass as a flat surface with no detail. The Wyeth painting uses realistic coloring without great contrasts, but the Chagall painting consists primarily of vivid, unmodulated or arbitrarily modulated colors. Once you begin to discover such differences through close perception, you have something to write about the two paintings. The simplest way of arranging your comparative detail is by discussing the aspects of one subject completely before beginning to discuss the second. Such an arrangement can be represented in a topic outline:

      I. Andrew Wyeth's painting "Distant Thunder"
         A. Use of perspective
         B. Use of detail
         C. Use of color
     II. Marc Chagall's painting "The Poet Reclining"
         A. Use of perspective
         B. Use of detail
         C. Use of color

The same arrangement can be represented in an abstract pattern that fits every such comparison pattern and is called the *half and half pattern,* shown on page 235.

After writing a comparison following this abstract pattern, you may have fulfilled your purpose and exhausted your interests. It is possible, however, that you will have discerned more subtle differences between aspects of the paintings and will wish to discuss them at more length, with more emphasis upon each aspect than is possible in the half and half pattern. You would then find the following outline useful:

I. Use of perspective
   A. The Wyeth painting
   B. The Chagall painting
II. Use of detail
   A. The Wyeth painting
   B. The Chagall painting
III. Use of color
   A. The Wyeth painting
   B. The Chagall painting

Since the aspects form the main divisions of this arrangement, we can call it the *aspects pattern* and represent it in abstraction as on page 235.

Now suppose that, as you worked with arranging significant differences, you began to discern significance in what you previously felt were superficial similarities—similarities in the mood of pastoral peace in both paintings, in the horizontal lines of the figures complemented by the vertical thrusts of the trees, in the proportions of the figures to their backgrounds, and in the proportions of land and sky areas in both paintings. (Yet the sense of space and breatheable air is exclusive to the Wyeth painting—another difference would emerge from your increasingly perceptive comparative thinking.) For this situation, in which both differences and similarities should be discussed in detail, there is the *similarities and differences pattern*, shown on the following page.

The three basic arrangements for comparative details, kept in mind as abstract patterns, will serve you well in your planning and writing of comparisons in any situation:

1. The half and half pattern
2. The aspects pattern
3. The similarities and differences pattern

The Half and Half Pattern

The Similarities
and Differences Pattern

The First Subject

Similarities

Aspect #1

Aspect #2

Aspect #3

Aspect #1

Subject #1

Subject #2

The Second Subject

Aspect #2

Aspect #1

Subject #1

Aspect #2

Subject #2

Aspect #3

Aspect #3

Subject #1

Subject #2

Differences

The Aspects Pattern

Aspect #1

Aspect #1

Subject #1

Subject #1

Subject #2

Subject #2

Aspect #2

Aspect #2

Subject #1

Subject #1

Subject #2

Subject #2

Aspect #3

Aspect #3

Subject #1

Subject #1

Subject #2

Subject #2

COMPARISON PATTERNS IN SELECTED COMPARISONS

After reading each of the comparisons, answer the questions following it.

A

FROM **Life of Pope**

1 The style of Dryden is capricious and varied; that of Pope is cautious and uniform. 2 Dryden observes the motions of his own mind; Pope constrains his mind to his own rules of composition. 3 Dryden is sometimes vehement and rapid; Pope is always smooth, uniform, and gentle. 4 Dryden's page is a natural field, rising into inequalities, and diversified by the varied exuberance of abundant vegetation; Pope's is a velvet lawn, shaven by the scythe, and levelled by the roller.

5 Of genius, that power which constitutes a poet; that quality without which judgment is cold, and knowledge is inert; that energy which collects, combines, amplifies, and animates; the superiority must, with some hesitation, be allowed to Dryden. . . . 6 If the flights of Dryden therefore are higher, Pope continues longer on the wing. 7 If of Dryden's fire the blaze is brighter, of Pope's the heat is more regular and constant. 8 Dryden often surpasses expectation, and Pope never falls below it. 9 Dryden is read with frequent astonishment, and Pope with perpetual delight.[1]

---

1. Is Samuel Johnson discussing differences, similarities, or both?
2. What are the subjects of the comparison?
3. Does Johnson complete his discussion of the first subject before beginning to discuss the second?
4. Since the same aspects of both subjects are discussed, one subject alternating with the other throughout the comparison, what pattern does this comparison follow?

B

FROM **What I Expected**

What I expected was
Thunder, fighting,
Long struggles with men
And climbing.
After continual straining
I should grow strong;
Then the rocks would shake
And I should rest long.

[1] Samuel Johnson, "Life of Pope," in *The Lives of the Most Eminent English Poets*, Vol. IV (London, 1794), pp. 160–61.

What I had not foreseen
Was the gradual day
Weakening the will
Leaking the brightness away,
The lack of good to touch
The fading of body and soul
Like smoke before wind
Corrupt, unsubstantial.

1. If Spender's poem is a comparison, what two subjects are being compared?
2. Does the comparison reveal similarities or differences or both?
3. "Before" and "after" are familiar subjects of comparison. What must the reader assume to have taken place between the two stanzas of this poem?
4. Since the poet finishes telling about the first subject before beginning to discuss the second, what comparison pattern does this selection follow?

C
FROM The Changing Face of Death

The funeral provides an excellent example of the changing nature of death in our society. Not many years ago the major function of the funeral was a ritualistic measure to help the soul get to its salvation in heaven. The funeral itself was not especially concerned with the body, although the body was to be kept intact and appropriately garbed.

The clergyman was responsible for the funeral, while the mortician was considered a skilled technician hired to do a mournful chore. However, the mortician also took it upon himself to give solace to the families of the deceased. Death was not hidden from the eyes of children; for example, the practice of kissing the dead, now looked upon as virtually a crime against children, was widely practiced without inducing the trauma so commonly associated with it today.

No one questioned the value of a funeral. Even cremation was considered heretical. A big funeral, like the potlatch it so closely resembled, meant that an affluent man had died. The number of people attending became a sign of pride. Consideration of a small, simple funeral, like a small, simple wedding, did not enter the picture.

Today the emphasis has shifted from the soul to the body. Death must be well-dressed, even pretty. The art of the embalmer is more ooh-ed and ahh-ed (He looks better than he did in life) than the fluency of the service. Along with the physician, the status of the embalmer has risen; the one keeps the body pretty and free of wasting ravages in life, while the other attains the same goal after life. The funeral service has become a eulogy of the dead, with little or no warning to the living to heed their own salvation. Indeed, hell and judgment are rarely touched upon in today's funeral service. . . .

From THE CHANGING FACE OF DEATH   By Richard A. Kalish. *The North American Review*, Winter, 1964. Copyright 1964 by Cornell College. Copyright 1969 by the University of Northern Iowa. Reprinted by permission.

As the role of death becomes more secular and less sacred, the role of the clergyman also moves in this direction. Thus many clergymen, especially those of less conservative Protestant and Jewish affiliation, perceive their major purpose in the funeral as that of comforting the bereaved, a function which has been that of the mortician since he replaced the coffin-maker and achieved a type of professional status. At the same time, by approaching funerals as a symbolic ritual rather than a necessary one, the contemporary minister is likely to discourage expensive funerals, elaborate caskets, and lavish display of flowers.

1. What are the subjects of this comparison?
2. What type of comparison is being made?
3. What pattern is used?
4. What is the stated purpose of this selection?
5. Is the pattern that the writer uses suitable to this purpose and to the comparative details given?

D
FROM **The Literature of Television**

1 . . . In using the phrase, "the literature of television," therefore, we are referring to those types of programs analogous in many of their purposes, if not in their form, to novels, short stories, plays, even essays. Before examining these types of programs in detail (we have called them "genres"), let us consider, in general, some of the similarities and differences between the literature of television and the more traditional forms with which we are all familiar.

2 Like all literary types, the literature of television reflects the assumptions and values of the men who create it and, to some extent, their assumptions about the audiences for whom they create. Thus, if there were few television plays of "social protest" in the 1950's, neither in literature nor in society were there many powerful and sustained expressions of social protest during the same period. Although we may criticize some of the literature of television for encouraging the acquisition of material comforts as an end in itself, we must concede that this tendency, too, is a genuine reflection of our times rather than an emphasis manufactured by latter-day Medicis. No doubt some of our collective virtues have also been reflected in the literature of television, as for example, our growing awareness of the dangers of class prejudice and ethnic stereotypes. In other words, to the extent that we may trust literature to reveal the prevailing attitudes of an era, television is perhaps as useful an index of the last decade as any other form of literature.

3 A second similarity is that, like the novel, short story, or play, the literature of television is uneven in quality. At its best, it is truthful and artistic.

From TELEVISION AND THE TEACHING OF ENGLISH   By Neil Postman and the Committee on the Study of Television of the National Council of Teachers of English, pp. 40–43. Copyright © 1961 by Appleton-Century-Crofts, Inc. Reprinted by permission of Appleton-Century-Crofts, Division of Meredith Corporation, and the National Council of Teachers of English.

Manhattan Skyline (Infrared Thermogram)

The Poet Reclining, Marc Chagall

Distant Thunder, Andrew Wyeth

Big Julie (1945), Fernand Léger

At its worst, it is trivial and formless. This is not to suggest that the best of television, say, Paddy Chayefsky's *Marty,* is the artistic equivalent of the best of twenty-four hundred years of the theater or even four hundred years of the novel. Such comparisons are unjust as well as unproductive. Rather, we are suggesting that in television, as in other literary forms, there are levels of value. *The Death of a Salesman* is a far cry from *Abie's Irish Rose* but perhaps no farther than is television's *Requiem for a Heavyweight* from *This Is Your Life.*

4 The literature of television is created within certain limitations, limitations imposed by the form of the medium. Limitations of form are, of course, well known to creators of novels, short stories, poems, journalism, stage plays, and films. The nature and extent of these limitations as they apply specifically to any medium define that medium's difference from other forms. For example, the form of the novel may be flexible enough to integrate, even exploit, lengthy philosophic discourse. The form of the film is not. The film, however, through the process of editing, lends itself to striking manipulations of time and space, while on "live" television such manipulations are less effective. The narrator may serve as a useful, perhaps essential, dramatic device on radio. In the theater, the Greek Chorus of *Electra* and the stage manager of *Our Town* notwithstanding, the narrator is less believable or, at least, less conventional.

5 The main part of this chapter will deal directly with the technical and artistic limitations and resources that make television unique. But some important differences between television and other forms of literature need mentioning before we begin.

6 In the first place, since the literature of television is transmitted simultaneously to millions of people, its creators are subject to limitations of theme, language, and style more severe than those in other media. In general, the wider the base of the audience, the greater the degree of restriction imposed on the creator, and no contemporary literary form has a more heterogeneous or massive audience than television.

7 In the second place, the line that separates commercial interests from literary interests in television is less distinct than in most other literary forms. To be sure, the publisher of novels and the producer of stage plays are concerned with making money. But in television . . . the advertiser, the man who pays the bills, is primarily concerned with the sale of a commercial product rather than an artistic one. At the same time, selling products and presenting high quality programs are not necessarily incompatible motives. There are, in fact, numerous examples of sponsors who have done both simultaneously.

8 [We] must remember, too, that the literature of television, unlike most types of literature, is highly ephemeral in character. At the moment, the libraries of television are its "reruns," but even so, a particular show must be seen at a specific time or it cannot be seen at all. As a result, studying or teaching about television presents certain problems not found in the study of other types of literature, except the legitimate stage.

9 Finally, unlike most types of literature, the literature of television defies easy classification. This poses a problem not only for those who would study or teach it but even for those who would praise it. For example, in 1948, when the National Academy of Television Arts and Sciences presented its first "Emmys," five awards were given, one of which was for "Best Film for Television" and another

for "Most Popular Television Program." The following year, neither of these categories was represented even though nine awards were given.

---

1. The literature of television (the first subject) is compared with what other subject?
2. The first paragraph tells us whether this comparison is to deal with similarities or differences or both. Which does it deal with?
3. What aspects are discussed in paragraphs 2, 3, and 4?
4. What do the comparisons of these aspects have in common?
5. Paragraph 5 functions as a transition paragraph. What does it indicate is to follow?
6. As you read the selection you probably realized that the author used the similarities and differences pattern because he found both similarities and differences worth discussing. But similarities and differences of two subjects may be treated under each aspect in the aspects pattern as well as in this more complex pattern. For what reasons do you think the author chose the similarities and differences pattern rather than the aspects pattern?
7. How does the similarities and differences pattern combine the other two patterns?

E
The Year 2000—The Trajectory of an Idea

Find examples of the three basic patterns of arranging comparisons in this selection (pp. 222–25), which you read for Dialog 9. List the number(s) of the paragraph(s) comprising each comparison pattern.

Summary

The use of a clear comparison pattern of arrangement guides the reader without confusion through your comparative details. But clear comparative writing also begins by telling the reader in a concise topic sentence or thesis statement what type of comparison is to follow. Locate and copy the general statements of comparison for Comparisons C and D; then write clear, appropriate statements for Comparisons A and B.

In conclusion, you will find that the use of one of the three patterns of arrangement combined with a general statement indicating the type of comparison to be made and the aspects to be discussed will help to ensure clarity and a sense of ease and control in your written comparisons. Add this to the sense and significance that can be achieved through the perceptive comparative thinking already discussed and you will have mastered some of the most essential elements of comparisons worth writing and reading.

REWRITING A COMPARISON

Writers at Work

E. B. White

Kenneth Roberts' working methods and ours differ so widely it is hard to realize we are in the same line of business. We've[1] just been looking through his book *I Wanted to Write* and marvelling at his stamina and his discipline. The thought of writing apparently stimulates Roberts and causes him to sit upright at a desk, put in requests to libraries, write friends, examine sources, and generally raise hell throughout the daylight hours and far into the night. He works at home (where his privacy is guarded), writes in longhand, counts the words, keeps a record of moneys received, and gets a great deal done. Now turn for a moment to your correspondent. The thought of writing hangs over our mind like an ugly cloud, making us apprehensive and depressed, as before a summer storm, so that we begin the day by subsiding after breakfast, or by going away, often to seedy and inconclusive destinations: the nearest zoo, or a branch post office to buy a few stamped envelopes. Our professional life has been a long, shameless exercise in avoidance. Our home is designed for the maximum of interruption, our office is the place where we never are. From his remarks, we gather that Roberts is contemptuous of this temperament and setup, regards it as largely a pose and certainly as a deficiency in blood. It has occurred to us that perhaps we are not a writer at all but merely a bright clerk who persists in crowding his destiny. Yet the record is there. Not even lying down and closing the blinds stops us from writing; not even our family, and our preoccupation with same, stops us. We have never counted the words, but we estimated them once and the estimate was staggering. The only conclusion we can draw is that there is no such thing as "the writing man," and that after you have waded through a book like *I Wanted to Write* you still don't know the half of it, and would be a fool to try and find out.

E. B. White, in this one-paragraph essay, "Writers at Work," compares differences between the working methods of Kenneth Roberts and himself. The pattern is obviously half and half, and since E. B. White is a careful craftsman (despite what he says about his working methods) he must have found this pattern suitable to his purposes and material. The directions below are designed to help you to think more deeply about the suitability of patterns to materials (comparative facts) and to purposes for writing.

WRITERS AT WORK   From *The Second Tree from the Corner* by E. B. White. Copyright, 1949 by E. B. White. Originally appeared in *The New Yorker*. Reprinted by permission of Harper & Row, publishers.

[1] E. B. White uses the first person plural in referring to himself.

1. White could have fulfilled a writing assignment, written the same number of words, or made the same amount of money by writing on any subject. Make a list of what seem to you to be White's probable purposes in writing this particular comparison.
2. In order to decide how the pattern that White uses fits his purposes, rewrite the essay following the directions given below.
   a. List, in parallel columns, details of the two men's working habits.
   b. Write a topic outline in the aspects pattern for these details (remember that conclusions are never included in outlines except *as* conclusions).
   c. Rewrite the essay, following your aspects pattern outline.
3. Consider which of the two patterns is more suitable for White's material by writing a brief paragraph comparing White's half and half arrangement with your aspects arrangement of the same material.

Transitional Expressions and Sentence Structure in Comparisons

DIALOG 10

Relationships Within and Between Parallel Sentences of Comparison

In writing comparisons, you will be concerned with comparative thoughts, whether similarities or differences, about parallel aspects of two subjects. Since your thoughts will be parallel or balanced, they can often be most effectively expressed in parallel or balanced form within compound sentences or in consecutive sentences, especially in the aspects and the similarities and differences patterns. Conscious control of the logical, grammatical, and rhetorical functions of the transitional expressions used in comparisons, as well as their punctuation, will increase your ability to integrate the content of your sentences with their form. Go through this dialog with paper ready and pencil in hand, as some questions should be answered in writing before you check the answers.

1. You have recently been reading the novels of Kenneth Roberts and essays and articles by E. B. White. The two thoughts, "E. B. White must be a productive writer" and "Kenneth Roberts certainly writes many novels," have occurred to you. Are these thoughts about the same aspects?	Yes, they both deal with the amount of writing produced by the subjects being compared. We can call them balanced thoughts, since both concern the same aspect.

2. Would the thoughts still be balanced if one of the writers had written many collected volumes and the other had produced only one?	Yes, they would still concern the same aspect.
3. What are the grammatical patterns of these two sentences?	$S(N_1)$ $LV(V)$ $SC(N_1)$ E. B. White must be a (productive) writer. $S(N_1)$ Kenneth Roberts (certainly) $TrV(V)$ $DO(N_2)$ writes (many) novels.
4. Are the sentences parallel in form?	No.
5. How could they be made parallel in form to reflect their balance in thought?	We could write "E. B. White is a productive writer. Kenneth Roberts is a productive writer." Both would be parallel S–LV–SC patterns.
6. We could write such sentences, but only when the sentences are long or we particularly wish to stress the similarity would we do so. Since these two sentences share common essential elements (verbs and subjective complements) in the predicate "is a productive writer," it seems elementary and repetitious to repeat that predicate. Combine the two sentences into one simple sentence by compounding the subjects to share the common elements.	E. B. White and Kenneth Roberts are productive writers.
7. Joining whole subjects, simple subjects, whole predicates, verbs, or complements with a coordinating conjunction (*and, but, for, nor, or, so, yet*) compounds them. Compounding essential sentence parts is natural, economical, and rhythmically pleasing to the ear. It is especially useful in stating similarities. Is such compounding of sentence parts possible with these two sentences emphasizing differences? "Kenneth Roberts wrote primarily novels. E. B. White is primarily a nonfiction writer."	No, they share no common element.

8. We could make these sentences parallel so that they do share a common essential element, the verb, and then compound the subjects and the direct objects in order to share that verb. What is wrong with the sentence "Kenneth Roberts and E. B. White write novels and essays and articles"?

Nothing, grammatically, but it does not make clear the difference you want to point out. The parallel differences have been "absorbed" by sentence structure suitable to expressing similarities.

---

9. But compounding of these two parallel ideas is possible, of course, since whole sentence patterns can be compounded as well as their essential and nonessential parts. (Parallel nonessential modification may be compounded also, and while such compounding is useful to comparative writing, it is not integral nor exclusive to the writing of comparisons and so will not be treated here.) The same coordinating conjunctions that can compound sentence parts can compound whole sentences. How would you join the two sentences in question 7 with a coordinating conjunction to form one compound sentence?

Kenneth Roberts wrote historical novels, but E. B. White writes articles and essays.

---

10. Why did we use *but* to join these two sentences when we used *and* to join sentences expressing similarities?

But logically "means" that the two elements joined by it are different in some way; *and,* when used for comparison, "means" that the two elements joined by it are similar.

---

11. *But* and *and* are the two *coordinating conjunctions* that express the logical relationships of comparison at the same time that they connect the two sentence patterns in a grammatical way. What they do grammatically is expressed in their descriptive name, "coordinating conjunctions." What does "conjunction" mean?

"Joiner"—the conjunction joins one thing with another. It is one of several types of connectors in English.

---

12. What does "coordinating" mean?

It means setting together in equal rank. The coordinating conjunction functions by joining together in equal rank the elements it appears between. Another word for this function is compounding.

13. In the sentence "Kenneth Roberts wrote historical novels, but E. B. White writes articles and essays," the coordinating conjunction functions by coordinating what two elements?	It coordinates two complete sentence patterns into one compound sentence, both parts of which are equal.
14. We have examined the logical and grammatical functions of the coordinating conjunctions *and* and *but*. How would you describe their rhetorical function? That is, when they are used between parallel sentence patterns, what sentence style results and what effect does it have on the reader?	The compound sentence is rhetorically balanced, a sentence type that gives equal weight and emphasis to the predication on either side of the coordinating conjunction. This sentence structure should cause its reader formally to balance in his mind the parallel halves of the comparison made by the sentence.
15. Form an abstract punctuation pattern to represent conventional punctuation of the compound sentence with a coordinating conjunction.	*Sentence pattern, coordinating conjunction sentence pattern.*
16. Review the four ways we have looked at the coordinating conjunction: a. What is its logical function? b. What is its grammatical function? c. What is its rhetorical function? d. What punctuation pattern fits its use between complete sentences?	a. To indicate the type of comparison between the elements it connects. *And* indicates that they are similar (when it is used comparatively—it very often is used to show simple addition or accumulation.) *But* indicates that they are different in some way. b. To coordinate the elements it appears between. If those elements are complete sentence patterns it forms a grammatically compound sentence. c. When used between complete parallel sentence patterns, it forms the rhetorically balanced sentence, its halves parallel and equal in emphasis. d. *Sentence pattern, coordinating conjunction sentence pattern.*
17. We have shown only one possible way to join two complete comparative sentences; in this dialog, we will discuss four more possibilities. We could, for instance, write "E. B. White is a productive writer; Kenneth Roberts, likewise, was a productive writer." Here *likewise* functions as the connector even though it is not placed between the sentence patterns. What other single words can you think of that could replace *likewise* in this sentence?	*Also, similarly.* (These are *conjunctive adverbs* that express similarity.)

18. We can also write a comparison of difference with the conjunctive adverb *however,* which expresses this logical relationship. "Mr. White is known for his nonfiction; Mr. Roberts, however, is best remembered for his historical novels." Could *but* replace *however* in this position?	No, "Mr. White is known for his nonfiction; Mr. Roberts, *but,* is best remembered for his historical novels" is not a sentence a native speaker of English would use. This difference in possible positions is one of the reasons coordinating conjunctions and conjunctive adverbs are classified as two different types of connectors.
19. Can *however* be used between the two sentence patterns as *but* and *and* can?	Yes, it is always grammatically correct, although sometimes stylistically awkward, especially with short sentences. ("Mr. White is known for his nonfiction; *however,* Mr. Roberts is best remembered for his historical novels.")
20. There is another difference in usable positions between the two types of connectors. *But* and *and* can join single words, phrases, and clauses as well as whole sentence patterns. Remember "E. B. White *and* Kenneth Roberts are productive writers"? Try to use *however* in place of *and* in this sentence.	"E. B. White *however* Kenneth Roberts are productive writers." It won't do. Conjunctive adverbs are used to "conjoin" only whole sentence patterns. This difference also helps to distinguish the two types of connectors.
21. Although they differ in possible positions, conjunctive adverbs and coordinating conjunctions are similar in several ways. Both express the logical type of comparison between the sentence patterns they join. Is the grammatical function of the conjunctive adverb also the same as that of the coordinating conjunction?	Yes. It too coordinates or joins two sentence patterns into one compound sentence.
22. Write the abstract punctuation pattern of the compound sentence joined with a conjunctive adverb.	*Sentence pattern; conjunctive adverb, sentence pattern.* If the conjunctive adverb is moved to within the second sentence pattern, the punctuation pattern is this: *Sentence pattern; subject, conjunctive adverb, predicate.* (This characteristic movability of the conjunctive adverb causes it to be classified as an adverb. Its position is purely a matter of stylistic choice.)

23. The *transitional phrase* is another type of transitional expression that can be used to connect two balanced sentences. "E. B. White prefers to write nonfiction; Kenneth Roberts, on the contrary, preferred to write fiction." Substitute other phrases for *on the contrary* in this sentence.

on the other hand, in contrast to this

24. What logical connection between sentences do such transitional phrases as *on the contrary* signify?

That of difference.

25. Transitional phrases indicating similarity are *in the same manner* or *in like manner.* The only difference between transitional phrases and conjunctive adverbs is that the phrases are phrases; that is, they consist of more than one word and conjunctive adverbs do not. Therefore, quickly review the common functions and punctuation of both the conjunctive adverb and the transitional phrase.
a. What is their logical function?
b. What is their grammatical function?
c. What is their rhetorical function?
d. With what punctuation patterns are they used?

a. To express that the sentence patterns they connect are similar or different.
b. To join two complete sentence patterns in equal rank—to compound them.
c. To create balanced sentences.
d. *Sentence pattern;*
$\left\{\begin{array}{c} \textit{conjunctive adverb,} \\ \textit{or} \\ \textit{transitional expression,} \end{array}\right\}$
sentence pattern.
or
Sentence pattern; subject,
$\left\{\begin{array}{c} \textit{conjunctive adverb,} \\ \textit{or} \\ \textit{transitional expression,} \end{array}\right\}$
predicate.

26. A very few *subordinating conjunctions* can also express the relationships of similarity and difference. Locate them and identify the logic expressed by them in the following two sentences:
"As E. B. White is a voluminous writer, so was Kenneth Roberts a voluminous writer."
"White edited anthologies, wrote scholarly works, articles for *The New Yorker* and *Harper's,* children's books, and some of America's wittiest essays, while Roberts confined himself primarily to writing American historical novels."

As . . . so indicates similarity (*just as . . . so* is a variation).
While indicates difference.

27. These connectors have the same logical function as the other types, but they differ in grammatical function, for, as their name states, they *subordinate* the sentence pattern that they head to another sentence pattern. A subordinating conjunction plus a sentence pattern becomes a modifier, an adverbial clause, and the sentence in which the modifier is used becomes complex. Looking at the sentences in question 26 above, construct punctuation patterns to fit this type of connector.

Adverbial clause, sentence pattern. (first sentence) *Sentence pattern, adverbial clause.* (second sentence) Notice that it is the first part of the two-part subordinating conjunctions *as . . . so* and *just as . . . so* that subordinates.

28. Another alternative way to connect two balanced sentences is by use of a semicolon. The following punctuation pattern represents a popular choice of form for a compound sentence: *Sentence pattern; sentence pattern.* Using our two subjects, write a sentence following this pattern.

"Kenneth Roberts wrote fiction; E. B. White does not." Or, "White has been a prolific writer; Roberts was a prolific writer."

29. How can the semicolon first indicate difference and then similarity?

It doesn't actually indicate either; it merely indicates a close relationship of some kind between the two sentence patterns it joins into one compound sentence. The reader must decide what that relationship is.

30. We started with two parallel sentences and used four different methods to combine them into compound comparative sentences. What are those four possibilities?

Using a coordinating conjunction, using a conjunctive adverb, using a transitional expression, and using just a semicolon.

31. A fifth alternative is to express the relationship in a complex sentence. How can two sentence patterns be joined this way?

Using a subordinating conjunction (as . . . so, just as . . . so, while).

32. There remains the very useful method of expressing balanced thoughts *without* combining the sentences. All of the transitional expressions we have shown, except for the subordinating conjunctions, can express relationships between separate, consecutive sentences. Write a pair of sentences following each of these punctuation patterns:

a. *Sentence pattern. Transitional phrase, sentence pattern.*

A few possibilities:
a. Mr. White writes many essays and articles. On the other hand, Mr. Roberts wrote early American historical novels.

b. *Sentence pattern. Coordinating conjunction, sentence pattern.*
c. *Sentence pattern. Subject, conjunctive adverb, predicate.*

b. Mr. White writes nonfiction exclusively. But Mr. Roberts preferred fiction.
c. Mr. White produces quantities of nonfiction. Mr. Roberts, similarly, was a voluminous writer.

---

33. We have exhausted many alternatives in expressing balanced comparative thoughts. Perhaps the best way to summarize would be for you to make a list of the expressions that can be used to signify the logic of difference and a list of those that can be used to signify the logic of similarity. Include with each expression the punctuation used before it when it joins two sentence patterns. The best final result of the dialog will be, of course, your use of varied, effective transitional expressions in your writing of comparisons.

Difference:
> *but* (comma precedes when it joins two sentence patterns)
> *however* (semicolon precedes)
> *on the contrary* (semicolon precedes)
> *on the other hand* (semicolon precedes)
> *in contrast to this* (semicolon precedes)
> *while* (comma precedes)
> *;* (can imply difference in context)

Similarity:
> *and* (comma precedes when it joins two sentence patterns)
> *likewise* (semicolon precedes)
> *similarly* (semicolon precedes)
> *also* (semicolon precedes)
> *in like manner* (semicolon precedes)
> *in the same manner* (semicolon precedes)
> *as . . . so* (comma) or *just as . . . so* (comma)
> *;* (can imply similarity in context)

EXERCISE 12

Transitional Expressions in Context

Here are transitional expressions in the context of sentences chosen from comparisons in Part III. Write out the information requested about each sentence or group of sentences.

1. "The future is not an overarching leap into the distance; it begins in the present."
   a. How are the two sentence patterns connected?
   b. What is the logical function of the connector?
   c. What is its rhetorical function?
   d. What is its grammatical function?

2. "The form of the film is not. The film, however, through the process of editing, lends itself to striking manipulations of time and space, while on 'live' television such manipulations are less effective."
   a. What are the two connectors used here?
   b. What type of connector is the first?
   c. What is its logical function?
   d. The second connector is what type of connector?
   e. What is its logical function?
   f. What is the grammatical function of the second connector?

3. "We have never counted the words, but we estimated them once and the estimate was staggering."
   a. What connector in this sentence expresses the logic of comparison?
   b. Which type of comparison does it signify?
   c. What is its grammatical function?
   d. What is the punctuation pattern of this sentence? (White has omitted the customary comma from between the last two complete sentence patterns connected by *and* because of their exceedingly short length.)

4. "Discussion about sex and the physical body is no longer restricted: families talk about sex at the breakfast table. . . . On the other hand, death and God are personal matters, not to be mentioned in polite society."
   a. What transitional expression is used here?
   b. What is its logical function?
   c. Which punctuation pattern is used?

5. "The real ship was 882.5 feet long; the fictional one was 800 feet."
   a. What is the punctuation pattern of this sentence?
   b. Which type of comparison is implied?
   c. This sentence is what rhetorical type?

6. "It is impossible, if no more than one opinion is uttered, to make choice of the best: A man is forced then to follow whatever advice may have been given him; but if opposite speeches are delivered, then choice can be exercised. In like manner, pure gold is not recognized by itself; but when we test it along with baser ore, we perceive which is the better."
   a. What are the three transitional expressions used here and which types of comparison do they signify?
   b. What are two differences between the connectors *but* and *in like manner*? (Notice that this writer used semicolons between two complete sentence patterns connected with *but* because commas are used within the patterns.)

7. "Just as the gridiron pattern of city streets in the nineteenth century shaped the linear growth of cities in the twentieth, so the new networks of radial highways, the location of new towns . . . and the like will frame the tectonics of the twenty-first century."

  a. What is the complete transitional expression used in this sentence?
  b. What is its grammatical function?
  c. What is its logical function?
  d. What is its rhetorical function?
8. "The style of Dryden is capricious and varied; that of Pope is cautious and uniform. Dryden observes the motions of his own mind; Pope constrains his mind to his own rules of composition. Dryden is sometimes vehement and rapid; Pope is always smooth, uniform, and gentle. Dryden's page is a natural field, rising into inequalities, and diversified by the varied exuberance of abundant vegetation; Pope's is a velvet lawn, shaven by the scythe, and levelled by the roller."

  a. Which grammatical type of sentence does every sentence in this excerpt exemplify?
  b. Which rhetorical type of sentence do they exemplify?
  c. Which logical type of comparison is implied by the punctuation in every sentence?
  d. Write the grammatical patterns of each of the first three sentences. (Notice the compounding of subject complements, and notice the exact parallelism between the two halves of each sentence. Is the author's [Samuel Johnson's] style more like his description of Dryden' style or of Pope's?)
  e. What is the rhetorical type of each half of the final sentence?
  f. What is the grammatical type of each half of the final sentence?
  g. What figurative comparisons are made in the final sentence?

SUGGESTED WRITING ASSIGNMENT

Imitating Sentences Expressing Comparisons

Choose three to five sentences or groups of sentences containing a variety of connectors from those you examined in Exercise 12. For each sentence or group of sentences, first write an abstract pattern describing its grammatical structure, then write a new sentence that imitates this grammatical structure exactly. For example, if you chose sentence 7, you would first write an abstract pattern like this:

Subordinating conjunction (first half)–Subject–Prepositional phrase–Prepositional phrase–Transitive verb–Direct object–Prepositional phrase–Prepositional phrase, Subordinating conjunction (second half)–Compound subject (Subject$_1$–Prepositional phrase–Subject$_2$–Prepositional phrase–Subject$_3$)–Transitive verb–Direct object–Prepositional phrase.

You would then write a sentence that contained all of the elements in the pattern and in the same order as you listed them. In writing your imitations do not write about the same subjects that the sentence you are imitating is about; for instance, if you are imitating sentence 7, you would not compare the tectonics of the nineteenth and twenty-first centuries. Your subjects and the words in which you express them will, of course, differ widely from those of the models you imitate; you are to imitate grammatical and rhetorical structures only.

In choosing subjects for these sentences, think about the different patterns of living that are possible in our society. Differing ways of living one's life are subjects of concern to most of us. On the following pages are a few of many contemporary glances at our varied and changing life-patterns, expressed in the diverse genres of cartoons and poems. Using the examples of either type as a springboard for comparative thought, and remembering to be as specific as possible, try to express your ideas in the structures you have outlined. You will find this kind of imitation time-consuming but challenging, and one of the very best methods of increasing your ease and skill with a variety of sentence structures and styles.

LOOK 10-17-67

"You heard me, Dad—I said you and Mom are creeps,
and I'm going to split and get adopted by a stockbroker and
join the Boy Scouts and play Little League ball!"

"Crazy!"   *"Crazy!"*

Life Cycle of Common Man

Howard Nemerov

Roughly figured, this man of moderate habits,
This average consumer of the middle class,
Consumed in the course of his average life span
Just under half a million cigarettes,
Four thousand fifths of gin and about
A quarter as much vermouth; he drank
Maybe a hundred thousand cups of coffee,
And counting his parents' share it cost
Something like half a million dollars
To put him through life. How many beasts
Died to provide him with meat, belt and shoes
Cannot be certainly said.

LIFE CYCLE OF COMMON MAN   From *New and Selected Poems,* University of Chicago Press, 1960.
Reprinted by permission of Margot Johnson Agency.

But anyhow,
It is in this way that a man travels through time,
Leaving behind him a lengthening trail
Of empty bottles and bones, of broken shoes,
Frayed collars and worn out or outgrown
Diapers and dinnerjackets, silk ties and slickers.

Given the energy and security thus achieved,
He did . . . ? What? The usual things, of course,
The eating, dreaming, drinking and begetting,
And he worked for the money which was to pay
For the eating, et cetera, which were necessary
If he were to go on working for the money, et cetera,
But chiefly he talked. As the bottles and bones
Accumulated behind him, the words proceeded
Steadily from the front of his face as he
Advanced into the silence and made it verbal.
Who can tally the tale of his words? A lifetime
Would barely suffice for their repetition;
If you merely printed all his commas the result
Would be a very large volume, and the number of times
He said "thank you" or "very little sugar, please,"
Would stagger the imagination. There were also
Witticisms, platitudes, and statements beginning
"It seems to me" or "As I always say."

Consider the courage in all that, and behold the man
Walking into deep silence, with the ectoplastic
Cartoon's balloon of speech proceeding
Steadily out of the front of his face, the words
Borne along on the breath which is his spirit
Telling the numberless tale of his untold Word
Which makes the world his apple, and forces him to eat.

The Unknown Citizen

W. H. Auden

(*To JS/07/M/378*
This Marble Monument
Is Erected by the State)

He was found by the Bureau of Statistics to be
One against whom there was no official complaint,
And all the reports on his conduct agree

That, in the modern sense of an old-fashioned word, he was a saint,
For in everything he did he served the Greater Community.
Except for the War till the day he retired
He worked in a factory and never got fired,
But satisfied his employers, Fudge Motors Inc.
Yet he wasn't a scab or odd in his views,
For his Union reports that he paid his dues,
(Our report on his Union shows it was sound)
And our Social Psychology workers found
That he was popular with his mates and liked a drink.
The Press are convinced that he bought a paper every day
And that his reactions to advertisements were normal in every way.
Policies taken out in his name prove that he was fully insured,
And his Health-card shows he was once in hospital but left it cured.
Both Producers Research and High-Grade Living declare
He was fully sensible to the advantages of the Instalment Plan
And had everything necessary to the Modern Man,
A phonograph, a radio, a car and a frigidaire.
Our researchers into Public Opinion are content
That he held the proper opinions for the time of year;
When there was peace, he was for peace; when there was war, he went.
He was married and added five children to the population,
Which our Eugenist says was the right number for a parent of his generation,
And our teachers report that he never interfered with their education.
Was he free? Was he happy? The question is absurd:
Had anything been wrong, we should certainly have heard.

REVISING SENTENCES AND CREATING ORIGINAL SENTENCES OF COMPARISON

A.

When you rewrote White's short essay, you did so thinking of the pattern but not particularly of the individual sentences comprising the pattern. Yet those individual sentences are important. If you reread White's original essay with sentence construction in mind, you will notice that his sentences fit his half and half structure very well. For example, read the sentences about Roberts' habits. Notice how the crisp, short sentences with many active verbs, little modification, and exact parallelism reflect in their very form their content—Roberts' brisk and businesslike approach to writing. And what happens to the sentence style after "Now turn for a moment to your correspondent?" The next sentence meanders vaguely and leisurely along, with much modification, getting nowhere in particular, evading action just as White is saying in it that he evades getting at his writing. Such is the subtlty writers can use in creating sentences. Since the half and half pattern, which White uses, treats one subject before discussing the next,

White does not need to use balanced sentences treating both subjects to the extent that your revision, which uses the aspects pattern, does. You are now ready to revise again your Roberts-White comparison by consciously combining sentence patterns to include the balanced sentence structure, the parallelism, and the precise connectors you have studied since your first revision. This study, plus your work with sentence imitation, should help you to bring your sentences to the most finished and mature comparative form possible.

B.

The preceding assignments have required you to imitate and to revise sentences expressing comparisons; the next step is obviously for you to create new sentence comparisons of your own. The goal of this assignment is to enable you to write sophisticated, varied, even exciting sentences expressing comparisons that are significant to you. Your choice and treatment of significant comparisons will indicate your individuality as well as your understanding of the devices available to you as a writer of comparative sentences. Remember that part of the fascination of writing is that the very process can help you to discover what you have to say. Again use the cartoons and poems on pages 252–55 as a basis for comparative thought. You may wish to use the cartoons merely as a suggestive take-off for your own thoughts on the two views of life they glance at, but if you choose to use the poems, you will probably wish to compare them as poems, considering both the ideas they embody and the form in which they embody them.

Create five original sentence comparisons, consciously formulating your balanced thoughts into superior balanced sentences, four using one of each type of transitional expressions and one using only punctuation. Try to write a few sentences expressing similarities as well as a few expressing differences. *After* creating the most finished sentences of which you are capable, which may take many rewritings, label their grammatical and rhetorical types.

The Essay of Comparison

SUGGESTED WRITING ASSIGNMENT

Writing a Comparison Essay

You should now be ready to write an essay comparing subjects of your own choosing. You may consider this an assignment to write a setting for the original sentences that you wrote for the preceding assignment, for you may incorporate them into your essay if you choose to further develop the comparisons you made there. Or you may wish to start fresh with new subjects. For instance, the two stanzas from Stephen Spender's short poem "What I Expected" on page 236 might suggest to you a comparison of your feelings before and after a disillusioning experience of your own. Whatever the subjects you choose to compare, the following steps will be useful to you in writing this essay or a comparison in any area of study. (A comparison item is very common in essay examinations; you may, for example, be asked in history to "Compare and contrast the social structure of France before and after the Revolution" or in art to "Compare Grecian and Roman art.")

Steps in Writing an Essay of Comparison

1. After you have chosen the general subjects of your essay, consider your past experiences, including reading, that relate to these subjects and jot down all possible aspects and relationships of the subjects that you can think of, no matter how wild or how dull.
2. Decide upon the aspects that you will use by considering which of them are the most significant and parallel and which of them you have the time and specific information to develop adequately. (This process of thinking of and evaluating aspects is an aid to memory; it helps you to recall and organize your experience of and knowledge about the subjects.)
3. With your material in mind, decide upon the types of comparison you will develop—similarities in kind or relationship, or differences in kind or degree.
4. Write your thesis statement, stating the type of comparison to be developed in the essay and listing the main aspects if possible.
5. Decide upon the pattern of arrangement (half and half, aspects, or similarities and differences) most appropriate for your central thesis, your materials, and your purpose. You may have to try fitting your facts into more than one pattern in outline form before writing. (For this first essay, at least, write outlines in two different patterns to hand in with your essay.)
6. Write the essay, following the better outline and developing each part of your comparison pattern with appropriate details, reports, and examples.

Notice that actually *writing* an essay is merely the final step in a process that includes many pre-writing steps. It is when these essential thinking-and-organizing steps are omitted that poor essays result. Even when writing under pressure of time limitations, as in essay examinations or the writing of essays in class, up to a third of that time can be best spent upon steps 1–5, the pre-writing steps.

COMBINING COMPARISON PATTERNS IN AN ESSAY

The following selection, the Foreword to *A Night to Remember*,[2] is an interesting combination of comparison patterns. After reading it, answer the

[2] From *A Night to Remember* by Walter Lord. Copyright © 1955 by Walter Lord. Reprinted by permission of Holt, Rinehart and Winston, Inc.

questions that follow. Keep in mind that you may find such combinations useful to your next writing.

In 1898 a struggling author named Morgan Robertson concocted a novel about a fabulous Atlantic liner, far larger than any that had ever been built. Robertson loaded his ship with rich and complacent people and then wrecked it one cold April night on an iceberg. This somehow showed the futility of every-thing, and in fact, the book was called *Futility* when it appeared that year, pub-lished by the firm of M. F. Mansfield.

Fourteen years later a British shipping company named the White Star Line built a steamer remarkably like the one in Robertson's novel. The new liner was 66,000 tons displacement; Robertson's was 70,000 tons. The real ship was 882.5 feet long; the fictional one was 800 feet. Both vessels were triple screw and could make 24–25 knots. Both could carry about 3000 people, and both had enough lifeboats for only a fraction of this number. But, then, this didn't seem to matter because both were labeled "unsinkable."

On April 10, 1912, the real ship left Southampton on her maiden voyage to New York. Her cargo included a priceless copy of the *Rubáiyát* of Omar Khayyám and a list of passengers collectively worth $250 million dollars. On her way over she too struck an iceberg and went down on a cold April night.

Robertson called his ship the *Titan;* the White Star Line called its ship the *Titanic.* This is the story of her last night.

---

1. What are the subjects of the comparison?
2. What type of comparison is made?
3. What pattern of arrangement is used in the second paragraph?
4. List the seven aspects being compared in the second paragraph.
5. Of what rhetorical type are the second and third sentences of the second paragraph?
6. Examine paragraphs one and three. What *pattern* of arrangement do they make up, taken together?
7. What do you think could have been Walter Lord's reason for retaining one aspect of the similarity for a final short paragraph?
8. Write a topic outline of the arrangement of the comparison in the selection. (Note: Each paragraph furnishes a main division in this instance.) Label the main divisions with their patterns of arrangement.

As you have probably concluded, the particular aspects of the subjects you wish to compare and the stress you wish to give them may require that you combine the comparison patterns imaginatively. If you do so for class assignments, indicate clearly that you are doing so by writing the patterns in the margin.

THE USE OF FACTUAL DETAIL AND EXEMPLIFICATION IN THE DEVELOPMENT OF COMPARATIVE IDEAS

When one has mastered the logic of comparing, the arranging of comparisons in patterns or combinations of those patterns, the writing of balanced and mature sentences with accurate transitions, and the steps in writing an essay, there remains one area of development to consider: developing the ideas in the comparative statements that form the parts of the pattern. Without support of some kind, your essay will remain skeletal, composed of statements your reader must take on faith rather than on the basis of the supporting evidence. Examining the development of other writers' comparisons may help you to understand how factual detail and exemplification are incorporated as evidence into comparative essays and to realize that your past work in this course is ready to be put to service in developing your comparisons.

[Socrates and the Sophists]

1 To some of his contemporaries Socrates looked like a sophist. 2 But he distrusted and opposed the sophists wherever possible. 3 They toured the whole Greek world; Socrates stayed in Athens, talking to his fellow-citizens. 4 They made carefully prepared continuous speeches; he only asked questions. 5 They took rich fees for their teaching; he refused regular payment, living and dying poor. 6 They were elegantly dressed, turned out like film-stars on a personal-appearance tour, with secretaries and personal servants and elaborate advertising. 7 Socrates wore the workingman's clothes, bare feet and a smock; in fact, he had been a stone-mason and carver by trade, and came from a working-class family. 8 They spoke in specially prepared lecture-halls; he talked to people at street corners and in the gymnasium. . . . 9 He fitted in so well there that he sometimes compared himself to the athletic coach, who does not run or wrestle, but teaches others how to run and wrestle better: Socrates said he trained people to think. 10 Lastly, the sophists said they knew everything and were ready to explain it. 11 Socrates said he knew nothing and was trying to find out.

1. What are the subjects being compared, the comparative relationship shown, and the pattern of arrangement?
2. What topic idea does the paragraph develop?
3. What logical type of statements make up this topic idea?
4. How does the paragraph develop the idea?
5. Although each statement develops the differences between Socrates and the sophists, is each statement itself developed? Does any other statement use factual details as do sentences 6 and 7? Would more development through detail improve the paragraph?
6. This paragraph is clear in its use of the aspects pattern. List the aspects common to both subjects treated in each compound sentence and in consecutive parallel sentences.

Anachronism

The boy playing the cello was eleven. His eyes were intent on the music stand before him, his rounded, child's features serious, the lips parted slightly, the tip of his tongue in a corner of his mouth. The short, stocky fingers of his left hand moved up and down the neck of the instrument, gripping the strings strongly, unhesitatingly, slapping the strings like pistons. His short bowing arm thrust and swept, but its movement was not reflected elsewhere in his set, purposeful body.

For fifteen minutes he had played without apparent diversion, yet on the floor beside him lay a fielder's glove, and on his head he wore a soiled, orange baseball cap, pushed back so that a shock of yellow hair hung over his bronzed forehead. His shirt was khaki, a Boy Scout shirt decorated with red and silver insignia, its tail hanging out over faded blue jeans that were patched on the knees that hugged the instrument. His feet, which had not moved from their set position, were square-toed, tanned, bare. The music he played was Baroque—a saraband—a dance of crystal-lighted, powder-wigged elegance.

1. What is the meaning of the title?
2. Is the comparison of this selection stated or implied?
3. What are the two subjects compared?
4. How is the comparison developed?
5. What rhetorical type of sentence is predominant? How is it appropriate to this type of development?
6. This selection is a journal entry; as such it is complete. If it were to be a complete essay, what would need to be added?

ANACHRONISM: A student journal entry reprinted by permission of the student.

7. What conclusions can you draw from consideration of this selection about the value of objective reporting to the development of comparisons?

Foreword to *A Night to Remember*

1. As you reread this selection with development in mind, you will probably be impressed by the amount and specificity of support. How would you characterize the development?
2. Notice how confident the author, Walter Lord, is that his support is convincing; he does not even feel it necessary to make a general summarizing statement. Is he right—do you get the message without its being stated for you?
3. In a formal essay, however, you would need the higher level of abstraction. What thesis statement would be appropriate to this development?

FROM **The Year 2000—The Trajectory of an Idea**

1. Reread the third paragraph of this article (on pp. 222–23). What is its topic sentence?
2. The development of the paragraph supports the second half of the comparative generalization that is its topic sentence. Of what does the development of this idea consist?
3. List the specific support used in this paragraph.
4. Question 2 uses the term "comparative generalization." Comparative generalizations form one common type of general statement for comparisons. Another possibility is a statement of straight comparison. Based on your knowledge of generalizations, what do you think is the difference between the two types?
5. Why is the topic sentence for paragraph 3 called a comparative generalization?
6. Your thesis statement for Walter Lord's Foreword is probably a straight comparison. If it is not, try to formulate a straight comparison for it.

The selections discussed in this section should prove helpful when you are writing your own comparison essays. The journal entry "Anachronism" can serve as a model for description suitable for developing comparisons. When you use factual details for developing a statement of comparison, keep the Foreword to *A Night to Remember* in mind as a model. And the third paragraph of "The Year 2000—The Trajectory of an Idea" is an excellent example of the use of exemplification in developing comparative ideas.

SUGGESTED WRITING ASSIGNMENT

Writing Another Comparison Essay

Before you write your final comparison essay in Part III, a quick review is in order. Your essay should include evidence of the following: (1) clear thinking about types of comparisons in your thesis and throughout, (2) individual use and probably mixtures of patterns of arranging your comparative details, (3) variety in balanced sentences and appropriate transitions, and (4) the use of many types of specific reports and examples, with their own diction and sentence structure, to develop and support your ideas. Especially review the steps in the writing of a comparison theme, on page 257, and add to this list the final, post-writing step of thorough proofreading and revision before considering this essay finished. Your instructor may wish to see your outline with the finished paper.

To stimulate your thinking and to give you suggested subjects for comparison, we have provided implied comparisons in three different forms: a painting, a poem, and a story. The poem "Trees" and the story "Digging the Weans" follow; the painting "The Great Julie" faces page 239. Each is suggestive of more than one set of comparisons; they are not intended as puzzles with "correct" answers but as sources of ideas to be developed from your own specific experience and thought. Exactly what you will do with any one of the implied comparisons is up to you. No questions accompany them, and there are no further directions other than to write a comparison that has significance to you as an individual living in a complex society.

Trees

Howard Nemerov

> To be a giant and keep quiet about it,
> To stay in one's own place;
> To stand for the constant presence of process
> And always to seem the same;
> To be steady as a rock and always trembling,
> Having the hard appearance of death
> With the soft, fluent nature of growth,
> One's Being deceptively armored,

TREES   From *New and Selected Poems*, University of Chicago Press, 1960. Reprinted by permission of Margot Johnson Agency.

One's Becoming deceptively vulnerable;
To be so tough, and take the light so well,
Freely providing forbidden knowledge
Of so many things about heaven and earth
For which we should otherwise have no word—
Poems or people are rarely so lovely,
And even when they have great qualities
They tend to tell you rather than exemplify
What they believe themselves to be about,
While from the moving silence of trees,
Whether in storm or calm, in leaf and naked,
Night or day, we draw conclusions of our own,
Sustaining and unnoticed as our breath,
And perilous also—though there has never been
A critical tree—about the nature of things.

Digging the Weans

Robert Nathan

Drawings by N. M. Bodecker

The inscription on the north wall of the temple at Pound-Laundry on the east coast of the Great West Continent has finally been deciphered by the team led by Sr. B'Han Bollek. This work brings us certain assurance of the theory expressed by Bes Nef, Hanh Shui, and Nat Obelgerst-Levy that a people of considerable numbers and power formerly inhabited this salt and desolate land. It is a triumph for those archaeologists who have been working ever since the fortunate discovery of an ivory cross and string of beads at the northeast, or "Bosstin" tumulus, along with a rusted iron wheel which seems to have been designed to run along some kind of track or trolley. These artifacts, as everyone knows, are now in the museum at Kenya.

What we have been unable to discover, is the fate of these ancient people. That they perished in some sort of upheaval many thousands of years ago is clear from the inscription itself, which Sr. B'Han Bollek translates as follows: "nor [for north?] rain nor hail nor snow . . ." there are some hieroglyphics missing, and the inscription ends with the phrase . . . "their appointed rounds."

However, it must be remembered that the *r* and the *w* are readily interchangeable, both in Hittite and in ancient Hivite, and Bes Nef prefers the reading: "their pointed wounds." This naturally suggests a catastrophe, possibly an invasion from the east, a belief, I may add, greatly encouraged by the findings in the Valley

of the Sun, which will be discussed later. On the other hand, if, as some believe, including B'Han Bollek, that the phrase should be read: "their appointed rounds," the meaning of the full inscription might well be as follows: "The north rain, the hail and the snow [also from the north] have accomplished their appointed 'rounds' [or tasks]" . . . namely, have annihilated the inhabitants.

So much, then, we do know; but very little else is known of these ancient people. Professor Shui believes that they may have been Brythons, and related to the still older, Druidic culture whose stones are still to be seen in the East Island. Professor Shui bases this theory upon a certain similarity in the two glyphs, the Brythonic "bathe" and the Wean "bath"; but his theory necessarily comes to grief when one examines the glyph for "that which rises"—the Brythonic "lift" and the Wean "elevator" having obviously no common root.

I have called these people the Weans, because certain archaeological findings incline us to the belief that they called their land the We, or the Us; actually, in the southern part of the continent, the word Wenus (or Weans) does appear, as well as the glyph for Wealls, and the word Theyuns.

To return for a moment to the theory of catastrophe, and the "pointed wounds" of Bes Nef. In the Valley of the Sun there have been unearthed many bronze, and tin, and even stone figures of what would seem to be a kind of huge praying mantis. There are many groups of such figures, usually including male and female, and sometimes with young; it is curious that in every case the male figure is larger and more powerful than the female, which we know to be untrue in the case of the actual praying mantis. These figures nevertheless have the small, cruel head, the long savage arms, the spindly legs, and the attenuated bodies of the mantis. Is it possible that a civilization of men and women, more or less like ourselves, might have been overwhelmed by an invasion of mantis-like insects? Where could they have come from? and where did they go? The conjecture is, of course, fascinating; but no mantis skeletons or remains of any kind have been found, except the above-mentioned statues.

Pound-Laundry is in itself the richest of the diggings. It is believed that at one time this city (for recent excavations indicate "the laundry," as we call it, to have been a city of considerable culture) may at one time have been, in fact, the capital of We, or at least to have had some political or historic importance. Obelgerst-Levy translates the first word of the name as "washing"; the second is obviously the sign for "weight." It is not known what—if anything—was washed there.

In the middle mound, or Cha'ago, near the Lakes, there have been unearthed several paintings; badly discolored, they yet show enough to prove that the inhabitants of Cha'ago were not entirely without visual art. However, they

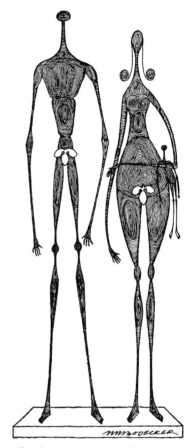

Praying mantises with young.

show almost nothing else. They portray squares, lines, lozenges, and mathematical figures; perhaps they were used in some way by the astrologers of the period. One finds no recognizable human face or figure. We cannot be sure what the Weans of Cha'ago looked like.

(In this relation, it is interesting to note that among the artifacts unearthed at Cha'ago were some unbroken jars and other ceramic objects; also statues of what appear to be eggs, and certain nightmare shapes in stone, iron, and bronze. One is allowed to wonder if there was not some correspondence between these art objects and the praying mantises who may have taken over the country. It is also believed that the Weans had music, but so far at least only a few brass instruments and some drums and cymbals have been found; no sounds have come down to us from those faraway people except a high rasping cry from a slender horn-like object found in Oleens.

To return again to the matter of what the Weans may have looked like; no human bones have been found. Although we have turned up many artifacts of the period, we have nothing for the anthropologists to work on. It is probable that the bones of these people were brittle, and turned to chalk soon after interment.

The greatest difficulty in reconstructing the life of the Weans has not been the deciphering of the inscriptions and the scrolls—due to the brilliant work of Professors Bollek and Shui—but the fact that the Weans, unlike the true ancients, used little gold, preferring to build everything of steel or other metal, and of some curious substance which Bes Nef translates as "gastric," or "plastric." As a result, little is left for the archaeologist. Stone was used mainly for monuments, as was bronze, but those which have been uncovered are too heavily encrusted with bird-droppings to be easily recognizable. One theory is that the Weans collected guano; but it is not known what they did with it.

It is here, for the first time, that I must take issue with my esteemed colleague, Professor Kowly of the Institute for Ancient Arts and Letters, who has discovered in one of the scrolls at Pound-Laundry a glyph of what he believes to be a bird-man. Professor Kowly sees in this some correspondence to the djinn of the even more ancient civilizations of Akad and Sumer. While agreeing in the translation of the glyph, I must dispute its meaning: I believe it to have a purely domestic significance, and not religious at all. For one thing, it is often found along with the glyph of a woman, and the sign of a host, or hosts; there seems to be another letter between the final *t* and the *s*, possibly an *a* or an *e*, which would make it hostas or hostes. I cannot help but see this as a picture of an ordinary family, the man in winged splendor, as befits a husband, the woman merely one of a number, or host (or hostes).

In this relation, it is interesting to note that the Hittite plural, in the feminine gender, often adds the *e*. I am not one of those who hold that these unknown Weans were actually Hittites, although I admit to some strange correspondences. In any case, a Sumerian djinn would never be found accompanied by a woman, unless she were a sorceress. There is no suggestion that the woman-hostes was in fact a witch or sorceress, which I believe effectively disposes of Kowly's untenable hypothesis.

Apropos of the mounds or tumuli of the Weans, each one of which appears to contain and cover the ruins of a city or congregation of habitations, an expedition under Hulay-Beneker has been for several seasons in the field in search of a mound thought to cover the most extensive congregation of all. The name of this lost city, or congregation, which is believed to have been more influential in Wean affairs than Pound-Laundry itself, was—as deciphered by both Eretebbe and Bes Nef—Mil Town. So far no trace of it has been found.

All that we have been able to learn of Wean manners and customs we have been obliged to decipher from the copper and silver tablets found in the mounds, and in the Valley of the Sun in the southwestern part of the country. As a matter of fact, it would appear that a considerable civilization flourished in the southwest, not in any way inferior to the middle mound at Cha'ago, or to the eastern tumuli such as n.yok. Here, in transcription, is Bes Nef's account of a religious occasion, translated from scrolls found in the Valley:

"Schwepps [schwaps?] was first."

"[for that] he did cause them . . . [by] rock and roll . . . to [give out] cries and screams . . . loudly . . . and . . . in the corridors[3] . . . in syncope[4] . . ."

The word "roll" or "rolls" suggests a feast, possibly a feast of communion on a grand scale. So far no one has been able to explain the presence of the word "rock."

However, it is apparent that the people came together, and were seized by an ecstasy of some sort in which they lost reason and decorum. This belief is further strengthened by another scroll found in the same tumulus, in which the scribe reports: "and the spirit came down."

So the evidence points to the fact that the Weans were a religious people. There is additional witness in a silver coin dug up in one of the smaller mounds, which carries the inscription "In God We Trust"—or "Trusted." The translation is by the Bantu scholar, Eretebbe; the tense of the verb "to trust" is obscure.

Neither Eretebbe nor any other member of the Academy has as yet been able to discover what god was meant. It is extremely unlikely that these ancient people had only one; inscriptions found among the ruins of Pound-Laundry suggest, in fact a number of religious differences among them. There are definite traces of Hebrew culture in the ruins of n.yok; and although nothing has so far been found at Pound-Laundry to suggest Babylonian or early Egyptian influences, there are hints here and there of the Cyprian cult of Antinous, particularly among the arts.

[3]"Columns"—Bollek. "Aisles"—Obelgerst-Levy.
[4]"Syncopation"—Obelgerst-Levy. But this makes no sense, apparently.

It is probable, too, that the Weans worshiped, among others, a sort of horse-god or centaur. Professor Rass points out that the fragment unearthed at s.nita, and known as the Rass fragment, contains the unmistakable glyph for "horse" and the simple statement: "Schwaps [schnaps?] was first." Yet another glyph, found not far from s.nita, is that of a bearded god; it, too, states that "Schwepps [schwaps?] was first."

In this regard, it is interesting to note that in a fragment unearthed at Oleens, and known as the Oleens fragment, the word "schnaps" is written: "coca-cola," which was the name of an Aztec root-deity.

In politics, we are on surer ground. It is possible to say with absolute certainty, from scrolls unearthed at Pound-Laundry, and also from the ancient city of Boxton, or Bosstin, known to archaeologists as mound x-5, that the Weans were divided into hegemonies or states, each ruled by a theocrat or autocrat, and all loosely joined in a confederacy under one ruler (who, however, was not a theocrat) whose duty it was to retire after an interval varying in length from four to twelve years, and to issue warnings and oracles. These groups, or states, were in turn divided into counties, which were in turn divided into wards. As for the system of government itself, it appears to have been conducted by means of barter, each county or state getting what it could for itself in exchange for helping its neighbor to do the same.

Public servants, we know, were paid little; they were expected to enrich themselves as best they could in private. When this enrichment, which was illegal, was discovered, they were beheaded. This curious fact did not keep the majority of Weans from seeking public office; but one is forced to conclude, from inscriptions found at Nassaw, that the most admired citizens lived in actual poverty, and rarely spoke at all, except in musical sounds or mathematical formulae. As we have already seen, no musical sounds have come down to us, which is unfortunate.

It is true that two scrolls, bound each in oblong form, were found by the team of Haph-Bukong and Sumer, digging one winter among the ruins of what may once have been some sort of library. That it may have been a repository of many such scrolls—or as we should say "books"—is suggested by the remains of metal shelves which may have held the scrolls (or else jellies, but informed opinion veers toward the scrolls).

Unfortunately, both scrolls, though easily legible, due to the brilliant work of the scholars Bes Nef and Obelgerst-Levy, are unintelligible; that is to say, the words, although translatable, make no sense when put together. One of these scrolls appears to be an account of a god or hero named Finigan, or Finnegan; the size of the scroll and its rare state of preservation attest to its importance as a religious or historical document, but it is impossible to make out what happens to him. The second scroll is in what appears to be a metrical, or verse form; nothing can be gathered from it at all.

A tablet unearthed at n.yok gives us a welcome glimpse into business transactions in We. "[Having] borrowed a million," it reads in the transcription of B'Han Bollek, "[I acquired] thereby credit to twice that amount." This suggests an economy not unlike our own: one thinks of the motto of our Treasury Department: "To the Borrower, All" Throughout history there has never been anything more useful than credit, to establish credit. Without a debt, there is nothing.

As for the history of these interesting and almost unknown ancestors[5] of ours, no more is known than is known of the Romans, and later the Brythons: they established themselves in the land by killing off the native tribes already there, and built their empire by the sword; when the sword rusted, they perished, along with Egypt, Babylon, and Greece, leaving behind them only these curious mounds, some scrolls, monuments, and glyphs, a few statues of eggs and mantises, and no music.

[5] Nat Obelgerst-Levy denies that the Weans were ancestors of ours.

PART IV
Explanation

Why?

Introduction

If we had placed the photograph that appears on page 271 in a writing assignment in Part I, we would have asked you to describe objectively what you could see in it, arranging details in a clear pattern, using transitions to emphasize the spatial relationships, and using concrete nouns and precise modifiers to make the details graphic. If we had placed it in a writing assignment in Part II, as one of a group of related photographs, we would have asked you to generalize upon what the photographs had in common, using the pertinent details of this photograph in an example supporting your generalization. If we had placed it in a writing assignment in Part III, we would have asked you to contrast the appearance of the young man in the sweater with the appearance of one of the military policemen or to contrast what you could infer to be the life style of the young man in the sweater with what you could infer to be the life style of the military policemen, treating parallel aspects according to a coherent pattern.

If we should place the photograph in a writing assignment in Part IV, we would ask you why the young man in the sweater is placing flowers in the policemen's gun barrels. Suppose that you should set out to answer this question for a reader who had not seen the photograph. You would first have to report the situation that prompted the question, and in doing so you would be able to use all of your descriptive skills. You would have to include any specific facts about the photograph that you could find through research—the time, the place, and the names of persons or their affiliations, or both—as you did earlier in your firsthand report. You might want to relate this incident to similar incidents through generalization before trying to account for it. In order to answer the question Why, you might interview the young man or someone who is in complete sympathy with him and listen to an explanation of his reason for the action. Then, from all that you know about the situation and from all that you are—your values and your ability to reason from past experiences—you would state what *you* interpret to be the reason or reasons for the action. Then you would support your interpretation with reasons, probably developing some of these with comparisons of the young man's values or the policemen's values with your own. In developing the comparisons, you would probably find occasion to use generalization and examples as support.

Thus, in this course, you have been accumulating skills in development that you can apply in writing explanations, since the explanation is a form so large that it can contain all of the forms of writing you have studied previously.

The central purpose of the interpretation developed by explanation is different, however, from the purpose of the other forms; this purpose is to explain *why* rather than *what*. *Why* seems a simple question, but *why* is a word with many meanings.

1. Why did an earthquake occur here yesterday? = What are the natural, inevitable causes?
2. Why does Johnny have a fever? = What are the irregularities of Johnny's physical condition?
3. Why did Felix give his dog away? = What was Felix's conscious reason for giving his dog away?
4. Why did Rupert shoot Governor Kline, whom he had not seen before? = What is there in Rupert's heredity, home environment, social milieu, and beliefs to explain such a shocking act?
5. Why do some teen-agers go steady? Why do many Americans keep guns in their homes? Why are so many actors engaging in politics? = If you took a poll of this group, which answers would be reported most often?
6. Why do we have ghettos in our cities? = What do you believe are the historical, political, and cultural reasons for this situation? To what extent do you think anyone is to blame?
7. Why does the speaker in "The Road Not Taken" say he will sigh in the future when he tells about choosing one of the roads that diverged in a yellow wood? = How does this detail act with other details in the poem to create effect or convey meaning?
8. Why is it wrong to cheat on examinations? = Which of your religious or philosophical convictions pertains to cheating on examinations?

This is quite a range of meaning for one word, but the diversity lies in the diversity of contexts to which *why* adapts itself, not in the procedures of thinking required to answer the questions. To answer the eighth question, one would reason deductively from an ethical principle, but to answer any of the others, one would follow a simple inductive procedure: (1) make an investigation, gathering as many pertinent facts as possible and (2) reason from the facts to causes, in the light of experience. The investigations would be conducted in the various situations by various means. The first investigator would check seismographic and topographical records; the second would look at Johnny's throat and into his ears; the third would interview Felix and ask him why he gave the dog away; the fourth would check medical and school records and interview many people who knew Rupert; the fifth would take a poll of a large number of persons in the group; the sixth would spend months or years studying many aspects of life in the ghettos in addition to laws, economic facts, and political forces on the outside that might be pertinent; and the seventh would investigate all of the details of form and content of the poem and the occasion of its composition. But whatever the differences in techniques, the principles of investigation would be the same and the process of reasoning to conclusions the same.

It is appropriate, then, that we approach the writing of explanations by studying the process of inductive reasoning that underlies most answers to the question *why*, as we shall do early in Part IV.

Explaining *why* requires the use of statements based on the relationship of reason to result. The typical grammatical patterns for the expression of this relationship and the typical connecting words within these patterns are presented in this part of the book. The discussion of the grammatical patterns and diction of the reason-result relationship also treats the concession-assertion and the condition-consequent relationships, since these relationships as well as the reason-result often occur in explanations.

The structure of an explanation that interprets facts derived from investigation tends to fall into one of two categories, which we will call *discovery* and *support*. In the *discovery structure* the writer proceeds inductively, "reliving" the process by which he reached his conclusion and stating the conclusion as the climax of his presentation. Two of the reading selections in Part IV, "S. Miami" and "Robert Frost: the Way to the Poem," have the discovery structure. In the *support structure* the author states his conclusion before presenting his support, even though he has formed or confirmed the conclusion through an inductive process of investigation. The support consists usually of reasons, statements by authorities, firsthand reports, generalizations and examples, and comparisons. If the composition is a long one, the writer usually describes, sometimes in considerable detail, *what* the subject is before he attempts to explain *why* it is. All of the prose selections in this part except the two mentioned above have the support structure. Some of these end with a section that goes beyond explanation to suggest a change that might occur or to recommend a course of action that might bring about a desired change.

The Logical Process: Formation of the Hypothesis

READINGS THAT ILLUSTRATE HYPOTHESES

As you read the following medical mystery story, observe the logical process by which Dr. McKernan gradually forms the hypothesis that solves the mystery.

S. Miami

Berton Roueché

Around five o'clock on Friday morning, June 4, 1954, an Upton, Massachusetts, garage mechanic whom I'll call Alfred Edison—a married man and the father of a three-year-old daughter—was wrenched from sleep by a grinding pain in the stomach. It doubled him up and turned him over and almost took his breath away. He began to groan, and his groans awakened his wife. He heard her asking what had happened, but before he could answer, a wave of nausea and diarrhea overwhelmed him. When he emerged from the bathroom some ten minutes later, the light was on in the nursery. His wife was holding the baby in her arms. The child was flushed and whimpering, and she had vomited in her bed. She was also, it soon developed, diarrheic. Frightened into a fleeting convalescence, Edison helped his wife calm and comfort the child, and presently she fell asleep. The Edisons then headed back to bed. At the door of their room, Mrs. Edison stopped. Her face went green. She turned and ran for the bathroom. Edison got as far as the nearest chair. He tumbled into it, gagging and retching, with another seizure of cramps. The baby awoke again and began to cry. There was no more sleep for anyone in the Edison house that night. Even the baby only dozed. Finally, toward

S. MIAMI   From *A Man Named Hoffman* by Berton Roueché, by permission of Little, Brown, and Company. Copyright © 1961 by Berton Roueché, originally appeared in *The New Yorker*.

seven o'clock, they decided to call the doctor. Edison dragged himself downstairs and telephoned a general practitioner named Bernard F. McKernan.

"Not that he had much choice," Dr. McKernan says. "I mean, if they wanted a doctor. Upton is a fair-sized village. It has a population of around three thousand. But I'm the only physician in town. Don't ask me why. It isn't my doing. I could use some help—in fact, I'd welcome it. I'd be more than happy to share the strain. I certainly would have been back there in June of 1954. However, I'm the doctor, and he called me. I was up and dressed—you have to get up early to handle a practice like mine—and was just sitting down to breakfast. It wasn't hard to get the picture. The symptoms told the story. I couldn't see much cause for alarm, but already had one house call to make in that neighborhood, so I told him I'd drop around. I got there a little after eight. I found no reason to change my first impression. It looked like a routine gastroenteritis. What I call summer diarrhea. Moreover, by then the worst appeared to be over. No more cramps and no more vomiting. Nobody had any fever. The only remaining symptom was diarrhea. I gave them each a dose of kaolin for that, and prescribed the usual bland diet and rest. Then, as a matter of course, I asked them what they had been eating in the past twenty-four hours or so. They couldn't think of anything unusual. They couldn't seem to think of anything at all. Just what they always ate, they said. I let it go at that. I told them to give me a ring the following day if the diarrhea continued, and went on to the next call on my list. They didn't call me on Saturday, so I put them out of my mind.

"Until Sunday. Sunday is nominally my day of rest. I realize that people can't always arrange their illnesses to suit my convenience, but I don't have office hours on Sunday, and I'm very much obliged when nobody calls me at home. Needless to say, that seldom happens. And it didn't happen that Sunday. My holiday ended at about three o'clock in the afternoon with a call from a man named, I'll say, Smith. He sounded pretty frantic. Could I come over right away? Both of his children—an eight-year-old boy and a girl of four—were violently ill. So was his wife. So were two members of her family who were spending the weekend with them—her father and one of her brothers. I asked him what seemed to be the trouble. Cramps, he said, terrible stomach cramps. Nausea and vomiting. Diarrhea. That made me perk up my ears. Summer diarrhea is a common complaint, but it isn't all that common. Two family outbreaks in less than three days in a village this size was something to think about. I told him I was on my way. I saw Mrs. Smith and the children first. Smith hadn't exaggerated. They were sick—really sick. Far sicker than the Edisons had ever been. Along with everything else, they were flat on their backs, too weak to lift a hand, and running quite a fever. Both children had a temperature of a hundred and three, and Mrs. Smith's was almost that high. I then had a look at her brother. The old man, it turned out, wasn't there. He didn't believe in doctors. When he heard I was coming, he left and went home—to Hopkinton, as I recall. No matter. His is another story. He died a week or two later, but not of gastroenteritis, although that might have been a contributing factor. The cause of death was a tibial-artery thrombosis. Well, to get back to the Smiths—I did what I could to make them comfortable. I also revised my original diagnosis. This was obviously no mere summer diarrhea. It was a full-fledged case of food poisoning—bacterial food poisoning, most likely.

"In the first place, it couldn't be chemical poisoning. That usually comes on within minutes of ingestion, and the time lapse is never more than a couple of hours. These people, however, took sick before breakfast. They didn't eat any breakfast. Their last meal was dinner on Saturday night. And the dinner menu eliminated the possibility that they had been poisoned by some inherently poisonous plant or animal substance. Toxic mushrooms, for example. Dinner was steak and fried potatoes, bread and butter, carrots and peas, and coleslaw, with milk for the children and watermelon for dessert. It had to be some form of bacterial poisoning. To judge from the clinical picture, the organism responsible could be either a staphylococcus or one of the salmonella group. My guess, in view of the onset time, was the latter. The staphylococcus toxin makes itself felt within two to seven hours. Salmonella takes from twelve to thirty-six hours. The next step was to try to determine just what food had served as the vehicle of infection. At a glance, there were three possibilities—the milk, the coleslaw, and the steak. But only at a glance. The children didn't eat any coleslaw, and they alone drank milk. That left the steak. Meat is an excellent medium for the growth of salmonella. Raw or rare meat, that is. Thorough cooking will safely destroy the organism. The Smith steak was fried to a crisp. Well, maybe the trouble went back to an earlier meal. I took up Saturday lunch and Saturday breakfast and dinner on Friday night. Lunch was out of the question. The boy had lunched at a neighbor's house, and the brother had also eaten somewhere else. Breakfast was completely innocuous. It consisted of fruit juice, doughnuts, and coffee. The children drank milk. Friday-night dinner was even less promising than dinner on Saturday night—fried fish and boiled potatoes, bread and butter, and string beans, with the usual milk for the children. Dessert, as on the following night, was watermelon.

"I've seldom felt so stumped. Or, a moment later, so stupid. I was just about ready to call it quits when the obvious suddenly dawned. The children were sick. Mrs. Smith was sick. Her brother was sick. And so, apparently, was her father. But Smith himself was well. How come? There was only one reasonable explanation. He hadn't eaten something that all the others ate. I was right. I asked him and he told me. It was watermelon. He never ate watermelon. He simply didn't like it. I don't know what I expected, but I'm sure it wasn't that. I'd never heard of watermelon as a vehicle for food poisoning. Nobody ever had. Nevertheless, it had to be considered. I asked Smith a few more questions and got a few more answers. They had bought the watermelon—it was half a melon, actually—at the supermarket in Milford, about five miles southeast of here, on Friday. There was some of it left. It was out in the refrigerator, if I wanted to take a look. I told him to keep it there. I'd probably want to have it analyzed.

"I got back home a little after four. I put the car away and went in the house and dropped my bag, and the doorbell rang. It was a woman I knew—Mrs. Brown, I'll call her. She and her husband and their four young children lived just down the street. Well, she hated to bother me on Sunday, but it couldn't be helped. It was mostly on account of the children. They had been sick and vomiting since nine or ten o'clock that morning. And now they were violently diarrheic. So was she, but it was the children that really concerned her. What did I think was the matter? I let that go for the moment. I had some questions of my own that I wanted answered first. She hadn't mentioned her husband. Did that mean that he wasn't sick? No, she said. Or, rather, yes—he was fine. I began to get a rather creepy feeling. Had they by any chance eaten any watermelon recently? She gave me a very odd look. Why, yes; they'd had watermelon for dinner only last night. I wondered if it might have come from the supermarket at Milford. It did—yes. That's where they always traded. And they had all eaten some of it? No. She and the children had, but not her husband. He didn't like watermelon. Neither did she, particularly. They had really bought it mainly for the children. I picked up my bag and opened the door and followed her out of the house.

"The first thing Monday morning, I put in a call to the Milford supermarket. I identified myself to the manager, and told him I had an outbreak of food poisoning on my hands that was tentatively traced to watermelon bought at his store within the past two or three days. Until the matter was settled, I'd be much obliged if he would withhold all watermelon still in stock from sale. All things considered, he took it very well. He didn't try to argue. He stuttered and stammered a little, but that was largely from shock. Or maybe just plain disbelief. If so, I could hardly blame him. I didn't entirely believe it myself. The idea of watermelon as a source of infection in food poisoning still seemed a trifle farfetched. There was reason to suspect it, but the evidence was purely circumstantial, and it was based on just two sets of circumstances. It could be a mere coincidence. I don't mean I really thought so, but it was possible to wonder. It was possible on Monday morning. By Monday afternoon, however, it was wholly out of the question. Two things accounted for the change. One was that I saw the Edison family again. I was called back there around noon. The kaolin hadn't seemed to help. They were all still miserably diarrheic. In view of what I now suspected, that wasn't too surprising. An attack of salmonellosis can hang on for four or five days. In fact, I've known of cases where the symptoms kept recurring for weeks, and even months. I did what I could—what I'd done for the others. I prescribed another adsorbent, and a regimen of penicillin and sulfasuxidine. I then brought up the subject of food again. With a little prompting, their memory revived. Enough to recall that on Thursday night they'd had watermelon for dessert. It was all gone now—they had only bought a slice. But, yes, it had come from the supermarket at Milford. Then came another outbreak—a young couple I'll call Miller. The Millers had been sick since Sunday with cramps, vomiting, and diarrhea. Mrs. Miller had a temperature of a hundred and two. On Saturday night, they had entertained another couple at dinner. Dessert was a slice of watermelon, from the Milford supermarket. There was some of it left in the refrigerator. Their guests, as it happened, hadn't eaten any. I took down the name of their friends, and when I got back to the office I gave them a ring. The wife answered the phone. Her husband was at work—and quite well. So was she.

"Well, that was the end of the argument. The watermelon was clearly in the picture. It was also clear that I had gone as far as I could alone. The rest was up to the State Department of Public Health. Food poisoning is a reportable disease in Massachusetts. I filled out the notification form and sent it off to the health officer for this district, in Worcester."

The district health officer to whom Dr. McKernan addressed his report was a physician named Gilbert E. Gayler. It reached Dr. Gayler on Tuesday. The following morning, he drove down to Upton for a preliminary survey of the outbreak. He first conferred with Dr. McKernan. There were now, he learned, not four but five striken families. The fifth was an elderly couple named (I'll say) Green. They had shared a slice of watermelon from the Milford supermarket on Friday night, they had become ill on Saturday, and on Tuesday, after nearly four days of misery, they had summoned Dr. McKernan. The Greens brought the number of cases to a total—the final total, as it turned out—of seventeen. Dr. Gayler spent the rest of the morning on a round of clinical calls. Accompanied by Dr. McKernan, he visited the Greens, the Smiths, and the Millers, and left with each of the several patients an enteric-specimen kit. The patients were instructed to mail the kits as soon as possible to the Diagnostic Laboratory of the Massachusetts Department of Public Health, in Boston. In addition, Dr. Gayler obtained from the Millers the remains of their Saturday-night watermelon. His next stop, after a hurried lunch with Dr. McKernan, was the supermarket at Milford. He interviewed the manager, the assistant manager, and three clerks assigned to the fruit-and-vegetable department. All five were in their normal state of health. None were, or recently had been, afflicted with any sort of skin, respiratory, or gastro-intestinal trouble. An examination of the fruit-and-vegetable department indicated that it was, if anything, better kept and cleaner than the average market. As requested by Dr. McKernan, the store's stock of watermelons—both whole and sliced—had been withdrawn from sale, but all the cut melons were still meticulously wrapped in cellophane, as they had been all along. Dr. Gayler took one of the slices with him to be analyzed along with the Miller sample. He then returned to his car, and headed for Boston and the Diagnostic Laboratory.

Dr. Robert A. MacCready, the director in charge, was not at the laboratory that afternoon when Dr. Gayler turned up with his samples of melon. He was attending a conference at the State House. It was not until his return the next day that he learned of the visit and i s purpose. He heard the news from his senior bacteriologist, Mrs. Marion B. Holmes, and he heard it with incredulity.

"I had no opinion of Dr. McKernan," Dr. MacCready says. "I didn't know him. I did know Dr. Gayler, though. I knew him well enough to know that he was a sound and sensible man. That's about all that kept me from scoffing at Dr. McKernan's hunch. There are innumerable vehicles of salmonella infection. The literature is full of outbreaks spread by almost any food you can name—meat, poultry, fish, eggs, milk, cheese, salads, pastries. Almost any food, that is, except fresh fruit. The incidence of salmonella in fresh fruit is so rare as to be almost negligible. Especially watermelon! That thick hide! The notion was almost whimsical. Mrs. Holmes thought so, too. Or, rather, she did at first. But now, after thinking it over, she wasn't entirely sure. She didn't attempt to explain just how a watermelon might come to harbor a colony of salmonellae. She simply pointed out that watermelon is rich in sugar and moisture. It could thus serve the organism very nicely as a medium for growth and proliferation. Which, of course, was perfectly true. I had to agree that watermelon was within the range of possibility. In my opinion, however, it still seemed quite unlikely. The inside of a whole watermelon is presumably sterile, and the cut melons had been carefully wrapped by clerks who were all in good health. I'd believe the implication when I saw some proof—when and if the laboratory could demonstrate the presence of salmonella in those melons. The procedure involved in such a test is a standard one.

Specimens of the suspected material are planted in certain culture mediums that especially favor the growth of salmonella. Then nature takes its course. The results, if any, can usually be obtained in two or three days. This was Thursday. We should have an answer by Saturday or Sunday. Meanwhile, there was nothing to do but wait.

"The only trouble was I didn't feel like just waiting. It wasn't impatience. I got over that long ago. It was simple curiosity. I was intrigued. Watermelon or no watermelon, it was a most unusual case, and I wanted to know a good deal more about it than Mrs. Holmes had learned from Dr. Gayler. That meant a trip to the scene. I made the necessary arrangements that afternoon, and drove down on Friday morning. For company, among other reasons, I took along a colleague— Joseph P. Reardon. He was, and is, the epidemiologist in the Department's Division of Communicable Diseases. As it turned out, Dr. Reardon more than paid his way. Our first stop was Dr. McKernan's office. Dr. Gayler joined us there. They gave us a full report. Dr. Gayler's contribution was a poll of the other doctors in the Milford area. I don't remember just how many he called, and it doesn't matter. The responses were all the same. None of the doctors had seen a case of acute gastroenteritis in the past ten days or two weeks. So the outbreak was confined to Upton. Before moving on to Milford, we had a look at some of the patients. That was mere routine. We didn't expect any revelations and we didn't find any. We did pick up another sample for the laboratory—the melon that Dr. McKernan had instructed the Smiths to save. Dr. Gayler had been favorably impressed by the look of the supermarket. So were Dr. Reardon and I. We inspected it practically foot by foot. There was no evidence of rats or mice. Animal droppings—particularly those of rodents—are a frequent salmonella reservoir. The store was as clean as good management could make it. Then we settled down in the fruit-and-vegetable department. We talked with the clerks and arranged for sample stools. The water-melons were still under embargo—some of them whole and some sliced and covered with cellophane. We were shown the knife that was used to slice them, and I took a sample swab of the blade for laboratory analysis. Dr. Reardon suggested a swab of the shelf where the knife was kept. I thought that was pretty futile—there was nothing there but dust. The possibility of salmonella's even existing there—let alone multiplying—was exceedingly remote. But I humored him. There was no harm in one more sample. We had little enough to show for the day.

"We left Dr. Gayler at Milford and Dr. Reardon and I drove back to Boston. After dropping him off, I stopped by the office. The only news from Mrs. Holmes was the arrival of the first lot of stool samples. I handed over our harvest of swabs and melon and went home. I wasn't exactly depressed. I just didn't feel quite comfortable. It was obvious that Dr. McKernan had done an excellent job. So good, in fact, that I hardly knew what to think. I still had certain misgivings about the watermelon theory. It still went against my grain. And yet, if the melon wasn't responsible, what was? The answer to that was: Nothing. There wasn't anything else. It had to be the melon.

"Our laboratory is on a skeleton basis over the weekend. We don't have the funds to function at full strength seven days a week. As a rule, however, there's always somebody there—the bacteriologists take turns—and this weekend it was

Mrs. Holmes. She kept me in touch with developments. As expected, there were several, and, as hoped, they told the story—the only possible story. Dr. McKernan was right. By Sunday night, the laboratory had confirmed his clinical diagnosis of salmonellosis. All of the patient stools were teeming with salmonellae. So were the Smith and Miller watermelon samples. That confirmed the melon as the vehicle of infection. It also pretty definitely linked the outbreak to the Milford super-market. Then, thanks to Dr. Reardon, the shelf swab completed the chain. It produced a magnificent culture. I still find that hard to believe. The odds against it were literally astronomical. It was an extraordinary stroke of luck. And a very fortunate one, as well. Because the swab I'd taken of the knife was negative. What happened, I suppose, was that the knife had been washed after Dr. McKernan embargoed the melons. The knife was our only disappointment. We got one other negative culture—from the melon slice that Dr. Gayler had picked up at the store—but that was hardly a blow. Just the reverse, as a matter of fact. It provided an acceptable answer to one of the two big questions that the positive cultures raised. It explained why the outbreak was confined to just those seventeen customers of the Milford supermarket. Dr. Gayler's melon was clean because the bulk of the melons were clean. If all, or most, or even many of the melons had been contaminated, the outbreak pattern would have been quite different. There would have been cases scattered all over the Milford area. But none of the doctors polled by Dr. Gayler had seen a sign of gastroenteritis. The conclusion was practically unavoidable. There must have been only two or three contaminated melons, and by some freak of circumstance they ended up in Upton.

"The other question was, of course, the essence of the problem. It was also the essence of my discontent—the root of all my misgivings. How did the contaminated melons get that way? How *could* something with so thick a hide have ever got contaminated? To answer that—to even attempt an answer—we needed to know a little more about the organism involved. We knew it was salmonella, but we didn't know the serotype—the species. When we did, we might have a lead. However, serotyping calls for antigenic analyses that most laboratories—including ours at that time—are not equipped to perform. We relied for such work on the New York Salmonella Center, at Beth Israel Hospital in Manhattan. Accordingly, on Monday morning we prepared a sample of culture and sent it off to the Center for specific identification. If all went well, we would have a report in a couple of days or so.

"The salmonella is a curious group of pathogens. It differs in many impor-tant respects from the other bacteria commonly associated with food poisoning—such as the staphylococci and *Clostridium botulinum,* the botulism organism. For one thing, salmonella is inherently infectious to man. The ingestion of food con-taining a quantity of living salmonellae commonly results in illness. Moreover, because salmonella is perfectly adapted for growth and reproduction within the human body, the quantity need not be an enormous one. With the others, the mechanism is quite different. Botulism and staphylococcus food poisoning are intoxications rather than infections. Their cause is not the living organism but a toxin excreted in the food by the organism in the course of its proliferation there. In other words, the food itself is poisonous. That largely explains why staphy-lococcus food poisoning comes on so much faster than salmonellosis. Botulism takes longer—sometimes three or four days—but it isn't a gastroenteritis. It's primarily a disease of the central nervous system. And an extremely serious one. Fortunately, it is easily controlled. *C. botulinum* lives in the soil and can grow and elaborate its toxin only in a total absence of oxygen. Most outbreaks of botulism in this country are traced to home-canned vegetables inexpertly washed and processed and eaten without further cooking. Although heat has little or no effect on the botulism organism itself, proper cooking will safely destroy the toxin. The staphylococci enterotoxin, on the other hand, is highly heat-resistant. In addition, the staphylococcus organism is ubiquitous in nature. It's even been isolated from the air of rooms. And it is perhaps the commonest cause of boils and other skin and wound infections. Nevertheless, the control of staphylococcus food poisoning is not—at least potentially—too difficult. Refrigeration will prevent the development of the toxin, and good common-sense hygiene on the part of food handlers will do the rest. Salmonellosis would seem to be as easily controlled. Cooking, refrigeration and cleanliness are all helpful precautions. The first will destroy the organism, and others will retard its growth. But the problem is more complicated than that. Infected human beings are not alone responsible for the spread of salmonellosis. Salmonella can live in the intestinal tract of almost any animal, including those that are closest to man—dogs, rats, mice, cows, chickens. And, to make matters worse, it appears to be a perfect parasite. It can live and propagate in most such animals without any visible signs of harm to the animal.

"Nor is that all. New species of salmonella turn up every year. Since 1885, when the first member of the group was described—by an American pathologist named Daniel E. Salmon—literally hundreds of species have been identified. The total now known is well in excess of four hundred. So far, I'm glad to say, most of them don't exhibit any unusual pathogenic powers. They produce a disagreeable but not usually fatal illness. But that doesn't mean they never will. A more virulent species might emerge tomorrow. The multitude of species is not in itself particu-larly disturbing. It actually has a certain epidemiological value. Many apparently unrelated outbreaks of salmonellosis have been linked through identification of the species involved. It also sometimes happens that the identity of the species will indicate the ultimate source of the trouble. It has been the custom for many years to name a newly discovered species for the place where it first was found. The names of some no longer have any geographical significance. In the inter-vening years, the species they denote have been found in many different places. *Salmonella montevideo* is one of that increasingly widespread group. So, among others, are *S. organienburg, S. newport, S. derby, S. bareilly,* and *S. panama.* A good many more, however, are still essentially regional species. Such as, to mention just a few, *S. dares-selaam, S. moscow, S. bronx, S. israel, S. marylebone, S. ndola, S. oslo,* and *S. fresno.* Another is *S. miami.* And that was the one we got. That was the Upton organism.

"I had a telegram from Dr. Ivan Saphra, the chief bacteriologist at the New York Salmonella Center, around four o'clock on Tuesday. The late Dr. Saphra, I should say—he died in 1957. A great pity. He was a fine man, and an outstanding one in his field, as his work in this case plainly testifies. Our culture didn't reach him until sometime Tuesday morning, but he had it typed that afternoon. It often takes longer than that to identify a relatively common species. To even think of

S. miami in this part of the country was remarkable. The implications of his report were even more so. *S. miami,* as its name suggests, is a Florida organism. It has been recovered in several human outbreaks in that area, and from many different animals. We could hardly have hoped for a more provocative lead. Or one that so comfortably simplified the problem. It was only necessary to find a link between Florida and Massachusetts. What might have transported *S. miami* from way down there to here? An animal host? Not likely. Our examination of the supermarket had produced no evidence of rodent infestation. A human carrier? The answer to that was on my desk in a laboratory report on the specimen stools from the fruit-and-vegetable clerks. They were negative for salmonella. What else? Well, unless I was very much mistaken, Florida was a major source of produce for the Northeastern market in the spring and early summer. I put in a call to the super-market at Milford and had a word with the manager. He was most cooperative. Their melons were Florida melons.

"That seemed to tell the story—the only reasonable story. We could scratch the store off the list. The trouble didn't originate there. It came up with the melons from Florida. To be sure, that was largely an inference, but it had the ring of truth. No other explanation was warranted by the facts. It wasn't, of course, the whole story. It didn't tell us how the contaminated melons got contaminated. That basic question still loomed. But it helped. We had sufficient data now to at least make a stab at an answer. We began with a train of assumptions. Suppose a melon had come in contact with infected animal droppings down there in some Florida field. Or, for that matter, after it was harvested and stacked in the local jobber's warehouse. Suppose some of that material adhered to the skin of the melon. Suppose it was still there when the melon arrived at the store. And suppose it was still there when the clerk took his knife and sliced up the melon for sale. What then? It was easy enough to find out. All we needed was a watermelon.

"I picked one up on the way to the office on Thursday. We lugged it into the laboratory, and Mrs. Holmes prepared a dilute suspension of *S. miami* from one of the positive cultures. She swabbed some of the material on the skin of the melon. Then, using a clean knife, she cut a slice out of the melon at that point. That pretty well reproduced our hypothetical situation. The next step was to demonstrate the result. We made two sets of cultures from the meat where it had come in contact with the knife. The first was made immediately after the melon was cut, and the second a few hours later—when the organism would have had time to establish itself better. We then tried a different approach. We deliber-ately contaminated the knife with our *S. miami* suspension and cut off another slice of melon and made a culture from that. The idea, of course, was to see if a knife could spread the infection from one melon to another. At that point, we called it a day. For good measure, however, we left the original slice of melon overnight on the laboratory table. Fifteen hours or so at room temperature would give the remaining *S. miami* a really good chance to grow. The following day, we made a culture from that exposed slice.

"We got the first results on Saturday. They weren't exactly discouraging. I went down to the laboratory and read them myself. On the other hand, they fell a bit short of convincing. The first set, made right after the first slice was cut, was practically nothing—just a hint of *S. miami.* There was a little more life in the two other Thursday cultures. They each produced a colony or two. That left the overnight culture. I won't pretend that we waited for Sunday with bated breath. The results of the other cultures were an indication that we might expect something fairly conclusive. So I was fully prepared for the best. But I wasn't prepared for what we actually got. It wasn't just a good solid cluster of colonies. It was any number of colonies—innumerable colonies. It was an *S. miami* metropolis."

The following newspaper article reviews a book concerned with a mystery that, unlike the one in "S. Miami," can never be indisputably solved. As you read the article, examine the kinds of evidence the hypotheses in the book are based on. Robert Nathan's "Digging the Weans," which you have probably read, is a satire on scholarly evidence. Do you think that the scholars who wrote *Pleistocene Extinctions: the Search for a Cause*, the book reviewed in the article below, could be as mistaken as the scholars in the satire?

Missing Mammals Case Intriguing Scientists

Carle Hodge

A new book re-opens this week what might be called *The Case of The Missing Mammals.*

It is about a mystery that has stayed unsolved for 11,000 years or so. The victims were the great ground sloths, the mammoths, camels and other giant animals that once roamed the earth.

They vanished from North America, as the last of the Ice Ages ebbed, during a relatively short span of some 1,000 years.

To deepen the riddle, the same sorts of big beasts disappeared almost simultaneously over much of the world. The smaller ones survived.

The book, "Pleistocene Extinctions: The Search for A Cause," was not fabricated for bedtime reading by the uninitiated. The content is as scientific as its title suggests.

There are, albeit, all the elements of a detective novel. And while no sure solution results (to everyone's satisfaction), the clues are intriguing.

For his part, Dr. Paul S. Martin, the volume's coeditor and one of four University of Arizona researchers who contributed chapters to it, sees only one explanation: "overkill."

He argues that ancient hunters erased the creatures: "Outside continental Africa and Southeast Asia massive extinction is unknown before the earliest known arrival of prehistoric man."

MISSING MAMMALS CASE INTRIGUING SCIENTISTS   From *Arizona Daily Star*, March 24, 1968. Reprinted by permission of *Arizona Daily Star*.

His position is more than mildly radical. Most concerned scholars have thought—and perhaps a majority still does—that the story is less a whodunit than a whatdidit. The "megafauna," the argument goes, simply could not cope with the enormous changes in climate.

Dr. Arthur J. Jelinek concurs with Martin—to a point. The UA anthropologist believes that humans and climate together brought about the extinction.

Prehistoric peoples hastened the extinction not only by slaughter but also by altering the environment. Certainly the aboriginals invaded the watering places that had been the private preserves of wildlife. They kindled fires that burned off woodlands and grassy prairies.

University of Minnesota geologist Dr. H. E. Wright, Jr., collaborated with Martin in editing the book.

In their sections, Dr. C. Vance Haynes, Jr., and Peter J. Mehringer more or less sidestep the issue of whether human hunters provided the critical factor. They are, like Martin, members of the UA Geochronology Dept.

Haynes, however, documents the fact that early man had made himself at home on our continent—and learned to fashion weapons—during the same period when the giant mammals were lost.

The oldest New World artifacts thus far positively carbon dated go back no more than 12,000 years, he says.

And Mehringer, using as evidence his work with fossil pollen and plant records, points out that climate could not have been responsible for the mass demise.

Climatic conditions for grazers and browsers were better than they had been during glaciation, he says, and better than they would become later, at least in the American West. The present deserts didn't develop until 7,000 to 7,500 years ago.

DIALOG 11

The Process of Forming a Hypothesis; the Difference Between the Inferential Generalization and the Hypothesis

Read this dialog after you have read "S. Miami" and "Missing Mammals Case Intriguing Scientists."

1. Suppose that while you are watching an F–104 flying overhead, you see a trail of black smoke suddenly appear behind it. You next observe that the plane is gradually decreasing in speed and losing altitude. Then you see the plane turn back toward the local Air Force Base. What conclusion do you draw?	The plane is having engine trouble.

2. Is this the only possible conclusion?	One might assume that the pilot is testing a new SOS device or playing a joke on his comrades in the control tower, but either of these conclusions is too farfetched to seem credible.
3. Why does the first conclusion seem more credible?	There are many recorded instances in which the signs observed were as a matter of fact associated with engine trouble. Conclusions that have been proved true a number of times in the past are credible.
4. From your position on the ground can you be absolutely certain that the plane is having engine trouble or do you merely think that this is highly probable?	One cannot be absolutely sure.
5. An interpretive conclusion like *the plane is having engine trouble*, which accounts for all observations and is contradicted by none, is commonly called a _____ .	hypothesis
6. You might have answered *inference. Inference* is a correct answer, but it is more general than *hypothesis*. The hypothesis is a _____ of inference.	type
7. What definition of *statement of inference* did we give in Dialog 1?	A *statement of inference* is a statement based on historical knowledge plus reasoning.
8. What is the historical knowledge upon which the hypothesis (or inference) *the plane is having engine trouble* is based?	From past experience and observation the observer knows that airplanes have engines, that black smoke comes from an engine when a fire breaks out in it, that a plane's speed can be decreased in the air, that a plane will lose altitude when something is wrong, that an F–104 could have taken off from the local Air Force Base and might return, and that the local Air Force Base is located southeast of his present position.
9. Is such knowledge as this necessary to the formation of the conclusion about the plane?	Yes. A being from another world who had never heard of a plane or an engine could not draw this conclusion.

10. Being able to draw inductive conclusions depends a great deal upon one's experience—the extent of one's historical knowledge. It depends also, of course, upon reasoning. What principle of inductive reasoning is involved in the process by which the conclusion about the plane is reached?	It is the principle that if two incidents are related as cause and effect in one situation they will be related in the same way in all like situations.
11. Then, because engine trouble has in the past caused black smoke, loss of speed, and loss of altitude and it has in the past been the practice of pilots to try to land when they are having engine trouble, you assume that engine trouble could produce the same set of results again?	Yes.
12. Suppose that at the same time the smoke appeared, the speed of the plane increased and it began to climb, would you draw the conclusion that the plane was having engine trouble?	No.
13. If not, why not?	One of the observed facts suggests this conclusion, but the two others do not.
14. What principle of inductive reasoning are you illustrating in your last answer?	Observations that support a hypothesis must not be contradicted by other observations.
15. What principle did you illustrate earlier in the lesson when you said *the plane is having engine trouble* was the most credible hypothesis?	The best hypothesis, other things being equal, is the one which is least far-fetched, that is, which is simplest and most commonly associated with the observations.
16. Dr. McKernan says at one point in "S. Miami," "The idea of watermelon as a source of infection in food poisoning still seemed a trifle farfetched." Why did this idea seem farfetched?	The doctor had never heard of watermelon's being "a vehicle for food poisoning," as he put it.
17. Why would it be unusual for watermelon to be the source of infection?	The outside of a fruit or vegetable is the part that is likely to be contaminated and the edible part of a watermelon is separated from the outside by a thick rind.

18. Why does Dr. McKernan make the far-fetched conclusion his working hypothesis?	All of the more-plausible conclusions were contradicted by observed facts. There was no conclusion left to work from but the farfetched one, which was supported by all of the observations.
19. Summarize the principles of inductive reasoning that we have discussed.	Patterns repeat themselves in like circumstances; a valid hypothesis must take all of the relevant observations into account and must not be contradicted by any; if two or more hypotheses are possible conclusions, the least farfetched hypothesis is the best.
20. Is a statement of hypothesis or any other kind of inference also a statement of fact?	No.
21. Why?	The reasoning—or the inductive leap, as it is sometimes called—makes the hypothesis a statement of probability.
22. Can a hypothesis be verified?	The hypothesis about the plane could be verified. Dr. McKernan's hypotheses in "S. Miami" are verified.
23. Once a statement of hypothesis has been verified, what is it called?	A statement of fact.
24. Can every hypothesis be verified?	No. The hypothesis that the giant mammals of prehistoric times were made extinct by hunters cannot be proved true or false.
25. Why?	No one left a firsthand report describing this process; the persons who might know cannot be interviewed as the pilot and mechanic of the F–104 can be; and the process cannot be reenacted as the contamination of watermelon meats was reenacted in "S. Miami."
26. Make a general statement about the types of hypotheses that cannot be verified.	Hypotheses that relate to the prehistoric past cannot be verified.
27. Can a hypothesis that relates to the future be verified?	It cannot be verified in the present, though it might be verified in the future.

28. In an earlier lesson we said that some generalizations were inferences. The classic example of this kind of generalization is *All men are mortal*. Why is this generalization an inference rather than a statement of fact?	Since it pertains to the future as well as to the present and the past, it cannot be completely verified.
29. When the generalization is an inference, it is a statement of probability, isn't it?	Yes.
30. Two types of inductive inference (statements of probability based on historical knowledge plus reasoning) are called the _____ and the _____ .	generalization, hypothesis
31. What is the principle of inductive reasoning involved in the formation of the inferential generalization *All men are mortal?*	If a generalization can be verified from all past incidents to which it pertains, we can assume that it will be verified by all present and all future incidents: for example, since in the past all creatures classified as men have died, we can assume that every creature classified in the present and in the future as a man will die.
32. In reasoning to both a generalization and a hypothesis, one works from perceptions or specific pieces of historical knowledge. Consider, however, the differences in the two processes of reasoning. If x stands for the characteristic that a group of specifics have in common, the process of reasoning to a generalization can be diagramed this way: (x) (x) (x) (x) (x) ⎯⎯⎯→ generalization. How would you define this kind of generalization?	It is a statement of what a group of specifics have in common.
33. Let a different alphabetical letter stand for each of the perceptions in the set with which we began this lesson. For example: a. Black smoke appeared in a trail behind the F–104. What would b, c, and d stand for?	b. The plane's speed decreased. c. The plane lost altitude. d. The plane turned back toward the Air Force Base.

34. We can then diagram the process of forming the hypothesis:

How does the process of forming a hypothesis differ from the process of forming a generalization?

When reasoning toward a generalization, a person works from the same fact observed again and again (Man$_1$ dies, Man$_2$ dies . . . Man$_n$ dies.) When reasoning toward a hypothesis, a person reasons from different facts.

---

35. A hypothesis may be defined as an inductive inference that is ——————— .

sufficient to explain the significance of a group of different but related facts.

---

36. Summarize the similarities and the differences between the inferential generalization and the hypothesis.

Both are inductive inferences, or logical conclusions derived from facts. The facts from which they are derived differ, however, in that the generalization is based on the repetition of the same fact and the hypothesis is based on a connection of different facts. Both are statements of probability, or probable truth, but the basis of the probability differs. The generalization says it is probable that something that has happened many times before will happen again. The hypothesis says it is probable that the interpretation stated in the hypothesis is true.

---

37. We said in an earlier lesson that some generalizations were statements of fact rather than inferences. What does this mean?

That some generalizations merely state what a tested group of specifics have in common without predicting anything about specifics that might be examined in the future or might never be examined. These are not statements of probability as inferential generalizations are.

---

38. Suppose that a house is standing where it has stood for years, and then a tornado hits it and the house immediately disintegrates, the pieces flying in all directions. Is the statement *this house was destroyed by a tornado* a statement of fact or a hypothesis?

A statement of fact.

---

39. Why is it not a hypothesis?

It is not a statement of probable cause; it is a statement of known cause.

40. Some generalizations are _____ , but others are _____ . Some statements of cause are _____ but others are _____ .	inferences, statements of fact, hypotheses, statements of fact
41. The element of _____ is essential to an inferential generalization or a hypothesis.	probability

Sentence Structure and Diction

THE SENTENCE STRUCTURE AND DICTION OF
LOGICAL STATEMENTS

One rarely, if ever, sees a long cumulative sentence with modifying present participial phrases used in a reasoned explanation. Such a sentence, as you saw in Part I, generally describes a subject performing two or more actions simultaneously or in quick succession, or a subject thinking or experiencing emotions while acting; and these are not the types of subjects ordinarily used in reasoned explanations. Likewise, one rarely, if ever, sees a balanced, cumulative, or periodic sentence employing *because, therefore, although,* or *unless* used in a description. Such a sentence expresses a logical relationship that is not appropriate to the translation of visual images or other types of sensory impressions into words. From such observations as these one can conclude that, to an extent not yet fully explored by rhetoricians, certain sentence structures are natural to certain rhetorical forms.

In this book we have in two instances coordinated the study of sentence structure with the study of rhetorical form. You studied cumulative sentences employing adjectival modifiers, nominative absolute phrases, and appositives when you needed them to write descriptions. You studied balanced sentences in which the clauses were joined by connecting words expressing comparative relationships when you needed them to write comparisons. It is appropriate now to study the types of sentences that you will most need when writing explanations. These sentences do not belong to one rhetorical type—they may be balanced, cumulative, or periodic. Nor do they belong to one grammatical type—they may be simple, complex, compound, or compound-complex. What they have in common is that they express the logical relationships of reason-result, concession-assertion, and condition-consequent and that they employ the connecting words that reinforce these types of relationships.

In the following discussion of these types of sentences, most of the examples of sentences are taken from selections in this book. The questions that test comprehension of the instruction in the discussion are not placed at the end of the discussion, but are interspersed with the examples, to make immediate application of grammatical principles possible. For easy reference these questions will be called Exercise 13. They are numbered consecutively throughout the discussion.

EXERCISE 13

The Reason-Result Relationship (*Which Includes Cause-Effect*)

Reason-Result in Simple Sentences

The simple sentence (a sentence with one sentence pattern) can make a straightforward statement that one thing is the reason for another, as in the following sentence: "Parental permissiveness is thought to be a major factor in Nancy's longevity." The meaning here is "Parental permissiveness is thought to be one of the causes contributing to Nancy's longevity." This approaches the simplest of all patterns to use in stating a reason-result:

$$S(N_1) \qquad TrV(V) \qquad DO(N_2)$$
$$\underline{\hspace{2cm}} \qquad \underline{\text{causes}} \qquad \underline{\hspace{2cm}}$$

A reason-result relationship may look complicated and still be based on this simple pattern, as in the following sentence: "This has given rise to a widespread skepticism not merely about the validity of the existing value structure of our contemporary society but [also] about the possibility of a valid value system of any kind." Here, *This* is a pronoun replacing the reason stated in the preceding sentence, *has given rise to* is the equivalent of *has caused*, and *a widespread skepticism*, the grammatical direct object, is the result.

1. Write a reason-result sentence using the pattern

$$S(N_1) \qquad TrV(V) \qquad DO(N_2)$$
$$\underline{\hspace{2cm}} \qquad \underline{\text{has caused}} \qquad \underline{\hspace{2cm}}.$$

Use any form of the verb *cause*.

The preposition is the only type of connector used in simple sentences to express the reason-result relationship, and the prepositions most commonly used for this purpose are *because of* and *on account of*. The following sentence illustrates a reason-result connected by *because of*:

Reason	Result

<u>Because of</u> the unusability of nuclear weapons, we have a military <u>deadlock</u> between the great powers on the major issues.

The next sentence uses a preposition to state the reason-result, but negates the relationship by means of <u>not</u>.

Result   Reason

On the whole, students do not riot <u>out of</u> sheer destructiveness.

The preposition *out of* is equivalent to *because of*.

> 2. Write a sentence using a preposition to connect a reason to a result.

Reason-Result in Complex Sentences

The complex sentence (a sentence with at least one subordinated sentence pattern—a noun clause, an adverb clause, or an adjective clause—and no more than one unsubordinated sentence pattern) is frequently used to express reason-result. The following sentence is an example of a reason-result with a noun clause:

> Result   Reason (Noun Clause)
>
> The reason power-politics is now out-of-date is that war is unusable as an instrument of national politics.

> 3. Write a sentence, imitating the pattern in the example above: <u>The reason</u> [Result] <u>is</u> [or <u>was</u>] <u>that</u> [completion of a noun clause].

Using a subordinating conjunction (*because, since,* or *as*) to introduce a reason in an adverb clause is perhaps the most common of all ways to express a reason-result relationship. Here are two examples:

> Result   Reason
>
> The owner is there <u>because</u> he is one of the forces in the poem.

> Result   Reason
>
> He has turned it away <u>because</u> he cannot answer it.

> 4. Rewrite the preceding sentence, using *since* instead of *because*. Place a comma before *since* to indicate that it states a cause, not a time.

The following complex sentences, in which the reason is stated in an adverb clause, are more complicated than the sentence you have just rewritten.

> Result
>
> But the McCarthy movement failed to realize its full potential, <u>because</u>
> Reason
> it failed to develop an organizational structure capable of permitting citizens to do their own thing effectively.

Result
A parent who tries to fathom the secret of Nancy's success is doomed to
                                    Reason
failure, <u>because</u>, strictly speaking, Nancy is terribly square.

Thus far, in the complex sentences used as illustrations, the statement of reason has followed the statement of result, or, in other words, the adverb clause has followed the independent clause. In the following examples the order is the reverse: the reason stated in the adverb clause precedes the result. Notice that a comma is placed after the adverb clause.

          Reason
<u>Since</u> the scientific method, as we have already observed, forced science to
                                                        Result
develop a value-free descriptive-explanatory conceptual system, the acceptance of the scientific method as a method of knowledge about the world
seems to rule out the possibility of value knowledge and to call into question the cognitive meaningfulness and semantic objectivity of all language.

          Reason
<u>Since</u> it still remains almost the only technique used in international rela-
          Result
tions, we can begin to understand why the world's main divisive issues . . .
are as far from solution as they were when they first arose.

5. Which subordinating conjunctions could be substituted for *since* in the sentences above?

6. Write two sentences on the reason-result pattern, using *because* to introduce the adverb clause. First, place the adverb clause after the independent clause; then reverse the order, placing the adverb clause at the beginning of the sentence. In the second sentence, be sure to use a comma after the adverb clause.

7. Write two sentences on the reason-result pattern, using *since* to introduce the adverb clause. First, place the adverb clause after the independent clause; then reverse the order, placing the adverb clause at the beginning of the sentence. Be sure to use a comma in the first sentence before the adverb clause, and a comma in the second sentence after the adverb clause.

The adverb clause expressing a reason in a complex sentence may appear in the middle of the independent clause, between the complete subject and the complete predicate, as the following sentence illustrates. Notice that commas are used before and after the adverb clause.

Subject of Result   Reason
Students,   <u>because</u> they possess youthful energy and idealism relatively
uncorrupted by experience and unconstrained by responsibility,
Predicate of Result
probably will keep things "stirred up."

8. Write a sentence in which the adverb clause stating a reason is placed
in the middle of an independent clause stating a result. Be sure to
punctuate correctly.

The complex sentence that might be called the "the . . . the" type can also
express the reason-result relationship, as the following sentence illustrates:

Reason   Result
<u>The</u> better we understand how young people view film, <u>the</u> more we have
to revise our notion of what film is.

The adverb clause in this sentence, *the better we understand film*, modifies *the*,
which modifies *more*. The two *the's* are descended from an Old English construction.

9. Imitate the "the . . . the" pattern, writing a sentence expressing a reason
and a result. Use a comma after the adverb clause.

Reason-Result in Compound Sentences, Compound-Complex Sentences and Combinations of Two Sentences

The compound sentence consists of two or more unsubordinated sentence patterns, or independent clauses. The compound-complex sentence consists of two or more unsubordinated sentence patterns, or independent clauses,
and at least one subordinated sentence pattern, or subordinate clause.

There is a tendency in modern English to state the reason-result relationship in two closely related sentences. The more traditional method of compounding the reason statement and the result statement in one sentence is
still used, however, especially when the clauses are short. Whether the reason
and result ideas are presented in two sentences or in one, the same connecting
words and phrases are used to reinforce the reason-result relationship. These
words and phrases fall into three categories:

Coordinating conjunctions: *for* and *so*
Conjunctive adverbs: *thus, therefore, consequently, hence,* and *accordingly*
Transitional phrases: *for this reason* and *as a result*

The coordinating conjunction *for* is always placed before the reason when it
joins a reason and a result. For example:

Like Hemingway's fisherman in *The Old Man and the Sea*, he may catch his
         Result   Reason
fish, but he can bring home only the bare bones, <u>for</u> the underlying anxiety
and despair will eat away and destroy everything of worth in it.

When a doctor in Boston, who had heard that in England a smallpox epidemic had been arrested by a serum that gave people a mild case of cow-
                                       Result
pox, proposed to vaccinate the people, they threatened to run him out of
           Reason
town, <u>for</u> they could no more think of resisting the administration of divine
justice than good citizens could bring themselves to free a legally condemned
man from the offices of the law preparing to hang him.

10. Write a sentence using *for* between a result and a reason, placing a comma
before *for*. Try imitating the first sentence above in all its complexity.

For often joins a result stated in the preceding sentence to a reason immediately following it. This is good form when the result and the reason are long and complicated, as in the example below.

Result
He simply found himself up against a difficulty he almost certainly had not
foreseen and he had to improvise to meet it. <u>For</u> in picking up the rhyme
from the third line of stanza one and carrying it over into stanza two,
Reason
he had created an endless chain-link form within which each stanza left a
hook sticking out for the next stanza to hang on.

The coordinating conjunction *so* is always placed before the result when it
joins a reason and a result. For example:

Reason   Result
They didn't call me on Saturday, <u>so</u> I put them out of my mind.

11. Write a reason-result sentence like the preceding, using *so* before the result.
Be sure to put a comma before *so*.

12. Can you reverse the clauses, placing *so* and the result at the beginning
of the sentence and the reason after the result?

Like *for, so* may be used at the beginning of a sentence when it joins long,
complicated ideas; but unlike *for*, it will always precede the result. The following sentence illustrates this use of *so*.

For in picking up the rhyme from the third line of stanza one and carrying
                                  Reason
it over into stanza two, he had created an endless chain-link form within

which each stanza left a hook sticking out for the next stanza to hang on.
Result
So by stanza four, feeling the poem rounding to its end, Frost had to do
something about that extra rhyme.

Conjunctive adverbs used to join independent clauses or to join sentences
differ from coordinating conjunctions in being movable: that is, they may
appear immediately before a clause, immediately after a clause, or in the
middle of a clause. Note the combination of two sentences below. *Therefore*
has to appear with the result statement, but it could appear after *empirical
science* or even after *reality,* though the last placement would be stylistically
inferior to the other two.

Reason
The modern mind, to a large extent, accepts the empirical scientific method,
including its common-sense counterpart, as the only way of obtaining knowl-
Result
edge about our world. Therefore the language of empirical science is identified with the language of knowledge and of reality.

If the two sentences in this example were compounded into one sentence, a
semicolon would be used before *therefore* and a comma after it.

The following sentence illustrates the internal placement of *therefore:*

Reason
Now "life-strife" and "life-rife" and "life-wife" seem to offer a combination
of possible ideas that can be related by more than just the rhyme. Inevitably,
Result
therefore, the poets have had to work and rework these combinations until
the sparkle has gone out of them.

13. Which coordinating conjunction could be used in place of *therefore* in
the combination of sentences above concerning the modern mind?

14. Can this coordinating conjunction be used in the place of *therefore* in
the second combination of sentences above (on "life-strife")?

15. Write a compound sentence, joining the two clauses with *therefore.* Be
sure to use a semicolon before *therefore* and a comma after it.

16. Using the ideas in the sentence you wrote for number 15, write a compound sentence in which *therefore* is used inside the second clause.

The following combination of two sentences illustrates the use of *accordingly*
as a conjunctive adverb:

Reason
They deliberately decided that the American economy was to be nonmonopo-
Result
listic. <u>Accordingly</u>, they passed the Sherman Anti-Trust Act, the Clayton
Act, and the Norris-LaGuardia Act.

These sentences could be compounded this way:

Reason
They deliberately decided that the American economy was to be nonmonopo-
Result
listic; <u>accordingly</u>, they passed the Sherman Anti-Trust Act, the Clayton
Act, and the Norris-LaGuardia Act.

17. Which other conjunctive adverbs could be used in place of *accordingly*
    in these sentences or the compound sentence constructed from them?

18. Write a complex sentence to express the ideas in this combination of
    sentences, making necessary changes in wording. You will need to use a
    subordinating conjunction.

The most literal connectors that can be used to join independent clauses or
whole sentences expressing the reason-result relationship are the transitional
phrases *for this reason* and *as a result*. Both of these connectors can be placed
before the second clause or the second sentence; but, whereas *for this reason*
points backward to the reason, *as a result* points forward to the result. As you
look at the following examples, notice that a comma follows the transitional
phrase. If the sentences were compounded, there would be a semicolon before
the transitional phrase and a comma after it.

Reason
The foregoing analysis of how young people look at film will appear to
some to constitute a simplistic eulogy to youth. <u>For this reason,</u>
Result
we may temper our optimism by a hard look at real problems with this
generation.

Reason
The foregoing analysis of how young people look at film will appear to
Result
some to constitute a simplistic eulogy to youth. <u>As a result,</u> we may temper
our optimism by a hard look at real problems with this generation.

19. Write two sentences to express the reason-result relationship, and use
    either *for this reason* or *as a result* as the transitional phrase at the
    beginning of the second sentence.

The Concession-Assertion Relationship

Concession-Assertion in Simple Sentences

When there is a concession-assertion relationship in a simple sentence, it is usually expressed by the preposition *in spite of*, as in the following sentence:

            Concession   Assertion

<u>In spite of</u> his previous victories, he feared that he would lose this chess match.

Concession-Assertion in Complex Sentences

The subordinating conjunctions that introduce adverb clauses expressing concessions are *although, even though,* and *though.*

The concession-assertion statement is often used in essays explaining reasons, because it generally denies that a reason and result exist as one might assume. One might feel, for example, that because people are equal at the human level, they are equal in all ways. Note that in the sentence below, equality at the human level is conceded, but equality in practical affairs is denied.

                   Concession

<u>Although</u> we all share a common office as human beings and thus at this

                           Assertion

level are equal, at more concrete levels we occupy positions defined by responsibilities and their correlative rights and are and must be quite unequal.

The subordinating conjunction in a sentence of this type always introduces the concession, but the whole concession statement is movable. Look at the order of the clauses in the sentence above, and notice that the order of the clauses is reversed in the sentence below.

                Assertion

Thus, the owner is a representative of an order of reality from which the

                                 Concession

poet has divided himself for the moment, <u>though</u> to a certain extent he ends by reuniting with it.

Notice that a comma follows a concession placed before an assertion and that a comma precedes a concession placed after an assertion.

Concession-Assertion in Compound Sentences, Compound-Complex Sentences, and Combinations of Two Sentences

The authors of essays in this book use two closely related sentences to express the concession-assertion relationship more often than they use a compound or compound-complex sentence. The coordinating conjunction *yet* is the connector they use most often. The following combination by John Ciardi is typical.

> Concession
> One may even have a sense that he knows the approximate center point of
> Assertion
> the ripples, the point at which the stone struck the water. <u>Yet</u> even then he has trouble marking it surely.

If these two sentences were written as one compound sentence, a comma would be used before *yet*. Like *for* and *so*, the coordinating conjunctions that express the reason-result relationship, *yet*, if it is to serve as a connector, must be placed before the second clause in a concession-assertion compound and at the beginning of the second sentence in a concession-assertion combination.

The conjunctive adverb most often used to connect clauses or sentences expressing the concession-assertion relationship is *nevertheless*. *Still* is also used in this way. The following sentence is an example of a concession-assertion in two sentences.

> Concession   Assertion
> All of this sounds as if the script is by McLuhan. <u>Nevertheless</u>, it is borne out by the experience of teaching contemporary film to university juniors and seniors . . . .

20. Compound the two sentences in the example above, using a semicolon before *nevertheless* and a comma after it.

21. Write a complex sentence stating the concession-assertion expressed in the sentence you composed above, using *though* as a subordinating conjunction to introduce the adverb clause.

The transitional phrase that expresses concession directly is *in spite of this fact*. The following sentence illustrates the use of this phrase:

> Concession
> Mitchell White studied less than any other freshman I have known at this
> Assertion
> university. <u>In spite of this fact</u>, he was always on the Dean's Honor Roll.

22. Write a sentence compounding the two sentences in the preceding example. Use a semicolon before *in spite of this fact* and a comma after it.

23. Which conjunctive adverbs could be used in place of *in spite of this fact?*

The Condition-Consequent Relationship

Condition-Consequent in Simple Sentences

To express a condition-consequent in a simple sentence, one must say, quite directly, that a consequent depends upon a condition, as in this sentence:

Consequent   Condition
His passing the course depends upon his making a B on the final examination.

Condition-Consequent in Complex Sentences

The noun clause beginning with *whether* can be used to express the consequent in a direct statement of condition-consequent. The following complex sentence is a variation of the simple sentence above.

Consequent (Noun clause)   Condition
Whether he passes the course depends upon his making a B on the final examination.

An adverb clause beginning with *if* or *unless* is more common in a complex sentence stating the condition-consequent than any other form. For example:

Condition   Consequent
If he makes a B on the final examination, he will pass the course.

Like other adverb clauses, the adverb clause expressing a condition can appear before or after the independent clause. When it comes before, it is followed by a comma. When it comes after, there is generally no punctuation between the two clauses.

24. Rewrite the condition-consequent sentence in the example above, reversing the order of the clauses.

Unless is the subordinating conjunction that often introduces conditions in complex sentences when the consequent is stated negatively, as in this sentence:

Condition   Consequent
Unless he makes a B on the final examination, he will not pass the course.

If . . . not can also be used to express a negative condition: "If he does not make a B on the final examination, he will not pass the course."

Unless may sometimes introduce a consequent that should be avoided, as the following sentence illustrates:

Consequent   Condition

And <u>unless</u> he is going to stop here forever, it is time to remember that he has a long way to go and that he had best be getting there.

Condition-Consequent in Compound Sentences

Though it generally is used to express an alternative, the coordinating conjunction *or* may be used to connect clauses in a condition-consequent sentence. For example:

Condition   Consequent

He will make a B on the final examination, <u>or</u> he will not pass the course.

The conjunctive adverbs that join condition and consequent clauses are *otherwise* and *else*. *Otherwise* is used as the connector in the following example, but *else* could be used.

Condition   Consequent

We must find some way to grow larger tomatoes; <u>otherwise</u>, we will have to sell the farm.

25. Write a complex sentence to express the condition-consequent in the compound sentence above. Place the adverb clause before the independent clause.

The condition-consequent relationship is similar to the reason-result relationship, because there is a logical dependence of the consequent upon the condition as there is a logical dependence of the result upon the reason. One cannot have the consequent without the condition, as one cannot have the result without the reason. But the relationships are not identical. The condition-consequent usually relates to the future, to a hypothetical situation, or to a situation in which there is some doubt about the condition, as in the following sentence:

Condition

Justified morale is the most important factor in life, for <u>if</u> there is valid high

Consequent   Condition

morale, whatever else is lacking, life is worth living; but <u>if</u> there is no morale,

Consequent

whatever else there is, life is not worth living.

The reason-result relationship pertains to situations in the past that can be proved to have existed or that someone firmly believes to have existed.

PUNCTUATION PATTERNS FOR COMPLEX SENTENCES WITH ADVERB CLAUSES AND FOR COMPOUND SENTENCES

Adv Cl (1)

┌─────────── adverb clause ───────────┐
Subordinating conjunction + sentence pattern,   sentence pattern.

Example:

If you would try to understand contemporary music, you would enjoy it.

Adv Cl (2)

                                    ┌─────────── adverb clause ───────────┐
Sentence pattern   subordinating conjunction + sentence pattern.

Example:

You would enjoy contemporary music if you would try to understand it.

Exceptions:

A comma is used between the sentence pattern and the subordinating conjunction when the subordinating conjunction is *although, even though, though, since* (when it means because), or *as* (when it means because).

Examples:

He holds his audiences spellbound when he sings, although he has never studied music.

We studied the Louisiana map carefully, since the last time we had tried to drive from New Orleans to Alexandria we had made a wrong turn and had gone to Opelousas.

Clauses beginning with *because* pose a special problem. Read the following sentences, trying to explain how the two sentences in each pair differ in meaning.

Examples:

I don't think they will prosecute him, because he is a Communist.
I don't think they will prosecute him because he is a Communist.
He did not kill his mother, because he loved her.
He did not kill his mother because he loved her.

Conj

Sentence pattern, coordinating conjunction   sentence pattern.

Examples:

We arranged his books by colors, and we filled his water jug with pink lemonade.

Advertising uses words to sell goods or services, but poetry uses words to increase awareness.

He will arrive by 6:00 P.M., or he will call us from Tulsa.

We stayed at home, for we had discovered that we did not have enough money for the voyage.

We discovered that we did not have enough money for the voyage, so we stayed at home.

Wilfred was only nine years old, yet he had just played his second piano concert at Carnegie Hall.

Semi (1)

Sentence pattern; sentence pattern.

Example:

Advertising uses words to sell goods or services; poetry uses words to increase awareness.

Semi (2)

Sentence pattern; conjunctive adverb, sentence pattern.

Example:

Mortimer reads poetry constantly; however, he seldom notices rhyme or meter.

Semi (3)

Sentence pattern; transitional phrase, sentence pattern.

Example:

James has moved six times in the last four years; for this reason, he has not made a satisfactory adjustment to school.

The Discovery Structure

The process of forming a hypothesis, like any other process, takes place in time. To recount it just as it occurred, therefore, produces a chronological structure. If the subject requires the thinker to move from place to place and talk with people, a narrative structure, like that of "S. Miami," emerges. There is in this structure a natural suspense, as there is a natural suspense in the original process of investigation, and the writer heightens the suspense through skillful selection of details. If the process of investigation occurs in a laboratory, the scientist making the investigation, or performing the experiment, will usually keep a log from day to day or from hour to hour. When he later explains the results of his experiment, he may take his readers or listeners from significant result to significant result, following the order of the log, moving gradually toward a conclusion. If he does this, he will be using what we call the *discovery structure.*

The discovery structure lends itself well to the interpretation of a short literary work. Since it is normal to read a work from beginning to end, it can often be satisfactory to move from beginning to end in the interpretation of a work, saving the comprehensive idea, or thesis of the interpretation, until all of the supporting evidence has been presented.

Perhaps the most famous of all literary critiques constructed in this way is John Ciardi's "Robert Frost: the Way to the Poem." The discovery structure is especially appropriate to this essay, because Ciardi's purpose is to teach the process of reading a poem closely, by "reading" one poem closely with his audience—from beginning to end. As you read this critique, please observe the structure carefully. In the second paragraph Ciardi states the basic question he intends to answer, but he withholds his answer, which he will state as his thesis near the end of the essay. After asking the basic question, he approaches the poem from a distance, taking first a swift glance at it to comprehend its general structure (as we are taking a swift glance at his essay to comprehend its general structure). He says that the poem "Stopping by Woods on a Snowy Evening" is a narrative and that it appears on the surface to be only a narrative, but that it is something more.

In paragraph 7, a transition paragraph, Ciardi tells the reader, in effect, "I will now proceed through the poem from beginning to end, observing its growing drama in what I shall call three scenes." Thus the reader expects the subdivisions of the close reading of the poem to be scene one, scene two, scene three, as indeed they are. But it is not Ciardi's intention just to retell the narrative. The challenge to him is in interpreting the "something more." He therefore digresses when he wants to raise a question for the reader to think about or when he wants to make a point, calling these digressions parentheses. The first parenthesis ends in paragraph 12. Notice that Ciardi in the last sentence of that paragraph sums up the ideas of the parenthesis before taking up the next subject.

The scene by scene progression, with parentheses, extends from paragraph 7 through paragraph 26. When you interpret a poem using the discovery structure, you probably will be ready to state your thesis at the end of the progression. What does Ciardi do after he has completed the progression? Why is he able to do this? Notice that this part of the development is essential to his thesis. In which paragraph is the thesis finally stated? Why does Ciardi say that an epilogue is necessary? How does the epilogue reinforce the thesis?

Robert Frost: the Way to the Poem

John Ciardi

Stopping by Woods on a Snowy Evening

Robert Frost

> Whose woods these are I think I know.
> His house is in the village though;
> He will not see me stopping here
> To watch his woods fill up with snow.
>
> My little horse must think it queer
> To stop without a farmhouse near
> Between the wood and frozen lake
> The darkest evening of the year.
>
> He gives his harness bells a shake
> To ask if there is some mistake.
> The only other sound's the sweep
> Of easy wind and downy flake.
>
> The woods are lovely, dark and deep.
> But I have promises to keep,
> And miles to go before I sleep,
> And miles to go before I sleep.

1 The School System has much to say these days of the virtue of reading widely, and not enough about the virtues of reading less but in depth. There are any number of reading lists for poetry, but there is not enough talk about individual poems. Poetry, finally, is one poem at a time. To read any one poem carefully

ROBERT FROST: THE WAY TO THE POEM   From *Dialogue with an Audience*, by John Ciardi, copyright © 1958 by John Ciardi. Published by J. B. Lippincott Co., and reprinted with their permission.

STOPPING BY WOODS ON A SNOWY EVENING   From *Complete Poems of Robert Frost*. Copyright 1923, 1930, 1939 by Holt, Rinehart and Winston, Inc. Copyright 1951, © 1958 by Robert Frost. Copyright © 1967 by Lesley Frost Ballantine. Reprinted by permission of Holt, Rinehart and Winston, Inc.

is the ideal preparation for reading another. Only a poem can illustrate how poetry works.

2 Above, therefore, is a poem—one of the master lyrics of the English language, and almost certainly the best-known poem by an American poet. What happens in it?—which is to say, not *what* does it mean, but *how* does it mean? How does it go about being a human reenactment of a human experience? The author—perhaps the thousandth reader would need to be told—is Robert Frost.

3 Even the TV audience can see that this poem begins as a seemingly-simple narration of a seemingly-simple incident but ends by suggesting meanings far beyond anything specifically referred to in the narrative. And even readers with only the most casual interest in poetry might be made to note the additional fact that, though the poem suggests those larger meanings, it is very careful never to abandon its pretense to being simple narration. There is duplicity at work. The poet pretends to be talking about one thing, and all the while he is talking about many others.

4 Many readers are forever unable to accept the poet's essential duplicity. It is almost safe to say that a poem is never about what it seems to be about. As much could be said of the proverb. The bird in the hand, the rolling stone, the stitch in time never (except by artful double-deception) intend any sort of statement about birds, stones, or sewing. The incident of this poem, one must conclude, is at root a metaphor.

5 Duplicity aside, this poem's movement from the specific to the general illustrates one of the basic formulas of all poetry. Such a grand poem as Arnold's "Dover Beach" and such lesser, though unfortunately better known, poems as Longfellow's "The Village Blacksmith" and Holmes's "The Chambered Nautilus" are built on the same progression. In these three poems, however, the generalization is markedly set apart from the specific narration, and even seems additional to the telling rather than intrinsic to it. It is this sense of division one has in mind in speaking of "a tacked-on moral."

6 There is nothing wrong-in-itself with a tacked-on moral. Frost, in fact, makes excellent use of the device at times. In this poem, however, Frost is careful to let the whatever-the-moral-is grow out of the poem itself. When the action ends the poem ends. There is no epilogue and no explanation. Everything pretends to be about the narrated incident. And that pretense sets the basic tone of the poem's performance of itself.

7 The dramatic force of that performance is best observable, I believe, as a progression in three scenes.

8 In scene one, which coincides with stanza one, a man—a New England man—is driving his sleigh somewhere at night. It is snowing, and as the man passes a dark patch of woods he stops to watch the snow descend into the darkness. We know, moreover, that the man is familiar with these parts (he knows who owns the woods and where the owner lives), and we know that no one has seen him stop. As scene one forms itself in the theatre of the mind's-eye, therefore, it serves to establish some as yet unspecified relation between the man and the woods.

9 It is necessary, however, to stop here for a long parenthesis: Even so simple an opening statement raises any number of questions. It is impossible to

address all the questions that rise from the poem stanza by stanza, but two that arise from stanza one illustrate the sort of thing one might well ask of the poem detail by detail.

10 Why, for example, does the man not say what errand he is on? What is the force of leaving the errand generalized? He might just as well have told us that he was going to the general store, or returning from it with a jug of molasses he had promised to bring Aunt Harriet and two suits of long underwear he had promised to bring the hired man. Frost, moreover, can handle homely detail to great effect. He preferred to leave his motive generalized. Why?

11 Any why, on the other hand, does he say so much about knowing the absent owner of the woods and where he lives? Is it simply that one set of details happened-in whereas another did not? To speak of things "happening-in" is to assault the integrity of a poem. Poetry cannot be discussed meaningfully unless one can assume that everything in the poem—every last comma and variant spelling—is in it by the poet's specific act of choice. Only bad poets allow into their poems what is haphazard or cheaply chosen.

12 The errand, I will venture a bit brashly for lack of space, is left generalized in order the more aptly to suggest *any* errand in life and, therefore, life itself. The owner is there because he is one of the forces of the poem. Let it do to say that the force he represents is the village of mankind (that village at the edge of winter) from which the poet finds himself separated (has separated himself?) in his moment by the woods (and to which, he recalls finally, he has promises to keep). The owner is he-who-lives-in-his-village-house, thereby locked away from the poet's awareness of the-time-the-snow-tells as it engulfs and obliterates the world the village man allows himself to believe he "owns." Thus, the owner is a representative of an order of reality from which the poet has divided himself for the moment, though to a certain extent he ends by reuniting with it. Scene one, therefore, establishes not only a relation between the man and the woods, but the fact that the man's relation begins with his separation (though momentarily) from mankind.

13 End parenthesis one, begin parenthesis two.

14 Still considering the first scene as a kind of dramatic performance of forces, one must note that the poet has meticulously matched the simplicity of his language to the pretended simplicity of the narrative. Clearly, the man stopped because the beauty of the scene moved him, but he neither tells us that the scene is beautiful nor that he is moved. A bad writer, always ready to overdo, might have written: "The vastness gripped me, filling my spirit with the slow steady sinking of the snow's crystalline perfection into the glimmerless profundities of the hushed primeval wood." Frost's avoidance of such a spate illustrates two principles of good writing. The first, he has stated himself in "The Mowing": "Anything *more* than the truth would have seemed too weak" (italics mine). Understatement is one of the basic sources of power in English poetry. The second principle is to let the action speak for itself. A good novelist does not tell us that a given character is good or bad (at least not since the passing of the Dickens tradition): he shows us the character in action and then, watching him, we know. Poetry, too, has fictional obligations: even when the characters are ideas and metaphors rather than people, they must be *characterized in action*. A poem does

not *talk about* ideas; it *enacts* them. The force of the poem's performance, in fact, is precisely to act out (and thereby to make us act out empathically that is, to *feel out,* that is, *to identify with*) the speaker and why he stopped. The man is the principal actor in this little "drama of why" and in scene one he is the only character, though as noted, he is somehow related to the absent owner.

15 End second parenthesis.

16 In scene two (stanzas two and three) a *foil* is introduced. In fiction and drama, a foil is a character who "plays against" a more important character. By presenting a different point of view or an opposed set of motives, the foil moves the more important character to react in ways that might not have found expression without such opposition. The more important character is thus more fully revealed—to the reader and to himself. The foil here is the horse.

17 The horse forces the question. Why did the man stop? Until it occurs to him that his "little horse must think it queer" he had not asked himself for reasons. He had simply stopped. But the man finds himself faced with the question he imagines the horse to be asking: what *is* there to stop for out there in the cold, away from bin and stall (house and village and mankind?) and all that any self-respecting beast could value on such a night? In sensing that other view, the man is forced to examine his own more deeply.

18 In stanza two the question arises only as a feeling within the man. In stanza three, however (still scene two), the horse acts. He gives his harness bells a shake. "What's wrong?" he seems to say. "What are we waiting for?"

19 By now, obviously, the horse—without losing its identity as horse—has also become a symbol. A symbol is something that stands for something else. Whatever that something else may be, it certainly begins as that order of life that does not understand why a man stops in the wintry middle of nowhere to watch the snow come down. (Can one fail to sense by now that the dark and the snowfall symbolize a death-wish, however momentary, *i.e.,* that hunger for final rest and surrender that a man may feel, but not a beast?)

20 So by the end of scene two the performance has given dramatic force to three elements that work upon the man. There is his relation to the world of the owner. There is his relation to the brute world of the horse. And there is that third presence of the unownable world, the movement of the all-engulfing snow across all the orders of life, the man's, the owner's, and the horse's—with the difference that the man knows of that second dark-within-the-dark of which the horse cannot, and the owner will, know.

21 The man ends scene two with all these forces working upon him simultaneously. He feels himself moved to a decision. And he feels a last call from the darkness: "the sweep / Of easy wind and downy flake." It would be so easy and so downy to go into the woods and let himself be covered over.

22 But scene three (stanza four) produces a fourth force. This fourth force can be given many names. It is certainly better, in fact, to give it many names than to attempt to limit it to one. It is social obligation, or personal commitment, or duty, or just the realization that a man cannot indulge a mood forever. All of these and more. But, finally, he has a simple decision to make. He may go into the woods and let the darkness and the snow swallow him from the world of

beast and man. Or he must move on. And unless he is going to stop here forever, it is time to remember that he has a long way to go and that he had best be getting there. (So there is something to be said for the horse, too.)

23 Then and only then, his question driven more and more deeply into himself by these cross-forces, does the man venture a comment on what attracted him "The woods are lovely, dark and deep." His mood lingers over the thought of that lovely dark-and-deep (as do the very syllables in which he phrases the thought), but the final decision is to put off the mood and move on. He has his man's way to go and his man's obligations to tend to before he can yield. He has miles to go before his sleep. He repeats that thought and the performance ends.

24 But why the repetition? The first time Frost says "And miles to go before I sleep," there can be little doubt that the primary meaning is: "I have a long way to go before I get to bed tonight." The second time he says it, however, "miles to go" and "sleep" are suddenly transformed into symbols. What are those "something-elses" the symbols stand for? Hundreds of people have tried to ask Mr. Frost that question and he has always turned it away. He has turned it away *because he cannot answer it.* He could answer some part of it. But some part is not enough.

25 For a symbol is like a rock dropped into a pool: it sends out ripples in all directions, and the ripples are in motion. Who can say where the last ripple disappears? One may have a sense that he knows the approximate center point of the ripples, the point at which the stone struck the water. Yet even then he has trouble marking it surely. How does one make a mark on water? Oh very well—the center point of that second "miles to go" is probably approximately in the neighborhood of being close to meaning, perhaps, "the road of life"; and the second "before I sleep" is maybe that close to meaning "before I take my final rest," the rest in darkness that seemed so temptingly dark-and-deep for the moment of the mood. But the ripples continue to move and the light to change on the water, and the longer one watches the more changes he sees. Such shifting-and-being-at-the-same-instant is of the very sparkle and life of poetry. One experiences it as one experiences life, for everytime he looks at an experience he sees something new, and he sees it change as he watches it. And that sense of continuity in fluidity is one of the primary kinds of knowledge, one of man's basic ways of knowing, and one that only the arts can teach, poetry foremost among them.

26 Frost himself certainly did not ask what that repeated last line meant. It came to him and he received it. He "felt right" about it. And what he "felt right" about was in no sense a "meaning" that, say, an essay could apprehend, but an act of experience that could be fully presented only by the dramatic enactment of forces which is the performance of the poem.

27 Now look at the poem in another way. Did Frost know what he was going to do when he began? Considering the poem simply as an act of skill, as a piece of juggling, one cannot fail to respond to the magnificent turn at the end where, with one flip, seven of the simplest words in the language suddenly dazzle full of never-ending waves of thought and feeling. Or, more precisely, of felt-

thought. Certainly an equivalent stunt by a juggler—could there be an equivalent—would bring the house down. Was it to cap his performance with that grand stunt that Frost wrote the poem?

28 Far from it. The obvious fact is that Frost could not have known *he was going to write those lines until he wrote them.* Then a second fact must be registered: *he wrote them because, for the fun of it, he had got himself into trouble.*

29 Frost, like every good poet, began by playing a game with himself. The most usual way of writing a four line stanza with four feet to the line is to rhyme the third line with the first, and the fourth line with the second. Even that much rhyme is so difficult in English that many poets and almost all of the anonymous ballad makers do not bother to rhyme the first and third lines at all, settling for two rhymes in four lines as good enough. For English is a rhyme-poor language. In Italian and in French, for example, so many words end with the same sounds that rhyming is relatively easy—so easy that many modern French and Italian poets do not bother to rhyme at all. English, being a more agglomerate language, has far more final sounds, hence fewer of them rhyme. When an Italian poet writes a line ending with "vita" (life) he has literally hundreds of rhyme choices available. When an English poet writes "life" at the end of a line he can summon "strife, wife, knife, fife, rife," and then he is in trouble. Now "life-strife" and "life-rife" and "life-wife" seem to offer a combination of possible ideas that can be related by more than just the rhyme. Inevitably, therefore, the poets have had to work and rework these combinations until the sparkle has gone out of them. The reader is normally tired of such rhyme-led associations. When he encounters "life-strife" he is certainly entitled to suspect that the poet did not really want to say "strife"—that had there been in English such a word as, say, "hife," meaning "infinite peace and harmony," the poet would as gladly have used that word instead of "strife." Thus, the reader feels that the writing is haphazard, that the rhyme is making the poet say things he does not really feel, and which, therefore, the reader does not feel except as boredom. One likes to see the rhymes fall into place, but he must end with the belief that it is the poet who is deciding what is said and not the rhyme scheme that is forcing the saying.

30 So rhyme is a kind of game, and an especially difficult one in English. As in every game, the fun of the rhyme is to set one's difficulties high and then to meet them skilfully. As Frost himself once defined freedom, it consists of "moving easy in harness."

31 In "Stopping by Woods on a Snowy Evening" Frost took a long chance. He decided to rhyme not two lines in each stanza, but three. Not even Frost could have sustained that much rhyme in a long poem (as Dante, for example, with the advantage of writing in Italian, sustained triple rhyme for thousands of lines in "The Divine Comedy"). Frost would have known instantly, therefore, when he took the original chance, that he was going to write a short poem. He would have had that much foretaste of it.

32 So the first stanza emerged rhymed a-a-b-a. And with the sure sense that this was to be a short poem, Frost decided to take an additional chance and to redouble: in English three rhymes in four lines is more than enough; there is no need to rhyme the fourth line. For the fun of it, however, Frost set himself

to pick up that loose rhyme and to weave it into the pattern, thereby accepting the all but impossible burden of quadruple rhyme.

33 The miracle is that it worked. Despite the enormous freight of rhyme, the poem not only came out as a neat pattern, but managed to do so with no sense of strain. Every word and every rhyme falls into place as naturally and as inevitably as if there were no rhyme restricting the poet's choices.

34 That ease-in-difficulty is certainly inseparable from the success of the poem's performance. One watches the skill-man juggle three balls, then four, then five, and every addition makes the trick more wonderful. But unless he makes the hard trick seem as easy as an easy trick, then all is lost.

35 The real point, however, is not only that Frost took on a hard rhyme-trick and made it seem easy. It is rather as if the juggler, carried away, had tossed up one more ball than he could really handle, and then amazed himself by actually handling it. So with the real triumph of this poem. Frost could not have known what a stunning effect his repetition of the last line was going to produce. He could not even know he was going to repeat the line. He simply found himself up against a difficulty he almost certainly had not foreseen and he had to improvise to meet it. For in picking up the rhyme from the third line of stanza one and carrying it over into stanza two, he had created an endless chain-link form within which each stanza left a hook sticking out for the next stanza to hang on. So by stanza four, feeling the poem rounding to its end, Frost had to do something about that extra rhyme.

36 He might have tucked it back into a third line rhyming with the *know-though-snow* of stanza one. He could thus have rounded the poem out to the mathematical symmetry of using each rhyme four times. But though such a device might be defensible in theory, a rhyme repeated after eleven lines is so far from its original rhyme sound that its feeling as rhyme must certainly be lost. And what good is theory if the reader is not moved by the writing?

37 It must have been in some such quandary that the final repetition suggested itself—a suggestion born of the very difficulties the poet had let himself in for. So there is that point beyond mere ease in handling a hard thing, the point at which the very difficulty offers the poet the opportunity to do better than he knew he could. What, aside from having that happen to oneself, could be more self-delighting than to participate in its happening by one's reader-identification with the poem?

38 And by now a further point will have suggested itself: that the human-insight of the poem and the technicalities of its poetic artifice are inseparable. Each feeds the other. That interplay is the poem's meaning, a matter not of WHAT DOES IT MEAN, for no one can ever say entirely what a good poem means, but of HOW DOES IT MEAN, a process one can come much closer to discussing.

39 There is a necessary epilogue. Mr. Frost has often discussed this poem on the platform, or more usually in the course of a long-evening-after a talk. Time and again I have heard him say that he just wrote it off, that it just came to him, and that he set it down as it came.

40 Once at Bread Loaf, however, I heard him add one very essential piece to the discussion of how it "just came." One night, he said, he had sat down after supper to work at a long piece of blank verse. The piece never worked out,

but Mr. Frost found himself so absorbed in it that, when next he looked up, dawn was at his window. He rose, crossed to the window, stood looking out for a few minutes, and *then* it was that "Stopping by Woods" suddenly "just came," so that all he had to do was cross the room and write it down.

41 Robert Frost is the sort of artist who hides his traces. I know of no Frost worksheets anywhere. If someone has raided his wastebasket in secret, it is possible that such worksheets exist somewhere, but Frost would not willingly allow anything but the finished product to leave him. Almost certainly, therefore, no one will ever know what was in that piece of unsuccessful blank verse he had been working at with such concentration, but I for one would stake my life that could that worksheet be uncovered, it would be found to contain the germinal stuff of "Stopping by Woods"; that what was a-simmer in him all night without finding its proper form, suddenly, when he let his still-occupied mind look away, came at him from a different direction, offered itself in a different form, and that finding that form exactly right the impulse proceeded to marry itself to the new shape in one of the most miraculous performances of English lyricism.

42 And that, too—whether or not one can accept so hypothetical a discussion—is part of HOW the poem means. It means that marriage to the perfect form, the poem's shapen declaration of itself, its moment's monument fixed beyond all possibility of change. And thus, finally, in every truly good poem, "How does it mean?" must always be answered "Triumphantly." Whatever the poem "is about," *how* it means is always how Genesis means: the word become a form and the form become a thing, and—when the becoming is true—the thing become a part of the knowledge and experience of the race forever.

CRITERIA FOR INTERPRETING POEMS

It is not right to suppose that every poem has just one meaning, especially a meaning that can be stated in a prose paraphrase or summary. At the same time, it is not right to suppose that just any interpretation of a given poem is as good as any other. Careful, perceptive reading is essential to sound interpretation of any poem, and knowledge of the writer's other works, the writer's life, the period when the poem was written, and the literary genre to which the work belongs are essential to the sound interpretation of some poems.

The poems following this explanation can be interpreted from their texts, without special knowledge of poets, periods, and genres. Your values and your knowledge of human nature will influence your interpretations (in fact, without values and a knowledge of human nature, you could not interpret these poems at all), but you will use your insight to read what the poet is saying, not, as some critics do, to create a different situation and different characters from his. In other words, sensitive objectivity is a good goal.

When a poem can be interpreted from the text alone, interpreting it is much like the process of forming a hypothesis. All of the evidence is in the poem, to be gathered bit by bit, and the same rules that pertain to the formation of the logical hypothesis—those that you listed in Dialog 11—pertain to the formation of the interpretive conclusion. The similarity between the hypothesis and the literary interpretation is developed in the following excerpt. Read it carefully so that you can recall Perrine's criteria as you interpret "My Last Duchess" and "Home Burial."

FROM **The Nature of Proof in the Interpretation of Poetry**

Laurence Perrine

The criteria used for judging any interpretation of a poem are two: (1) A correct interpretation, if the poem is a successful one, must be able to account satisfactorily for any detail of the poem. If it is contradicted by any detail it is wrong. Of several interpretations, the best is that which most fully explains the details of the poem without itself being contradicted by any detail. (2) If more than one interpretation satisfactorily accounts for all the details of the poem, the best is that which is the most economical, i.e., which relies on the fewest assumptions not grounded in the poem itself. Thomas Huxley illustrates this principle of judgment in a different area in one of his essays. If, he says, on coming downstairs in the morning we find our silverware missing, the window open, the mark of a dirty hand on the window frame, and the impress of a hobnailed boot on the gravel outside, we logically conclude that the silverware has been stolen by a human thief. It *is* possible, of course, that the silverware was taken by a monkey and that a man with dirty hands and hobnailed boots looked in the window afterwards; but this explanation is far less probable, for though it too accounts for all the facts, it rests on too many additional assumptions. It is, as we would say, too "far-fetched."

These two criteria, I ask you to notice, are not different from those we bring to the judgment of a new scientific hypothesis. Of such we ask (1) that it satisfactorily account for as many as possible of the known facts without being contradicted by any fact, (2) that it be the simplest or most economical of alternative ways of accounting for these facts.

FROM "THE NATURE OF PROOF IN THE INTERPRETATION OF POETRY" From *The English Journal*, September, 1962. Reprinted by permission of the National Council of Teachers of English and the author.

A POEM FOR CLOSE READING

My Last Duchess

Robert Browning

Ferrara[1]

That's my last Duchess painted on the wall,
Looking as if she were alive. I call
That piece a wonder, now: Frà Pandolf's hands
Worked busily a day, and there she stands.
Will't please you sit and look at her? I said
"Frà Pandolf" by design, for never read
Strangers like you that pictured countenance,
The depth and passion of its earnest glance,
But to myself they turned (since none puts by
The curtain I have drawn for you, but I)   10
And seemed as they would ask me, if they durst,
How such a glance came there; so, not the first
Are you to turn and ask thus. Sir, 'twas not
Her husband's presence only, called that spot
Of joy into the Duchess' cheek: perhaps
Frà Pandolf chanced to say, "Her mantle laps
Over my lady's wrist too much," or "Paint
Must never hope to reproduce the faint
Half-flush that dies along her throat"; such stuff
Was courtesy, she thought, and cause enough   20
For calling up that spot of joy. She had
A heart—how shall I say—too soon made glad,
Too easily impressed; she liked whate'er
She looked on, and her looks went everywhere.
Sir, 'twas all one! My favor at her breast,
The dropping of the daylight in the West,
The bough of cherries some officious fool
Broke in the orchard for her, the white mule
She rode with round the terrace—all and each
Would draw from her alike the approving speech,   30
Or blush, at least. She thanked men—good! but thanked
Somehow—I know not how—as if she ranked
My gift of a nine-hundred-years-old name
With anybody's gift. Who'd stoop to blame
This sort of trifling? Even had you skill
In speech—(which I have not)—to make your will
Quite clear to such a one, and say, "Just this

---

[1]During the Renaissance, the time in which this poem is set, Ferrara was the central city in the duchy of Ferrara, in Northern Italy. The speaker is the Duke of Ferrara.

Or that in you disgusts me; here you miss,
Or there exceed the mark"—and if she let
Herself be lessoned so, nor plainly set   40
Her wits to yours, forsooth, and made excuse
—E'en then would be some stooping; and I choose
Never to stoop. Oh sir, she smiled, no doubt,
Whene'er I passed her; but who passed without
Much the same smile? This grew; I gave commands;
Then all smiles stopped together. There she stands
As if alive. Will't please you rise? We'll meet
The company below, then. I repeat,
The Count your master's known munificence
Is ample warrant that no just pretense   50
Of mine for dowry will be disallowed;
Though his fair daughter's self, as I avowed
At starting, is my object. Nay, we'll go
Together down, sir. Notice Neptune, though,
Taming a sea horse, thought a rarity,
Which Claus of Innsbruck cast in bronze for me!

---

1. How much do you learn from reading the first line?
2. Why does Browning use the word *last* in the title and in the first line? How does the meaning of *last* in *my last Duchess* differ from the meaning of *late* in *the late Duchess*?
3. What evidence is there in lines 3–12 that the Duke is proud of the painting?
4. What do you learn about the Duke from the parenthetical clause in lines 9–10?
5. What do you learn about the Duchess in lines 3–12?
6. What has the listener presumably asked before line 13?
7. According to the Duke, what could delight the Duchess so much as to bring that glance, the "spot of joy," to her countenance?
8. After reading to line 34, do you like the Duchess? Why, or why not?
9. Why had the Duke been displeased with the Duchess?
10. After reading to line 34, do you like the Duke? Why or why not?
11. The Duke says in lines 34–43 that he had not told the Duchess that her manner displeased him. Why had he not?
12. Had the Duchess been ill-tempered toward the Duke?
13. What were the commands the Duke gave (line 45)?
14. Where do you learn why the listener has come to visit the Duke? Why has he come?
15. Does the Duke expect a dowry from the Count whose daughter he is arranging to marry?
16. Does the Count probably think he is making "a good match" for his daughter? Why?
17. Can you be sure whether the Duke is sincere when he says that the "daughter's self," rather than the dowry, is his object? Why does the ex-

pression "his fair daughter's self . . . is my object" carry more force in this
context than it usually does?

18. Has the Duke had a special purpose in telling the Count's emissary about his *last* Duchess?

19. You know from the Duke's statement in lines 53–54—"Nay, we'll go/ Together down, sir"—that the emissary has said something. What do you suppose he has said?

20. What is the purpose (or what are the purposes) of the last three lines?

HOW TO PROCEED FROM A CLOSE READING OF A POEM TO A WRITTEN INTERPRETATION

1. Decide what the central subject of the poem is. For example, it seems after a close reading of the dramatic monolog "My Last Duchess" that it is not about the Duchess, but the Duke.

2. Look for divisions that mark steps in the illumination of the subject, or, to put it another way, steps in the reader's progress toward deeper levels of awareness. "My Last Duchess" can be divided this way:

    Phase 1 (lines 1–13): Exposition of the situation and introduction of the subject to be discussed.

    Phase 2 (lines 13–34): The Duke's revelation of his resentment because the Duchess was not completely absorbed in him.

    Phase 3 (lines 34–47): The Duke's revelation of his extreme pride and his brutality.

    Phase 4 (lines 47–56): Evidence upon which the reader will judge the Duke's purpose in talking with the Count's emissary.

3. Set up the general outline for the *discovery structure:*

    I. An overview of the poem

    II. The progression, with parentheses

    III. The thesis

4. Write the interpretation.

    In the first part, the overview, classify the poem and indicate the general subject, without stating the thesis.

    Begin the progression by stating the number of divisions in the poem. Use an appropriate name for these divisions. John Ciardi called the divisions in "Stopping by Woods on a Snowy Evening" scenes. Please turn back to Ciardi's critique and notice the use of the scene numbers as transitional expressions at the beginning of paragraphs 8, 14, 16, 20, 21, and 22. Use the division numbers of the poem to mark the lines of division in your interpretation. Use connectors effectively to give your theme coherence.

    When you can support inferences in your interpretation with evidence and reasons, do so. If, to fill out the interpretation, you need to make inferences from only hints, guard them with expressions like *perhaps* and *possibly,* so that the reader will be fully aware that you are answering a question raised by the text and not paraphrasing the text.

The following interpretation is one that you might write from the instructions above after doing a close reading of "My Last Duchess." The structural divisions and summary statements are labeled in the margin. Connectors expressing reason-result, concession-assertion, and condition-consequent relationships are set in boldface. Words that guard inferences are italicized, and the inferences are labeled in the margin.

An Interpretation of "My Last Duchess," by Robert Browning

Overview
Classification of the poem

Browning's "My Last Duchess" is a dramatic monolog set in Renaissance Italy. At first glance, it seems to be about a Duchess, **since** the speaker, the Duke of Ferrara, is talking about his last Duchess as he and a guest look at a portrait of her, but the real subject of the poem is the character of the Duke, which he himself reveals as he speaks.

Indication of the general subject

Progression
The number of divisions
Summary statement on the first division

Paraphrase

Inference

Reason supporting an inference

There are four phases in the Duke's monolog, and, **hence,** four levels of awareness for the reader. The first phase (lines 1–13) sets the stage for the Duke's self-revelation. The reader learns that the Duke is showing a lifelike portrait of his former wife to some unidentified man called simply a stranger. The Duke is proud of the painting as a work of art, but it does not seem that he is showing the painting just to impress the listener with his artistic taste, **because** he seems intent upon having the listener observe the expression on the Duchess' countenance—"the depth and passion of its earnest glance."

Summary statement on the second division

Long paraphrase

This glance, or "spot of joy," as the Duke calls the expression in his second reference to it, is the ostensible subject of the next phase of the poem (lines 13–34). As the Duke lists several simple experiences that could bring that joyful expression to his wife's face—a courteous compliment from the portrait painter Frà Pandolf, a sunset, a bough of cherries given her by a person of no special importance, the white mule she rode—the reader becomes aware that the Duke resented every pleasure the Duchess had except those he gave her. She received a brooch from him, an ornament she was wearing in the portrait, with the same joyful expression that she received other favors. What offended the Duke most deeply, though, was the Duchess' failure to appreciate, with a special reverence, the "nine-hundred-years-old name" he had given her. The reader knows at the end of this phase that pride of birth is the mainspring of the Duke's being.

Inference

Inference	A man of rank with less pride could have discussed with his young wife whatever characteristic of her manner displeased him. **If** the Duke had done this, the Duchess might
Value judgment	have defended herself, **because** she had really done nothing wrong; but it is just as likely that she would have taken
Value judgment	counsel from her husband. Certainly, to have talked about the problem with her would have been the fair thing to
Reason supporting a value judgment	do, **since** even in the Duke's portrayal of her, the Duchess seems not to have known of her husband's resentment.
Summary statement on the third division	In the third phase (lines 34–47) the reader begins to realize the precariousness of the Duchess' situation when the Duke says that he did not tell the Duchess of his repugnance, **even though** he knew she might have changed
Guarded inference	her manner to please him. *Perhaps* he knew that even **if** she did respond submissively, she would know that he was unreasonable in his jealousy and absolute in his possessiveness. The **reason** he states for not talking with her **is**
Paraphrase	**that** in talking in this way he would have been stooping. The Duke, with his "nine-hundred-years-old name," is not a man to stoop.
Summary and transition	The reader, even knowing that the Duke is proud, jealous, and possessive, is not prepared for his next statement: "This grew; I gave commands;/Then all smiles stopped
Anticipatory questions	together." Why should the Duke be telling a stranger not only that he was too proud to imply to his wife that he was jealous of her simple pleasures, but also that he would actually give commands to have her killed (for this seems the most likely meaning of his commands)?
Summary statement on the last division	In the last phase, lines 47–56, the reader suddenly understands the Duke's purpose in talking to a stranger in
Paraphrase	a previously unaccountable way. This stranger is an emissary of a Count whose daughter the Duke is arranging to marry. The Duke's price is high: he not only expects a dowry in line with the Count's "known munificence," but he also
Guarded inference	*apparently* expects the "fair daughter" to learn from the fate of her predecessor that he is a man who demands a woman's complete devotion. Of course he cannot stoop
Guarded inference	to tell her this himself, but he *may be* trying to tell her indirectly through her father's emissary.
	Browning does not tell the reader what the emissary thinks of what the Duke has said about his last Duchess. With only this statement of the Duke's to go on—"Nay,
Guarded inference	we'll go/Together down, sir"—*one might hazard a guess* that the emissary has been shocked by the Duke's revelation and by an ominous statement of the Duke's that not the dowry, but the "fair daughter's self" is his "object."
Guarded inference	*Perhaps* the emissary is trying to get away from the Duke

Inference

to talk with the Count, who has apparently just arrived below, before he makes the marriage arrangement final. But the Duke does not let him get away.

Guarded inference

As the Duke and the emissary descend together to meet the company, *probably* the Count's company, the Duke points out to the emissary a statue of Neptune taming a sea horse. He may be simply revealing again his pride in

Reason supporting an inference

his art collection, **since** he says that the statue is a rarity cast in bronze especially for him by Claus of Innsbruck,

Guarded inference

but *it is possible* that this statue appeals to him **because** it is an expression of dominance that harmonizes with his own penchant for dominance; at least, for the reader it stands as an appropriate symbol for the domineering spirit of the Duke.

Thesis

Thus, Browning is able in twenty-eight rhymed couplets to open for the reader deepening levels of awareness—curiosity, concern, shock, and awed disgust—as he creates a self-portrayal of the Duke of Ferrara in his jealousy, pride, shrewdness, and brutality.

SUGGESTED WRITING ASSIGNMENT

An Interpretation of "Home Burial," by Robert Frost

1. Read Robert Frost's "Home Burial" closely, trying to understand the husband and the wife and the attitude of each toward the other. Write down details that reveal character and attitude. Does your attitude toward either or both change as you read? Remember that changes in your thinking and feeling form a progression.
2. After mastering the details, decide what the poem is about. What is Frost trying to say? Or, what kind of experience is he trying to give the reader? Is he on the side of the husband, on the side of the wife, or on neither side? What evidence do you have to support your opinion?
3. Look back at "How to Proceed from a Close Reading of a Poem to a Written Interpretation," and follow the directions there.

Home Burial

Robert Frost

He saw her from the bottom of the stairs
Before she saw him. She was starting down,
Looking back over her shoulder at some fear.
She took a doubtful step and then undid it
To raise herself and look again. He spoke
Advancing toward her: 'What is it you see
From up there always—for I want to know.'
She turned and sank upon her skirts at that,
And her face changed from terrified to dull.
He said to gain time: 'What is it you see,'   10
Mounting until she cowered under him.
'I will find out now—you must tell me, dear.'
She, in her place, refused him any help
With the least stiffening of her neck and silence.
She let him look, sure that he wouldn't see,
Blind creature; and awhile he didn't see.
But at last he murmured, 'Oh,' and again, 'Oh.'

'What is it—what?' she said.

                'Just that I see.'

'You don't,' she challenged. 'Tell me what it is.'

'The wonder is I didn't see at once.   20
I never noticed it from here before.
I must be wonted to it—that's the reason.
The little graveyard where my people are!
So small the window frames the whole of it.
Not so much larger than a bedroom, is it?
There are three stones of slate and one of marble,
Broad-shouldered little slabs there in the sunlight
On the sidehill. We haven't to mind *those*.
But I understand: it is not the stones,
But the child's mound—'

              'Don't, don't, don't, don't, she cried.   30

She withdrew shrinking from beneath his arm
That rested on the bannister, and slid downstairs;
And turned on him with such a daunting look,

He said twice over before he knew himself:
'Can't a man speak of his own child he's lost?'

'Not you! Oh, where's my hat? Oh, I don't need it!
I must get out of here. I must get air.
I don't know rightly whether any man can.'

'Amy! Don't go to someone else this time.
Listen to me. I won't come down the stairs.'   40
He sat and fixed his chin between his fists.
'There's something I should like to ask you, dear.'

'You don't know how to ask it.'

                                        'Help me, then.'

Her fingers moved the latch for all reply.

'My words are nearly always an offense.
I don't know how to speak of anything
So as to please you. But I might be taught
I should suppose. I can't say I see how.
A man must partly give up being a man
With women-folk. We could have some arrangement   50
By which I'd bind myself to keep hands off
Anything special you're a-mind to name.
Though I don't like such things 'twixt those that love.
Two that don't love can't live together without them.
But two that do can't live together with them.'
She moved the latch a little. 'Don't—don't go.
Don't carry it to someone else this time.
Tell me about it if it's something human.
Let me into your grief. I'm not so much
Unlike other folks as your standing there   60
Apart would make me out. Give me my chance.
I do think, though, you overdo it a little.
What was it brought you up to think it the thing
To take your mother-loss of a first child
So inconsolably—in the face of love.
You'd think his memory might be satisfied—'

'There you go sneering now!'

                                'I'm not, I'm not!
You make me angry. I'll come down to you.
God, what a woman! And it's come to this,
A man can't speak of his own child that's dead.'   70

'You can't because you don't know how to speak.
If you had any feelings, you that dug
With your own hand—how could you?—his little grave;

I saw you from that very window there,
Making the gravel leap and leap in air,
Leap up, like that, like that, and land so lightly
And roll back down the mound beside the hole.
I thought, Who is that man? I didn't know you.
And I crept down the stairs and up the stairs
To look again, and still your spade kept lifting.   80
Then you came in. I heard your rumbling voice
Out in the kitchen, and I don't know why,
But I went near to see with my own eyes.
You could sit there with the stains on your shoes
Of the fresh earth from your own baby's grave
And talk about your everyday concerns.
You had stood the spade up against the wall
Outside there in the entry, for I saw it.'

'I shall laugh the worst laugh I ever laughed.
I'm cursed. God, if I don't believe I'm cursed.'   90

'I can repeat the very words you were saying.
"Three foggy mornings and one rainy day
Will rot the best birch fence a man can build."
Think of it, talk like that at such a time!
What had how long it takes a birch to rot
To do with what was in the darkened parlor.
You *couldn't* care! The nearest friends can go
With anyone to death, comes so far short
They might as well not try to go at all.
No, from the time when one is sick to death   100
One is alone, and he dies more alone.
Friends make pretense of following to the grave,
But before one is in it, their minds are turned
And making the best of their way back to life
And living people, and things they understand.
But the world's evil. I won't have grief so
If I can change it. Oh, I won't, I won't!'

'There, you have said it all and you feel better.
You won't go now. You're crying. Close the door.
The heart's gone out of it: why keep it up.   110
Amy! There's someone coming down the road!'

'You—oh, you think the talk is all. I must go—
Somewhere out of this house. How can I make you—

'If—you—do!' She was opening the door wider.
'Where do you mean to go? First tell me that.
I'll follow and bring you back by force. I *will!*—'

PATTERN OF THE SUPPORT STRUCTURE FOR EXPLANATIONS

> Existing Situation

> The Basic Question,
> evoked by the situation

> The Thesis Statement
> (the answer to be explained)

Support

> First Supporting Reason: causal generalization, authority, or straight generalization, developed by firsthand report, statistics, quotations from authorities, analysis of parts, classification, subgeneralization and examples, and/or comparison

> Second Supporting Reason: causal generalization, authority, or straight generalization, developed by firsthand report, statistics, quotations from authorities, analysis of parts, classification, subgeneralization and examples, and/or comparison

> Continues for as many supporting reasons as seem necessary or desirable.

The Support Structure

Often writers are not interested in explaining the processes by which they have formed hypotheses or interpretations, so they do not use the discovery structure. They wish only to state their conclusions and support them well enough to convince the reader of their validity, and almost inevitably they use a structure similar to that diagramed above. The *basic question* may be only implied; the *thesis* may be stated before the *situation* is described; and there may be other variations, but the ingredients of this pattern will be present.

If the situation is assumed to be well known to the reader, it will be described briefly. If it is assumed not to be well known, it will be described in detail with firsthand reports, statistics, analyses of parts, definitions, classification and examples, generalization and examples, or comparisons, or some combination of these. The purpose in this division is always to tell *what*. Sooner or later, however, the subject shifts from *what* to *why* or *so what*. The *thesis statement* is the answer to the *basic question*.

The thesis statement in an explanation is generally a reason-result statement. It may be specific, stating a specific reason for a specific situation, or it may be general, in which case it is called a causal generalization. The causal generalization, like the straight generalization, may express a value judgment. Exercise 14 will clarify the difference between the causal generalization and the straight generalization and between the causal generalization with value judgment and the causal generalization without value judgment. This exercise is intended to be instructive rather than evaluative. Please check your answers against the answers following the exercise.

EXERCISE 14

The Causal Generalization

Examine the following sets of sentences, and answer the questions beneath each set.

Set 1

A. Many astronomers oppose NASA's plans to develop satellites that would, like mirrors, reflect the sun and illuminate two hundred miles of Earth at night.

B. Professor Edgar Everhart of the University of Connecticut, a serious amateur astronomer, has begun writing letters to thousands of fellow scientists, alerting them to what he considers the inherent dangers in NASA's Project Able.[2]

    1. What is the logical relationship of the second statement to the first statement?

    2. Is there a reason-result relationship in the first sentence?

    3. What kind of conclusion is the first sentence?

Set 2

A. Students often withdraw from college because their reading comprehension is low.

B. Because Thomas B. Childers, who scored in the fourteenth percentile on the Princeton Reading Comprehension Test 463, did not read well enough to pass any of his courses, he withdrew from the university.

[2]The facts in this example were taken from *Time*, January 13, 1967, p. 56.

1. What is the logical relationship of the second statement to the first statement?
2. Is there a reason-result relationship in either of the statements? In both?
3. What kind of conclusion is "Students often withdraw from college because their reading comprehension is low"?

Set 3

A. The wife's extravagance ruins many marriages.
B. Mrs. Pamela Andress was so extravagant in her buying of clothes and jewels that her husband divorced her.
    1. What is the logical relationship of the second statement to the first statement?
    2. Is there a reason-result relationship in either statement? In both?
    3. Are *extravagant* and *extravagance* value terms?
    4. What kind of statement is "The wife's extravagance ruins many marriages"?

ANSWERS TO EXERCISE 14

Set 1

1. The second statement is more specific than the first; it is an example of the first.
2. No.
3. A generalization (report, not inference).

Set 2

1. The second statement is more specific than the first; it is an example of the first.
2. Yes. Yes.
3. It is both a generalization and a reason-result statement: a causal generalization.

Set 3

1. The second statement is more specific than the first; it is an example.
2. Yes. Yes.
3. Yes.
4. A causal generalization with value judgment.

The causal generalization used as a thesis statement may be supported in part by firsthand reports, statistics, quotations, analyses of parts, classification and examples, subgeneralization and examples, and comparison; but the main divisions in the support are usually reasons. The following excerpt from Neil Postman's *Television and the Teaching of English* illustrates support by a list of reasons. Since there is very little development of the reasons, the reason-structure is easy to see.

> 1 Television writers worked for years within these limitations and produced a substantial body of serious drama. 2 But for various reasons, the fifty-two minute live drama has become increasingly rare. 3 In the first place, some writers abandoned television altogether because they felt it did not provide sufficient artistic freedom or financial reward. 4 They objected, for example, to the intrusion of commercial messages and to the imposition of thematic limitations by sponsors. 5 And, of course, they have found that writing for the movies is far more lucrative.
>
> 6 In the second place, many producers abandoned the fifty-two minute hour because a weekly series demanded a constant source of talent that was simply not available. 7 Television is a ravenous consumer of talent and material. 8 It must be fed eighteen hours a day, seven days a week. 9 The most gifted find it difficult to survive such a relentless challenge of their creative resources. 10 Even if Paddy Chayefsky, Tad Mosel, J. P. Miller, and all the others were still writing for television, they probably could not produce distinguished hour-long dramas week after week. 11 Finally, many sponsors abandoned the form because it was more expensive than filmed half-hour shows and not quite as magnetic as the ninety-minute or two-hour "special."[3]

The second sentence in this excerpt states the causal generalization developed in the two paragraphs. Notice that the first reason is introduced by *in the first place* (sentence 3); the second reason, by *in the second place* (sentence 6), and the third reason, by *finally* (sentence 11). All three of the reasons are stated in one of the forms that you studied under "The Sentence Structure and Diction of Logical Statements"—result-reason (with the reason being stated in an adverb clause introduced by *because*).

SUGGESTED WRITING ASSIGNMENT

A Paragraph Stating Reasons

Write a paragraph stating three general reasons why you like or dislike Thurber's cartoons or a photograph on one of the following pages: 13, 96, 101, 143, 271, or 392. Assume that the reader has seen the cartoons or the photograph and that for this reason it is unnecessary to describe the situation. Imitate the form of Postman's result-reason statements.

---

[3]New York: Appleton-Century Crofts, 1961, pp. 49–50. Reprinted with the permission of Appleton-Century-Crofts and the National Council of Teachers of English.

ILLUSTRATIONS OF THE SUPPORT STRUCTURE

Now that all parts of the explanation based on the support structure have been discussed and the relationships of the parts shown in a diagram, three selections that illustrate the applicability of the structure will be examined. The first selection below is a short student composition altered slightly in order to emphasize transitions. The next two selections are longer essays, one written by a recent graduate of Yale University and the other by a professor of philosophy at the University of North Carolina. The styles of these selections differ greatly, but the same logic is at work in their structures.

The Volkswagen and the Accident

The situation, developed by description

 The time was 11:30, on a cold, dark night. Our Volkswagen rounded the unexpectedly sharp turn in the mountain road. Suddenly, some rocks on the road became visible under the car lights—it was too late to miss them. The Volkswagen leaped to the left and spun around twice, the tires screeching. Then it skidded over the dirt embankment, tumbling end over end, then side over side, and finally coming to rest on its top seventy-five yards down the mountain side, its body "totaled."

The basic question

 Why did this accident occur? What were the major factors in its cause? The rocks and the speed of the car were factors, of course; but I suggest that certain features in the design of the Volkswagen itself contributed.

The thesis

Support
The first and the second reasons

 One of these features was the light weight of the Volkswagen, and another, closely related to it, was the imbalance of the weight, the back being heavy in comparison to the front. The Volkswagen simply did not hold the road as a heavier car would have. The impact caused a swerve that a heavier car would not have made, and the imbalance increased the centrifugal force. The Volkswagen skidded 114 feet, spinning, before we went over the embankment.

The third reason

 The third feature is the narrow wheel base of the Volkswagen. Just as a closed fist resting fingers down on a table is harder to knock over than a fist resting on its side, so an automobile with a wide base in comparison to its height is harder to knock over than a Volkswagen, as high as it is wide, its base small, its wheels close together. In our

THE VOLKSWAGEN AND THE ACCIDENT   Reprinted by permission.

accident, the impact of hitting the rocks caused the car to leap, whereas if the base of the car had been resting on a larger area, it would have resisted the impact.
Sometimes economy is expensive.

The student, writing in a composition class, was trying to follow the recommended support structure, but Strobe Talbott, in the essay that follows, is simply trying to answer a timely question in a clear, readable way. Note, however, that his essay has all of the major divisions of the support structure, arranged in the order of the pattern on page 325. In the support he does not list reasons as Postman does in explaining why television drama has become rare. Instead, he explains a chain of reactions in which a result becomes a reason for another result. Reduced to a simple form, the chain of reactions is this:

1. Dissatisfied students tried using conventional means of reform, but were ignored by authorities.
2. They therefore tried types of civil disobedience that had been successful in civil rights campaigns in the South, but they met, not the widespread approbation given their efforts in these campaigns, but widespread condemnation, often carrying legal punishment.
3. Because of the frustration caused by this resistance, they have become cynical about all authority and about all means of redress except violence.

In developing the support division of his explanation, Mr. Talbott uses mainly generalized statements of reasons and results, supported often by straight generalizations. A few of the causal generalizations are developed by examples.

What Student Riots Are All About

Strobe Talbott

Situation

1 Europe and Asia have long suffered from student riots, but the United States has always thought of itself as a nation at peace with its students. Until recently we have regarded the college campus as a quiet realm where the homecoming queen reigns on Alumni Day and the bespectacled college dean is her prime minister.

WHAT STUDENT RIOTS ARE ALL ABOUT   From *Parade*, June 16, 1968. Reprinted by permission of Parade Publications, Inc.

2 The events of the last two months have shattered this peaceful image. An estimated 3,000 students on at least 15 campuses, ranging from Stanford in California to Columbia in New York, have crippled their schools with militant demonstrations and taken administration offices by storm.

3 At Duke University in North Carolina, students invaded the president's house and held him prisoner. At Columbia over 700 students were hauled off in paddy wagons after they occupied five buildings and brought the university to a standstill.

Basic question

4 University administrators, trustees, mayors, police chiefs, teachers, the public at large are all asking: Why has this happened? Why has student activism in America become so violent?

5 Before anyone decides that students have all gone crazy or that they are being duped into a seditious conspiracy by professional agitators, we should look at the context in which this new wave of student militancy has developed.

Thesis (causal generalization)

6 On the whole, students do not riot out of sheer destructiveness. They riot against the inattention, intransigence, and condescension of administrations with which they have lost patience.

Restatement of thesis

7 Most of the riots of the past few months have been based on long-standing grievances which university officials have been too slow to recognize and too reluctant to redress. Often the students involved had tried to call attention to their complaints by the conventional and legitimate means of petitions, letters, resolutions, peaceful demonstrations.

Straight generalization

Support

First result in chain reaction

Reason

8 Too frequently they found that this kind of protest simply did not work. The established administration tends too often not to listen to soft, polite voices. Or, if it does listen, it tends to fend off the requests for reform in a patronizing way which sooner or later wears down student patience and respect for the standard, democratic channels of communication.

Result

9 Thus, they resort to more violent resistance to authority, to which those in charge must pay heed.

Example

10 This, for example, is what happened at Columbia University. For years, the student leadership—especially the Negro student leadership—asked for some voice in the university's relations with the surrounding community. It was the last straw when Columbia announced plans to build a gymnasium in a nearby Harlem park without consulting either the students or the already much oppressed citizens of the neighborhood.

Comparative example

11 Similarly the handful of Negro students at Wellesley College near Boston found the only way they could get the administration to accept more than a token number of Negroes was to go on a hunger strike. First, they had tried petitions. Petitions did not work. The hunger strike did.

Historical report

12 The very generalized and deep-seated revolution which the recent campus protests represent began in the late 1950's and early 1960's. It began with the civil rights movement, when busloads of students ventured into the American South to help stage sit-ins and voter registration drives.

Causal generalization

13 The injustice and oppression which they saw there charged them with an impulse to challenge and set right those wrongs which the rest of society seemed willing to tolerate and even condone.

Causal generalization

14 The campaign against the segregated lunch counters, the redneck police departments, the all-white juries, and some of the feudal legislatures of the South also taught these students to distrust the laws on the books.

Result

15 They learned that local statutes and state laws, as well as the courts and officers that often administer them, can be instruments to protect the repressive interests of those in power and to deprive others of their most basic rights to equality and self-respect.

Result

Straight generalization

16 In Selma, Montgomery, and Birmingham, students learned firsthand the necessity and effectiveness of civil disobedience. There, the deliberate violation of standing laws was used to protest, to challenge, and ultimately to overthrow legislation which has since been found to be unconstitutional.

Straight generalization

17 Not only did their civil disobedience work, but the young men and women who frequently spent the night in small-town Southern jails were vindicated by the Supreme Court and honored by large segments of society.

Causal generalization

18 Much of the more recent anti-Vietnam activity in this country, which has accounted for so much unrest on the campuses, owes its impetus, its ideology, and its methodology directly to the civil rights movement. Many students consider America's war in Vietnam to be just as unconscionable, just as inhumane, just as unconstitutional and therefore just as "illegal" as segregation and poll-taxing.

Report of value judgment

Concession-assertion

19 Yet unlike their predecessors in the civil rights movement, these new dissenters have not been vindicated either by the courts or by the American society at large.

Straight generalization

20 The jail terms which many of them risk are no longer matters of a few nights in some hinterland pokey. They face years in federal prison. They face lasting disgrace in the

eyes of their fellow citizens and severe curtailments in their career possibilities.

Straight generalization

21 Many of these young people, who are so often called traitors, consider their motivations to be basically patriotic.

Reason

Result

They see themselves fighting for the good of a society that reviles them. Therefore, their activism is often charged with bitter frustration and anger.

Causal generalization

22 The resulting sense of despair easily breeds the kind of cynicism and destructiveness which have had such a field day during the worst moments of the recent student riots, when a protest turns into a frenzy of obscenity-chanting and rock-throwing.

Straight generalization

23 Students are also fed up with being told they should conduct themselves peacefully while the nation fights violently in Vietnam and its universities continue to participate in federal programs connected with the Vietnamese war, such as the Institute for Defense Analyses and military contracts.

Subclass and example

Straight generalizations

24 The most militant student activists of the New Left have developed a deep hate for established authority in any form. Many of them have rejected the principles of a nonviolent democratic society which such youth groups as the Students for a Democratic Society and the Student Non-Violent Coordinating Committee were originally meant to champion.

Example

25 During the siege laid against the Dow Chemical Company recruiter at Harvard University last fall, one of the SDS leaders was asked why, in a free society, a recruiter for Dow Chemical or the Marines or the CIA should not be as free to come on campus as a recruiter for the Peace Corps or the Communist Party. "Because," he replied indignantly, "some things are just too evil."

Quotation (value judgment)

Hypothesis

26 What this also means is that some people and some institutions are not, in the eyes of their student opponents, worth preserving for reformation.

Straight generalizations

27 The kind of student leadership that had its way at Columbia is fed up with the old traditions of collective bargaining and the adjudication of disputes by compromise. It is fed up with its more moderate contemporaries who will not repudiate everything that so smacks of the Establishment. It has given up on talking and spends most of its time shouting.

Report, with value judgment

28 When leaders of the Columbia riot were asked to sit down and explain their demands to the university vice president David B. Truman, they used the interview to vilify him with obscenities and charges of "fascism."

Hypothesis, with value judgment

29 That futile confrontation was a stark demonstration of how helpless the leadership of the academic establishment is, even when it is trying to be most responsive, and of how hopeless and irresponsible much of the student leadership has become, even when it is exercising its most terrifying power.

Causal generalization

30 The riots, the unrest, the bitter arrogance, the new impulse to halt the university in its tracks, all reflect a common discouragement among the students at the center of the

Comparative generalizations

fracas. They tend to believe that the entire nation is just as much on the brink of chaos as Columbia was at the height of the riots. They believe that there is just as much a breach of communication among the constituent sectors of this society as there was between Columbia's vice president Truman and the SDS leaders. They believe that the United States is committing far more senseless violence in Vietnam than they are committing on campus.

Comparative generalizations

31 Many other students do not agree with this grim attitude of the militants. But those students who have reached this stage of impatience and disaffection are suddenly

Hypothesis

making themselves heard with frightening clarity. In America we are witnessing the irrefutable proof to the belief that violence breeds violence, peace breeds peace, and understanding breeds understanding. It's just that we seem to have fallen in short supply of the last two virtues in the society at large.

In this essay, Strobe Talbott refers to immediate reasons for student violence. In the next essay, E. M. Adams probes the deeper reasons for unrest, of which student violence is one dramatic manifestation. Adams' scope is broad, and all parts of his explanation are developed at length, but the explanation is built on the support structure as surely as the student's and Talbott's explanations are.

There is a variation in structure at the beginning of the essay. Before describing the situation in detail, Adams mentions the situation (in paragraph 1), summarizes the reasons usually given for this situation (in paragraph 2), and then expresses his dissatisfaction with these reasons (in paragraph 3). From paragraph 4 through paragraph 16 he explains the situation in detail. The key expression in his discussion of the situation is *low morale*. He analyzes the problem of low morale by dividing the demoralized into two groups—people incapable of succeeding in our complicated society and people who are successful but disenchanted. He explains what he means by low morale in general by comparing it in an analogy, point by point—in paragraphs 8–10—with low job morale, which most people understand. In this comparison, he develops an example at length, explaining what happened to a colleague of his who had lost his morale.

In paragraphs 18–21, he lists the surface reasons for unrest. It becomes clear in paragraph 22, however, that the basic question of his explanation is "What are the deeper reasons for low morale in the twentieth century?" In paragraph 22, he implies this question and states this thesis: there are three philosophical reasons for this low morale—the death of God, the death of man, and the death of authority. From paragraph 23 through paragraph 53, he discusses each of these—the first in paragraphs 23–31, the second in paragraphs 32–39, and the third in paragraphs 40–53.

Adams' support includes several of the forms we have studied. When discussing the second reason for unrest, he develops by classification (in paragraphs 34–47) the following generalization, stated in the last sentence of paragraph 33: "Yet the language of science tends to crowd out or to render inapplicable the rational appraisal use of value concepts just as much as it does the explanatory use." The examples he uses to support this generalization are introduced by the transition "Let us consider several cases." Throughout, he uses reason-result and concession-assertion statements, some of them quite complicated, but most of them clearly tagged by connectors like *thus, therefore, yet,* and *although.* He occasionally uses quotations to support his ideas or to elucidate the attitudes of other people.

In his conclusion, in paragraphs 54–56, Adams restates, in more general terms "the compelling problem of our time"; he offers no solution to the problem, nor even any hope that finding a solution seems likely. His purpose in the essay is merely to explain a philosophical problem, without making any recommendation for improvement, and to relate that problem to a current situation.

A Changing America: Morale and Morality

E. M. Adams

1 No one can say that morale is high in America today. President Johnson, in his State of the Union Message in January, spoke of "a certain restlessness" in the land. This is the understatement of the century. The "restlessness" looks dangerously like nothing less than a widespread loss of faith in America, in our political institutions, and in our whole middle class, technological civilization.

2 Editorial writers say that everywhere we look, something is wrong. But they usually point to the war in Vietnam and the Negro poverty problem in our

A CHANGING AMERICA: MORALE AND MORALITY   From *Vital Speeches,* July 15, 1968. Reprinted by permission of the publisher and the author.

cities as the causes of most of our troubles. Many think that if we could only end the war and apply the money and the effort being expended there to the problems of our cities, all would be made right.

3 But, this I think, is superficial. Our problems cut much deeper. Even if we could end the war on terms acceptable to us and could solve the poverty problems at home, we would still have all the problems inherent in our democratic, middle class, technological civilization. There is perhaps more profound lack of morale today among those fully participating in the best that our society has to offer than in the Negro ghettos of our decaying cities.

4 We can understand the despair and frustration of those unequipped to pull their weight in our complicated, industrial society and separated off and crowded out of sight in unbelievable squalor. We know in general how their peculiar problems can be solved; or at least we know what would constitute a solution and something about how to begin. They must, we think, be brought into the mainstream of American life so that they can fully participate with others in the riches of our civilization.

5 But the increasing restlessness, frustration, and rebellion of those who have made it in our way of life, those who are prepared to and have participated fully in the best that our civilization has to offer, are much more difficult to understand and far more alarming. I refer to the disenchantment and rebellion of the younger generation, especially the best educated from upper middle class families. The beatniks and the hippies are the most extreme. They repudiate our civilization and have dropped out of our society. The new radical activists led by such men as Tom Hayden of the Students for a Democratic Society and Mario Savio of the Free Speech Movement at Berkeley are not content to drop out of society. They want to tear it down, for they believe that it is rotten to the core. Although these extremists may not be large in number, they seem to be expressing a widespread spirit of discontent and rebellious attitude that is just beneath the surface and could erupt in any crisis.

6 Justified morale is the most important factor in life, for if there is valid high morale, whatever else is lacking, life is worth living; but if there is no morale, whatever else there is, life is not worth living. But this is likely to be misleading. It suggests that morale is simply one factor among others in the fabric of life; that it can be added or subtracted, leaving other things unaffected. This is not so. A person lacking morale cannot achieve it without reconstituting his life as such, or at least coming to see his life under a new image that has a transforming effect.

7 Many today seem to think that morale is a state of consciousness casually produced. Some even take a chemical approach. This is nothing new. Throughout the ages men have turned to alcoholic drinks to boost their morale. Because such drinks seem to elevate or to heighten one's spirit, at least for a time, they are still called "spirits." In some early religions, even in the Christian Eucharist, we find an association or even identification of alcoholic drinks and the life or spirit of a divine being. Today many are turning to "mind expansion" or hallucinogenic drugs like mescalin and LSD. It seems to be an era of "Better living through chemistry." New religious cults are being built around the use of such drugs in a kind of "communion service." One of our former students at the University of

North Carolina is defending himself in court against a charge of illegal possession of mescal buttons by pleading the right to freedom of religious worship.

8 It is misleading, indeed erroneous, to think of morale in casual terms, for it is, I suggest, a mode of awareness, a form of perception. One's job-morale, for example, is his sense of the normative state of his job. To have good job-morale is (1) to feel that one's job is an important part of a worthwhile enterprise; (2) to feel that it is worthy of oneself; (3) to feel challenged and engaged by its demands; (4) to feel oneself worthy of the job and competent to handle it; and (5) to feel that one is functioning well in the job.

9 I had a colleague in philosophy one time who had spent years of study in preparing himself to be a philosopher because he was excited by the subject, he felt that it was concerned with vitally important problems, and to him no vocation seemed more significant than work on them. Yet he became convinced along in his thirties that the philosophical problems that had seemed so important were really pseudo-problems caused by linguistic confusions. His morale sank terribly. He made an attempt to prepare himself for medicine, but soon gave it up. It was too late. He felt that he reached a point of no return in a profession which seemed to him pseudo and trivial, with colleagues whom he could not respect because he did not value their work. He was soon on a psychiatrist's couch.

10 Life-morale is similar to job-morale. High life-morale involves feeling that the human enterprise itself is eminently worthwhile. One may try to run away from this issue, to avoid it, by busying oneself with this or that special enterprise— with being a student, a lawyer, a physician, an educator, a traveler, and the like. But these will be empty and meaningless minor campaigns in a lost cause if life itself is not felt to be worthwhile. They may provide some temporary excitement and fill some of the years, but they will add up to nothing in the end. Like Hemingway's fisherman in *The Old Man and the Sea,* he may catch his fish, but he can bring home only the bare bones, for the underlying anxiety and despair will eat away and destroy everything of worth in it.

11 To feel that the human enterprise is worthwhile involves, of course, believing that there is a human enterprise, that there is something for one to be or to become as a human being, that to be a human being is to have an office as it were, to have a responsibility to fulfill, to be under an imperative that defines for him a way of life. We judge men as teachers, lawyers, brickmasons, carpenters, designers, and the like. We judge them on the basis of their competence, skill, and performance in fulfilling the imperative that defines their trade or profession. When we judge men morally we are judging them in terms of their competence, skill and performance in fulfilling the office of a human being. Every office is defined not only by some imperative or responsibility but by certain rights and privileges. The rights that pertain to an office consists of the areas of freedom that the officeholder must have in order to fulfill the responsibilities of the office. The privileges of an office are those areas of freedom that can safely be left to the office-holder in the performance of his duties. Human rights and privileges are those that go with the responsibility of being a human being. This package, the responsibility of one as a human being together with its correlative rights and privileges, constitutes the human status, station, or position. We distinguish between the respect appropriate to one by virtue of his office or position as a human

being and the respect he merits by virtue of the way he fulfills the office just as we distinguish between the respect due the President of the United States by virtue of his office and that due him by virtue of his performance in that office.

12 One cannot, of course, just be a human being. The office is highly determinable and becomes determinate in a variety of ways. We are male or female and here roles and functions divide. We have different talents and capacities and find ourselves in different places and times. And so the specific imperatives that shape and define our lives in detail vary immensely. Although we all share a common office as human beings and thus at this level are equal, at more concrete levels we occupy positions defined by responsibilities and their correlative rights and privileges that are and must be quite unequal.

13 Physical space is that in which physical objects exist or have spacial position. We may speak in a parallel manner of social space in which people exist, in which people have social positions or offices, the most basic one being that of being a human being. Social space, like physical space, must be three dimensional, for there must be higher and lower social positions as well as those on the same social plane. It must also be correlated with time to provide a four dimensional continuum. People are not only related socially to their contemporaries, but to their ancestors and to future generations. Traditional religions think of social space as extended in such ways as to make possible the existence or position of God and certain other personal beings in the divine hierarchy.

14 Life-morale involves an awareness of a social space-time continuum and of oneself as having a position in it. It further involves a sense that one's position is important, that it is worthy of him and he of it, that it challenges and engages his total being, and that he is filling the position well.

15 The social space-time continuum is such that it makes possible the existence of certain quasi-persons like institutions that function as agents, having responsibilities, rights and privileges. These range all the way from small clubs, churches, colleges and universities, business corporations, cities, states, nations, and the United Nations.

16 National morale, for us in the United States, has to do with how we the people feel about the normative state of the nation. This involves how we feel about the office or station of the United States in the world—its responsibilities and correlative rights and privileges; whether that station is worthy of it and it of its station; how well it is fulfilling its responsibilities and exercising its rights and privileges. It further involves our sense of the normative state of that vast structure of social positions held by persons and other agents within the nation and how well they are performing.

17 Our present low morale as a nation is a response to three obvious conditions:

18 (1) The United States has felt it to be its responsibility in the wake of World War II, because of its great power, to contain the Communist powers in the world and in doing so it has involved itself in problems all over the world at great cost and sacrifice to the country. There is a growing sense that we are neither worthy nor competent to hold the office and that we are not performing well in it. Furthermore, it is increasingly felt that it is not a proper office for any nation.

19 (2) Many have become acutely conscious of the fact that our society has been throughout its history and still is a racist society. By that I mean that in our society there is the social position or office of the Negro, the White Man, the Indian, the Oriental, etc. This permeates our social structure. Many feel that this morally invalidates our society. Paul Wolff, Professor of Social and Political Philosophy at Columbia University, said recently in a letter to the Editor of *The New York Times*, that no decent citizen has any moral obligation to obey any law in the United States because of the racial injustice in our society on which our political institutions are built. The new militant Negro leaders no longer seek to gain admission of their people into our White society. They want to destroy it. Racial integration has become the desperate effort of the white man to save his society. Segregation was the White man's way of making the Negro invisible; now integration has rapidly become his way to achieve the same objective. But the office, the position, of the Negro cannot be abolished without also abolishing the office of the White Man.

20 (3) Many, especially the younger generation under thirty, feel that in our complicated technological society, the key social positions are held by big government, big business corporations, big universities, and the like, and that people as such no longer have an important place. They are sacrificed to the efficiency of the technological system. Many of our most promising young people are, as Jacobs and Landau say, in their book, *The New Radicals* (New York: Vintage Books, 1966), in "revolt against the postwar 'over developed society,' with its large bureaucracies in government, corporation, trade unions, and universities. To those in The Movement the new technologies of automation and cybernation, with their computers and memory-bank machines, are instruments of alienation, depersonalizing human relations to a frightening degree . . . All that remains is nineteenth century rhetoric about democracy and freedom, and technology has drained the words of their content."

21 Mario Savio, leader of the student revolt at Berkeley, said from the steps of the University Administration Building: "There is a time when the operations of the machine become so odious, make you so sick at heart, that you can't take part, you can't even tacitly take part, and you've got to put your bodies upon the gears and upon the wheels, upon the levers, upon all the apparatus, and you've got to make it stop. And you've got to indicate to the people who run it, to the people who own it, that unless you're free the machine will be prevented from working at all."

22 So far we have been concerned with a straightforward moral appraisal of our society as reflected in the present discontent and low national morale. The problems brought into focus are threatening and staggering, but perhaps they would be manageable in time if they were our basic problems. There are symptoms, however, of a deeper derangement in our civilization that adversely affects our basic life-morale and threatens our capacity to cope with our problems. I refer to certain philosophical assumptions deeply ingrained in the modern mind that have brought about what I shall call dramatically the death of God, the death of man, and the death of authority.

23 First, let us consider the ways in which people of our culture talk about why things happen the way they do, particularly things important to us. In the

Bible, which is still read as part of living literature by many in our own time, disasters like the destruction of Sodom and Gomorrah are explained as punitive acts of God for the wickedness of the people. Spectacular escapes from or victories over their enemies are explained by Israel as divine acts of deliverance. The great smallpox epidemic in New England in the eighteenth century was interpreted by the Puritans as divine punishment for the sins of the people. When a doctor in Boston, who had heard that in England a smallpox epidemic had been arrested by a serum that gave people a mild case of cowpox, proposed to vaccinate the people, they threatened to run him out of town, for they could no more think of resisting the administration of divine justice than good citizens could bring themselves to free a legally condemned man from the offices of the law preparing to hang him. They could not in good conscience forcibly resist respected authority. Furthermore, they reasoned that the punishment so far had not been anything compared to what they would receive if they lifted their hand against God and thus defied his authority and provoked his anger. Even in our own time, there are communities where prayer meetings are held to pray for rain in time of drought, for the healing of the desperately sick, and for many other desired things that seem beyond the reach of human powers.

24 Many today who would not think of explaining an earthquake in Alaska that destroyed a town or a landslide in Italy that buried a village as an act of God to punish the people, nor think of explaining the stunning and spectacular victory of little Israel over the Arab Nations in 1967 as the deliverance of the "chosen people" by a miraculous act of God, still ask *why* certain crucial events in their lives happen the way they do with a sense that demands an answer that would make each such event intelligible by placing it in a value structure in which things happen in fulfillment of what ought to be and therefore would show that it was good for the particular event to have occurred regardless of how disturbing it might seem. If an anguished widow asks in her grief why her husband, a man in his prime, a brilliant success but with a still more promising future, had to die so young when he had so much to live for and so much to offer the world, her "why?" asks for quite a different kind of answer than the "why?" of the medical examiner. The autopsy report that describes the condition of his heart and the adjacent arteries and explains scientifically why the fatal heart attack occurred is irrelevant to her question. It leaves the untimely death unintelligible, senseless, and absurd from within the framework of ideas that she experiences the death of her husband and asks her question.

25 Not many in our culture today would attempt to answer her question with any confidence. Most people would not take it to be a genuine question at all but a rhetorical way of expressing grief. Some, however, would take the question seriously and at face value but contend that there was no reason for the happening; that it was simply senseless, unintelligible, absurd, and that this is true of all history, including human existence itself. The *Book of Job*, Macleish's *J. B.*, Camus' *Myth of Sisyphus*, and Agee's *A Death in the Family* are classic studies of this problem.

26 Many who would not feel this kind of problem nor ask this kind of question about any "natural" event (any occurrence that is independent of or uncaused by human action) speak of some happenings in a behavioral situation

as senseless or absurd in just this way. The death of a nineteen year old college student in a silly fraternity initiation seems senseless and absurd. Many Americans feel that the deaths in the Vietnam war are senseless. On the other hand not many Americans, however much they grieved the loss of a relative or friend in World War II, felt the death to be senseless. The difference lies in the fact that most Americans understood and thought about our involvement in World War II in such a way that the risks and losses were seen to be worthwhile and necessary. In any behavioral situation in which the values at issue are trivial but the risks and losses are great, the losses are felt to be senseless and absurd. The mother of the fraternity pledge killed in the trivial initiation ceremony cannot be consoled, for the death is meaningless, it does not make sense, it cannot be rendered intelligible by being placed in a value structure that would show it to be worthwhile in any way. Mrs. Jacqueline Kennedy's lament, upon learning that President Kennedy's assassin was a long, alienated, would-be-communist misfit, "It had to be a dirty little communist. He didn't even have the satisfaction of dying for civil rights" expresses poignantly the demand for intelligibility in terms of values.

27 Some have contended that intelligibility *per se* consists of explanation in terms of values. Socrates says: "When I was young . . . I had a prodigious desire . . . to know the causes of things . . . I heard someone reading, as he said, from a book of Anaxagoras, that mind was the disposer and cause of all, and I was delighted at this notion, . . . and I said to myself: If mind is the disposer, mind will dispose all for the best, and put each particular in the best place; and I argued that if anyone desired to find out the cause of the generation or destruction or existence of anything, he must find out what state of being or doing or suffering was best for that thing . . . and I rejoiced to think that I had found in Anaxagoras a teacher of the causes of existence such as I desired, and I imagined that he would tell me first whether the earth is flat or round; and whichever was true, he would proceed to explain the cause and the necessity of this being so, that this was best; and if he said the earth was in the center, he would explain further that this position was the best, and I should be satisfied with the explanation given, and not want any other sort of cause." (Plato, *Phaedo*, 96–97; tr. B. Jowett. New York: Random House, 1937, I. V 480–82) W. M. Urban, an American philosopher, wrote in 1929: "The ultimate inseparability of value and reality is . . . almost axiomatic; to attempt to divorce them can issue only in unintelligibility . . . Traditional Metaphysics is . . . a value-charged scheme of thought. . . . It represents the 'Natural Metaphysic of the human mind,' a natural bent of the intellect which it is impossible to unbend." (*The Intelligible World:* New York: The Macmillan Company, 1929, p. 3.) Yet, as previously remarked, modern science seeks a value-free framework of thought in terms of which to describe and to explain whatever happens, whether an earthquake that destroys a city, a smallpox epidemic, an historical event, a social movement, or even the order of the observable world.

28 In our culture we have come, for the most part, to regard the empirical scientific method as the only way to get at truth about reality. "Superstition" is defined in some school textbooks as any belief which cannot be scientifically verified. Our whole educational system tends to reinforce this naturalistic view of experience, thought, and reality.

29 Thus our culture, taken as a whole, teaches us to ask two "whys?"

They seek intelligibility of the same things in terms of two teams of concepts that seem incompatible with one another. Some have tried to resolve the conflict by saying that science doesn't ask "Why?" only "How?" Those who accept this solution to the apparent conflict obviously take "Why?" to ask for an explanation that would involve a value as an explanatory reason. They interpret science as giving only a partial account of things to be supplemented by theology or philosophy. But our culture increasingly regards science to be in search of the full account of why things are the way they are and firmly believes that only an empirical scientific account can be intellectually respectable. In fact, the scientific "Why?" has gained such grip upon the modern mind that it has all but crowded out the traditional "Why?" in most areas of thought. Thus philosophical perplexity generated by the conflict is not so intense nor widespread as it was in earlier generations.

30 But the matter is not a dead issue in our own times and certainly not in the lives of many individuals. The "death of God" controversy is news in the public press and elicits serious discussion and debate. Nietzsche's Madman proclaimed in the nineteenth century "whither is God . . . I shall tell you. We have killed him—you and I. All of us are his murderers. But how have we done this? How were we able to drink up the sea? Who gave us the sponge to wipe away the entire horizon? What did we do when we unchained this earth from its suns? Whither is it moving now? Whither are we moving now? Away from all suns? Are we not plunging continually? Backward, sideward, forward, in all directions? Is there any up or down left? Are we not straying as through an infinite nothing? Do we not feel the breath of empty space? Has it not become colder? Is not night and more night coming on all the while? . . . God is dead. God remains dead. And we have killed him."

31 How did we kill God? One answer is that we switched "Whys?" Those for whom God is not dead have not switched, and many of them would rather fight than switch. But the revolution takes place imperceptibly in the foundations of one's thought and it may take time for the superstructure to collapse. What Nietzsche's Madman said of the culture may be true of the individual: "I come too early, . . . My time has not come yet. This tremendous event is still on its way . . . it has not yet reached the ears of man. Lightning and thunder require time, the light of the star requires time, deeds require time even after they are done, before they can be seen and heard. This deed is still more distant from them than the most distant stars *and yet they have done it themselves."* (From Walter Kaufmann, *Nietzsche,* New York: Meridian Books, 1956, p. 81 Originally *Die Frohliche Wissensdeaft,* 1882, p. 125).

32 A second problem concerns the ways in which we talk about human behavior. We appraise human behavior as rational or irrational, responsible or irresponsible, justified, or unjustified, appropriate or inappropriate, praiseworthy or blameworthy, excusable or inexcusable, defensible or indefensible, correct or in error, and the like. We so appraise, at least in part, our sensory experiences, feelings, emotions, attitudes, desires, longings, ambitions, purposes, intentions, decisions, plans, policies, promises, projects, beliefs, thoughts, assumptions, memories, statements, charges, and actions of whatever kind. We would not be

agents engaged in knowing, doing and undertaking things without being subject to such appraisals.

33 We are, however, deeply committed in our culture to bringing human behavior, including our experiences, thoughts, and overt acts, under the blanket of science. We ask the modern scientific "Why?" of behavioral events and demand a scientific description and explanation of them as events among other events, as subject to the same kind of change and causality as physical and biological happenings. We are largely committed, or so it seems, to the development of psychology and the social sciences after the model of the natural sciences. We look to them for the kind of knowledge of behavior, society, and social change that will be power for the manipulation and control of behavior in a process of human and social engineering. Yet the language of science tends to crowd out or to render inapplicable the rational appraisal use of value concepts just as much as it does the explanatory use.

34 Let us consider several cases. Suppose a man gets up one morning with a radical change in his personality. All his life he has been a quiet, even tempered, cautious, considerate, and thoroughly responsible person in word and deed. Yet on a particular morning and thereafter he behaves in quite a contrary manner. He is loud, abusive, aggressive, quick to anger, wild, inconsiderate, unpredictable, and undependable. Let us suppose further that a medical examination reveals that he suffered a mild stroke during the night before the change. In so far as his family and associates accepted the medical report as the explanation for his unusual behavior, they would not feel that he was subject to rational appraisal. He would not be taken at face value as a person, to be confronted on equal terms with oneself and to be reasoned with; rationally appraised, and held responsible for what he says and does. They would treat him more as a thing to be explained, manipulated, causally controlled and changed.

35 Look at our response to the Negro riots in our cities. On the one hand the police, the courts, the law-makers, and the public at large rationally appraise the rioters for their destruction, brutality, and lawlessness. Some are arrested, convicted, and sent to prison. Yet we give sociological and psychological explanations of why the riots occur. In so far as we think of the conditions cited in these explanations as causes of the riots, in the usual scientific sense of causation, we tend to become bothered about rational appraisal of the persons involved in much the same manner as we do with the man who has suffered the stroke.

36 As we extend and more widely accept the scientific study of criminal behavior in general, we become more uneasy with rational appraisal of criminals. We tend to think that criminals need treatment, being changed through the manipulation of the causes of their behavior, rather than punishment, which is increasingly regarded as primitive and unenlightened. Those who used to be called wicked are now almost universally regarded as sick. This represents a basic category shift.

37 But science does not restrict itself to the study of erratic and criminal behavior. It seeks to give a scientific description and explanation of the ordinary as well as of the extraordinary. This means that all behavior, including the experience and thought of scientists, is brought under the observational language of

science and the categories of scientific explanation. When this happens, rational appraisal language seems to be crowded out completely. It is left no territory at all.

38 The result for the modern mind is not simply philosophical perplexity. "The same presuppositions and intellectual operations that have given us such unprecedented power over nature when extended to ourselves," Dr. Hobart Mowrer, a clinical psychologist at the University of Illinois, says, "produces a pervasive feeling of helplessness, confusion, resignation, desperation . . . By the very principles and premises that have led to the conquest of the outer world, we ourselves lose our autonomy, dignity, self-mastery, responsibility, indeed, our very identity." Little wonder, then, he continues, "that we feel weak, lost, fearful, 'beat.' Being part of nature, we, too, apparently obey strict cause-and-effect principles. And if this be true, . . . the whole notion of purpose, responsibility, meaning seems to vanish" ("Psychiatry and Religion," *Atlantic Monthly,* July, 1961, p. 8).

39 Thus it is not only God who is dead. Man is also. From within the Naturalistic view of scientific thought, there are no persons, only objects; no social space, only physical space.

40 So far we have seen how the scientific conceptual system seems to crowd out the explanatory and rational appraisal uses of value language wherever it is applied. But this is not the end of the matter. The modern mind, to a large extent, accepts the empirical scientific method, including its commonsense counterpart, as the only way of obtaining knowledge about our world. Therefore the language of empirical science is identified with the language of knowledge and of reality. Sensory observation is taken to be our only data-gathering or knowledge-yielding mode of experience and thus our only experiential ground for semantic ties between language and the world. This is not a thesis accepted only by philosophers. It is an assumption widely operative in our culture and strongly reinforced by our educational system all the way from elementary school through the University. Since the scientific method, as we have already observed, forced science to develop a value-free descriptive-explanatory conceptual system, the acceptance of the scientific method as the method of knowledge about the world seems to rule out the possibility of value knowledge and to call into question the cognitive meaningfulness and semantic objectivity of all value language. This has given rise to a wide spread skepticism not merely about the validity of the existing value structure of our contemporary society but about the possibility of a valid value system of any kind. All value judgments are, for the most part, taken to be subjective and private and therefore value disagreements are not regarded as subject to rational resolution except in so far as they may result from factual disagreements.

41 In the area of religion, politics, morals, and all other basic value issues, we feel that everyone is not only entitled to his opinion, but that everyone's opinion is just as good as anyone else's, which is to admit that, as far as truth is concerned, no one's is worth anything. Where we hold that there is the possibility of truth, we do not believe that everyone is entitled to his opinion. We do not believe, for example, that one is entitled to his opinion that five times six is thirty-six, or that the capital of the United States is in North Carolina. Many of us take great pride in our tolerance. We count it a virtue to be able to grant

to others their moral judgments which are contrary to our own without feeling any disturbance whatever. In areas where we really think that we are getting at truth, contrary opinions on the part of others disturb us, unless we are prepared simply to reject theirs as false. While tolerance may prevent conflict, it may be the product of indifference, of the conviction that nothing really matters, that everything goes, that everything is permitted. Peace won through tolerance at the price of a world-view without values would be a poor bargain.

42 We hold that factual beliefs can be formed either by conditioning or by instruction. In general, we tend to oppose efforts to instill beliefs in people by causal influence. We call it propaganda, indoctrination, or brain washing. In the field of education, at least, we insist on instruction—on appeal to experience, reason, and insight.

43 The contrast between the techniques of propaganda, advertising, and indoctrination on the one hand and instruction on the other are well known. Briefly, the difference is this; the goal of propaganda or indoctrination is to produce a certain frame of mind or set of beliefs and the means are chosen on the basis of their effectiveness in achieving this end. Passive, docile minds are preferred. An environment free from opposing influences is better. Only one side of issues is allowed to be voiced if possible. Everything unfavorable to the desired end is avoided. People are exposed over and over again under the most favorable conditions to expressions of the desired beliefs and attitudes. The aim of instruction, on the other hand, is to help those being taught to arrive at the truth, or at least the most probable beliefs, about the subject matter through the exercise of their own rational powers. Alert, active, critical minds are necessary for success. The student is taught to free himself through self-criticism of any perverting bias or prejudice. He is encouraged to examine all sides of the issues involved and to weigh carefully all relevant considerations. In education, more emphasis is put on developing the skills for success in such inquiries than in getting a student to accept a particular body of alleged truths.

44 While we hold, in our culture, that instruction is desirable in factual and formal matters, we tend to believe that only one approach is possible in the area of value judgments, namely, the way of conditioning, causal influence, propaganda, and indoctrination. If a political scientist in a course on American government, for example, leaves the facts and makes value judgments, he will be opposed by this faction or that. If he makes so-called "liberal" value judgments, he will be attacked by conservatives for interjecting his own bias, for expressing his own personal and private opinions. If he makes conservative value judgments, he will be accused of being prejudiced. Whenever a person makes value judgments, he is regarded as being subjective, as merely expressing his own feelings and sentiments. This is a reflection of the widespread skepticism in our culture, not just about our existing value system, but about the very possibility of a valid value system of any description.

45 The rejection of the possibility of an objective, valid value system has given rise to apparently contradictory results. It causes some to regard the structure of society, its customs, institutions, and laws, as simply residues of the sentiments and volitions of others and therefore a threat to an individual's freedom and individuality. He feels compelled to rebel, to free himself, to follow only his own

will. He has to reject society and its ways in order to be a genuine, authentic individual.

46 This is the gospel of popular existentialism and the present Student Movement. A young man in Sartre's *Age of Reason* felt that he had to reject all the values of his culture in order to be free. When he found that he could not steal some money when he had the opportunity to do so, he concluded that his efforts to escape from his class were in vain. Freedom eluded him. "I am a bourgeois," he said to himself, "I couldn't take Lola's money, I was scarred by their taboos." The idea was that in order to be a free, authentic person he would have to be able to do anything he wanted to do without feeling any restraint or guilt.

47 According to Sartre, the free man is one who recognizes or feels no restraints or obligations from any source other than his own will, which he regards as subject to nothing, not even an objective situation. There are no requirements or guidelines. Everything is permitted. "The existentialist," Sartre says, "does not think that man is going to help himself by finding in the world some omen by which to orient himself. Because he thinks that man will interpret the omen to suit himself. Therefore, he thinks that man, with no support and no aid, is condemned every moment to invent man."

48 A nationally known professor of philosophy recently said, that morality, like religion, is something to outgrow. To grow up, to become a man, he contended, involves being able to do what you want without any felt inhibitions of restraints.

49 But moral judgments are not dismissed. They are simply regarded as expressions of one's personal decisions, decisions made without objective reasons or guidelines, decisions that are not subject to being appraised as well-grounded or ill-grounded, as valid or as invalid, except in the sense that they are one's very own and thus authentic. The only way a moral judgment can be condemned, according to this view, is for it not to be authentically one's own. The only thing that can be said to be objectively wrong is for one to act as though there were an objectively right thing to do, for one who so acts acts by judgments that are not expressions of his own authentic decisions.

50 On such a view one cannot acknowledge any authority. One cannot say that one is obligated to obey laws and policies of the society when they happen to be in conflict with his own personal judgment. Some spokesmen for the Students for a Democratic Society say that the only kind of collective action possible is through participatory democracy according to which no one is obligated to do anything, except insofar as it happens to be his own personal decision to do so. No one is obligated to do anything because it is the law or the policy of the government. Therefore, any effort on the part of the government of a representative democracy cannot obligate its citizens. It has no authority over them. It is only a force oppressing them. Tom Hayden of Students for a Democratic Society speaks of creating widespread "disrespect for law and order." Our local George Vlasits, in a letter to several North Carolina newspapers, says: "There can be no democratic government if people are required to obey laws if their personal moral judgments are *not* in line with them."

51 Good citizenship used to be counted as a virtue, as identical with being a civilized person, being qualified for living in a community with other

people. But it is now rapidly becoming something to be condemned. Many think that no authentic person can be a good citizen of society today. We still ask references for a candidate for admission to our Graduate School at the University of North Carolina to evaluate the candidate with respect to citizenship. I recently saw a recommendation from a nationally known professor of religion in which, in reply to this question concerning the student's citizenship, he wrote, "What is that?" In a committee of our own professors, one recently remarked that to be evaluated "poor" in citizenship was the highest recommendation. What is working here is the idea that a good citizen respects the authorities of the society and its law and order and that no authentic person can do so. It is not just that our present authorities and laws are considered unworthy of respect and thus lacking in authority, but rather that an authentic person can acknowledge no authority and no law as binding on him, for there are no objective moral requirements that impinge upon man. A Harvard professor of philosophy recently wrote me: "Do you really believe there are ontic imperatives? In my world there are only mere actualities."

52 Although belief in the subjectivity and personal character of moral judgments gives rise to the death of all authority and to resistance to the established ways of society on the part of individuals in search of their personal identity and authentic existence, it naturally leads to efforts on the part of society to control the attitudes and the value judgments of people, for these are their springs of action. Where there is no conviction that free inquiring minds will move toward agreement by discovering an objective truth, it is felt that propaganda, indoctrination, censorship, speaker bans, and the like must be employed to safeguard and to protect cherished institutions and ways of living, indeed to assure that minimum consensus in attitudes and judgments necessary for society to function at all.

53 These are not contradictory results. The one is simply the reaction of the individual and the other the response of society to the loss of faith in the possibility of moral knowledge or wisdom.

54 In light of our cultural climate, there is little wonder that homes and schools are battlegrounds between the generations, that there is a youth revolution stirring in the land, that all establishments are under attack. For in the very nature of the case, if there is no possibility of moral knowledge, all authority collapses into naked power and all law into oppression. The only options become anarchy or tyranny. Youth will opt for anarchy and the power structure for tyranny.

55 In the sense in which our first problem was said to be responsible for the death of God and our second for the death of man, our third is responsible for the death of authority and indeed of the whole social space-time continuum. These specific painful trouble spots in our culture, combined with the earlier problems we discussed, are indeed alarming. They are compelling reasons for thinking that our society faces grave moral problems that necessitate radical change while at the same time our culture is operating on false philosophical assumptions about the categorical principles of the mind and of the world in such a way that we are being thwarted in our efforts to know and to cope with reality and to live successfully.

56 "The modern sickness," Walter Lippmann wrote in 1964, "is the despair James Thompson called 'the insufferable inane.' It is to be found among the rich

and the poor, among the grandees and the groundlings, and it has nothing to do with an unbalanced budget, a swollen bureaucracy, with communism or anti-communism, with the New Deal or the New Frontier." Some forty years ago, he says, "I was writing that the promises of liberalism have not been fulfilled. We are living in the midst of that vast dissolution of ancient habits which the emancipators believed would restore our birthright of happiness. We know now that they did not see very clearly beyond the evils against which they were rebelling . . . The poignant question not yet answered, is how, with the ancestral order dissolved and with the ancient religious certainties eroded by science, the modern man can find meaning which binds his experiences and engages his faculties and his passions." This remains the compelling problem of our time.

SUGGESTED WRITING ASSIGNMENT

A Structural Analysis

Read either "The Secret of Nancy Drew," by Arthur Prager, or "Can Science Prevent War?" by Arthur Larson; then write an analysis of the structure of the essay, describing the extent to which it illustrates the *support structure* and explaining how techniques of development—like analysis, quotation, description, classification and examples, generalization and examples, definition, and comparison—are used as support in the divisions.

The Secret of Nancy Drew—Pushing Forty and Going Strong

Arthur Prager

1 A few karmas ago, circumstance compelled me to raise a small daughter, without benefit of wife and mother, in the insecure atmosphere of a large hotel. Emily was ten, and because of my busy schedule, she had to spend a great deal of time alone, inventing her own amusements. One evening I observed her curled up in a ball on the sofa, shoes off, face unusually serious and preoccupied. Interrogated, she answered in a manner so vague, so ruminative, that if I had been a husband of ten years instead of a father I would have been certain she had taken a lover. She had discovered Nancy Drew.

THE SECRET OF NANCY DREW: PUSHING FORTY AND GOING STRONG   From *Saturday Review*, January 25, 1969. Copyright 1969, Saturday Review, Inc. This selection will be part of a book on children's series, by Arthur Prager, to be published by Doubleday and Company, Inc. in the fall of 1970.

2 In a local bookstore, mixed in among out-of-date Little Golden Books and the misadventures of improbable animals, my daughter had found a row of blue-jacketed volumes, each bearing in a printed medallion the intrepid girl detective's seductively *nice* face. Emily bought *The Secret of the Old Clock*, identified as the first in the series by the small numeral (1), and promising countless hours of pure happiness ahead. By the time she was ready for *The Hidden Staircase* (2), she was hooked, like so many bored, lonely kids before her. "So many" means 30,000,000, reading Nancy's adventures in seventeen languages over a period of thirty-eight years.

3 My daughter is grown now, and oriented toward more sophisticated pleasures, but Nancy's magic still galvanizes the nine- to eleven-year-old set in the same wonderful way. The dauntless, bewitching girl detective is still happening, while other favorites dwindle and disappear. Bomba the Jungle Boy crumbles into dust. Tom Swift is replaced by Tom Swift, Jr., but Nancy is still a smash at the box office. In a world of gaudy exhibitionism, subteens find refuge in Nancy's enviable, secure, conservative world.

4 Nancy is written in East Orange, New Jersey, by "Carolyn Keene," who is really a grandmotherly lady named Harriet S. Adams, abetted by her partner Andrew Svenson and four anonymous ghost writers. This group also writes the "Tom Swift, Jr." series, the "Hardy Boys," the "Bobbsey Twins," and a number of others. Mrs. Adams has written forty-three Nancys, the latest of which will appear this year. The girl sleuth is the financial star of the list. Last year Nancy sold 1,500,000 copies compared to 1,000,000 for the Hardy Boys and a paltry 250,000 for the Bobbseys. Mrs. Adams's publisher, Grosset & Dunlap, is understandably reticent about how much actual cash Nancy has brought her creator, but simple arithmetic tells us that since 1930 she has probably netted her author considerably more than $1,000,000.

5 Augmenting this profit, Nancy came to the attention of Warner Brothers in 1938, and they decided to film her, with Bonita Granville in the title role. There were four films in all, beginning with *The Hidden Staircase*, loosely based on the book of the same name. The other three, dreamed up and "improved" by contract script writers, were *Nancy Drew, Detective* (1938); *Nancy Drew, Reporter* (1939); and *Nancy Drew, Trouble Shooter* (1939); after which the series petered out having failed to achieve the popular following of, say, Andy Hardy or Charlie Chan. What Grosset & Dunlap calls "contract complications" have prevented Nancy from appearing as a TV series, although she would probably make a good one.

6 A girl usually gets her introduction to Nancy Drew from someone else: a gift or loan from some friend or relative. After initial exposure, she mounts a campaign of wheedling and cajoling until she has extracted the other forty or so from her parents. Advances are begged on allowances. Hints are dropped before birthdays and Christmas. Once a kid is hooked she has no scruples about infecting her friends and classmates, and Nancy reaches epidemic proportions in the fourth, fifth, and sixth grades. Strict reciprocal trade agreements are drawn up, and woe to anyone who tries to slip in a "Dana Girls" or a "Judy Bolton."

7 A parent who tries to fathom the secret of Nancy's success is doomed to failure, because, strictly speaking, Nancy is terribly square. Yet she appeals to

subteeny-boppers today just as she did in the Thirties. Apparently there is a rock-ribbed streak of conservatism in the nine-to-eleven group. They will participate in outlandish fads for the sake of show, but they like things simple, basic, well organized. Just as the brashest smart aleck will still gulp down a massive lump of anguish when Amy, in *Little Women,* comes in out of the snow and says, "Beth, the baby's dead . . . ," the loudest little cynic will retire to her room, curl up among the psychedelic posters and "Legalize Pot" buttons, and devour some forty Nancy Drews in a row with deep concentration and heartfelt involvement.

8 Parental permissiveness is thought to be a major factor in Nancy's longevity. Women of my generation passed their worn copies to their daughters fondly, and with (as Nancy would say) a suspicious moisture in their eyes. Mothers who have never read the series examine it and find it harmless if not downright wholesome. Parents who don't care one way or another tolerate Nancy because she keeps the children quiet and arouses in them an interest in books and reading. These reasons do little to explain Nancy's attraction. On the contrary, any one of them is sufficient to poison a little girl's mind against the series. Nancy appeals to her readers in spite of parental approval, not because of it.

9 The books have an odd, timeless quality. I looked for anachronisms in our 1930 first edition of *The Secret of the Old Clock.* Except for Nancy's roadster, with its running boards and rumble seat, there were none. Like the Land of Oz, Nancy Drew Country is in another time dimension, untouched by the outside world. The Depression came and went, followed by three wars, but they passed unnoticed in Midwestern, suburban River Heights, where Nancy and her chums and their well-to-do country-clubbing parents live. Teen-agers all have new cars there. They buy unlimited pretty clothes, and they summer at fashionable resorts. They give lovely parties. At the height of World War II Nancy went on a pleasure cruise to Buenos Aires, untroubled by U-boats in the sea-lanes. There was always plenty of gasoline for her convertible. Hungry kids, shattered by the announcement of bubble-gum rationing, drowned their sorrows in Nancy's world.

10 When I asked my daughter why she had loved Nancy, she thought for a moment, and then said simply, "You can *identify* with her." She meant that a little girl can plausibly pretend to be Nancy. She is an example of the fantasy world in which pre-pubescent girls live in daydreams. A boy can imagine that he is swinging from tree to tree, ululating the victory cry of the bull ape, but he knows in his heart it will never happen. Nancy, on the other hand, is within reach. She is pretty but not beautiful ("like a quaint little princess"). Her hair is a lovely gold color, and naturally wavy. She is small, with a slight but good figure at sixteen. She is graceful, the result of ballet lessons; and she dresses well, with as many changes of costume as any paper doll. She is respected by difficult grownups, such as salespeople, waitresses, and policemen, all of whom address her courteously as "Miss Drew."

11 Lest any reader think her keen mind is restricted to solving mysteries, it should be noted that Nancy also has a rich vein of pure culture, although at sixteen she shows no signs of attending school or preparing to enter a university. Invited by the parents of her beau, Ned Nickerson, to accompany them to the

big Thanksgiving Day football game at Emerson College, where Ned is on the team, Nancy replies that she will enjoy going to the game, but she will "also enjoy the Shakespearean play the Drama Club is presenting afterwards." A clue appears in an obscure document and:

> George and Bess studied the paragraph to which Nancy had pointed. It was a quotation in Old English, and they could not make it out. Nancy, who had learned to read the works of the old English poet Chaucer in school, eagerly translated it.

12 Asked to a college weekend, she is just as much at home in a deep discussion with a young faculty member on "the subject of bringing lost relatives together" as she is on the dance floor. She is not above pausing in her gardening to instruct a family servant:

> These larkspurs are also called "delphinium" because they were the sacred flower of the temple at Delphi, Nancy explained. I believe they have other names too.

13 For all her intellectual attainments, Nancy is no bluestocking as we shall see. She rides and swims in Olympic style, not only besting the Amateur Champion of fashionable Sylvan Lake, but on one occasion leaping into a bayou with all her clothes on and doing a rapid 500 yards to the shore. She can fix a balky outboard motor with a bobby pin. With no effort, she climbs a rose trellis to the second floor. Pursuing an escaped crook, she puts the police on his trail by drawing a perfect likeness of him for them. When the River Heights Women's Club charity show faces disaster because of the defection of its leading lady, Nancy steps in at a moment's notice and wins general kudos with a creditable ballet, although she is recuperating from a sprained ankle. At 100 yards, she plugs a lynx three times with a Colt .44 revolver. Her delphiniums win first prize at the flower show. She floors "Zany" Shaw, a full-grown lawbreaker, with a right to the jaw. She is always a barrel of fun at a party, and she " . . . received a lot of applause for her impersonation of Helena Hawley, a motion-picture star who played parts in old-time Westerns."

14 What hero or heroine of modern fiction can top that?

15 One of Nancy's greatest victories comes at an Emerson College dance, when the master of ceremonies announces:

> Now, as you all know, it is our custom to select each year a beautiful young lady to preside over this event—one who will wear the Festival Robe and Crown. After careful consideration a choice has been made by a committee of faculty and students.
>
> "Gosh, I wonder who the lucky girl will be?" Bill Tomlin commented. "It always goes to the prettiest and most popular one in the audience."
>
> "Will Miss Nancy Drew please come to the stage?" he requested. Everyone began to clap and whistle, for beyond question the choice was a pleasing one.

16 Put that in your daydream if you dare, no matter how old you are. Poor Nancy doesn't wear the Festival Robe and Crown very long, because the

auditorium lights are suddenly extinguished, and she is abducted, robe, crown, and all, and hustled away in a speeding car by a masked man and a hard-faced woman.

17 Nancy's mysteries follow a simple but inflexible pattern. First there is an anonymous warning to her to get off the case or face dire consequences, which she bravely ignores. In every one there is a wild chase, either on foot through crowded streets or in Nancy's convertible. Nearly all are concerned with the withholding of sums of money or jewelry from deserving people by thieves or embezzlers. There are missing wills, treasure maps, hidden rubies, secret codes, long-separated relatives reunited. Occasionally there is an oddball crime like the forgery of ancient Chinese porcelains, or the plagiary of popular tunes. There are several attempted arsons to conceal evidence, but murder is never allowed.

18 Kidnapping abounds, and in almost every book someone, usually Nancy, is spirited away, bound and gagged, and abandoned. Rescue is swift. No one is ever permitted to die. Even the unlucky lynx, shot by Nancy in *The Secret at Shadow Ranch,* staggers off into the underbrush, presumably to get well after having learned his lesson.

19 Violence in the series usually takes the form of atrocious assaults on Nancy's person. Again and again, just as she sees an important clue and reaches for it, everything goes black as she is sapped from behind with a blunt instrument. There are more than thirty occasions on which Nancy is bludgeoned into unconsciousness by blows on the head, enough to reduce her to a lifetime of hanging around Stillman's Gym looking for odd jobs. She is struck by lightning, hurled down a flight of stairs, and even blown through a plaster wall by a charge of dynamite. None of this seems to have any effect, and she always bounces back, bright as a button, to foil the caitiff responsible.

20 The protagonists in the stories are generally poor, but well educated, having seen better days. They are patient and deserving, people of family, who have nice but run-down old houses with a few good antiques. They are ladies and gentlemen in every sense. Crooks are easily identifiable, because they are vulgar, bad-tempered, and have an unfortunate tendency to raise their voices to people. They have red or coarse, bushy black hair, and nicknames like "Spike," "Red," "Snorky," or "Flip." They further identify themselves by their regrettable preference for checkered suits, yellow overcoats, elevator shoes, and (for the oilier, better-educated crook) striped pants, spats, and goatees. Criminals always have a physical oddity: a long nose, or a missing middle finger.

21 The surest clue to an evil-doer in the series is grammar. A Nancy Drew felon reveals himself at once by his garbled syntax. In *The Quest of the Missing Map* Nancy receives an anonymous letter:

> Dear Miss Drew: I tuk yere boat cos I need money but I can't sell it. You kin hev it back fer five dollars. It says sumthin important inside. Don't tell the perlice and come alone on foot to 47 White Street.

22 Who but a miscreant would write such a letter? Nancy hurries to the White Street address, is captured, bound, gagged, and shoved in a broom closet from which she is eventually rescued by her father and Ned.

"Are you hurt, Nancy?" her father asked apprehensively. "No, I'm all right, Dad," she reassured him, "but I'm afraid the worst has happened."

23 It is characteristic of Nancy that this remark is never for a moment interpreted as meaning that her abductor has taken liberties. Her rescuers assume at once, and correctly, that she means the crooks have stolen her half of the missing treasure map.

24 In addition to bona fide felons with long police records, each book contains an evil couple, a shrewd, wickedly handsome man and a hard-faced, overdressed woman. Every volume also contains a homily of some sort, a little lecture on some obscure but marginally educational subject: Ming Dynasty porcelains, the impasto technique in modern painting, conchology, old ships figureheads, New Orleans trade and commerce, dye-making from whelks, button manufacture, stained glass painting—all are woven painlessly into the plot to instruct the curious little reader.

25 The characters who support Nancy in her adventures seem pallid compared to their heroine. Her beloved and indulgent father, Carson Drew, a "noted lawyer engaged largely in mystery cases," discusses his law practice with her and finds her opinions to be "astonishingly sound for one so young." He supplies her considerable logistical needs, replenishing her wardrobe and her private savings and checking accounts; and buys her a shiny new convertible when crooks disable hers (as they do periodically) by sawing through its brake or steering mechanism. When he is not engaged in uttering platitudes ("Success is one-tenth inspiration and nine-tenths perspiration"), he is usually on his way out of town on a business trip. He looks distinguished, carries a cane, worries a lot about whether Nancy will get hurt, and always listens with interest to what she has to say. From the pre-teen point of view, this makes him a perfect Daddy. Nancy adores him, and shows it by tweaking his distinguished ear mischievously, or ruffling his well brushed gray hair.

26 Left motherless at an early age, Nancy was raised by elderly Hannah Gruen, who does the cooking and the heavy housework. Hannah and Nancy never depart from their servant-mistress relationship, and there is no doubt about who is the boss. Hannah is too old, too plain, and too working-class to pose a threat to Nancy's freedom or her relationship with her father, as a real mother might. When the chores get too hard for Hannah, she is assisted by her niece, Effie, a giggling cretin about Nancy's age.

27 Ned Nickerson, Emerson College football hero, is Nancy's sincerest admirer. Big and good-natured, malleable and self-effacing, he knows Nancy is smarter than he is and doesn't care. An Emerson sophomore for the past thirty-two years, Ned easily beats out Lord Fancourt Babberly for the all-time undergraduate longevity record. Although he makes it plain in his blunt, outspoken way that he expects to make Nancy his bride some day, Ned is allowed no physical contact or visible sign of affection. Occasionally, pursuing a hot clue in Nancy's car (faster and larger than Ned's), he will make a leading remark, pointing out that they are alone and there is moonlight. This boldness makes Nancy blush to her fingertips (a frequent habit of hers) and change the subject to "something less personal."

28 Poor unkissed Ned is unceremoniously brushed off in most of the books; brought in for a chapter only when a strong back is needed. Often he is a mere mention. "Where is Ned?" someone will ask. "Oh, he is in South America," Nancy will reply, without further embellishment. During the school year, he is conveniently away at college, and in the summer he works as a camp counselor. In one horrid sequence the reader is led to believe that he has shown a little gumption and asked another girl to the big Emerson dance. Nancy bears up well ("After all he has a perfect right to"), but it turns out to be a mistake, and the two are reunited.

29 Nancy is helped in her detective work by her dearest chums, George Fayne and Bess Marvin. George (who is a girl) has short hair, a boyish voice, and a boyish figure. She hates frilly clothes, jewelry, and people who call her "Georgina" or "Georgette." Bess is pretty but slightly plump, and is terrified by rats and spiders, a feminine weakness that causes endless merriment to her bolder companions. George has an unfortunate tendency to fall into wells, creeks, bayous, and other muddy water holes. Sometimes the girls are joined by Helen Corning, but she is a weakling, and too lah-de-dah to contribute anything to the excitement.

30 Nobody ever tells a lie in the series, and there are none of the commoner vices. Whiskey only appears once, in *The Bungalow Mystery*, in which a silly watchman allows himself to be seduced into taking one too many by would-be burglars and abandons his post. He is roundly punished for this transgression. Parents don't drink at dinner parties, and Nancy and her chums are never exposed to beer, even at the numerous fraternity functions held at Emerson College. No one smokes cigarettes. Nancy herself eschews stimulants to the extent of substituting milk or cocoa for breakfast coffee.

31 There is some sex in the series, but nothing that would have caused Colette a moment's envy. It is all of the pre-pubescent giggly kind, which doesn't need boy and girl contact to titillate. In *The Clue in the Crumbling Wall*, George falls into a lily pond, and, soaked to the skin, lays out her clothes to dry. She is forced to pop into a summer house with nothing on when a naughty twelve-year-old boy comes prowling around and steals all her garments, leaving her in a fine pickle indeed until Bess comes to the rescue with a raincoat. In *The Scarlet Slipper Mystery*, Nancy spots a suspect during a ballet class, and rushes into the street in a revealing leotard, unaware until she is reminded of her improper costume by the disapproving stares of passers-by. In *The Hidden Window Mystery*, a sneak thief rifles the girls' luggage and makes off with not only an important clue, but intimate bits and pieces of their underwear as well. This sort of harmless, pre-teen ribaldry serves to relieve the routine of the mysteries with an occasional blush and titter.

32 Negroes in the earlier books were minstrel-show stereotypes with names like Mandy and Beulah. They said things such as "Lawsy me!" and "Yassuh!" and spoke a kind of pidgin English:

> Scuse me, sah, but de bank am closin'. Ah jest natcherly got to shet de do'.

33 By 1957, although they still drop their consonants, Negro characters have become articulate and informative. Uncle Rufus, bayou dweller and voodoo practitioner, says:

> It was my ancestors that invented the first long distance com-mun-i-ca-tions. We made drums that could carry sounds for miles and miles. The folks in one place sent signals an' messages by beatin' on the drums with their hands. Then the next village would pick it up an' send the signal on to another place far away. That's how they get all the members of a tribe together for special meetin's and for fightin' wars.

34 Uncle Rufus is still being patronized, but there is an improvement. By the 1960s the earlier books had been rewritten to expunge objectional matter (also cleaning up vulgar, pushy Johnny and Kitty Blair, who had changed their name from Sellerstein, and smirking, cringing disbarred lawyer Abe Jacobs).

35 Mrs. Adams is presently engaged in writing *The Invisible Intruder,* forty-third in the series, and undoubtedly the sixteen-year-old girl detective will go on forever. My daughter will never read *The Invisible Intruder,* and neither will many other girls who have achieved puberty and have begun to notice boys and create another fantasy world of a very different kind. But they are expendable in Nancy's world. There is a whole new generation of stupefied pre-teens with puffy red-rimmed eyes from staying up too late so that they can finish one more chapter. They can *identify* with Nancy. Following them is another generation of first-graders, spelling out their A-B-Cs, with no idea of the thrills and joys in store for them. A day will come when each of them will discover, either on her own or through the instrument of some fond relative who remembers her own girlish past, the irresistible girl detective and *The Secret of the Old Clock,* and will turn to chapter one, page one, and read:

THE LOST WILL

> "It would be a shame if all that money went to the Tophams! They will fly higher than ever!" Nancy Drew, a pretty girl of sixteen, leaned over the library table and addressed her father, who sat reading a newspaper by the study lamp . . .

and the cycle will start all over again.

Can Science Prevent War?

Arthur Larson

1 In physical science man has to an impressive degree learned to control and direct the forces and materials supplied by nature, for better or for worse. In human affairs he has not.

CAN SCIENCE PREVENT WAR   From *Saturday Review,* February 20, 1965. Copyright 1965 Saturday Review, Inc. Reprinted by permission of the Saturday Review and the author.

2 The reason is that man has seldom applied to the conduct of human affairs even the most elementary techniques that he has used for generations in discovering facts and putting them to work in the physical sciences.

3 There are three ways to approach knowledge: scientific, nonscientific, and pseudoscientific.

4 The scientific approach begins with finding the facts through direct examination and experiment, and then applying to these facts tested methods of analysis and verification.

5 The nonscientific approach merely reacts blindly to the environment, guided by nothing but instincts, emotions, prejudices, and superstitions.

6 The pseudoscientific approach borrows the trappings of the scientific, including elaborate paraphernalia, complex demonstrations and polysyllabic terminologies, but suffers from two oversights: failure to get the facts in the first place, and failure to test results against reality.

7 The tragedy of man's attempt to bring order into his political and social relations is that this attempt has floundered between the nonscientific and the pseudoscientific without ever coming to rest on the scientific.

8 Before the Age of Science, if you wanted to find out what the inside of the human body was like, you did not open a human body; you opened Aristotle. When Galileo, to test whether the speed of falling objects increased with their weight, dropped two balls of differing weights from the Leaning Tower of Pisa instead of accepting the answer contained in the books, it was considered a piece of impertinence. Today this fact seems almost unbelievable—yet for the most part our conduct of political and international affairs is still dominated by pre-Galileo methods.

9 World wars have been started with what seems to have been less real investigation of the facts bearing on the probable outcome than a scientist would put into the dietary habits of an obscure insect. How much research did the Kaiser conduct to support his conviction that the British would never enter World War I, not to mention the United States? With this lesson of history behind him, Hitler nevertheless made precisely the same error of fact, with similar results.

10 Similarly, millions of Soviet citizens have repeatedly been brought to the verge of starvation because of slavish adherence to doctrinaire ideology rather than reliance on observable facts on how to get crops and livestock produced. The Communists display the most grandiose example of the pseudoscientific approach to human affairs in history. Their jargon is shot through with appeals to the scientific method, but their starting-point is a *priori* dogma. Their gaze is still riveted on a state of facts dated 1850. They are fighting a kind of raw capitalism that may or may not have existed a century ago, but certainly does not exist now. Their pure ideology presupposes a species of human creature with motivations that direct observation would quickly show do not exist except in rare cases.

11 By contrast, the United States has at times seemed to symbolize the nonscientific approach—a kind of assumption that if everyone just does what comes naturally, the good life for all will somehow emerge. This view is typified by the economics of Adam Smith, and, indeed, the lusty surge of industrial development in the Western world owes much to the drives engendered by this attitude. One of the products of this experience is the fragment of phony American folklore

that teaches that our society came into being as unself-consciously as the unfolding of the petals of a flower, and that although in personal and business life planning is the key to success, in public life planning is un-American and unqualifiedly evil. Even now, many politicians think that the most devastating insult you can apply to an opponent is to call him a "planner." This attitude was no doubt reenforced by the fact that, in the Thirties, planning came to be associated with Communism and socialism. Other sweeping ideas to change society such as technocracy came under the same cloud.

12 The true fact is that at certain key points in our history Americans have applied the genuine scientific approach by first studying the facts, then conceiving a definite design and building toward it.

13 The outstanding example is our Constitution—the product of a gigantic effort of intellectual research and creativity.

14 When the great farm lands of the Midwest opened up, Americans concluded that the West was going to be a country of small-family farms. The result was the Homestead Act, a concept of breathtaking scope and imagination, which methodically translated this blueprint into reality.

15 In somewhat the same way, although the persistence of *laissez-faire* thought permitted the growth of the cartel system in Europe, Americans looked at the facts rather than the pages of Adam Smith and saw that the end result of supposedly perfect competition was all too often the death of competition. They deliberately decided that the American economy was to be nonmonopolistic. Accordingly, they passed the Sherman Anti-Trust Act, the Clayton Act, and the Norris-LaGuardia Act.

16 Again, Americans perceived that the bargaining power of organized labor was not equal to that of employers, and therefore set out to try to make it at least approximately so by devising and subsequently revising the Wagner Labor Relations Act.

17 On the international scene, after World War II, the facts showed that everyone's peace and welfare depended on economic and technical rebuilding and development, first by the devastated countries of Europe, and then by the underdeveloped countries of Asia, Africa, and Latin America. The magnificent concept of economic and technical aid was the deliberately designed result.

18 The area outside the physical sciences where the authentic scientific approach has been most successfully applied is that of economics, particularly in the prevention of severe recessions and in the reconciling of free enterprise with orderly growth through careful observation of an array of "economic indicators" and skillful manipulation of such controls as discount rates, taxes, government purchase policy, social insurance, and fiscal measures.

19 Of all areas in which the need to control events rather than be controlled by them is urgent, that of international relations should have the highest priority.

20 How well are we doing in applying the power of intelligence to this task? The answer is that, until recently, it never seems to have occurred to the world's leaders that the techniques of intellectual research had anything to contribute to solving the problem of war between nations.

21 A rational approach to any problem begins with getting the facts—facts

which are accurate and current. International relations today are being conducted on the basis of facts that are from eighteen to 300 years out of date.

22 A partial check-list of current misconcepts of fact bearing on the ultimate issue of war and peace may serve to support this statement.

23 The first misconcept is that diplomacy is the only valid method of settling international disputes. The fact is that old-fashioned power-politics diplomacy is virtually obsolete as a method of settling major disputes. Since it still remains almost the only technique used in international relations, we can begin to understand why the world's main divisive issues—divided Germany, divided Korea, and divided Viet Nam, to name only the most obvious—are as far from solution as they were when they first arose.

24 The reason power-politics is now out-of-date is that war is unusable as an instrument of national policy. It is unusable legally, because we have made it so in the United Nations Charter. It is unusable practically, because the possible extinction of all life in the northern hemisphere that might result is, in the language of the Pentagon, unacceptable. What is not adequately understood is that, when war becomes obsolete, methods of dispute-settling that depended upon the ultimate availability of war also become obsolete. Old-fashioned diplomacy was not typically an exercise in finding the intrinsic rights and wrongs of a controversy such as a boundary dispute. What the parties really were concerned about was which one could defeat the other if matters came to a military showdown. If country A could convince country B that it had decisively superior military power, the boundary would move to the disadvantage of B. But if neither could convince the other of such superiority, sooner or later there would be a military collision. One side would lose; one would win; and the process would start over again. This, somewhat simplified, has been the story of international dispute-settling through most of human history.

25 But now something new has been added. Because of the unusability of nuclear weapons, we have a military deadlock between the great powers on the major issues. The new fact of life is that when you have military deadlock you also have diplomatic deadlock. Yet in the teeth of this observable fact, we go on trying to settle disputes by diplomacy as if we were still living in the days of Machiavelli or Metternich.

26 The second misconcept, closely related to the first, is that in all international situations it is power that ultimately counts. We have just seen that, as between the nuclear giants, the effect of power is not to gain advantage but to preserve a stalemate. But even as between a nuclear power and a small nation, nuclear power is virtually useless when disputes arise.

27 For example, at the time of the Korean conflict, the use of nuclear weapons to bring a quick end to the struggle and save the lives of thousands of American soldiers was apparently never a serious enough possibility to warrant public discussion. There is no evidence that the Soviet Union in its contest with the People's Republic of China is enjoying any advantage because of its overwhelming superiority in military strength. Poland and other satellites are taking a more independent line toward Moscow than before Russia acquired effective nuclear armaments. The awesome destructive capacity of the United States is of no use to it in relation to Cuba, and does not prevent such a humiliating episode

as the Bay of Pigs invasion; nor is nuclear strength of any relevance in South Viet Nam, Malaysia, Yemen, Cyprus, the Northern India border, and the many other trouble-spots in Africa, Asia, and around the world.

28 The third misconcept is that nations cannot bring themselves to accept settlement of their important disputes by peaceful means such as arbitration and adjudication. The fact is that nations have repeatedly submitted controversies involving high interests and high public excitement to peaceful settlement. During the nineteenth century 177 major disputes between nations were resolved by arbitration, including seventy-nine to which the United States was a party. Nor will it do to try to explain this fact away by saying that nations only submit unimportant issues to peaceful settlement. No type of controversy in international affairs is more emotion-packed than a dispute over territory. One recalls Hamlet's soliloquy about how nations will fight over a strip of ground too small to bury the dead in. Yet Norway (which was the country that prompted Hamlet's observation) gave up East Greenland to Denmark as the result of a court decision. In the last few years, boundary disputes important enough to provoke armed conflict between Nicaragua and Honduras, and between Cambodia and Thailand, have been settled in the World Court. The fact is that adjudication or arbitration on the merits is usually the only way a hotly contested boundary dispute can be settled. The reason is that no government could make a diplomatic settlement giving away the sacred soil of the motherland and still survive politically at home, but a judicial settlement reaching the same result involves no such political disaster.

29 The fourth misconcept is that, since there is no world government with overwhelming military power to enforce law, nations will not pay any attention to judicial or arbitral decisions that they do not like. The fact is that there is no case on record of disobedience to a decision of the Permanent Court of International Justice, and only one case of disobedience to a decision of the current International Court of Justice; and among the hundreds of other judicial and arbitral awards, there are only a few cases in which the losing party has refused to give effect to the decision. It is generally agreed by scholars that the record of compliance with international decisions compares favorably with that of compliance with domestic decisions.

30 When we come to the area of the peacekeeping potential of the United Nations, we encounter similarly erroneous notions. For example, it is constantly said that the usefulness of the organization is limited because it can only act when there is great power unanimity. Yet even the most cursory look at the record shows that every major peacekeeping action of the U.N. was undertaken despite the opposition of at least one power possessed of the Security Council veto: Korea, opposed by the Soviet Union; the Middle East force, opposed and indeed vetoed by Great Britain and France in the Security Council; and the Congo action, opposed in greater or less degree by every major power except the United States.

31 Running through all our international misconcepts is an entire network of outdated ideas about the Soviet Union, Communism, and the cold war. One such idea is the notion that the Soviet Union never changes. The fact is that when the events in that area since the death of Stalin are seen in historical perspective

it may well be concluded that Khrushchev worked a greater change in the Soviet Union than has ever been achieved without revolution in a major country in a comparable period of time. An allied fallacy is the assertion that all totalitarian regimes are alike, and that there is really no difference between today's Soviet Union and Hitler's Germany. For present purposes, there may be cited just one interesting difference. The entire force of Hitler's immense propaganda machine was devoted to preparing the German people to accept war; whereas everywhere one travels in the Soviet Union today one encounters nothing but propaganda for peace. This is not for the benefit of outsiders; this is for the home folks. This is not to ignore the problem of reconciling Russian words and policies in this area of seeking peace; the point here is merely that if the Soviet Union at some future time were to decide to plunge into the kind of flagrantly warlike course that Hitler took, it would have to reckon with a generation that, instead of having been trained to regard war as noble and inevitable, as was the case with the Hitler youth, has been suffused with the message that war is the greatest evil, and peace the highest good for which mankind can hope.

32 In the same bundle of outdated notions is the idea that all conflicts in the world can ultimately be explained as Communism versus anti-Communism. It would be difficult to calculate how many blunders of policy and errors of strategy this persistent fallacy has produced and may still produce. A large part of the quarrels now going on around the world go back to animosities and rivalries that were old before Communism was even heard of: between Arabs and Jews, between Hindus and Moslems, between dozens of African tribes, between Greeks and Turks, between innumerable nations, groups, religions, and factions in all parts of the world with old scores to settle and new frictions attendant upon the decolonialization process. True, Communism is not averse to fishing in these troubled waters; but this is quite a different matter from supposing that if Communism could somehow be made to go away the world's conflicts would largely disappear.

33 The bipolar picture of global conflict is discredited even more decisively by the break between the Soviet Union and Communist China. It has become clear that this is no mere ideological debate. It is a dead-earnest national struggle between two natural rivals, involving the largest territorial dispute in the world, a life-and-death battle for the allegiance of a large part of the world's population, and a growing racial conflict that could dwarf any other such conflict we have yet seen, as the Communist Chinese try to mobilize racialism on a global basis.

34 This, then, is a mere sampling of erroneous notions that too often take the place of accurate facts in the conduct of international affairs. The list could be extended to dozens of other items, large and small. What then is to be done about this dangerous state of affairs?

35 The fundamental requisite is acceptance of the idea that the techniques of research, scholarship, and the scientific method have much more to contribute to the amelioration of human and international troubles than has ever been suspected. It is curious how difficult it is to get this point accepted. At one of our Soviet-American Citizens' Conferences we were trying to demonstrate that a three-man "troika" instead of a single Secretary-General of the United Nations simply would not work. Professor Louis Sohn cited a research study done at

Harvard, investigating the workings of various kinds and sizes of international boards, panels, and commissions. The study showed that, of all possible bodies, the three-man group worked worst. One reason was the tendency, familiar to all seasoned committee workers, of two men in a three-man group to gang up on the third. Every triumvirate has its Lepidus and its Caesar. We reminded the Russians that they had recently had a demonstration of this phenomenon in the triumvirate that succeeded Stalin. On the other hand, a board of five or seven or nine members was found by the study to eliminate most of these kinds of difficulty. We pointed out to the Russians that if a comparable study with a comparable mass of data had shown what happens when you combine two hydrogen atoms with one oxygen atom, they would not hesitate to accept the validity of the study's findings. But merely because the subject of the study was human behavior, it is all too easy to ignore the observed facts and go on and on making the same mistakes forever.

36 About six years ago there was a significant turning in this entire story: the upsurge of what may be called the peace research movement. The central conviction of this movement is that the scholarly and research community have an important and indeed vital role to play in building the structures and procedures and attitudes that are essential to peace. The physical sciences should probably be credited with having taken the lead. At a time when, for example, inspection was the cornerstone of our disarmament position, it became apparent that no meaningful political discussion of inspection could be undertaken unless a vast amount of scientific data was developed, bearing on such obvious questions as the distance from which particular kinds of underground blasts could be detected. To continue the example of disarmament: the lawyers and economists soon saw that their disciplines also bore upon crucial points. As a matter of law, could our negotiators really promise that Russian inspectors could enter private plants in the United States even if the owners objected? As a matter of economics, could disarmament be accomplished without severe depression and unemployment?

37 Research centers began to be formed for the express purpose of methodically supplying the needed data and analysis. A Peace Research Committee, which produced designs for research in law, science and technology, economics, communications, and decision-making, was formed. Over 500 projects are described in these books. The Committee then led to the Peace Research Institute, Inc., with Ambassador James J. Wadsworth as its first president. Now there are active peace research institutes and programs in dozens of countries. The new importance of research is seen in the prominent place occupied by research in the purposes and budget of the Arms Control and Disarmament Agency.

38 The significance of all this is that, for the first time, we are witnessing a methodical intellectual assault upon the stubborn problems, both fundamental and detailed, whose solution is a precondition to any workable and structured peace. This is not a matter of preaching peace in generalities or slogans, nor is it a matter of constructing shining models of a utopian world order. It is a matter of beginning from where we are, working with what we have and within the limits of the possible, and finding ways both to handle the day's troubles more effectively

and to construct gradually better procedures, laws, and institutional arrangements for the settling of all disputes and the prevention of all threats to the peace of the world as they arise.

THE ADAPTABILITY OF THE SUPPORT STRUCTURE

The support structure is adaptable to an endless number of occasions for writing. It can be used whenever one wishes to answer a question about any situation in life or art. There are, of course, other structures which can at times be used for such explanations, but the support structure is always adequate. When a critic wishes to interpret any work of art, he usually begins by explaining what the situation in criticism is, as far as that work is concerned; then he states his thesis against this background and supports it, using some of the forms of support listed in the "Pattern of the Support Structure for Explanations" (page 325). When a financial expert wishes to explain to the public why interest rates are high, he usually begins by stating what the rates are and how they compare with rates the year before, two years before, and so forth. After he has described the situation, he must state an interpretation in a thesis sentence or paragraph and give reasons to support it. A judge on the Supreme Court rendering a formal opinion on a case will first explain the facts in the case, next state his thesis, expressing his opinion of the complaint, and, finally, support his opinion.

It is not surprising that the Report of the National Advisory Commission on Civil Disorders,[4] popularly known as the Kerner Report, on the race riots of 1967, has these three main divisions:

What happened? (in the riots)
Why did it happen?
What can be done to prevent it from happening again?

In Part I the situations in ten cities where riots occurred are described in detail. The question—Why did it happen?—is answered in a thesis section called "The Basic Causes," on page 5, and the thesis is supported through a historical sketch of relations between blacks and whites and an analysis of aspects of life in racial ghettos—family structure, health and sanitary conditions, unemployment and its effects. The explanation ends with Part II. Part III, the recommendations, is the kind of addition which can always be made to an explanation without changing its structure.

Whenever you are asked in any course to explain *why*, in a formal paper or on an examination, the support structure is appropriate to use. Knowing it well

[4]Issued by the United States Government, March 1, 1968.

enough to remember it when the occasion for use presents itself and knowing the various kinds of support by which a thesis in this structure can be defended will insure an appropriate beginning to the paper, a clear thesis, and adequate development.

SUGGESTED WRITING ASSIGNMENT

An Explanation of an Existing Situation

Write a composition to explain why a situation with which you are acquainted exists or why it is desirable or undesirable.

Choosing a situation: Choose a situation in real life that you know well or one that you are curious about.

Deciding on the basic question: Form a question which asks, in effect, why this situation exists or whether it is desirable.

Investigating: If you do not know the chosen situation from the inside, it will probably be necessary for you to make a survey or hold a few interviews; or it may be that by simply listening more carefully you can gather the information you need. This phase of the work is very important, because the support section of your composition cannot be stronger than the facts, statistics, examples, and descriptive details that you collect during the investigation. (Consider as evidence the reasons given by the persons involved in the situation. For example, if you ask six women why they work outside the home, you must assume that the reasons they give you are the real reasons.)

Interpreting the evidence: You probably will have formed an answer to your question as a working hypothesis when forming the question itself. But your evidence gathered during the investigation may lead you to another answer. Be sure to follow the rules for the formation of a hypothesis when making your interpretation.

Setting up the structure: Use the support structure. Decide how much information about the situation needs to be given, and select the forms of development most appropriate for the presentation of this information. Your basic question may be stated or implied, but the thesis should be stated. Decide upon a pattern of organization for the support, after considering various patterns that you have seen.

Writing: First, write your thesis and your summary statements or lead-in statements for each division. Then fill in details, using specific words and concrete class words in examples and using descriptive detail, wherever appropriate, to make your subjects graphic. Read and revise, adding transitional expressions, using connectors to reinforce logical relationships, and improving sentence structure.

Application

Four Essays, With Suggested
Writing Assignments

The following essays are built upon the support structure, but unlike the essays in Part IV, they explore effects rather than causes. The anonymous author of "The T.V. Generation" examines the effects of television on a generation that has grown up with it. The authors of the other three essays speculate upon future effects of situations that have recently emerged. After describing several modern movies in detail, Anthony Schillaci, in "The Now Movie," explains the effects that these movies are having on the young, after which he suggests effects that the young will have on film-making in the future. Donald Fleming, in "On Living in a Biological Revolution," maintains that ever increasing biological discoveries forecast a future in which the majority of human beings will give up some of their freedom of choice to physicians and sociologists in order to gain greater measures of sanity, serenity, and social order. Lee Benson maintains, on the contrary, in "The Irrepressible World Revolt," that the present world-wide revolt of the young prefigures a future in which individualism will spring as a matter of course from scientific, economic, and educational advancement.

Each of these provocative essays is followed by writing assignments to which techniques of writing treated in this book are applicable. Key words such as *describe, classify, generalize, compare,* and *explain* are used in the assignments to help you relate your new subjects to the specific techniques of development that you have studied.

The TV Generation

Anonymous

If you're over 30, you can remember when there weren't any television sets. If you're over 21, you can probably remember when your family got its first TV set. But few children born in the last 15 years can remember a time *without* television. They're truly the first TV generation. Most of these kids have always had one or more TV sets available at home. To them the TV set, like the kitchen table, is just there—and it's there to be used.

Boy, do they *use* it. The average child today spends more total time in front of a TV screen than he does in school. Educators figure that by the time the typical American student graduates from high school, he has spent just under 11,000 hours in class and just over 15,000 hours watching TV.

What's the result of so much exposure to "the tube"?

Some critics have said it would produce a "generation of spectators" who won't be able to make a move without directions from a TV set. Others have feared it would produce a "generation of juvenile delinquents" spurred on by TV's "electronic crime school."

On the other hand, some authorities pooh-poohed the idea that TV would have any bad influence. They said it satisfies a child's fantasy needs, as comic books and radio did for earlier generations.

Both extremes appear to be off the mark. The dire predictions of harm remain unproved, and children's exposure to TV remains a matter of serious concern, for comic books, radio, movies and other mass media have not had the powerful, day-in-day-out impact of television.

It's hard to measure TV's impact accurately because there's no comparable group of American children who haven't been exposed to it. However, by studying these kids who've spent a large part of their lives watching television, researchers believe they have found at least some partial answers to questions about TV's influence. The information can help clear up some confusion, help reduce some fears, and—most important of all—help parents and other adults cope with the viewing habits of future TV generations.

The possibility that television would work great physical harm on children, particularly on their sight and posture, was much feared in the early 1950's. It proved to be a groundless fear.

True, unrestricted television viewing may cause some isolated physical problems. Occasionally, a child will be fatigued by lack of sleep. There are even reports of a "tired-child syndrome," in which children complained of chronic fatigue, loss of appetite, headaches and vomiting. It turned out that they had been watching TV three to six hours daily on weekdays and six to ten hours on Saturdays and Sundays. When their televiewing was prohibited, the symptoms vanished.

THE TV GENERATION   Reprinted by permission from *Changing Times*, the Kiplinger Magazine (July, 1968 issue). Copyright 1968 by The Kiplinger Washington Editors, Inc., 1729 H Street N.W., Washington, D.C. 20006.

Another early fear that proved invalid was that television would lower school grades and lessen book reading. Later reports claimed TV enhances academic achievements. But recent research indicates that such TV influence is slight. For instance, listen to the latest findings of Dr. Paul A. Witty, an educator who has made continuing studies of televiewing from 1949 to 1967:

"In our early studies, we found that elementary school pupils read about the same amount after TV came to them as they did before its advent. In recent studies, we have found few pupils who state that TV *has caused* them to read less. And many indicate that TV *has motivated* them to read. Our studies suggest that pupils may be reading a little more than before TV came to them. But the picture is by no means a bright one since most pupils do not read widely.

"Little relationship was found between the amount of televiewing and marks in school. Similarly, reading achievement as measured by standardized tests showed little relationship to amount of televiewing."

TV does contribute to the vocabularly development of preschool children. Some teachers claim that the vocabulary of youngsters entering school now is a year ahead of pre-TV first graders. But critics ask: What good is a pre-school vocabulary full of names of beer, cigarets and advertising slogans? Dr. Witty discovered that older pupils also make some vocabulary gains from TV. But here, too, the value is questionable. For instance, new words learned by a group of sixth graders included seiche, hemoglobin, espionage and torso.

The most written about, talked about and worried about aspect of TV's impact centers on children's incessant exposure to crime, violence and brutality. Indeed, the statistics are fearsome: By the time he reaches age 14, the average child has witnessed the violent destruction of 13,000 human beings on TV.

But does such exposure to violence make a child more violent? There are three schools of thought on that question.

The first is the "generation of delinquents" school, represented best by the congressional committee that several years ago concluded: "The excessive amount of televised crime, violence and brutality can and does contribute to the development of attitudes in many young people that pave the way for delinquent behavior."

At the opposite pole is the "catharsis" school, based on the psychiatric theory that TV violence offers a healthy outlet for a child's hostilities and aggressions. He gets them out of his system vicariously.

The third and now most popular school contends that TV itself rarely *causes* crime or aggression but that it can be a contributing factor. How it contributes supposedly depends on what the child brings to his viewing. If the child brings emotional disturbance, for instance, TV violence may arouse his aggressive impulses. Even proponents of this school disagree on whether or not these impulses will be expressed in real-life situations. And if they are, will the child imitate the violent act he sees on TV or will the aggressiveness take another form?

Such questions will have to remain unanswered until there's more adequate research on TV violence with less contradictory results.

TV violence may have an impact on children, however, that's unrelated to aggressive behavior. Some psychologists say that children who are heavy viewers appear to become less sensitive to television violence because they see so much of it. Also, a growing number of children don't distinguish between the soldier who dies on the 6 o'clock news and the one who dies on "Garrison's Gorillas" and returns to life tomorrow on another channel. In other words, children are confusing fantasy and reality.

No doubt TV does distort the young child's world. Young children readily believe what they see and hear, and much of what they see and hear today comes from television.

"Seeing is believing," says Boston University psychology professor Ralph Garry. In the Association for Childhood Education International's recent study *Children and TV*, Prof. Garry warns that children's belief in the truth of television "can lead to startling misconceptions, e.g., only bad guys bleed, or that the commercials tell you what is good to buy. Inevitably, misconceptions, whatever their source, must stand the test of experience and be corrected. Where they do not, they become a base for preconceptions and prejudice."

Most of the blame for any adverse impact of TV is placed at the feet of broadcasters of commercial television and the advertising messages that sustain them.

Critics say the TV commercial not only *distorts* reality (toothpaste doesn't really make you happy) but creates distrust when the toys advertised as so big, so sturdy and so realistic turn out to be so small, so frail and so phony. Many fear that this distrust will breed "a generation of cynics."

As a matter of fact, the commercial message may have more direct impact than any other aspect of television. A leading TV ad salesman proudly claims that "70% of the kids ask their parents to buy products advertised on television and 89% of the parents *do it.*"

Commercials plague children's programs, as any adult who watches with the kids knows. The National Association for Better Broadcasting, which monitors and publicly evaluates TV programs, found that each hour of network broadcasting on Saturday morning typically includes 18 or 19 commercials.

The content of commercials causes as much concern as their number. The NABB charges: "The *nature* of the commercial messages directed to children often indicates a carefully planned exploitation of children's special appetites for war games, candy, lavish dolls, soft drinks, oversweetened cereals, etc. There is little evidence of restraint on the part of many program 'emcees,' broadcasters and advertisers in the manipulation of immature viewers."

The association worries even more about programing. It says values taught at home and school are often contradicted by TV shows that glorify the smart aleck, ridicule authority and solve all problems through violent, thoughtless action. In the view of NABB members who monitor TV shows: "As far as children are concerned, 1968 television is the worst in the history of TV." They charge the majority of TV broadcasters, including the national networks, with "gross negligence" for giving America's 30,000,000 juvenile viewers entertainment dominated by triviality, ugliness, noise, violence and horror.

Many other critics give broadcasters the benefit of the doubt on motives but still castigate programing. Some say it's hard to find a "good" TV program for children. That depends on your definition of good, of course. But even the NABB lists a number of "excellent" children's TV programs, such as "Captain Kangaroo," "Discovery" and "Animal Secrets," and even some good creative cartoon shows.

Then, too, criticism of television usually ignores some programs' positive effects. Though it's often just a convenient baby-sitter, television does offer amusement, entertainment and many rewarding experiences. While it may distort some concepts, it also enlarges a child's view of the world, exposing him to the arts and sciences, sports and current events.

However, you can't expect children to search out on their own, or limit themselves to, good programs or rewarding experiences. That's where adults come in.

Most adults agree that there's too much indiscriminate televiewing by children of all ages. Yet those who could best control this viewing—parents and teachers—aren't doing it.

In most families, Dr. Witty's studies indicate, the young child watches TV almost as much as he wishes and views programs of his own choice. Researchers at Columbia University discovered that as little as 5% of families control TV viewing, and even those families limit their control to the amount of watching and ignore the content of what's watched.

Effective control requires that both time and type of viewing be supervised by parents.

Limiting time. Parents can establish reasonable time limits for young children, perhaps one hour a day, with consideration given to additional programs of particular interest. The National Congress of Parents and Teachers recommends a "selective dialing" rule—the set is turned on only for a preselected program and must be turned off when it ends.

Rules for limiting time will vary for different families and different children. Some parents provide effective guidance through family planning councils. The entire family draws up weekly schedules of leisure activities, making a place for television, reading and various kinds of outdoor recreation.

Limiting type. The best way for a parent to check the content of programs his children view is to watch the programs himself.

Outside help is available. Many local newspapers offer comments on programs in their TV listing, though their guidance is usually minimal. Some parents and teachers find the NABB's evaluation publication to be a valuable aid. *The PTA Magazine* also carries regular program appraisals.

The network of educational TV stations rapidly developing throughout the U.S. gives some parents an alternative to commercial TV. But since commercial TV is so much more pervasive than ETV, upgrading the commercial programs will have a greater impact on children.

To get better programing, many authorities recommend putting pressure on broadcasters, individually or through groups like the PTA. Letters to networks, station managers, program producers, directors and sponsors are effective, especially if you commend as well as complain. A thank-you note or a congratulatory letter to a broadcaster for a patricularly enjoyed or well-done program not only wins his moral support but gives him ammunition to use on the sponsors for continuing such programs.

A child's viewing can't be controlled from afar. Parents must share the experience of TV with their children. That doesn't mean watching with the kids every day. It does mean watching *some* programs with your child and discussing their good and bad features. It does mean offering alternative values and opinions to ones that children get from TV.

Though the research on TV's impact is still inadequate and in some respects inconclusive, the vast majority of authorities agree that whether a child's world is or isn't distorted by TV's violence, fantasies or commercials depends in large part on the adult guidance he gets. A child may not be equipped to distinguish between fantasy and fact or between acceptable and unacceptable behavior. An adult should be around to help sort them out.

"This places adults, parents in particular, in a crucial role," says Ralph Garry, whose findings are quoted above. Prof. Garry, along with most investigators, maintains that any disturbing effects that TV may have on kids are likely to be minimized if adults—

take the time to view and discuss programs with children,
make their own beliefs and attitudes clear in words and deeds, and
maintain healthy emotional relationships with children.

SUGGESTED WRITING ASSIGNMENT

1. Explain why some parents do not control their children's watching of television. Remember to develop a situation and to support reasons with examples.
2. If you have evidence of any effects that watching television has had on children, write a composition on these effects, developing a causal generalization with examples.
3. Interview a number of children to find out which television shows they like best, and write a composition classifying their preferences.

The Now Movie: Film as Environment

Anthony Schillaci

The better we understand how young people view film, the more we have to revise our notion of what film is. Seen through young eyes, film is destroying conventions almost as quickly as they can be formulated. Whether the favored

THE NOW MOVIE: FILM AS ENVIRONMENT   From *Saturday Review*, December 28, 1968. Copyright 1968 Saturday Review, Inc. Reprinted by permission of the publisher and the author.

director is "young" like Richard Lester, Roman Polanski, and Arthur Penn, or "old" like Kubrick, Fellini, and Buñuel, he must be a practicing cinematic anarchist to catch the eye of the young. If we're looking for the young audience between sixteen and twenty-four, which accounts for 48 per cent of the box office today, we will find they're on a trip, whether in a Yellow Submarine or on a Space Odyssey. A brief prayer muttered for Rosemary's Baby and they're careening down a dirt road with Bonnie and Clyde, the exhaust spitting banjo sounds, or sitting next to The Graduate as he races across the Bay Bridge after his love. The company they keep is fast; Belle de Jour, Petulia, and Joanna are not exactly a sedentary crowd. Hyped up on large doses of *Rowan and Martin's Laugh-In,* and *Mission: Impossible,* they are ready for anything that an evolving film idiom can throw on the screen. And what moves them must have the pace, novelty, style, and spontaneity of a television commercial.

All of this sounds as if the script is by McLuhan. Nevertheless, it is borne out by the experience of teaching contemporary film to university juniors and seniors, staging film festivals for late teens and early adults, and talking to literally hundreds of people about movies. The phenomenon may be interesting, and even verifiable, but what makes it important is its significance for the future of film art. The young have discovered that film is an environment which you put on, demanding a different kind of structure, a different mode of attention than any other art. Their hunger is for mind-expanding experience and simultaneity, and their art is film.

Occasionally a young director gives us a glimpse of the new world of film as environmental art. The optical exercise known as *Flicker* came on like a karate chop to the eyes at Lincoln Center's Film Seminar three years ago. One half-hour of white light flashing at varied frequency, accompanied by a deafening sound track designed to infuriate, describes the screen, but not what happened to the audience. As strangers turned to ask if it was a put-on, if they had forgotten to put film in the projector, they noticed that the flickering light fragmented their motions, stylizing them like the actions of a silent movie. In minutes, the entire audience was on its feet, acting out spontaneous pantomimes for one another, no one looking at the flashing screen. The happening precipitated by *Flicker* could be called the film of the future, but it was actually an anti-environment that gives us an insight into the past. By abstracting totally from content, the director demonstrated that the film is in the audience which acts out personal and public dramas as the screen turns it on. The delight of this experience opened up the notion of film as an environmental art.

Critics have noted the trend which leaves story line and character development strewn along the highways of film history like the corpses in Godard's *Weekend.* The same critics have not, in general, recognized that the growing option for nonlinear, unstructured experiences that leave out sequence, motivation, and "argument" is a vote for film as environment. Young people turn to film for a time-space environment in which beautiful things happen to them. The screen has, in a sense, less and less to do with what explodes in the audience. This new scene could mean either that film is plunging toward irrelevant stimulation, or that there is a new and unprecedented level of participation and involvement in young audiences. I prefer to think the latter is the case. Young people want to talk about Ben's hang-up, why Rosemary stayed with the baby, or what it feels like to be in the electronic hands of a computer like Hal. They do not forget the film the minute they walk out of the theater.

The attention given the new style of film goes beyond stimulation to real involvement. A generation with eyes fixed on the rearview mirror tended to give film the same attention required for reading—that is, turning off all the senses except the eyes. Film became almost as private as reading, and little reaction to the total audience was experienced. As the Hollywood dream factory cranked out self-contained worlds of fantasy, audiences entered them with confidence that nothing even vaguely related to real life would trouble their reveries. As long as one came and left in the middle of the film, it was relatively noninvolving as environment. When television brought the image into the living room, people gave it "movie attention," hushing everyone who entered the sacred presence of the tube as they would a film patron who talked during a movie. One was not allowed to speak, even during commercials. It took post-literate man to teach us how to use television as environment, as a moving image on the wall to which one may give total or peripheral attention as he wishes. The child who had TV as a baby-sitter does not turn off all his senses, but walks about the room carrying on a multiplicity of actions and relationships, his attention a special reward for the cleverness of the pitchman, or the skill of the artist. He is king, and not captive. As McLuhan would put it, he is not an audience, he *gives* an audience to the screen.

The new multisensory involvement with film as total environment has been primary in destroying literary values in film. Their decline is not merely farewell to an understandable but unwelcome dependency; it means the emergence of a new identity for film. The diminished role of dialogue is a case in point. The difference between *Star Trek* and *Mission: Impossible* marks the trend toward self-explanatory images that need no dialogue. Take an audio tape of these two popular TV shows, as we did in a recent study, and it will reveal that while *Mission: Impossible* is completely unintelligible without images, *Star Trek* is simply an illustrated radio serial, complete on the level of sound. It has all the characteristics of radio's golden age: actions explained, immediate identification of character by voice alone, and even organ music to squeeze the proper emotion or end the episode. Like *Star Trek,* the old film was frequently a talking picture (emphasis on the adjective), thereby confirming McLuhan's contention that technologically "radio married the movies." The marriage of dependence, however, has gone on the rocks, and not by a return to silent films but a new turning to foreign ones. It was the films of Fellini and Bergman, with their subtitles, that convinced us there had been too many words. Approximately one-third of the dialogue is omitted in subtitled versions of these films, with no discernible damage—and some improvement—of the original.

More than dialogue, however, has been jettisoned. Other literary values, such as sequential narrative, dramatic choice, and plot are in a state of advanced atrophy, rapidly becoming vestigial organs on the body of film art as young people have their say. *Petulia* has no "story," unless one laboriously pieces together the interaction between the delightful arch-kook and the newly divorced surgeon in which case it is nothing more than an encounter. The story line wouldn't make a ripple if it were not scrambled and fragmented into an experience that explodes from a free-floating present into both past and future simultaneously. *Petulia* is like some views of the universe which represent the ancient past of events whose light is just now reaching us simultaneously with the future of our galaxy, returning from the curve of outer space. Many films succeed by virtue of what they leave out. *2001: A Space Odyssey* is such a film, its muted understatement creating gaps in the action that invite our inquiry. Only a square viewer wants to know where the black monolith came from and where it is going. For most of the young viewers to whom I have spoken, it is just there. *Last Year at Marienbad* made the clock as limply shapeless as one of Salvador Dali's watches, while *8½* came to life on the strength of free associations eagerly grasped by young audiences. The effect of such films is a series of open-ended impressions, freely evoked and enjoyed, strongly inviting inquiry and involvement. In short, film is freed to work as environment, something which does not simply contain, but shapes people, tilting the balance of their faculties, radically altering their perceptions, and ultimately their views of self and all reality. Perhaps one sense of the symptomatic word "grooving," which applies to both sight and sound environments, is that a new mode of attention—multisensory, total, and simultaneous—has arrived. When you "groove," you do not analyze, follow an argument, or separate sensations; rather, you are massaged into a feeling of heightened life and consciousness.

If young people look at film this way, it is in spite of the school, a fact which says once more with emphasis that education is taking place outside the classroom walls. The "discovery" that television commercials are the most exciting and creative part of today's programing is old news to the young. Commercials are a crash course in speed-viewing, their intensified sensations challenging the viewer to synthesize impressions at an ever increasing rate. The result is short films like one produced at UCLA, presenting 3,000 years of art in three minutes. *God Is Dog Spelled Backwards* takes you from the cave paintings of Lascaux to the latest abstractions, with some images remaining on the screen a mere twenty-fourth of a second! The young experience the film, however, not as confusing, but as exuberantly and audaciously alive. They feel joy of recognition, exhilaration at the intense concentration necessary (one blink encompasses a century of art), and awe at the 180-second review of every aspect of the human condition. Intended as a put-on, the film becomes a three-minute commercial for man. This hunger for overload is fed by the television commercial, with its nervous jump cuts demolishing continuity, and its lazy dissolves blurring time-space boundaries. Whether the young are viewing film "through" television, or simply through their increased capacity for information and sensation (a skill which makes most schooling a bore), the result is the same—film becomes the primary environment in which the hunger to know through experience is satisfied.

Hidden within this unarticulated preference of the young is a quiet tribute to film as the art that humanizes change. In its beginnings, the cinema was celebrated as the art that mirrored reality in its functional dynamism. And although the early vision predictably gave way to misuse of the medium, today the significance of the filmic experience of change stubbornly emerges again. Instead of prematurely stabilizing change, film celebrates it. The cinema can inject life into historical events by the photoscan, in which camera movement and editing liberate the vitality of images from the past. *City of Gold,* a short documentary by the National Film Board of Canada, takes us by zoom and cut into the very life of the Klondike gold rush, enabling us to savor the past as an experience.

Education increasingly means developing the ability to live humanly in the technological culture by changing with it. Film is forever spinning out intensifications of the environment which make it visible and livable. The ability to control motion through its coordinates of time and space make film a creative agent in change. Not only does film reflect the time-space continuum of contemporary physics, but it can manipulate artistically those dimensions of motion which we find most problematic. The actuality of the medium, its here-and-now impact, reflects how completely the present tense has swallowed up both past and future. Freudian psychology dissolves history by making the past something we live; accelerated change warps the future by bringing it so close that we can't conceive it as "ahead" of us. An art which creates its own space, and can move time forward and back, can humanize change by conditioning us to live comfortably immersed in its fluctuations.

On the level of form, then, perhaps the young are tuned in to film for "telling it like it is" in a sense deeper than that of fidelity to the event. It is film's accurate reflection of a society and of human life totally in flux that makes it the liberating art of the time. We live our lives more like Guido in *8½*—spinners of fantasies, victims of events, the products of mysterious associations—than we do like Maria in *The Sound of Music,* with a strange destiny guiding our every step. Instead of resisting change and bottling it, film intensifies the experience of change, humanizing it in the process. What makes the ending of *The Graduate* "true" to young people is not that Ben has rescued his girl from the Establishment, but that he did it without a complete plan for the future. The film may fail under analysis, but it is extraordinarily coherent as experience, as I learned in conversations about it with the young. The same accurate reflection of the day may be said of the deep space relativity of *2001,* the frantic pace of *Petulia,* or the melodramatic plotting of *Rosemary's Baby.* Whether this limitless capacity for change within the creative limits of art has sober implications for the future raises the next (and larger) questions of what young people look for and get out of film.

When the question of film content is raised, the example of *Flicker* and other films cited may seem to indicate that young people favor as little substance as possible in their film experiences. A casual glance at popular drive-in fare would confirm this opinion quickly. Nevertheless, their attitude toward "what films are about" evidences a young, developing sensitivity to challenging comments on what it means to be human. The young are digging the strong humanism of the current film renaissance and allowing its currents to carry them to a level deeper than that reached by previous generations. One might almost say that young people are going to the film-maker's work for values that they have looked for in vain from the social, political, or religious establishments. This reaction, which has made film modern man's morality play, has not been carefully analyzed, but the present state of evidence invites our inquiry.

As far as the "point" of films is concerned, young people will resist a packaged view, but will welcome a problematic one. The cry, "Please, I'd rather do it myself!" should be taken to heart by the film-maker. It is better to use understatement in order to score a personal discovery by the viewer. Such a discovery of an idea is a major part of our delight in the experience of film art. A frequent answer to a recent survey question indicated that a young man takes his girl to the movies so that they will have something important to talk about. It is not a matter of pitting film discussion against "making out," but of recognizing that a rare and precious revelation of self to the other is often occasioned by a good film. The young feel this experience as growth, expanded vitality, more integral possession of one's self with the consequent freedom to go out to others more easily and more effectively.

Very little of the business of being human happens by instinct, and so we need every form of education that enlightens or accelerates that process. While young people do not go to films for an instant humanization course, a strong part of the pleasure they take in excellent films does just this. Whether through a connaturality of the medium described earlier, or because of a freer viewpoint, young audiences frequently get more out of films than their mentors. It is not so much a matter of seeing more films, but of seeing more in a film. The film-as-escape attitude belongs to an age when the young were not yet born; and the film-as-threat syndrome has little meaning for the sixteen to twenty-four group, simply because they are free from their elders' hang-ups. A typical irrelevance that causes youthful wonder is the elderly matron's complaint that *Bonnie and Clyde* would teach bad driving habits to the young.

The performance of youthful audiences in discussions of contemporary film indicates their freedom from the judgmental screen which blurs so many films for other generations. In speaking of *Bonnie and Clyde,* late high school kids and young adults do not dwell upon the career of crime or the irregularity of the sexual relationship, but upon other things. The development of their love fascinates young people, because Clyde shows he knows Bonnie better than she knows herself. Although he resists her aggressive sexual advances, he knows and appreciates her as a person. It is the sincerity of their growing love that overcomes his impotence, and the relationship between this achievement and their diminished interest in crime is not lost on the young audience. The reversal of the "sleep together now, get acquainted later" approach is significant here. These are only a few of the nuances that sensitive ears and eyes pick up beneath the gunfire and banjo-plucking. Similarly, out of the chaotic impressions of *Petulia*, patterns are perceived. Young people note the contrasts between Petulia's kooky, chaotic life, and the over-controlled precision of the surgeon's existence. The drama is that they both come away a little different for their encounter. Instead of a stale moral judgment on their actions, one finds open-ended receptivity to the personal development of the characters.

Youth in search of identity is often presented as a ridiculous spectacle, a generation of Kierkegaards plaintively asking each other: "Who am I?" Nevertheless, the quest is real and is couched in terms of hunger for experience. SDS or LSD, McCarthy buttons or yippie fashions, it is all experimentation in identity, trying on experiences to see if they fit. The plea is to stop the world, not so that they can get off, but so they can get a handle on it. To grasp each experience, to suck it dry of substance, and to grow in that process is behind the desire to be "turned on." But of all the lurid and bizarre routes taken by young people, the one that draws least comment is that of the film experience. More people have had their minds expanded by films than by LSD. Just as all art nudges man into the sublime and vicarious experience of the whole range of the human condition, film does so with a uniquely characteristic totality and involvement.

Ben, *The Graduate,* is suffocating under his parents' aspirations, a form of drowning which every young person has felt in some way. But the film mirrors their alienation in filmic terms, by changes in focus, by the metaphors of conveyor belt sidewalk and swimming pool, better than any moralist could say it. The satirical portraits of the parents may be broad and unsubtle, but the predicament is real and compelling. This is why the young demand no assurances that Ben and the girl will live happily ever after; it is enough that he jarred himself loose from the sick apathy and languid sexual experimentation with Mrs. Robinson to go after one thing, one person that he wanted for himself, and not for others. Incidentally, those who are not busy judging the morality of the hotel scenes will note that sex doesn't communicate without love. Some may even note that Ben is using sex to strike at his parents—not a bad thing for the young (or their parents) to know.

Emotional maturity is never painless and seldom permanent, but it can become a bonus from viewing good films because it occurs there not as taught but experienced. Values communicated by film are interiorized and become a part of oneself, not simply an extension of the womb that parents and educators use to shield the young from the world. Colin Smith, in *The Loneliness of the Long Distance Runner,* IS youth, not because he did it to the Establishment, but because he is trying to be his own man and not sweat his guts out for another. The profound point of learning who you are in the experience of freedom, as Colin did in running, is not lost on the young who think about this film a little. Some speak of Col's tragedy as a failure to realize he could have won the race for himself, and not for the governor of the Borstal. Self-destruction through spite, the pitfalls of a self-justifying freedom, and the sterility of bland protest are real problems that emerge from the film. The values that appeal most are the invisible ones that move a person to act because "it's me" (part of one's identity), and not because of "them." Because they have become an object of discovery and not of imposition, such values tend to make morality indistinguishable from self-awareness.

It should be made clear, however, that it is not merely the content, but the mode of involvement in the film experience that makes its humanism effective. In terms of "message," much of contemporary film reflects the social and human concerns that Bob Dylan, the Beatles, Simon and Garfunkel, and Joan Baez communicate. But the words of their songs often conceal the radical nature of the music in which they appear. The direct emotional appeal of the sound of "Eleanor Rigby," "Give a Damn," "I Am a Rock," or "Mr. Businessman" communicates before we have the words deciphered. Films with honest human concern, similarly, change audiences as much by their style as their message. *Elvira Madigan*'s overpowering portrait of a hopeless love, *A Thousand Clowns'* image of nonconformity, *Zorba*'s vitality, and *Morgan*'s tragedy are not so much the content of the images as the outcome of their cinematic logic. If these films change us, it is because we have done it to ourselves by opening ourselves to their experiences.

Expo 67 audiences were charmed by the Czech Kinoautomat in which their vote determined the course of comic events in a film. Once again, we find here not a peek into the future, but an insight into all film experience. In one way or another, we vote on each film's progress. The passive way is to patronize dishonest or cynical films, for our box-office ballot determines the selection of properties for years to come. We have been voting this way for superficial emotions, sterile plots, and happy endings for a generation. But we vote more actively and subtly by willing the very direction of a film through identification with the character, or absorption into the action. The viewer makes a private or social commitment in film experience. He invests a portion of himself in the action, and if he is changed, it is because he has activated his own dreams. What happens on the screen, as in the case of *Flicker,* is the catalyst for the value systems, emotional responses, and the indirect actions which are the by-products of a good film. Film invites young people to be part of the action by making the relationships which take the work beyond a mere succession of images. The reason why young people grow through their art is that they supply the associations that merely begin on the screen but do not end there. When parents and educators become aware of this, their own efforts at fostering maturity may be less frantic, and more effective.

It is not only the films that please and delight which appeal to the young, but also those which trouble and accuse by bringing our fears into the open. The new audience for documentary films highlights a new way of looking at film as an escape *into* reality. From *The War Game* to *Warrendale,* from *The Titicut Follies* to *Battle of Algiers,* young audiences are relishing the film's ability to document the present in terms of strong social relevance. *Portrait of Jason* is more than a voyeuristic peek into the psyche of a male whore; it is a metaphor for the black man's history in America, and this is what young people see in that film. Even the most strident dissenters will appreciate the ambiguities of *The Anderson Platoon,* which leaves us without anyone to hate, because it is not about Marines and Vietcong, but about men like ourselves. In these as in other films, the social content is intimately wed to the film experience, and together they form a new outlook. Ultimately, we may have to change our views on what film art is about.

The foregoing analysis of how young people look at film will appear to some to constitute a simplistic eulogy to youth. For this reason, we may temper our optimism by a hard look at real problems with this generation. There is a desperate need for education. Although they cannot all be structured, none of the better youthful attitudes or responses described came about by chance. Mere screening of films, for example, whether they be classics or trash, does little good. Colleges can become places where the young are taught hypocrisy, being told they "should" like Fellini, Bergman, Antonioni, or Godard. They can accept these film-makers just as uncritically as their parents adulated movie stars. Unless there is encouragement to reflect on film experience, its impact can be minimal and fleeting. Most of the responses I have mentioned came from students who were well into the habit of discussing film. These discussions are best when they flow from the natural desire we have to communicate our feelings about a film. Non-verbalization, the reluctance to betray by treacherous abstractions the ineffable experience of the film, arises at this point. Real as it is, there must be found some middle ground between a suffocatingly detailed dissection of a film, and the noncommunicative exclamation, "like WOW!" Reflecting on one's experience is an integral part of making that experience part of one's self. Furthermore, one can see an almost immediate carry-over to other film experiences from each film discussed.

A problem more crucial than lack of reflection is the poverty of critical perspective. The young can plunge into their personal version of the *auteur* theory and make a fad or fetish out of certain films and directors. Roman Polanski has made some bad films, that is, films which do not reflect his own experience and feelings honestly as did *Knife in the Water*. Fascinating as *Rosemary's Baby* is, it suffers from an uncertain relationship of the director to his work. Some directors are adulated for peripheral or irrelevant reasons. Joseph Losey is a good film-maker, not because of a cynical preoccupation with evil, but because, like Hitchcock and Pinter, he makes us less certain of our virtue. And Buñuel, far from being a cheerful anarchist attacking church and society with abandon, is a careful surgeon, excising with camera the growths of degenerate myth on the cancerous culture.

In their own work, young people can celebrate bad film-making as "honest" and voyeuristic films as "mature." Criticism of poor films is not "putting down" the director for doing his own thing, especially if his thing is trite, dishonest, or so personal that it has no meaning accessible to others. Criticism means taking a stand on the basis of who you are. The current preference of spoof over satire is not just another instance of cool over hot, but is symptomatic of a noncritical stance. *Dr. Strangelove* makes comic absurdity out of the cold war from a certain conviction about what mature political action should be. The *Laugh-In* has no convictions but a lot of opinions. If it is accused of favoring an idea or cause, it will refute the charge by ridiculing what it holds. The cynical, sophisticated noninvolvement of the "won't vote" movement in the recent election has its counterpart in film viewing.

A question that should perhaps have been asked earlier is: Why should we be concerned with asking how young people look at film? Tired reasons, citing *Time's* Man of the Year, the under-twenty-five generation, or the youthquake menace of *Wild in the Streets* (they'll be taking over!) are not appropriate here. Anyone who is interested in the direction taken by cinema, and its continued vitality in the current renaissance of the art, will have to take the young into account as the major shaping force on the medium. If the age group from sixteen to twenty-four accounts for 48 per cent of the box office, it means that this eight-year period determines the success or failure of most films. Fortunately, there has not yet appeared a formula for capturing this audience. *Variety* described the youth market as a booby trap for the industry, citing the surprise success of sleepers such as *Bonnie and Clyde* and *The Graduate*, as well as the supposed youth-appeal failures (*Half a Sixpence*, *Poor Cow*, *Here We Go Round the Mulberry Bush*). The list may suggest a higher level of young taste than producers are willing to admit. In any case, if the young have influenced the medium this far, we cannot ignore the fact. It is for this reason that we are encouraged to speculate on the future in the form of two developments revolutionizing the young approach to film: student film-making and multi-media experiences.

More and more, the answer to how young people look at film is "through the lens of a camera." In coming years, it will be youth as film-maker, and not simply as audience, that will spur the evolution of the cinema. Students want a piece of the action, whether in running a university, the country, or the world; in terms of our question, this means making films. There is a strong resonance between film-making and the increasingly sophisticated film experience. Young people delighted by a television commercial are tempted to say: "I could do that!" Considering the cost and artistry of some commercials, this is a pretty naïve statement, but it doesn't stop the young from taking out their father's Super-8 or buying an old Bolex to tell their story on film. Today, anyone can make a film. Although Robert Flaherty's longed-for parousia, when film is as cheap as paper, has not yet arrived, the art has come into the reach of almost everyone. The Young Film-Makers Conference held by Fordham University last February drew 1,200 people, 740 of them student film-makers below college age. On a few weeks' notice, some 120 films were submitted for screening. Kids flew in from Richmond, California, and bussed in from Louisville, Kentucky, with twenty-seven states and Canada represented. Numbers, however, do not tell the story. One of the notable directors and actors present sized up the scene by saying: "My God, I'm standing here in the middle of a revolution!" It was the quality of the films that caused Eli Wallach to remark, only half in jest, that some day he'd be working for one of these film-makers. The young look at film as potential or actual film-makers, and this fact raises participation to an unprecedented critical level. The phenomenon also removes the last residue of passive audience participation from the Golden Forties box-office bonanza.

Foolhardy though it may be, one can predict that the new interest in film will take the direction of multi-media experimentation. Expo 67, it seems, is *now*. Our new and growing capacity to absorb images and synthesize sounds demands a simultaneity that cannot be met by traditional forms of film-making. The response so far has been the halfhearted multiple screens of *The Thomas Crown Affair*, not part of the conception of the film, but inserted as fancy dressing. The object of multiple images is not so much to condense actions as to create an environment such as the Ontario pavilion film, *A Place to Stand*. My own students have begun to relegate location shots such as street scenes or mood sequences to peripheral attention on side screens and walls, while the action takes place on the main screen.

It is symptomatic that the staged novelty of the Electric Circus is giving way to a new and interesting experiment in Greenwich Village, Cerebrum—where for a modest fee parties can set up their own media platforms equipped with projectors, tape recorders, and lights to stage their own happening. The idea being developed here is central to multi-media art, that is, the orchestration of contemporary media instruments. Young people are not afraid to carry a running projector around, spraying the images on walls and ceilings for distortions which communicate. An older generation is inclined to think of the media hardware as "machines" to be screwed to the floor or locked in a booth while they "produce" images and sounds. The young, in contrast, recognize this hardware as part of the information environment of electronic technology, and they use it accordingly.

Spontaneity, the chance synchronization, overload that leads to breakthrough—these are all part of the excitement that draws people to media rather than film alone.

The young look at film is a revolutionary one, motivated more by love of the medium than hatred of the Establishment. In a sense, the new taste is liberating film for a free exploration of its potential, especially in the area of humanizing change. The hunger for a relativity of time and space will extend to morality, producing films that explore problems rather than package solutions. Nevertheless, the very intensity of young involvement gives promise of profound changes in the youth audience as people open themselves to the reality of the medium. Whether as young film-maker or multi-media entrepreneur, the young will have their say. If we take the time to cultivate their perspective, we may learn an interesting view of the future of media, and a fascinating way to stay alive.

SUGGESTED WRITING ASSIGNMENT

1. State that a given movie has humanistic values, and illustrate by describing scenes that you think express these values; or, state that a film raises important questions about human relations, and illustrate by describing scenes that raise these questions.
2. Contrast the treatments of the same theme in two films.
3. Explain why a given movie appeals to many young people or why a given movie appeals to you.
4. Describe the responses of a specific audience (or specific persons in an audience) to specific scenes in a film; then interpret these responses.

On Living in a Biological Revolution

Donald Fleming

Here are a dozen things that we have discovered in the last fifteen years.

1. We have discovered the structure of the genetic substance DNA—the double helix of Watson and Crick—the general nature of the process by which the chromosomal strands are replicated.

2. We have discovered in viruses how to achieve the perfect replication of DNA molecules that are biologically effective.

ON LIVING IN A BIOLOGICAL REVOLUTION   From *The Atlantic*, February, 1969. Copyright © 1969 by Donald Fleming. Reprinted by permission of the author.

3. We have discovered the code by which DNA specifies the insertion of amino acids in proteins.

4. We have discovered how to produce hybrid cells between the most diverse vertebrate species, including hybrids between man and mouse; and some of these hybrids have gone on multiplying for several (cellular) generations.

5. We have discovered the power of viruses to invade bacterial and other cells and to insert the genes of the virus into the genome of the host; and we have good reason to conjecture, though not yet to affirm, that this phenomenon is involved in cancer.

6. We have discovered hormonal contraceptives and grasped in principle the strategy for devising a contraceptive pill for *both* sexes, by knocking out certain hormones of the hypothalamus, the master sexual gland of the body.

7. We have discovered on a large scale in the livestock industry that deep-frozen mammalian sperm, suitably mixed with glycerol, can be banked indefinitely and drawn upon as desired to produce viable offspring.

8. We have discovered in human females how to produce superovulation, the release of several eggs into the oviduct at the same time instead of the customary one, with the possibility on the horizon of withdrawing substantial numbers of human eggs for storage, culture in test tubes, or surgical manipulation, without destroying their viability.

9. We have discovered in rabbits how to regulate the sex of offspring by removing fertilized ova from the female before they become implanted in the wall of the uterus, "sexing" the embryos by a technique entailing the deletion of some 200 to 300 cells, flushing embryos of the "wrong" sex down the drain, and then in a substantial minority of cases, successfully reinserting in the uterus embryos of the desired sex that proceed to develop normally.

10. We have discovered drugs, above all the hallucinogens, that simulate psychotic states of mind; and have thereby rendered it plausible that the latter are the product of "inborn errors of metabolism" and as such remediable by the administration of drugs.

11. We have discovered in principle, and to a certain extent in practice, how to repress the immunological "defenses" of the body.

12. We have discovered a combination of immunological and surgical techniques by which the kidney, liver, or heart can be transplanted with fair prospects of the recipient's survival for months or even years—the first constructive proposal for turning our death wish on the highways to some advantage.

Each of these is a major discovery or complex of discoveries in itself, but they add up to far more than the sum of their parts. They constitute a veritable Biological Revolution likely to be as decisive for the history of the next 150 years as the Industrial Revolution has been for the period since 1750.

Definitions of what constitutes a revolution are legion. An undoctrinaire formulation would be that every full-scale revolution has three main components: a distinctive attitude toward the world; a program for utterly transforming it; and an unshakable, not to say fanatical, confidence that this program can be enacted—a world view, a program, and a faith.

In this sense, Darwinism did not usher in a full-scale biological revolution. Darwinism was a profoundly innovating world view, but one that prescribed no steps to be taken, no victories over nature to be celebrated, no program of triumphs to be successively gained. Indeed, one of the most plausible constructions to be put upon it was that nothing much *could* be done except to submit patiently to the winnowing processes of nature.

This defect was not lost upon Darwin's own cousin Sir Francis Galton, who tried to construct an applied science of eugenics for deliberately selecting out the best human stocks. But Galtonian eugenics was sadly lacking in any authentic biological foundation. Once the science of Mendelian genetics came to general notice about 1900, a more promising form of eugenics began to commend itself, the effort to induce artificial mutation of genes in desirable directions.

This was long the animating faith of one of the most extraordinary Americans of the twentieth century, the geneticist Herman J. Muller. He was the actual discoverer, in 1927, of artificial mutation through X rays. But this great achievement, for which he got the Nobel Prize, was a tremendous disappointment to Muller the revolutionary. There was no telling which genes would mutate in which direction, and he came to suspect that the vast majority of mutations were actually harmful in the present situation of the human race.

Muller at the end of his life—he died in 1967—was thrown back upon essentially Galtonian eugenics. He did bring this up to date by his proposal for sperm banks in which the sperm of exceptionally intelligent and socially useful men could be stored for decades and used for artificial insemination. He also envisioned, in the not too distant future, ova banks for storing superior human eggs. But none of these modern touches, these innovations in technique, could conceal the fact that this was still the old eugenics newly garbed, but equally subjective and imprecise.

BIOLOGICAL ENGINEERING

The Biological Revolution that Muller failed to bring off was already in progress when he died, but on very different terms from his own. There is a new eugenics in prospect, not the marriage agency kind, but a form of "biological engineering." When this actually comes to pass, chromosomes, segments of chromosomes, and even individual genes will be inserted at will into the genome. Alternatively, germ cells cultured in laboratories will be enucleated and entire tailor-made DNA molecules substituted. Alternatively still, superior genes will be brought into play by hybridization of cells.

The detailed variants upon these general strategies are almost innumerable. They all have in common the fact that they cannot be accomplished at present except in viruses and bacteria or in cell cultures. But it would be a bold man who would dogmatically affirm that none of these possibilities could be brought to bear upon human genetics by the year 2000.

That is a long way off for the firebrands of the Biological Revolution. The Nobel Prize winner Joshua Lederberg in particular has been pushing the claims of a speedier remedy, christened by him "euphenics," and defined as "the engineering of human development." The part of human development that fascinates Lederberg the most is embryology, seen by him as the process of initially translating the instructions coded in the DNA into "the living, breathing organism." Embryology, he says, is "very much in the situation of atomic physics in 1900; having had an honorable and successful tradition it is about to begin!" He thinks it will not take long to mature—"from 5 to no more than 20 years." He adds that most predictions of research progress in recent times have proved to be "far too conservative."

The progress that Lederberg has in mind is the application of new embryological techniques to human affairs. He is at once maddened and obsessed by the nine-months phase in which the human organism has been exempted from experimental and therapeutic intervention—such a waste of time before the scientists can get at us. But the embryo's turn is coming. It would be incredible, he says, "if we did not soon have the basis of developmental engineering technique to regulate, for example, the size of the human brain by prenatal or early postnatal intervention."

SEX CONTROL

Nothing as sensational as this has yet been attempted, but the new phase in embryology that Lederberg heralded is undoubtedly getting under way. The most conspicuous figure at present is Robert Edwards of the physiology laboratory at Cambridge University. In 1966 Edwards reported the culture of immature egg cells from the human ovary up to the point of ripeness for fertilization. He made tentative claims to have actually achieved fertilization in test tubes. The incipient hullabaloo in the newspapers about the specter of "test tube babies" led Edwards to clamp a tight lid of security over his researches in progress.

In the spring of this year, however, he and Richard Gardner announced their success in "sexing" fertilized rabbit eggs before implantation in the wall of the uterus and then inducing 20 percent of the reinserted eggs to produce normal full-term infants. The aspect of these findings that attracted general attention, the prospect of regulating the sex of mammalian offspring, is not likely to be of permanent interest. For this purpose, Edwards and Gardner's technique is obviously a clumsy expedient by comparison with predetermining the "sex" of spermatozoa—presently impossible but certainly not inconceivable within the next generation.

The real importance of Edwards and Gardner's work lies elsewhere. They have opened up the possibility of subjecting the early embryo to microsurgery, with the deletion and "inoculation" of cells at the will of the investigator, *and* the production of viable offspring from the results. The manufacture of "chimeras" in the modern biological sense—that is, with genetically distinct cells in the same organism—is clearly in prospect.

Work in this vein has just begun. The only branch of euphenics that has already become something more than a promising growth stock in science is the suppression of immunological reactions against foreign tissues and the accompanying, highly limited, successes in the transplantation of organs.

BIOLOGICAL REVOLUTIONARIES

The technical details and immediate prospects in eugenics and euphenics, however fascinating, are less important than the underlying revolutionary temper in biology. The most conspicuous representatives of this temper are Lederberg himself, the biochemical geneticist Edward L. Tatum, and Francis Crick of the model—all of them Nobel Prize winners, with the corresponding leverage upon public opinion. Robert Edwards, though slightly singed by the blast of publicity about test tube babies, is clearly in training for the revolutionary cadre.

One of the stigmata of revolutionaries in any field is their resolute determination to break with traditional culture. For a scientist, the most relevant definition of culture is his own field of research. All of these men would angrily resent being bracketed with biologists in general. Biology has always been a rather loose confederation of naturalists and experimentalists, overlapping in both categories with medical researchers. Today even the pretense that these men somehow constitute a community has been frayed to the breaking point.

At Harvard, for example, the revolutionaries have virtually seceded from the old Biology Department and formed a new department of their own, Biochemistry and Molecular Biology. The younger molecular biologists hardly bother to conceal their contempt for the naturalists, whom they see as old fogies obsequiously attentive to the world as it is rather than bent upon turning it upside down.

In one respect, the molecular biologists do overlap with the contemporary naturalists and indeed with most creative scientists in general—in their total detachment from religion. In a way, this is a point that could have been made at any time in the last seventy-five years, but with one significant difference. Herman Muller, for example, born in 1890, had no truck with religion. But he was self-consciously antireligious.

The biological revolutionaries of today are not antireligious but simply unreligious. They give the impression not of defending themselves against religion but of subsisting in a world where that has never been a felt pressure upon them. They would agree with many devout theologians that we are living in a post-Christian world, to such an extent that some of the most doctrinaire biological revolutionaries are able to recognize without embarrassment, and even with a certain gracious condescension, that Christianity did play a useful role in defining the values of the Western world.

The operative word here is in the past tense. Francis Crick says that the facts of science are producing and must produce values that owe nothing to Christianity. "Take," he says, "the suggestion of making a child whose head is twice as big as normal. There is going to be no agreement between Christians and any humanists who lack their particular prejudice about the sanctity of the individual, and who simply want to try it scientifically."

This sense of consciously taking up where religion left off is illuminating in another sense for the revolutionary character of contemporary biology. The parallel is very marked between the original Christian Revolution against the values of the classical world and the Biological Revolution against religious values.

All the great revolutionaries, whether early Christians or molecular biologists, are men of good hope. The future may or may not belong to those who believe in it, but cannot belong to those who don't. Yet at certain points in history, most conspicuously perhaps at intervals between the close of the Thirty Years' War in 1648 and the coming of the Great Depression in 1929, the horizons seem to be wide open, and the varieties of good hope contending for allegiance are numerous. But the tidings of good hope don't become revolutionary except when the horizons begin to close in and the plausible versions of good hope have dwindled almost to the vanishing point.

For the kind of good hope that has the maximum historical impact is the one that capitalizes upon a prevalent despair at the corruption of the existing world, and then carries conviction in pointing to itself as the only possible exit from despair. Above everything else, revolutionaries are the men who keep their spirits up when everybody else's are sagging. In this sense, the greatest revolutionaries of the Western world to date have been precisely the early Christians who dared to affirm in the darkest days of the classical world that something far better was in process and could be salvaged from the ruins.

Both of these points are exemplified in the Biological Revolution that has now begun—despair at our present condition, but infinite hope for the future if the biologists' prescription is taken. Anybody looking for jeremiads on our present state could not do better than to consult the new biologists. "The facts of human reproduction," says Joshua Lederberg, "are all gloomy—the stratification of fecundity by economic status, the new environmental insults to our genes, the sheltering by humanitarian medicine of once-lethal genes."

More generally, the biologists deplore the aggressive instincts of the human animal, now armed with nuclear weapons, his lamentably low average intelligence for coping with increasingly complicated problems, and his terrible prolificity, no longer mitigated by a high enough death rate. It is precisely an aspect of the closing down of horizons and depletion of comfortable hopes in the second half of the twentieth century that conventional medicine is now seen by the biological revolutionaries as one of the greatest threats to the human race.

Yet mere prophets of gloom can never make a revolution. In fact, the new biologists are almost the only group among our contemporaries with a reasoned hopefulness about the long future—if the right path is taken. There are of course many individuals of a naturally cheerful or feckless temperament, today as always, but groups of men with an articulated hope for the future of the entire race are much rarer. The theologians no longer qualify, many Communists have lost their hold upon the future even by their own lights, and the only other serious contenders are the space scientists and astronauts. But just to get off the earth is a rather vague prescription for our ills. Few people even in the space program would make ambitious claims on this score. In a long historical retrospect, they may turn out to have been too modest.

This is not a charge that is likely ever to be leveled against the new biologists. It is well known by now that J. D. Watson begins his account of his double-helix double by saying that he had never seen Francis Crick in a modest mood. But after all, modesty is not the salient quality to be looked for in the new breed of biologists. If the world will only listen, they *know* how to put us on the high road to salvation.

CUSTOM-MADE PEOPLE

What exactly does their brand of salvation entail? Perhaps the most illuminating way to put the matter is that their ideal is the manufacture of man. In a manufacturing process, the number of units to be produced is a matter of rational calculation beforehand and of tight control thereafter. Within certain tolerances, specifications are laid down for a satisfactory product. Quality-control is maintained by checking the output and replacing defective parts. After the product has been put to use, spare parts can normally be supplied to replace those that have worn out.

This is the program of the new biologists—control of numbers by foolproof contraception; gene manipulation and substitution; surgical and biochemical intervention in the embryonic and neonatal phases; organ transplants or replacements at will.

Of these, only contraception is technically feasible at present. Routine organ transplants will probably be achieved for a wide range of suitable organs in less than five years. The grafting of mechanical organs, prosthetic devices inserted in the body, will probably take longer. Joshua Lederberg thinks the embryonic and neonatal intervention may be in flood tide by, say, 1984. As for gene manipulation and substitution in human beings, that is the remotest prospect of all—maybe by the year 2000. But we must not forget Lederberg's well-founded conviction that most predictions in these matters are likely to be too conservative. We are already five to ten years ahead of what most informed people expected to be the schedule for organ transplants in human beings.

The great question becomes, what is it going to be like to be living in a world where such things are coming true? How will the Biological Revolution affect our scheme of values? Nobody could possibly take in all the implications in advance, but some reasonable conjectures are in order.

It is virtually certain that the moral sanctions of birth control are going to be transformed. Down to the present time, the battle for birth control has been fought largely in terms of the individual couple's right to have the number of babies that they want at the desired intervals. But it is built into the quantity-controls envisioned by the Biological Revolution, the control of the biological inventory, that this is or ought to be a question of social policy rather than individual indulgence.

Many factors are converging upon many people to foster this general attitude, but the issue is particularly urgent from the point of view of the biological revolutionaries. In the measure that they succeed in making the human race healthier, first by transplants and later on by genetic tailoring, they will be inexorably swamped by their own successes unless world population is promptly brought under control. The irrepressible Malthus is springing from his lightly covered grave to threaten them with catastrophic victories.

LICENSED BABIES

The only hope is birth control. The biologists can contribute the techniques, but the will to employ them on the requisite scale is another matter. The most startling proposal to date for actually enforcing birth control does not come from a biologist but from the Nobel-Prize-winning physicist W. B. Shockley, one of the inventors of the transistor. Shockley's plan is to render all women of childbearing age reversibly sterile by implanting a contraceptive capsule beneath the skin, to be removed by a physician only on the presentation of a government license to have a child. The mind boggles at the prospect of bootleg babies. This particular proposal is not likely to be enacted in the near future, even in India.

What we may reasonably expect is a continually rising chorus by the biologists, moralists, and social philosophers of the next generation to the effect that nobody has a right to have children, and still less the right to determine on personal grounds how many. There are many reasons why a couple may not want to be prolific anyhow, so that there might be a happy coincidence between contraception seen by them as a right and by statesmen and biologists as a duty. But the suspicion is that even when people moderate their appetite in the matter of babies, they may still want to have larger families than the earth can comfortably support. The possibility of predetermining sex would undoubtedly be helpful in this respect, but might not be enough to make people forgo a third child. That is where the conflict would arise between traditional values, however moderately indulged, and the values appropriate to the Biological Revolution.

This issue is bound to be fiercely debated. But some of the most profound implications of the Biological Revolution may never present themselves for direct ratification. In all probability, the issues will go by default as we gratefully accept specific boons from the new biology.

Take, for example, the role of the patient in medicine. One of the principal strands in Western medicine from the time of the Greeks has been the endeavor to enlist the cooperation of the patient in his own cure. In certain respects, this venerable tradition has grown much stronger in the last century. Thus the rising incidence of degenerative diseases, like ulcers, heart trouble, and high blood pressure, has underscored the absolute necessity of inducing the patient to observe a healthful regimen, literally a way of life.

This has been the whole point of Freudian psychiatry as a mode of therapy, that cures can be wrought only by a painful exertion of the patient himself. We often forget, for good reasons, how traditional Freudianism is after the one big shock has been assimilated. In the present context, it actually epitomizes the Western tradition of bringing the patient's own personality to bear upon his medical problems.

Where do we go from here? The degenerative diseases are going to be dealt with increasingly by surgical repair of organs, by organ transplants, and later on by the installation of mechanical organs and eventually by the genetic deletion of weak organs before they occur. The incentive to curb your temper or watch your diet to keep your heart going will steadily decline.

As for mental illness, the near future almost certainly lies with psychopharmacology and the far future with genetic tailoring. Though the final pieces stubbornly decline to fall into place, the wise money is on the proposition that schizophrenia and other forms of psychosis are biochemical disorders susceptible of a pharmacological cure. If we are not presently curing any psychoses by drugs, we are tranquilizing and antidepressing many psychotics and emptying mental hospitals.

Neuroses, the theme of Freudian psychoanalysis, are another matter. It is not easy to envision a biochemical remedy for them. But even for neuroses, we already have forms of behavioral therapy that dispense with the Freudian tenet of implicating the patient in his own cure. For the *very* long future, it is certainly not inconceivable that genetic tailoring could delete neurotic propensities.

Everywhere we turn, the story is essentially the same. Cures are increasingly going to be wrought upon, done to, the patient as a passive object. The strength of his own personality, the force of his character, his capacity for re-integrating himself, are going to be increasingly irrelevant in medicine.

GENETIC TAILORING, BOON OR BANE?

This leads to what many people would regard as the biggest question of all. In what sense would we have a self to integrate under the new dispensation? The Princeton theologian Paul Ramsey has now been appointed professor of "genetic ethics" at the Georgetown University Medical School, presumably the first appointment of its kind. He thinks that genetic tailoring would be a "violation of man." To this it must be said that under the present scheme of things, many babies get born with catastrophic genes that are not exactly an enhancement of man. Our present genetic self is a brute datum, sometimes very brutal, and anyhow it is hard to see how we can lose our identity before we have any.

As for installing new organs in the body, there is no evident reason why the personality should be infringed upon by heart or kidney transplants per se. Brain transplants would be different, but surely they would be among the last to come. States of mind regulated by drugs we already possess, and obviously they do alter our identity in greater or lesser degree. But even here we must not forget that some identities are intolerable to their distracted possessors.

We must not conclude, however, that the importance of these developments has been exaggerated. The point is that the immediate practical consequences will probably not present themselves as threatening to the individuals involved—quite the contrary. Abstract theological speculations about genetic tailoring would be totally lost upon a woman who could be sure in advance that her baby would not be born mentally retarded or physically handicapped. The private anxieties of individuals are likely to diminish rather than increase any effective resistance to the broader consequences of the Biological Revolution.

One of these is already implicit in predicting a sense of growing passivity on the part of patients, of not participating as a subject in their own recovery. This might well be matched by a more general sense of the inevitability of letting oneself be manipulated by technicians—of becoming an article of manufacture.

The difficulty becomes to estimate what psychological difference this would make. In any Hegelian overview of history, we can only become articles of manufacture because "we" have set up as the manufacturers. But the first person plural is a slippery customer. We the manufactured would be everybody and we the manufacturers a minority of scientists and technicians. Most people's capacity to identify with the satisfactions of the creative minority is certainly no greater in science than in other fields, and may well be less.

The beneficiaries of the Biological Revolution are not likely to feel that they are in control of the historical process from which they are benefiting. But they will not be able to indulge any feelings of alienation from science without endangering the specific benefits that they are unwilling to give up.

The best forecast would be for general acquiescence, though occasionally sullen, in whatever the Biological Revolution has to offer and gradually adjusting our values to signify that we approve of what we will actually be getting. The will to cooperate in being made biologically perfect is likely to take the place in the hierarchy of values that used to be occupied by being humbly submissive to spiritual counselors chastising the sinner for his own salvation. The new form of spiritual sloth will be not to want to be bodily perfect and genetically improved. The new avarice will be to cherish our miserable hoard of genes and favor the children that resemble us.

SUGGESTED WRITING ASSIGNMENT

1. Discuss the difference between being antireligious and being unreligious. Use concrete terms and specific examples in developing your comparison.
2. Generalize that genetic tailoring is badly needed, and develop your generalization by using subgeneralizations and examples.
3. Explain why you would approve or disapprove of licensing parenthood. Remember to describe *what* before explaining *why*.
4. Discuss the use of drugs in the treatment of mental illness, describing in detail behavior before medication and after.

The Irrepressible World Revolt

Lee Benson

Barring nuclear war, the 1968 worldwide revolt for autonomy and against authoritarianism not only will continue but will accelerate during the 1970's.

In the US, that revolt expressed itself most powerfully, and prophetically, in the movement that made Senator McCarthy its symbolic leader and President

THE IRREPRESSIBLE WORLD REVOLT   From *The New Republic*, January 18, 1969. Reprinted by permission of *The New Republic*, © 1969, Harrison-Blaine of New Jersey, Inc.

Johnson its enemy. But almost everywhere last year, the "power elites" experienced angry challenges to their authority and contemptous denials of their legitimacy. This "global unrest," wrote Saville R. Davis in *The Christian Science Monitor,* was symptomatic of:

> ". . . a world trying to become young. In the capitalist West and the communist East and the underdeveloped South, people are revolting politely or impolitely against the systems that have been handed down to them.
> "The students, or at least the more thoughtful among them, have produced a word for it. They want 'participation.' They want to take part in the big decisions that affect their lives. They don't want their orders merely handed down to them—by parents or employers or politicians who represent some established order and try to impose it on their underlings. . . .
> "In a word: Power has been traditionally exercised from the top down, whether it dealt with nuclear weapons, politics, the community, or the family. The people of the modern age seem to have decided this is too arbitrary."

On December 15, 1968 *The New York Times* reported that middle-class Catholic laymen had been joining the "2-year-old Revolt by Local Priests" against the "authoritarian rule" of the 77-year-old Archbishop of San Antonio, the Most Rev. Robert E. Lucey. The report began on this arresting note:

> "'We're headed for a more democratic church, one that belongs to the people.'
> "The speaker was Joe Bernal, a dapper 42-year-old Mexican-American State Senator who is part of a grassroots revolt that is seeking to bring about radical changes in the style of government of the Roman Catholic Archbishop of San Antonio."

Both the priests and the laymen, the report continued, are demanding a greater role in church governance. "Both [groups] are also becoming increasingly impatient with what they regard as a contradiction between the authoritarian ecclesiastical traditions of their church and the current secular movement for human rights." The report concluded by quoting Msgr. Martin, chairman of the fact-finding board appointed by Archbishop Lucey:

> "'The church will never be the same,' he said. 'Twenty years ago we priests were pawns on the board, but now there is a realization that people have rights. Even an institution that we would claim is divinely instituted cannot deprive people of their personhood.'"

Impressed by the Pandora-like box of troubles opened by the Second Vatican Council, which ended in 1965, *Life* magazine sounded this variant on the theme:

> "All major sources of authority seem to have rebellions on their hands—universities, parents, US law, the Russian Communist party, and now even the Roman Catholic Church, to name a few. A general question arises: once such an authority is seriously challenged or even undermined, how can it re-establish itself?"

Now, a self-styled "realist" might dismiss such quotations as superficial observations rhetorically escalated. "Take Czechoslovakia," he might say. "By December, where had all the flowers gone? Where was the springtime missionary ardor inspired by the 'truth-spreading raids' of pre-Reformation Hussite 'field armies?' Did Alexander Dubcek continue exultantly to proclaim, 'We want to play our role in making socialism more appealing for the whole world'? The whole world was watching Czechoslovakia—as it had watched Chicago in late August. But did the spectacle look the same in the wintry light of December as in the warm sunshine of May?"

To ask these questions, realists contend, is to answer them. And not only for Czechoslovakia. At year's end, did not the established order stand essentially unchanged everywhere? How can 1968 compare, the realist says, with such a genuinely historic year as 1848 when, to quote Eric Hobsbawn:

> "Almost simultaneously revolution broke out and [temporarily] was in France, the whole of Italy, the German states, most of the Hapsburg

Empire and Switzerland [1847]. In a less acute form the unrest also affected Spain, Denmark and Rumania, in a sporadic form Ireland, Greece and Britain. There has never been [as of 1962], anything closer to the world-revolution of which the insurrectionaries of the period dreamed than this spontaneous and general conflagration. . . . What had been in 1789 the rising of a single nation [France], was now, it seemed, 'the springtime of peoples' of an entire continent."

But the "realistic" assessment just sketched, is not realistic. Admittedly, in the short-run, the revolutions of 1848 brought about greater political changes than the rebellions of 1968. But several considerations negate the force of that admission.

For one thing, the 1848 revolutions affected only part of one continent, Central and Western Europe. For another, they primarily were restricted to attacks upon governmental institutions and, to a more limited extent, economic institutions. Other major institutions—the family, churches, universities, voluntary associations—remained essentially untouched. Finally, most of the reforms proclaimed in 1848 either never were implemented or were cancelled by 1852. Reaction set in, the revolutionary rhythm was broken, disillusionment spread widely.

I predict that the rhythm of the 1968 revolt will continue essentially unbroken during the 1970's. Temporary reverses or consolidations doubtless will occur in some places, particularly where ultraleftists manage to snatch defeat out of the jaws of victory. But general reaction and disillusionment à la 1848–1852 will not set in. Out of fashion during the 1950's, Utopias again are on the agenda everywhere; they will remain there. The permanent revolt against anti-humanistic institutions and modes of conduct and thought is here. Only in societies that have experienced great humiliations from foreigners, however, is it likely to take that form of sustained revolutionary violence advocated by Mao's "Great Cultural Revolution" or Castro's contemporary version of Babouvism (ultra-left-wing communism).

In short, I see the worldwide revolt of 1968 as having given irreversible impetus to what Dr. Glenn Seaborg, Nobel Prize winner and chairman of the United States Atomic Energy Commission, recently forecast as "the dawn of a new scientific era, a scientific-humanistic era, a 'quiet revolution that will prevail—simply because it speaks a prevailing truth'."

To demand that human institutions be constructed or reconstructed so as to enable everyone to "do his own thing"—the central premise underlying and linking the 1968 anti-bureaucratic and anti-authoritarian revolts—is to restate in contemporary idiom the radical prophetic element of Renaissance humanism: namely, the belief that men ought to choose and practice life styles compatible with their own natures, aptitudes and constitutions. As Montaigne later stated the Renaissance formula for the prevention of alienation, "the greatest thing in the world is to know how to belong to oneself."

Humanistic individualism must not be confused with that egoistic individualism that sees the world as a jungle in which atomistic individuals (or interest groups) live by the philosophy: "It's all right, Jack," and as for you, "well, sorry 'bout that." Erasmus, for example, cherished his autonomy. But he did not see himself as pitted against other men in a series of egoistic struggles. On the contrary, he emphasized the harmony of interest among self-determined individuals and justified doing his own thing on social rather than egoistic grounds. The welfare of society was best served, he maintained, when social institutions facilitated men's making right use of their distinctive gifts or talents. "Human happiness depends mainly on this," he observed, "that everyone should apply himself to that for which he is naturally fitted."

But in a world that lacked modern science and technology, humanistic individualism could function only as prophecy, not program. Since the sixteenth century, however, an increasingly direct and dynamic interaction has linked the principle of self-determination and the process of modernization that has transformed the world. And by modernization, I mean "the process by which historically evolved institutions are adapted to the rapidly changing functions that reflect the unprecedented increase in man's knowledge, permitting control over his environment, that accompanied the scientific revolution." (C. E. Black, *The Dynamics of Modernization.*)

The events of 1968, I believe, have undermined the assumptions of the ideology developed after World War I by Max Weber, Roberto Michels, George Orwell, Aldous Huxley, Reinhold Niebuhr, and other latter-day secular or theological Augustinian pessimists. Weber, Michels and Orwell based their predictions about the consequences of modernization on a skewed sample of early twentieth-century returns. That modernization brings agony doesn't need demonstration. The terrible wars of the 16th and 17th centuries, the even more terrible wars and bureaucraticized "purges" of the 20th century, indicate how difficult men find the process of adapting "historically evolved institutions" to "rapidly changing functions." But 1968 suggests that Weber, Michels, and Orwell were wrong when they mechanically extrapolated some bureaucratic and authoritarian tendencies into all-embracing inevitabilities.

From the downfall of Stalinist Party Secretary Novotny of Czechoslovakia in January to the forced "abdication" of President Johnson in March, to the near overthrow of President de Gaulle in May, to the resignation of President Kirk of Columbia University in August, to the outcries of Pope Paul VI against the increasing defiance of his authority by bishops and priests and laymen in December 1968—all these have exposed the fallacies in Orwell's prediction that men are doomed to life on a 1984-style Animal Farm, and in Michels's prediction that democracy is impossible due to the organizational needs of political parties in modern societies "and the ineluctable tendencies of human psychology."

Characterized by Stuart Hughes as "the most cosmopolitan of the leading intellectuals of the early twentieth century," Michels thought that:

> "The psychology of the crowd is fairly the same in the socialists and the nationalists, in the liberals and the conservatives. In group movements, with rare exceptions everything proceeds naturally, and not 'artificially'. The fact that the people follow their leader is quite a natural phenomenon. 'To use the term exactly' Rousseau has said, 'there has never existed a true democracy, and none can ever exist. It is against natural order that the great number should govern and that the few should be governed.'

> Our consistent knowledge of the political life of the principal civilized nations of the world authorizes us to assert that the tendency toward oligarchy constitutes one of the iron laws of history, from which the most democratic modern societies and, within those societies, the most advanced parties, have been unable to escape."

On November 14, 1968 in Moscow, Pyotr G. Grigorenko, a former major general of the Soviet army, refuted Michels's "iron law." Standing over the open coffin of one of his comrades (the writer Aleksei Y. Kosterin), he denounced the "totalitarianism that hides behind the mask of so-called Soviet democracy."

Kosterin had repeatedly charged that Stalinism was returning to the Soviet Union. As a result, despite his membership for 52 years in the Communist Party, he had been expelled from it and from the Union of Soviet Writers shortly before his death. Grigorenko accused the men responsible for Kosterin's expulsion of responsibility for his death and pledged himself and the other 300 mourners around the coffin to fight "the damned machine" against which his comrade had struggled.

> "In farewells, it is usually said, 'Sleep quietly, Dear Comrade,'" the tall, straight, bald general said, his voice choked and near breaking. "We shall not say this. In the first place, he will not listen to me. He will continue to fight anyway.
>
> "In the second place, it is impossible for me without you, Alyosha. You sit inside me and you will stay there. Without you, I do not live. Therefore, do not sleep Alyoshka! Fight Alyoshka!
>
> "Burn all the abominable meanness with which they want to keep turning eternally that damned machine against which you fought all your life. We, your friends, will not be far behind you. Freedom will come! Democracy will come!"

Why accept Grigorenko's prediction rather than Michels's, particularly in light of the circumstances under which General Grigorenko's was made? First, *because* of the circumstances contrary to Michels's prediction, after five decades of development and consolidation, the bureaucratic "damned machine" had been unable to prevent Soviet citizens from, in his words, functioning as "thinking being[s]" whom "nature has given . . . a striving for knowledge that is critically evaluating reality, drawing one's own convictions and opinions." Nor was Grigorenko's action an isolated bit of heroics within the Soviet Union; it represented a growing tendency among Soviet intellectuals, artists and scientists.

Secondly, Grigorenko's action was part of a world wide pattern—Czech progressives against Stalinist party dogmatists; Senator McCarthy, relatively unknown and without power, leading a "Children's crusade" against the "unbeatable" incumbent President Johnson; Columbia students against immovable President Kirk; French students against centralized educational hierarchy.

The Weber-Michels school postulated that modern societies must be dominated by oligarchic, centralized bureaucracies. But 1968 showed that the fatal weakness of modern bureaucracies is precisely their inability to satisfy humanist needs.

Henry Kissinger is not likely to be characterized as a self-deluded, visionary Utopian. His paper in the Brookings Institution book, *Agenda for the Nation* (December, 1968) published to guide the new Presidential Administration taking power in 1969, makes the point that:

> "The modern bureaucratic state, for all its panoply of strength, often finds itself shaken to its foundations by seemingly trivial causes. Its brittleness and the worldwide revolution of youth—especially in advanced countries and among the relatively affluent—suggest a spiritual void, an almost metaphysical boredom with a political environment that increasingly emphasizes bureaucratic challenges and is dedicated to no deeper purpose than material comfort."

To appreciate the prophetic quality of Grigorenko's "heroic act" (and to recognize its lineal descent from Luther's "heroic act" of 1517 when he nailed his Ninety-five Theses to the door of the court church at Wittenberg), we need to shift from an empirical to a theoretical level of discussion. My basic proposition is this: by its very nature, modernization functions as a revolutionary process that strongly tends to develop forms of social organization capable of realizing the humanist principle of self-determination. Although centralized bureaucracies tend to increase with institutional size and complexity, at a certain point in the modernizing process and at a certain stage of the communications revolution, the tendency reaches its peak and begins to decline. 1968 suggests that this point has already been reached in many societies and in many institutions. It suggests the validity of what, only semi-facetiously, might be called the domino theory of falling bureaucratic or authoritarian institutions. In a modernizing world increasingly connected by a global communication network, the fall of one bureaucratic or authoritarian institution tends to release energies that then bring about the fall of similar institutions. The affected institutions need not be geographically contiguous, nor of the same type, nor at the same level of bureaucratic unresponsiveness or authoritarianism. Thus, the Czech progressives *visibly* toppled Novotny in January and thereby stimulated student and faculty participation in the McCarthy-led "crusade" against the Johnson Administration; the McCarthy crusade visibly scored a stunning victory in March by forcing Johnson's abdication, and in turn, lent fuel to the Columbia revolt in April, that helped to spark the French student uprising in May, that. . . .

Defeats can and do occur to brake momentum and damp down enthusiasm, particularly when ultra-leftists take command and activists let their reach exceed their grasp (the French student leaders who intoxicated themselves with their own rhetoric and confused May 1968 with July 1789). But in the contemporary world the potential sources of anti-bureaucratic and anti-authoritarian revolts are so numerous and so diverse that they cannot all be simultaneously rooted-out. Temporarily contained in August in Czechoslovakia, they burst out in December in Italy and Portugal and in new form in Czechoslovakia (workers joining enthusiastically in the movement previously sparked by students and intellectuals).

I am unable to advance a rigorous and comprehensive theory to explain the unprecedented phenomena of 1968. But it seems possible to suggest three propositions that help us make sense of what we saw last year, as well as support the prediction that the "autonomous revolution" has become irrepressible.

To gain some control over and freedom from brute necessity, men have always been forced to try to act as *homo sapiens, homo faber*—man the thinker, man the maker. But necessity does not necessarily mother successful invention; witness the relatively slow, sporadic, discontinuous, unorganized evolution of science and technology before the modern era. After 1700 in the Western world, however, science became so dynamic and pervasive a social activity, impelled and conducted by so powerful a complex of institutions and processes, that we can now view it as virtually a self-sustaining and self-generating enterprise. Since 1945, moreover, the "international demonstration effect" has produced a worldwide desire to gain the benefits of the Scientific Revolution, particularly the improved material well-being that so visibly accomplished its development in the West. For the first time in history, it has become a matter of "common knowledge" that abundance for all is possible and that men are not *necessarily* doomed to struggle with each other in a zero-sum game in which gains for some inevitably mean losses for others.

Granted the accuracy of those observations, my first proposition is: the accelerating development of science and technology, and its geographic expansion throughout the world, is irreversible. The second proposition derives from the first It is the nations whose people are motivated by the goal of continually raising their level of material well-being must continually upgrade their scientific and technological enterprises and thus must continually upgrade their median educational level.

My third proposition derives from the first and second: the higher the level of scientific and technological development, the higher the median level of education, the higher the level of economic development of a nation, then the greater the individual and culture group (e.g., French Canadians, Afro-Americans) autonomy and the greater the participation of all men in all forms of collective decision-making.

Can that third proposition be reasonably derived from the first and second? In a world that daily shows us men's terrible capacity to treat other men inhumanly, why predict the displacement of competitive egoism by humanist altruism?

Ernest Havelock, a leading classicist, offered persuasive answers to those questions in his brilliant exegesis on Aeschylus' *Prometheus Bound.* Writing in 1950, at the beginning of that dreadful decade that led sensitive observers to pen premature epitaphs to ideology, Havelock asserted that the development of contemporary scientific method:

> ". . . has created a definition of the intellect of man more precise and more formidable than man in the past has been willing to entertain. . . . The process of training men in the habits of measurement and calculation and analysis and hypothesis goes on over most of the civilized world, and it is still accelerating. . . . In sum total, the extension of scientific method combines with the literacy of the masses to produce a type of *homo sapiens* specific to this century. . . .

"Literacy releases certain spiritual energies in man. It confers freedom of occupation and movement upon him. . . . The wine of intellectual activity, diluted but still active, is distilled throughout the entire body politic. Men breathe a freer and larger air. They respect themselves and their neighbors more. The education of the masses, as a kind of by-product of itself, kindles the concept of the preciousness of human life."

Havelock then suggested some subtle interrelationships between the scientific revolution and changes in the administrative structure of Western society.

"While the banners under which political reform has marched have been emblazoned with the noun 'liberty,' first political and now economic, it would seem on second thought that these political changes reflect rather the underlying revolution wrought by scientific method. . . . Whatever class or group may demand democratic reform, and perhaps attain it by revolution, the form itself is operative only by the services of an increasing number of intelligent people. In fact, the form may be said to be a necessary response to the multiplication of procedures which are technological and complex and exact, whether in science or industry or the multitude of professions which have to use the results of science. These cannot be operated by the illiterate, *and they require a type of intelligence which within its own job is independent*" [emphasis added].

Following Havelock, my third proposition can be extended and clarified. The more intellectually demanding the job, the more forceful the jobholder's demand for personal autonomy. The greater the proportion of intellectually demanding jobs and jobholders in a nation, the more forceful the demand that *all men enjoy personal and group autonomy.*

What justifies the great qualitative transformation represented by those two sentences, that is, the leap from egoistic individualism into altruism? Here I follow Havelock's use of the myth of Prometheus as a parable for modern man which interprets altruism "as a close relation of science."

Havelock emphasizes that Pro-metheus means the "Forethinker" in Greek. The "Forethinker" is portrayed by Aeschylus as a lesser god who, because he was a "philanthropist," or "lover of man," stole fire from heaven and thereby released men from primitive bondage to the natural environment. By making philanthropy an integral part of the Forethinker's character, Aeschylus dramatized the "inner connection between intellectual foresight on the one hand, and philanthropic action on the other."

"'Forethought' . . . is what it is because it represents the ability to visualize the end beyond the end beyond the end. It is always shaping and then reshaping the means to embrace an objective which becomes wider and wider . . . . If man cares to prethink far enough, his forethought becomes increasingly moral and philanthropic in its direction. Man cannot prethink evil, but only good.

"This quality of intellectual prevision is close kin to the scientific imagination, and it needs the patience, the precision and the analysis of science to accomplish the stages of forethought; it calls for the discipline of measurements and a large dose of experimental courage. Philanthropy may commonly be regarded as the motive which causes forethought 'on behalf of' others, but in a more profound sense, it is really the product created by forethinking."

If one grants Havelock's argument, and also grants that the development of science and technology is a (perhaps *the*) most critical determinant of modernity and affluence, it follows that, *in time,* the more modern and affluent the nation, the greater the forethought, philanthropy and, *therefore,* autonomy its people will exhibit and enjoy.

Still, abstract principles and value systems are not self-realizing. To bring them to life, real-life men must articulate them and fight sustained battles on their behalf. Which social group or groups have the capacity to do that?

Karl Marx, in observing how the Industrial Revolution had developed by the mid-nineteenth century, identified the working-class, "the proletariat," as the main social group that would produce the New Prometheans. However accurate Marx's proposition was for the late 19th and early 20th centuries—and I think more can be said for it than some recent critics grant—Marx erred when he assumed that the same social group would continue to play this role until a genuinely humanist society was achieved. The proletariat is not the main social group likely to produce the New Prometheans of the 1970's and 1980's. (The proletariat, of course, can be defined so inclusively and so "Un-Marxianly" as to render the concept worse than useless. To do this, one artificially links together in close communion social groups radically different in consciousness, life styles and direct interests. Nobel Prize-winning theoretical physicists, like unskilled workers on the Ford assembly line, do not "own the means of production." But to view both types of "workers" as members of "the proletariat," as some New Leftists do, is to caricature Marx and forfeit claims to attention on any subject.)

My answer to the question, "Who are likely to be the new Prometheans?", derives from the three propositions advanced above. Given the increasingly critical role played by colleges and universities in modernized and modernizing nations, given the growing size and power of the "non-academic intellectual class" that develops as a result of the increasing size and power of the "academic class," the social groups that now constitute the vanguard of the permanent worldwide revolt for autonomy can be identified as the academic-scientist-intellectual complex. Undergraduate and graduate students—particularly those from middle- and upper-income families, for whom education has less of a "making it" character— probably are the most activist, unflagging, "purist" component of this complex. but because university (broadly defined) students constitute a short-lived, physically and psychically mobile generation group who play a relatively large number of social roles in a relatively short time, they are unlikely to formulate the basic ideas, or create and sustain the organizations required to translate the *desire* for autonomy into the *achievement* of autonomy.

The delusion that conflicts against bureaucratic or authoritarian organizations can be won without counter-organizations that have some rational structure and differentiated set of roles dies hard; hopefully, it will tend to disappear when thoughtful activists in the US take time to study the "lessons of 1968." The diffuse movement that made Senator McCarthy its symbol can serve as a classic example. It permanently changed the structure of American politics by demonstrating that participatory democracy *could* change the direction of American governmental policy. Tens of thousands of students (and non-students) passionately responded to the opportunity it provided them to help shape political decisions. But the McCarthy movement failed to realize its full potential, because it failed to develop an organizational structure capable of permitting citizens to do their own thing *effectively*. It vividly illustrated the tendency among contemporary rebels to rely on "anarchic spontaneity." It also demonstrated the necessity to overcome that tendency if one wants to engage in serious politics.

And it can be overcome. Thus, when young Czechs came to West Berlin recently to discuss mutual problems with students of the Free University, the correspondent of the *Christian Science Monitor* reported that their "tone and style were very different from those of radical Berlin activist students. They were reserved, careful, mannerly." Sharp ideological differences quickly manifested themselves, the West Berliners taking an ultra-leftist line. One Czech girl responded: "You're only interested in playing with theories. We've had 20 years of trying to deal with those theories in practice." Another said:

> "We are the vanguard of the progressive movement [in Czechoslovakia]. . . . We can express the feelings and opinions of the whole people because we are young and freer than most. The rest of the population supports us, and we feel a great respnsibility to them."

Particularly in countries such as the United States, where academic freedom is strongly rooted, where the "knowledge industry" is the fastest growing segment of the economy, where the material and social status of professors continue to rise, it is the "professoriate," I believe, who will form the vanguard of the movement for autonomy. Students, because they possess youthful energy and idealism relatively uncorrupted by experience and unconstrained by responsibility, probably will keep things "stirred up." The most important "gadfly" role of students, judging from my own and my friends' experience, however, will be to serve as models of altruism in action. I anticipate that, by their example, they will prod into socially responsible action other components of the academic-scientist-intellectual complex, particularly the professoriate, who have for many reasons, good and bad, concentrated heretofore on their "own work" to the neglect of "burning problems" of the larger society.

SUGGESTED WRITING ASSIGNMENT

1. Is Lee Benson in sympathy with the world revolt he discusses? Explain why you think he is or is not (after explaining the situation—the world revolt as he conceives it).

2. Generalize upon contradictory aspects in the predictions of the new biologists (discussed by Donald Fleming) and the predictions of Lee Benson. Be sure to use examples as one kind of support in your comparison.
3. Do you think Benson is right in supposing that the new Prometheans will be college professors? After explaining his prediction about the future role of college professors in the world revolt (your situation), explain why you think he is or is not right.

Index

Italic numbers indicate diagrams.